VIOLENCE AND THE VIOLENT INDIVIDUAL

VIOLENCE AND THE VIOLENT INDIVIDUAL

Proceedings of the Twelfth Annual Symposium,
Texas Research Institute of Mental Sciences,
Houston, Texas, November 1-3, 1979

Edited by
J. Ray Hays, Ph.D.
Texas Research Institute of Mental Sciences
Thomm Kevin Roberts, Ph.D.
University of Houston
and
Kenneth S. Solway, Ph.D.
Texas Research Institute of Mental Sciences
Lore Feldman
Technical Editor

SP MEDICAL & SCIENTIFIC BOOKS
New York

SPECTRUM PUBLICATIONS, INC.
175-20 Wexford Terrace, Jamaica, N.Y. 11432

Library of Congress Cataloging in Publication Data

Main entry under title:
Violence and the violent individual.

Includes index.
1. Violence—Congresses. 2. Violence—Etiology—Congress. 3. Criminal psychology—Congresses. 4. Psychodiagnostics—Congresses. 5. Psychotherapy—Congresses. I. Hays, James Ray, 1942- II. Roberts, Thomm Kevin. III. Solway, Kenneth S. IV. Feldman, Lore. V. Texas Research Institute of Mental Sciences.
RC569.5.V55V56 616.85'84 80-24

ISBN 0-89335-116-4

Printed in the United States of America

Contributors

GENE G. ABEL, M.D.
New York State Psychiatric Institute
and
Department of Psychiatry
College of Physicians and Surgeons
Columbia University
New York, New York

ERNEST S. BARRATT, Ph.D.
Behavioral Science Laboratory
Department of Behavioral Sciences
University of Texas Medical Branch
Galveston, Texas

JUDITH V. BECKER, Ph.D.
New York State Psychiatric Institute
and
Department of Psychiatry
College of Physicians and Surgeons
Columbia University, New York, NY

EDWARD BLANCHARD, Ph.D.
Department of Psychology
and
Clinical Psychology Program
State University of New York at Albany
Albany, New York

ARTHUR M. BODIN, Ph.D.
Mental Research Institute
Palo Alto, California

RAMSEY CLARK, J.D.
Former Attorney General of the U.S.
New York, New York

KAREN H. COLEMAN, M.Ed.
Marriage and Family Clinic
Texas Research Institute of Mental Sciences
Houston, Texas

NANCY E. DAWSON, B.S.
Psychiatric and Psychosomatic Research Laboratory
Veterans Administration Medical Center
and
Birkman-Mefferd Research Foundation
Houston, Texas

HAROLD K. DUDLEY, JR., M.A.
Texas Department of Mental Health and Mental Retardation
Austin, Texas

VICTOR H. ELION, Ph.D.
Behavioral Sciences Research Section
Texas Research Institute of Medical Sciences
Houston, Texas

DIANA SULLIVAN EVERSTINE, Ph.D.
Mental Research Institute
Palo Alto, California

LOUIS EVERSTINE, M.P.H.
Mental Research Institute
Palo Alto, California

BARRY FLANAGAN, B.S.
New York State Psychiatric Institute
New York, New York

ROBERT D. HARE, Ph.D.
Department of Psychology
University of British Columbia
Vancouver, Canada

J. RAY HAYS, Ph.D.
Texas Research Institute of Medical Sciences
and
Department of Psychology
University of Houston
and
Department of Psychiatry
Baylor College of Medicine
Houston, Texas

KAREN HOLDEN, M.A.
Department of Psychology
University of Illinois
Champaign, Illinois

EDWIN E. JOHNSTONE, M.D.
Psychiatry Residency Training Section
Texas Research Institute of Mental Sciences
and
Department of Psychiatry
University of Texas Medical School
Houston, Texas

BLAIR JUSTICE, Ph.D.
Department of Psychology
University of Texas School of Public Health
Houston, Texas

RITA JUSTICE, Ph.D.
Southwestern Institute for Group and Family Therapy
Houston, Texas

A. JOAN KLEBBA, M.A.
Division of Vital Statistics
National Center for Health Statistics
Hyattsville, Maryland

JOHNE M. LENNON, B.S.
Psychiatric and Psychosomatic Research Laboratory
Veterans Administration Medical Center
Houston, Texas

RODNEY LININGER, B.A.
Buena Park Police Department
Buena Park, California

JOHN R. LION, M.D.
Clinical Research Program for Violent Behavior
Institute of Psychiatry and Human Behavior
University of Maryland School of Medicine
Baltimore, Maryland

DAVID MARRERO, M.A.
Program in Social Ecology
University of California
Irvine, California

ROY B. MEFFERD, JR., Ph.D.
Psychiatric and Psychosomatic Research Laboratory
Veterans Administration Medical Center
and
Departments of Physiology and Psychiatry
Baylor College of Medicine
Houston, Texas

EDWIN I. MEGARGEE, Ph.D.
Department of Psychology
Florida State University
and
Crime and Delinquency Specialty Program
Tallahassee, Florida

WALTER J. MEYER III, M.D.
Departments of Human Biological Chemistry, Genetics, and Psychiatry
and
Division of Endocrinology, Department of Pediatrics
University of Texas Medical Branch
Galveston, Texas

LOU ANN TODD MOCK, Ph.D.
Department of Psychiatry
Baylor College of Medicine
Houston, Texas

RUSSELL R. MONROE, M.D.
Department of Psychiatry
and
Institute of Psychiatry and Human Behavior
University of Maryland School of Medicine
Baltimore, Maryland

JAMES M. MULLEN, Ph.D.
Research Project on Dangerousness
Texas Department of Mental Health and Mental Retardation
Austin, Texas

JULIAN RAPPAPORT, Ph.D.
Community Psychology Training Program
University of Illinois
Champaign, Illinois

LINDA RICHARDSON, M.S.N.
Department of Psychology
University of Houston
Houston, Texas

THOMM KEVIN ROBERTS, Ph.D.
Texas Research Institute of Mental Sciences
Houston, Texas

ELI A. RUBINSTEIN, Ph.D.
Department of Psychology
University of North Carolina
Chapel Hill, North Carolina

PETER SCHARF, Ed.D.
Program in Social Ecology
University of California
Irvine, California

SALEEM A. SHAH, Ph.D.
Center for Studies of Crime and Delinquency
National Institute of Mental Health
Rockville, Maryland

S. I. SHUMAN, Ph.D., J.D.
Department of Psychiatry
Wayne State University Medical School
and
Lafayette Clinic
Michigan Department of Mental Health
Detroit, Michigan

KENNETH S. SOLWAY, Ph.D.
Behavioral Sciences Research Section
and
Clinical Psychology and Social Sciences Training Section
Texas Research Institute of Mental Sciences
and
Harris County Juvenile Probation Department
and
Department of Psychiatry
Baylor College of Medicine
Houston, Texas

HENRY J. STEADMAN, Ph.D.
Special Projects Research Unit
New York State Department of Mental Hygiene
and
State University of New York at Albany
Albany, New York

HANS TOCH, Ph.D.
School of Criminal Justice
State University of New York at Albany
Albany, New York

PAUL A. WALKER, Ph.D.
The Gender Clinic
and
Departments of Psychiatry and Behavioral Sciences, and Pediatrics
University of Texas Medical Branch
Galveston, Texas

CHARLES WEIGEL II, J.D., LL.M.
South Texas College of Law
Houston, Texas

MAXINE L. WEINMAN, Dr.P.H.
Psychosomatic Research Section
Texas Research Institute of Mental
Sciences
Houston, Texas

MARVIN E. WOLFGANG, Ph.D.
Center for Studies in Criminology and
Criminal Law
University of Pennsylvania
Philadelphia, Pennsylvania

Preface

This volume contains the proceedings of the 12th in a series of national symposia held annually at the Texas Research Institute of Mental Sciences. The conferences bring together scientists from different disciplines to discuss research of current interest in the mental sciences. We chose violence as our topic in 1979 because it is an issue of worldwide concern, and because professionals in the mental health field are increasingly being charged with responsibility for care of dangerous and violent individuals.

Our institute's interest in criminal behavior and violence has a long history dating from the late 1950s and early 1960s, when our psychology and psychiatry trainees began to provide clinical services to the Harris County Juvenile Probation Department. Parallel to the research of delinquency, Texas Research Institute scientists and clinicians have been involved in investigations of mental illness related to acts of violence and crime.

This book has three major components: the causes of violent behavior, measurement and prediction of violence, and treatment of the violent individual. These topics are thoughtfully discussed by researchers and clinicians who are on the leading edge of knowledge in their field. Their chapters present the latest information on the scientific understanding of violence. The authors fill the dual criteria of scientific integrity and broad-ranging understanding of the topic.

The chapters vary greatly in the depth and specificity with which the authors approached their task. The contrast, from Ramsey Clark's broad view of health to Ernest Barratt's study of evoked potentials, shows that the concern with violence must take many forms, and forward movement in science comes most frequently from incremental steps in the laboratory and clinic. As scientists, we must not become so enmeshed in our laboratory ventures as to disregard the larger view; to do so is not a wise thing when dealing with a topic such as violence and in treating and studying violent individuals.

Our symposium could not have been nearly so comprehensive or complete without the generous support of the Law Enforcement Assistance Administration, Sandoz Pharmaceuticals, and Merck Sharp & Dohme Postgraduate Program. We acknowledge their financial support with deep appreciation. We thank Joseph C. Schoolar, director of the institute, for supporting our pursuit of this topic. Special thanks to our secretaries, Anita Smith, Mildred Dickson, Stella Harrison, and Debbie Johnston, whose outstanding work made the program a success, and to Marcia Tibbets who typed the edited manuscripts so competently. Many institute staff members have participated in the organization of these symposia over the years; their experience and aid were invaluable.

J. RAY HAYS
THOMM KEVIN ROBERTS
KENNETH S. SOLWAY

Contents

VIOLENCE AND THE VIOLENT INDIVIDUAL

CHAPTER 1

A Few Modest Proposals to Reduce Individual Violence in America

RAMSEY CLARK

There are many types of violence. It is well to remember this when considering interpersonal violent crime. Foremost is war and its threat where violence is supreme, slaughters millions and imperils all. Insurrection, terrorism, and politically motivated violence cannot be ignored. Poverty with its extremes of starvation, malnutrition, sickness, ignorance, and want is a form of violence as deadly as gunfire. Environmental pollution, slum housing, bad air and water, excessive noise and fear are as traumatizing as a mugging in their insidious ways. Countless forms of economic exploitation, of discrimination, and hopelessness are constant violent experiences.

These are all part of the world as it is. They are part of the environment in which interpersonal violence occurs.

The causes of violence are many. Their effects in different societies vary. Cultural anthropology and comparative studies of violence in contemporary societies and economic, social, racial, ethnic, religious, age, sex, and other groups within our society help us analyze causes of violence. What we see are apparently enormous variations: Murder in Houston compared to London; Watts to West Los Angeles; Pakistan to Thailand; Aztecs to Tasadays; Thuggees to Franciscans; the Weimar Republic to Nazi Germany; China to Taiwan.

How much do we really know about the occurrence of violence? What measure do we really have of assaults? How many children are beaten? Has violence in America increased or decreased since 1776, 1886 or 1976? How can we find out? A stern scepticism will probably best serve judgment; our ignorance is vast.

Greater study of who commits violent crime and who are its victims is important. We know in a general way that violent acts are far more common among poor, urban, young, male minorities, school drop-outs, persons from broken homes, the emotionally disturbed, slum dwellers. Areas of high violent crime can be located on the maps of every American city. It is where those people live. Their victims live there, too.

The principal proposal is that healthy children raised in decent conditions among loving people in a gentle and just society where freedom and equality are valued will rarely commit violent acts toward others. The capacity for interpersonal violence will increase as a society varies from these.

Physical and emotional health are a major factor in violent conduct. With the National Institute of Mental Health predicting 10 percent of the American people will suffer protracted periods of mental illness, we know how difficult violence will be to control. Dr. Thomas S. Langner of the New York University Medical School found mental illness in 28 percent of the children of the poorest families living in Manhattan. The proportion of the American prison population that is classified "retarded" is a substantial multiple, five or more, of the proportion of all "retarded" to the total population. Ten million alcoholics and serious drug abuse by hundreds of thousands contribute enormously to violence. Dyslexia and physical and psychological reading handicaps contribute to social failure, school drop-out, and violence. Congenital and later brain damage caused by trauma or disease, malnutrition, physical defects and illness causes differences among people that sometimes lead to violence.

Health care is both a major opportunity for reducing violence and a real risk. Comprehensive health service reaching the most deprived could obviously prevent many conditions leading to violence. This is particularly true where the services reach families before and during pregnancy, at birth, during infancy, and childhood. But many illnesses, physical and emotional, are caused by conditions that make it very difficult for health care to cure. Emotional stability is hard to establish in people living in Bedlam. Care for alcoholism and drug addiction in a drug culture that seems to offer little other relief is not readily within the ability of medical science. The ability of health care to help an adult with a propensity to violence is limited, although it is an important human service and a preventive opportunity.

The risks of viewing violence as a sickness that can be treated like cancer are real. The treatment model may be harmful to most who have committed violent crime. Surgery, sedation and behavior modification have not been proven helpful, nor have they reconciled with principles of individual freedom. Medical semantics applied to the criminally violent often are inapplicable and they handicap problem-solving. It is important to acknowledge the limits of the medical solution.

Early interpersonal relationships are perhaps the most important in forming capacities for violence. A society that loves its children will not know much violence. Family stability is conducive to personal stability, and family crisis intervention is the surest early warning system of the probability of violence. Running away is the first conflict with society for most later convicted of serious crime. Child abuse including brutal assaults on infants, babies, and children may condition many to use violence themselves. Social services supporting families, or families living together with adequate housing, income assurance, instruction in child care and training, family counseling, good child care, and babysitting services can maintain themselves and raise their children in love. Equality is the mother of justice, Philo tells us. Mothers need to know this. We cannot overestimate the power of compassion to create character.

Plato observed "poverty is the mother of crime." While we can inventory countless facts to contradict the proposition, these facts are, as Cervantes observed, the enemy of truth. An expanding imagination will reveal the antihumane effects of poverty in its broadest meaning.

America, an affluent society, is particularly afflicted by materialism. Success is money. Communications, advertising, conspicuous consumption constantly condition us to this. The poor are more painfully aware of their low economic state, and the possibility of more, than ever before. Poverty rations health, food, housing, family stability, personal safety, education, opportunity, comfort, justice itself.

Economic crime by poor people—burglary, larceny, and theft—is 90 percent of all "index" crimes in the Uniform Crime Reports. Economic crimes by the middle class and the wealthy illegally and immorally convert a thousand times annually the conversions by the poor. Crimes against corporations total $45 billion annually, the American Management Association estimates, including $5 billion for pilfering. Corporations return the favor many times over. Consumer fraud, price-fixing, usury and other crimes usually visit those who can least afford them.

The poor are at least subjectively aware of our value patterns. They see the hypocrisy of the system which sends them to prison for property crime while, as Shaw observed, the rich are often "sent to Parliament" for similar, if more profitable, conduct. You cannot make the world safe for hypocrisy. Economic insecurity may be the single most destabilizing factor in our society, leading to emotional stress and violence.

For the maturing youth, poverty forges values that often lead to violence. No decent home, no family, a relative afflicted with alcoholism and idleness, school drop-out, no jobs, no money, no organized activity or recreation, nothing to do, gangs seeking some release from miserable circumstances, success seen in gambling, drugs, and prostitution, the elderly, weak and sick left in their midst for want of love, all these and more make that period when personal choices are being made at 10 to 20 years of age likely to lead to violence. It often does.

Inequality is an important factor. "The chief and universal cause of the revolutionary impulse is the desire for equality," Aristotle reports. Inequality in lives can hammer people into rage. Patent racism in America created interpersonal violence long before Nat Turner was rewarded for his violent uprising by having his head placed on a pole. It continues today. The inequality continues even to the use of violence. Murder of a policeman brings a death penalty. Murder by a policeman is rarely punished. Police killed 39 people, including ten hostages, in retaking the Attica prison, shot 128 and brutally beat 700. No police officer was ever tried, but a teen-aged inmate was given a 20-year to life sentence for assaulting the one guard killed by inmates. Events like these create impressions that affect conduct. Efforts at equality can reduce violence.

A punitive society causes violence by its sanctions. When we use aversive techniques to have others act as we would have them act, we teach them to do the same. We instruct in the utility of force, failing to see how unstable and sad is a society in which people are not violent only because they are afraid. The total experience of some drives them to violence for which society then punishes them. When they see a way to avoid punishment they will use force. Since not one serious crime in 50 results in conviction, they see the probability of apprehension as slight and take their chances. Others are so out of self-control and discipline that they will act violently whatever the probability of punishment. And some will use violence because they want to be punished.

Prison manufactures crime. A higher capacity for violence walks out of prisons than enters. Alternatives to incarceration should be used for all but the immediate and uncontrollably violent. Prisons should be abolished. Prisons with the word "hospital" over the door will serve no better. Punishment is itself a crime and the death penalty tells the people to kill those they choose to kill, however capricious the choice for murderer and executioner. We should abandon punishment to reduce violence.

The paramilitary concept of police is the antithesis of the free society. The idea of a civil police involves human services, not force. Community relations, integration, family crisis intervention, youth training, athletic leagues, referral to effective social agencies, training in cultural differences, and psychology are but a few of the services police can provide to reduce violence. Marksmanship, manacling, arrests for drunkenness—a problem police can never solve—will only make police the enemy of the people and America a police state. We should enlarge the social service capacity of police and reduce the role of force.

Finally, America glorifies the power of violence and ignores its pity. Nonviolence is seen as cowardly. For a man to be gentle is for him to be weak. From the school yard fight to "Kojak" on television, we equate might with right. Our folklore is full of criminal heroes like Jesse James and Bonnie and Clyde. We respect force, and it is very human to want respect. Give me death, or life in prison, but don't ignore me, Son of Sam cries out. Few Americans are strong enough to adhere to nonviolence under pressure. "Winning" is everything and force is the way.

By commitment and conduct we must make gentleness a virtue. We must see violence as the ultimate human degradation. Disputes should be resolved by reason, by compassion, by democratic processes. Freedom and equality should be our practice as they are our preachment. Fear must be recognized as the ultimate despot driving us to force and violence.

Violence measures the moral temperature of a people. A society that loves children and cares about its character will have as its highest priority the reduction of violence.

Part I

ETIOLOGY OF VIOLENT BEHAVIOR

CHAPTER 2

Psychological Aspects of the Etiology of Violence

THOMM KEVIN ROBERTS
LOU ANN TODD MOCK
EDWIN E. JOHNSTONE

Violence has been written about and studied from many different perspectives, from a criminological point of view (Beattie and Kenney, 1966) as well as from the perspective of morality (Feshbach, 1971). We have studied genetics and its effects on the development of certain personality types believed to be predisposed to violent behavior (Crowe, 1974) while also being interested in family influences in relation to violent behavior (Curtis, 1963; Kopernik, 1964; Silver et al., 1969). Investigations of violence have ranged from the molecular pursuits of laboratory scientists (Aufreiter, 1969; Nordlicht, 1972; Hamburg and Brodie, 1973; Plutchik et al., 1976) through the vast undertakings of scientists concerned with cultures and societies (Ball-Rokeach, 1973; Lester, 1967), to the immense efforts of investigators studying the imponderable phenomena of evil (Gruen, 1974), mass violence (Serban, 1970), and war (Meade, 1973).

Recently, David Hamburg (1977), president of the National Institute of Medicine, stated that "if infectious disease was the chief life limiting factor for children, adolescents, (and) young adults at the turn of the twentieth century, then accidents, suicide and homicide are now the prime causes of very early death" (p. 5). Violent acts, then, are viewed as a serious threat to life and the quality of life, so serious, in fact, that the social scientist Kenneth Clark (1971), in a controversial paper, pleaded with medical scientists to develop a biochemical intervention that could stabilize and make dominant the moral and ethical side of human beings. He supported experimentation with human subjects in developing such an intervention, and suggested that all national and international leaders take these drugs as soon as they are available. So much for the gravity of the situation with regard to violence.

We shall highlight the difficulty of semantics and of definition of the topic, briefly outline the philosophical tracings and influences on theory, present the major psychological theories, and some psychiatric and psychological descriptions of violent individuals along with psychological variables associated with violence.

The first thing one is struck by is the ambiguity of the term *violence* as it is used in the literature. A given investigator will purport to be writing about violent people, while examination of the characteristics of the subject sample will reveal that criminals guilty of passing bad checks, or theoretically even income tax evaders, were included in the study. Criminality is not synonymous with violence. Further, one is apt to be reading results of a study whose author is generalizing about violent behavior, and, recalling the procedures, realize that the experimental behavior under investigation was administration of mild electric shocks by one college sophomore to another.

As Megargee (1969) wrote, "no definition of violence has ever proved completely successful. Although everyone 'knows what violence is' no one has ever been able to define it adequately so that every possible instance of violent behavior is included within the definition while all the excluded behavior is clearly nonviolent" (p. 1038). Bemoaning the state of scientific and semantic disrepair, many scientists believe that worthwhile investigations cannot be done until the situation is changed. Others believe that a universally accepted definition is unattainable but that this does not mean that violence and aggression cannot be studied. As Plutchik et al. (1976) stated, "science does not start with definitions, it ends with them" (p. 71). Several authors have offered definitions that may more or less serve as conventional thought in the area. Ilfeld (1969) viewed violence as an act of intense, willful, physical harm committed by an individual or a group against himself or another individual or group. Megargee (1969) described violence as overtly threatened or overtly accomplished application of force which results in the injury or destruction of persons or property or reputation, or the illegal appropriation of property. More recently, Feshbach (1971) characterized violence as the more severe forms of physical aggression.

In the literature, a number of features are often attended to in reflecting about, describing, evaluating, and classifying an act of violent aggression. The characteristics to follow represent a compilation and synthesis of facets of violence discussed by Buss (1961), Megargee (1969), and Feshbach (1971), and are offered as a useful heuristic method in conceptualizing violence or aggression. Considering the nature of the act, one is likely to ask whether it was physical or verbal, active or passive, direct or indirect. Then one is likely to take into account the legality, intentionality, and intensity of the behavior. One will probably be concerned with the factors of personal as opposed to social motivation, degree of personal responsibility, options available to the individual, defensive or initiated basis of the act, degree of emotional disturbance, age and sex of the victim, and more generally, appropriateness of the target. Lastly, in examining the violent or aggressive aspects of an act, one will probably introduce the notion of fair play and one's own attitude toward the objectives of the act.

Research that focuses directly on human violence is extremely difficult to do. Psychologists and behavioral scientists generally use two basic research strategies, naturalistic and experimental. From the standpoint of morals and ethics, the naturalistic method is ruled out; one cannot study an incident of human violence as it is happening without attempting to interfere and somehow stopping it. Even more anathematic is the notion of a behavioral scientist's constructing an experiment in which human beings perpetrate some form of violence on one another. Witness the reaction to Milgram's studies in which subjects were simply led to believe they were being violent. Given these ethical and moral restraints, we have few adequate data on which to build and test theories of violence. All we do have are what Megargee (1969) termed "armchair" or "philosophical" theories. As a result, theories presented here, which are to some degree empirically based, are theories of aggression, an aspect on which we have sounder data. As Megargee (1969) reminds us, "whether or not these theories can be extrapolated to account for violence is another question" (p. 1042).

In *Discourse on Method,* Descartes told us that of the subjects he had studied in his youth, mathematics pleased him most because its conclusions were demonstrated with certainty. And in the dawning of early modern empiricism, physics was to Sir Francis Bacon what mathematics was to

Descartes: a model for true and usable knowledge about humankind and its world (Morgan, 1950; Ramsperger, 1950). Surely, psychologists fleeing the basements of university philosophy buildings near the turn of the twentieth century hoped that in the fleeing they, as scientists devoted to the study of behavior, were freeing themselves to deploy some of their emerging empirical method. Presumably, they had grown weary of and felt hamstrung by more speculative thinking. Reading the psychological theories of aggression, we do indeed find the influences of empiricism, but we also find the tracings of seventeenth century social philosophers. More than that, if one sifts through psychological theories of aggression, one discerns religious and biblical influences, often in the form of the issue of human goodness or evil. This is not to say that psychological theories are nothing more or less than latter-day distillations of the thinking of philosophers long since deceased. Rather than being embarrassed by these influences, as a developing, self-conscious science might have been in the past, a science more firmly rooted and confident would now do well to acknowledge its roots and try to explain their effects and get on with it.

The social philosophers of the seventeenth and eighteenth centuries who, apart from those already cited, seem to have influenced, directly or not, psychological theories of aggression are Thomas Hobbes, John Locke, and Jean Jacques Rousseau. They were concerned with the legitimization of government and political authority, and they were much enamored of the notion of a social contract. The terms of such a contract were subject to varied formulations, according to the particular philosopher's concept of man's essential nature (Lefkowitz et al., 1977). Hobbes's view was that man is essentially aggressive; conflicted, he desires preservation of individual liberty while also wanting dominion over others, the resolution being man's impulse of self-preservation and his consequent essential aggressiveness. Locke took a different view. His term, *tabula rasa,* or blank slate, connotes his notion of innate ideas, but Locke's opinion of human nature was that man is essentially virtuous. Rousseau rejected the idea that man has a fundamental nature—aggressive or virtuous, good or bad—and began with the premise that man would be good; the institutions governing his life made him bad. For Rousseau, in current terms, what a child becomes is consequent to his learning history (Lefkowitz et al., 1977).

ETHOLOGICAL THEORY

Ethological research seems to fall into the area of comparative psychology and behavior genetics, although ethologists are usually trained, not in psychology, but in medicine, physiology, or zoology (Megargee, 1969).

Unlike some of the other behavioral sciences, ethology applies the method of biology to behavioral phenomena (Lefkowitz et al., 1977), examining similarities and differences between species by both naturalistic observation and experimentation. This is done with the notion that hypotheses derived from the study of infrahuman organisms will provide insights into human behavior as well (Megargee, 1969).

Perhaps the best known figure in this area is Konrad Lorenz, whose book, *On Aggression* (1966), became widely read in a short time (Fromm 1973). From his study of fish, bird, and mammalian species, Lorenz concluded that human aggressiveness is an instinct fed by a constant source of energy to neural centers that govern the instinct, and it is not necessarily reaction to outer stimuli. Primarily an inner excitation, aggression seeks release and will be expressed regardless of the adequacy of the outer stimulus (Fromm, 1973). As Lorenz (1966) tells us, "it is the spontaneity of the instinct that makes it so dangerous." The hydraulic characteristic of the model is clear. Another part of the model is the notion that aggression is in the service of life: aggression among members of the same species serves natural selection, providing a balanced distribution of a species over the available territory and aiding in the gathering of food. Rival fighting serves to provide the best mate and thereby the strongest offspring (Fromm, 1973; Lefkowitz et al., 1977).

In human beings, intraspecific aggression has gone awry. According to Lorenz (1966), lower animals able to kill one another have innate inhibitory mechanisms, such as ritualistic displays of appeasement, that help to fend off aggressors with little or no physical contact. Innate aggressive and inhibitory instincts are balanced in lower animals. In man, basically a harmless omnivore, these mechanisms presumably have been rendered ineffective by the rapid advance of cultural evolution (Lefkowitz et al., 1977).

Aggressive instincts have become grotesquely exaggerated in man, whose endless supply of aggressive energy is augmented by the technology of violence. The ethological view, then, as represented by Lorenz, is that man's aggressive behavior is instinctual, spontaneous, inevitable, and the result of phylogenetic processes.

Observing the territoriality of several species, Robert Ardrey (1966) found many parallels to human forms of aggression. In a later book, *The Social Contract* (1970), Ardrey generally holds to the view that man is innately "a killer"; territorial defense and thereby aggression is an innate human characteristic. All of these sentiments with regard to man are extrapolations from animal studies (Megargee, 1969).

Tinbergen (1968) takes a more moderate approach. Based on his investigations of infrahuman organisms, Tinbergen believes that much of the internal predisposition to aggression must be inborn, yet he describes the complex interaction of heredity and environment to produce overt behavior (Megargee, 1969). According to Tinbergen (1968): "On the one hand, man is akin to many species of animals in that he fights his own species. But on the other hand, he is, among the thousands of species that fight, the only one in which fighting is disruptive. . . . Man is the only species that is a mass murderer, the only misfit in his own society" (p. 1412).

The ethological theories of Lorenz, Ardrey, and others have not gone unchallenged. Megargee (1969) suggests that the cited ethologists have emphasized the similarities between man and other animals without acknowledging the dangers of uncritically applying animal data to human problems. Crook (1968) observes that the primates nearest to man in the evolutionary sequence lack territoriality, while Zegans (1971) believes that emergent man was endowed with a milder disposition to dominance and a weaker instinctive link to territory than his herbivorous ancestors. Commenting on the self-preservation aspect of aggression described by Lorenz, Zegans (1971) says that "little adaptive purpose could be served by the inheritance of an endogenous, self-stimulating aggressive drive. Such an internal summons to combat would have retarded the difficult task of forging larger, more cooperatively differentiated social organization" (p. 358). Concerning Lorenz's theories of self-stimulating and spontaneous aggression, Scott (1962) finds that available data indicate that "fighting behavior among the higher mammals, including man, originates in external stimulation and that there is no evidence of spontaneous internal stimulation" (p. 173). According to Lefkowitz et al. (1977), Scott further states that certain chemical and physical changes would have to precede spontaneous aggression for the concept to have any validity. "For example . . . the physiological concomitants of hunger are lowered blood sugar in the cells, stimulation of the brain cells, stimulation of the brain centers associated with this factor, and the consequent hunger contractions in the stomach which lead to food seeking and eating behavior. Such a mechanism has not been demonstrated with regard to spontaneous aggression as far as we know" (Lefkowitz et al., 1977, p. 14).

The ethological approach has also been criticized sharply by anthropologists and sociologists involved in cross-cultural study. Eisenberg (1972) and Montagu (1968, 1976) suggest human beings are by nature neither aggressive nor peaceful but may be molded into either type. Support for this position is found in many accounts that demonstrate great diversity in aggressive patterns found in various cultures (Megargee, 1969). Whiting (1965) and Paddock (1975)—the former studying nearby towns and the latter towns in Okinawa, New England, Mexico, the Phillipines, India, and Africa—conclude that culture has a tremendous influence on behavior, including violent and aggressive behavior. They found considerable differences in the incidence of violence in the various societies. The number of totally nonviolent cultures challenges the view that human beings are instinctively and inevitably aggressive.

PSYCHOANALYTIC THEORY

Sigmund Freud was trained as a physician and conducted considerable physiological research before the psychological complexities of human behavior became the focus of his attention. That personal history along with the Darwinian spirit of the times seemed to lead Freud to a theory of human behavior strongly tied to the notion of man's animalistic nature. His thinking with regard to human aggression was similar to Lorenz's, in that he saw it as instinctual and inevitable. Constantly examining and revising his theories, however, Freud held different views at different times, and this is true also in the area of aggression. Most psychoanalytic research depends upon the observation of humans, and Freud obtained most of his ideas from psychoanalytic treatment of patients and analysis of his own inner psychological life. The clinical tradition in psychoanalytic research has remained prevalent to this day. Where the ethological theorists use animal investigations, psychoanalytic theorists use the consulting room.

Buss in 1961 and Zegans in 1971 discussed the evolutionary nature of Freud's thoughts on aggression. His views on the topic may be divided into three stages. In his very early writings, Freud was primarily concerned with stages of psychosexual development and the notion of libidinal energies in his attempt to confirm the idea that sexuality, broadly conceived, underlies all neurotic conflicts. This concentration on libido resulted in relegating aggression to a minor role, that of becoming manifest only in relation to the psychosexual stages of development. For example, in the late oral stage of psychosexual development, the child acquires teeth and the tendency to bite objects. Freud saw this as an expression of oral-sadistic impulses. He believed the zenith of aggression is reached during the anal period, the second stage of psychosexual development, in which sadistic urges to hurt and dominate others are frequent and intense. Finally, in the oedipal period, competition and rivalry with the same-sex parent for the love of the opposite-sex parent lead to death wishes toward the hated rival (Buss, 1961). Thus, in Freud's theories, aggression is directed outwardly but always to sexual energies and in an ancillary role to that of libido and the psychosexual stages (Buss, 1961).

In his next phase of theorizing about aggression, Freud placed more emphasis on the "ego instincts" in which nonlibidinal urges occupy a more important role. Ego instincts are directed to self-preservation, their major constituent being aggression. In this reformulation, which moved aggression from being an aspect of libido to part of the ego instincts, Freud thought that aggressive impulses could occur in the absence of sexual conflict. Now emphasizing the reactive nature of aggressive urges, Freud postulated that the source of aggression is not biological, as are sexual urges, but the self-preserving tendency of the ego to strike back at whatever threatens or denies it satisfaction. Here aggression was at the disposal of the ego (Buss, 1961; Zegans, 1971).

In the third and final phase of his concept of aggression, Freud postulated a death instinct, which he felt represented the organism's wish to return to the state of nothingness from which it had emerged (Buss, 1961). Fromm (1973) quotes from a 1930 paper by Freud:

> Starting from speculations on the beginning of life and from biological parallels I drew the conclusion that, besides the instinct to preserve living substance, there must exist another, contrary instinct seeking to dissolve those units and to bring them back to their primeval, inorganic state. That is to say, as well as Eros there was an instinct of death. (p. 15)

The death instinct, then, is directed against the organism itself, being a self-destructive drive, or it is directed outward, tending to destroy others (Fromm, 1973).

According to Buss (1961), Freud believed the more powerful an individual's death instinct, the greater the need to direct aggression outward against objects and people. Aggression that cannot be discharged against external objects will be turned back on the self.

Thus, in Freud's final position, he gave aggression a role comparable to that of life itself—life and death instincts were in a constant struggle—and as instinctive and inevitable as sexual energies.

Freud wrote, "the aim of all life is death" (Megargee, 1969, p. 1057). Destructive instinct derives from death instinct. "Freud realized that there is no direct evidence for the existence of a death instinct, but he reasoned that the absence of its manifestation was due to its being a silent instinct" (Buss, 1961, p. 186). Freud was not overly occupied with trying to prove the existence of the death instinct; he felt that its proof was best left to chemists. He hoped that instinct eventually would be placed on a firm physiological foundation (Buss, 1961).

Little psychological experimentation has been done on this question, but there has been a good deal of clinical and theoretical reaction to Freud's position within the psychoanalytic school of thought and a great deal of reaction from nonpsychoanalytic researchers. Some experimental studies have been done on the relationship between sex and aggression (Barclay, 1971; La Torre, 1973). These researchers have used various ways of stimulating subjects by presenting sexually arousing, anxiety-arousing, or laughter-arousing visual or reading material, then administering some dependent measure that purports to measure aggression, particularly sexual arousal in relation to aggressive behavior. These researchers believe they have demonstrated that sexually arousing material increases aggressive behavior. The presumed link between sex and aggression also has been discussed by Gardner (1950).

Some non-Freudian psychoanalytic theoreticians viewed aggression differently. Adler early in his career characterized aggression as instinctive but later defined it as "a partly conscious, partly irrational reactive tendency toward overcoming obstacles and everyday life tasks" (Buss, 1961, p. 192). Jung did not write much on aggression but, in contrast to Freud, he started with a single instinct from which he developed the polar opposites of life and death instincts. Horney rejected both death and aggressive instincts, stating that aggression and hostility are responses to basic anxiety (Buss, 1961). More recent writers, Hott in 1970 and De Rosis in 1971, believe aggression is not instinctual. Bender (1969), also disagreeing with the view of aggression as instinctive, sees in her clinical work with children instances of extreme aggression as a form of developmental pathology, usually the result of an unsympathetic and disturbing environment.

Having outlined the criticisms and arguments in psychoanalytic thought, we find that the criticisms outside of it are similar to those directed at Lorenz. The cross-cultural studies mentioned earlier question Freud's instinctivist position much as they do Lorenz's. There is also objection to the inevitable as well as instinctive aspects of aggression proposed by Freud, which the critics see as speculative and unsubstantiated. Meade (1973), for example, calls warfare an invention and not a biological necessity, whereas Freud in a letter to Einstein concerning war "argued against the feasibility of ridding man of his aggressive instincts" (Lefkowitz et al., 1977, p. 8).

One criticism aimed at psychoanalytic theory of aggression has been lodged at psychoanalytic theory generally, that is, that the concepts are ambiguous, often abstract, and do not lend themselves to experimental rigor. The psychoanalytic research method generally, and specifically with regard to aggression, has been criticized for its clinical emphasis on patient pathology as a basis for generalization, and for the fact that its procedure does not allow controlled research.

FRUSTRATION-AGGRESSION THEORY

Frustration-aggression theory was originally proposed by psychologists John Dollard, L. W. Dobb, Neal Miller, O. H. Mowser and Robert Sears at the Institute of Human Relations at Yale University in 1939, (Megargee, 1969). The research procedures they and subsequent investigators used were laboratory-based, experimental studies with animals and human subjects. Investigative techniques included an approximation or diminished form of frustration or aggression such as the delivery of mild electric shocks or some form of verbal aggression. The psychologists stated their hypotheses clearly and unambiguously. In so doing, while perhaps oversimplifying the problems of studying a complex behavior like aggression, they did facilitate hypothesis-testing for empirical investigation. The frustration-aggression theory has over the years spawned a great deal of empirical research.

Frustration was "initially defined as something that interferes with an ongoing goal response" (Megargee, 1969, pp. 1059-1060), while aggressive behavior was defined as "an act whose goal response is injury to an organism or organism surrogate" (Lefkowitz et al., 1977, p. 24). Here, aggressive behavior is a result of aggressive drive produced by frustration. The frustration-aggression hypothesis as quoted by Lefkowitz et al. (1977) stated that "the occurrence of aggressive behavior always presupposes the existence of frustration and, contrariwise, that the existence of frustration always leads to some form of aggression." The theorists went on to state that "the strength of instigation to aggression should vary directly with: 1) the strength of instigation to the frustrated response; 2) the degree of interference with the frustrated response; 3) the number of frustrated response sequences" (Lefkowitz et al., 1977, p. 24).

Criticized immediately, the view that aggression is always a result of frustration was rephrased to state that "frustration produces instigations to a number of different types of response, one of which is an instigation to some form of aggression" (Lefkowitz et al., 1977, p. 25).

According to Megargee (1969), two important implications of the frustration-aggression position are "first, that the aspects of frustration can remain active over a period of time, and second, that the frustration from different events can summate." The theorists raised two additional questions, when in infancy their hypotheses were applicable and whether frustration-aggression is innate or learned.

Buss (1963) demonstrated experimentally that frustration does not necessarily lead to aggression but may also lead to anxiety or depression. Berkowitz (1960), testing the notion that an act of aggression by an individual reduces the strength of his aggressive drive, found no evidence for the cathartic effect. He believed that guilt over the initial display inhibits further aggressive behavior. A number of studies examined the relationships between frustration, anxiety, level of physiological arousal, overt aggression, and physical attack (Hokanson, 1961; Holmes, 1966; Taylor and Pisano, 1971). Their findings were mixed; for example, experimentally frustrated subjects delivered more shocks to their frustrator but they had higher blood pressure and heart rates than subjects not permitted to respond with aggression. Taylor and Pisano (1971) specifically suggest studying antecedents like anxious stimuli. Scientists, they say, should investigate effects of attacks (experimentally, the delivery of noxious stimuli) and of intended attack on the expression and inhibition of physical aggression. Palmer (1960), in a field study of the effects of frustration, found from interviews and ratings gleaned from the families of male murderers that the murderers did indeed experience more frustration in growing up than did their nearest male sibling.

The frustration-aggression theorists have been criticized for oversimplifying the phenomena of aggression. Their willingness to generalize findings from experimentally induced mild forms of aggression and frustration to phenomena in the natural environment has also been criticized, as have their methods. Megargee (1969) writes: "Typically, all one can measure is the overt behavior that results from a given situation and often there is no way of determining whether the experimental manipulations have influenced the instigation, the inhibition, or the stimulus factors" (p. 1061).

SOCIAL-LEARNING THEORY

Miller and Dollard's *Social Learning and Imitation* was published in 1941, followed in 1954 by Rotter's *Social Learning and Clinical Psychology,* and by Bandura and Walters' *Social Learning and Personality Development* in 1963.

Most of the research done by the social-learning theorists has been laboratory-based, of the milder forms of aggression in animals and human beings, and often with children. Typically, the studies are done in academic settings by psychologists trained clinically but with the behaviorists' strong emphasis on experimental psychology.

Social-learning theory holds that aggressive behavior is learned or acquired in the same way any other behavior is learned. "Compared with theories holding that aggression is innate or the result of an aggressive drive, social learning theory seeks the external rather than the internal impellers to aggression" (Lefkowitz et al., 1977, p. 26). The concern should be with predisposing conditions rather than with predisposed individuals (Lefkowitz et al., 1977). Bandura (1973) states, "The social learning theory of human aggression adopts the position that man is endowed with neurophysiological mechanisms that enable him to behave aggressively, but the activation of these mechanisms depends upon appropriate stimulation and is subject to cortical control" (p. 29). Bandura questions, not the notion of motivated behavior, but whether or not it is explained by instincts, drives, or inner forces. There is a difference, he believes, between ascribing motivational properties to social inducements and acquired incentives as opposed to invoking acquired drives.

The social-learning theory of aggression is based on a three-part model: the way in which aggressive behavior is learned, is activated or provoked, and maintained (Lefkowitz et al., 1977).

Social-learning theorists believe that aggressive behavior is acquired in two basic ways, the first being imitation. The major sources of this kind of learning are familial influences, subcultural influences, and symbolic modeling. Simply stated, youngsters who display aggressive behavior tend to come from families in which parents behave aggressively or in which there is an attitude that favors aggressive solutions to problems. Physical punishment in such families can serve as an aggressive model. A subculture that encourages and offers live modeling of physical aggression as a prestigious way of being is a source of learning that involves imitation. Symbolic modeling, by way of pictures and words, is believed to be a source of imitative learning, the prime example of this mode being television (Lefkowitz et al., 1977).

The second basic way of learning aggressive behavior according to social-learning theory is that of direct experience. Here we delve into terms like reinforcement—both positive and negative, punishment, and extinction. Social-learning theory suggests that behaviors that are reinforced are more likely to occur again. As Megargee (1969) states, "social learning has its greatest effect in teaching the child that aggression can satisfy a number of needs" (p. 1064). If aggression works in getting what one wants, the implications are clear.

In discussing activation or provocation of aggressive behavior, Bandura outlines the major instigators: modeling influence, aversive treatment, incentive inducements, instructional control, and bizarre symbolic control. Someone who has seen others acting in an aggressive way learns the behavior but also is more likely to carry it out. This is so when the modeled acts serve as cues through association with past reinforcement, and when modeled aggressive behavior is reinforced or treated indifferently, thereby disinhibiting the observer and increasing the probability of his performing aggressively. Aversive treatment, Bandura believes, tends to increase arousal in the recipient, and, depending on his/her hierarchy of responses, increase the likelihood of aggression.

As to incentive inducement, the expectation of positive consequences of an aggressive act may instigate aggression. A similar mechanism operates for instructional control. Bizarre symbolic control means that, under certain pathological conditions, e.g., delusions, an individual may be provoked to act aggressively (Lefkowitz et al., 1977).

In maintaining a behavior, social-learning theory delineates the major categories of reinforcement as external, vicarious, and self-reinforced. External reinforcements may be tangible rewards and social and status rewards. Vicarious reinforcement occurs when the aggressive behavior is observed as rewarded. Self-reinforcement may serve to maintain aggressive behavior if, for example, one's aggressive behavior produces feelings of self-worth and esteem (Lefkowitz et al., 1977).

Studying modeling processes, Soares and Soares (1969) found that children in a stress situation tend to respond imitatively rather than with initial trial-and-error behavior. The authors found that children with low self-esteem, feelings of incompetence, and high dependence seem to be especially susceptible to imitative learning. Bandura and Walters (1963) demonstrated that individuals who see others act aggressively are also more apt to behave aggressively. Milgram (1963) found that, in a laboratory investigation, people would violate their own values and administer stimuli thought to be painful when they were instructed to do so by an authoritative figure.

Criticisms of the social-learning approach to understanding aggression are somewhat similar to those directed at frustration-aggression theory. Because of its emphasis on parsimony, little speculation, few hypothetical or unobserved variables, along with the emphasis on empirical studies, the theory is seen as dry and mechanistic (Megargee, 1969). Many critics believe that social-learning theory, because of its reductionism and concern with rigor, has missed the mark in understanding the richness and subtlety of what it is to be human. In regard to research on aggression, social-learning approaches have been criticized for their emphasis on controlled experimentation in laboratory settings, which used mild forms of aggression in testing the theory. The critical outcry is that this is not the way the world is, that the results have limited generalizability at best, and at worst are irrelevant in relation to severe physical aggression or violence.

The attempt to discover psychological aspects of the etiology of violence led us to examine three different kinds of information. The first, the coherent psychological theories posited as reasons for violence, has been presented. The others, examination of several variables in relationship to violence, and a description of violent individuals or groups, are less easy to present in concise form. Definitions of violence vary widely, and while we have attempted to limit this survey to studies of violence defined as physical harm to other human beings, some citations of particular interest were included that are less directly related to violence so defined. Work having to do with violence as a result of alcohol or drug use, or of a psychotic process, was generally excluded.

Before discussing personality variables and individual characteristics of violent people, it is necessary to comment on the possible futility of examining personality for causes of violence. Berkowitz (1968) found evidence of the importance of such immediate cues as guns in triggering violence, while Fischer et al. (1969) found that aggression may be intensified by the presence of potential weapons. Goldstein (1975) believes that situational factors largely determine aggression, and suggests that scientists investigate "aggressible environments." Similarly, according to Monahan (1975), not much success has been achieved in predicting violence-prone individuals because of too many false positives. He suggests that, given the evidence for situational determinants in violence, researchers should look for situations conducive to violence. Having identified those, researchers could investigate (1) ways to modify the situations, (2) modification of an individual's response to the situation, and (3) how to avoid such situations. The fact remains that personality variables and descriptions comprise a great deal of the literature on violence, and they are the subject of the concluding section of this chapter.

Recent studies have dealt with childhood and violence or aggression (Gardner, 1971; Bolman, 1974; Owens and Straus, 1975; Hoover, 1976). While some researchers believe that learning disabilities may predispose a child to violent behavior (Berman, 1972), Gardner (1971), in a study of deprived children, suggested that an excess of traumatic incidents and violent events during the first six years of life produced a great deal of fear in the children; defending against these fears then forms the basis for a neurotically determined learning disability. Gardner states that the type of defense relates to the type of learning disability. Bolman (1974), studying violent and aggressive children, developed a typology of violent children; he concluded that the best approach to treating aggressive children is to view violent behavior as a symptom of problems in relationships, and the violence as the child's attempt to solve the problems. In a nationwide survey, Owens et al. (1975) found that approval of violence by adults is related to their exposure to violence in childhood as either the victim, perpetrator, or observer. Several investigators indicate that wife-battering often occurs in couples who were exposed to domestic violence as children (Straus, 1971; Gayford, 1975; Gelles, 1975). Hoover (1976) found a relationship between lack of physical affection in infancy and violence in adulthood. Finally, Eisen (1976) posits the idea that the failure of the mother to appease and console the infant's rage provides the cornerstone for subsequent violence. Eisen suggests that the child needs to incorporate consolation and comforting from the mother, and that without it the child will not be able to develop control over his own rage.

Another area of investigation has been the study of the relationship between violence and body buffer zones, the imaginary "bubble" around one's body sometimes referred to as "personal space" (Kinzel, 1970; Hildreth et al., 1971; Roger and Schalekamp, 1976; Curran and Blatchley, 1978). Studies reviewed in the recent literature demonstrated that violent prisoners compared to nonviolent ones imagined having a larger body buffer zone (Kinzel, 1970; Hildreth et al., 1971; Roger and Schalekamp, 1976; Curran and Blatchley, 1978). This was found not only from use of subjective measures but also from tests of galvanic skin response (Curran and Blatchley, 1978).

Attitudes and values with regard to violence have also been investigated (Kahn, 1972; Ball-Rokeach, 1973). Kahn's (1972) nationwide survey of attitudes of American men found that most men are prepared to justify use of substantial force for social control but not social change. Ball-Rokeach (1973), surveying men in and outside of prisons, discovered no relationship between violent experience and attitudes and values held toward violence. He concluded that another variable must be looked for in understanding the violent behavior, since attitudes and values do not seem to determine it. This finding is at odds with Wolfgang and Ferracutti's (1976) "subculture of violence" theory discussed elsewhere in this volume.

The relationship between sex roles and violence is another area of psychological research interest (Brownmiller, 1975; McConahay and McConahay, 1977; Straus, 1976; Toby, 1966). In urban industrial societies, Toby argues, family structure in which the father is absent weakens confidence in masculinity. This, the author believes, results in "compulsive masculinity," which is viewed as an exaggerated insistence on characteristics differentiating males from females. Violence remains a clandestine masculine ideal. Brownmiller (1975) believes that the culture's tradition of male dominance over women is asserted most dramatically in the act of rape, a violent behavior which the author believes is the manifestation of a political act of humiliation. One cause of wife-beating, according to Straus (1976), is sex-role rigidity in which there is a heavy emphasis on male authority. McConahay and McConahay (1977), in an investigation of 17 cultures, found sex-role rigidity highly correlated with the incidence of violence.

Investigating the nature of the relationship between perpetrator of violence and victim, one group of studies examines the attitudes toward victims and the phenomena of dehumanization that often occur in the context of war or slaughter (Bernard et al., 1971; Gault, 1971; Kelmon, 1973; Pinderhughes, 1972; Sanford and Coustoch, 1971). Dehumanization occurs when victims are perceived as less than human; other attitudes that increase the likelihood of violence include increased emotional distance from other human beings, a diminished sense of personal responsibility, increased involvement with procedural problems, inability to oppose dominant group pressure, and feelings of personal helplessness (Bernard et al., 1971).

In terms of relationship, the perpetrators are likely to feel that the victims deserve the attack (Pinderhughes, 1972); given such feelings, the perpetrators then sense that they have permission to enact the violence (Sanford and Coustoch, 1971). Another focus of these investigations has been victim precipitation (Gold, 1965; Amir, 1967; Curtis, 1974), in which the victims are somehow seen as directly or indirectly "causing" their own demise, often by having been the first ones in the sequence to have used physical force (Curtis, 1974). The relationship notion is explored also in the investigation of intimate relationships and the violation of the rules of those relationships (Cormier, 1962; Gold, 1965; Kardener and Fuller, 1970; Mohr and McKnight, 1971; Ruotolo, 1968, 1975; Hepburn, 1973; Lystad, 1975; Tidmarsh, 1976; McGrath, 1977). Like Cormier (1962), Mohr and McKnight (1971) conclude that homicides seem to occur when a relationship can no longer be sustained but cannot be given up. Hepburn (1973) views structural factors and cultural norms as most important in domestic violence, and he believes that violation of "relational rules" provokes negotiation and possible violence. Gorney (1971) argues that intense interpersonal bonding produces cultural achievement, aggression, and mental illness. He suggests that increased synergy (individual goals also being society's goals) will reduce aggression and mental illness as it reduces intrasocial competition. Ruotolo (1968,

1975) and Kardener and Fuller (1970) describe some violence as defensive in that the perpetrator perceives the victim as blocking a return to a formerly successful neurotic adjustment.

Psychodiagnostic testing and personality description of various kinds of violent offenders have provided a fruitful area of study. The instruments often used are the Wechsler Adult Intelligence Scale (WAIS) (Deiker, 1973; Kunce et al., 1976; Ruff et al., 1976; Shawver and Jew, 1978), the Rorschach (Perdue and Lester, 1972, 1973), the Thematic Apperception Test (TAT) (Matranga, 1976), and the Minnesota Multiphasic Personality Inventory (MMPI) (Martin and Channell, 1964; Megargee, 1966, 1967; Blackburn, 1968, 1971; Anderson, 1969; Carrol and Fuller, 1971; Davis and Sines, 1971; McCreary, 1976; Lothstein, 1978). Deiker (1973), matching subjects for sex, race, age, and education, and using the WAIS, found the mean full-scale IQ of men indicted for capital offenses did not differ from normal men. Kunce et al. (1976) found that violent prisoners scored lower in the similarities subtest of the WAIS than did nonviolent ones, while Shawver and Jew (1978), in a study published two years later, failed to replicate the Kunce group's finding. Ruff et al. (1976) found lower intelligence quotients in rapists as compared to nonrapist convicts. Perdue and Lester (1972), using the Rorschach, found no differences between rapists and men convicted of aggressive, nonsexual crimes. In another study with the Rorschach, these authors found that murderers of kin appeared healthier than murderers of nonkin. Matranga (1976) found an inverse relationship in male adolescent delinquents between measures of aggression and aggressive content on the TAT. Among MMPI studies, Carrol and Fuller (1971) found that nonviolent offenders exhibit the most deviant profiles, and they found no differences between violent offenders and sexual offenders. According to Anderson (1969), parents of aggressive boys are more deviant than parents of normal or neurotic children. Megargee (1966, 1967) demonstrated both an undercontrolled and an overcontrolled personality type in terms of violence, and Blackburn (1968, 1971) corroborated those findings. Various clinical scale patterns of the MMPI have been suggested as being related to violence. Persons and Monks (1971) and Davis and Sines (1971) showed an apparent relationship between violent-assault offenders and a 4-3 profile.

Perhaps most used are studies that are primarily descriptive. The literature is filled with psychiatric and psychological descriptions of murderers (Guttmacher, 1960; Toch, 1969), dangerous sex offenders (Cormier, 1969), delinquents (Malmquist, 1971), military men who "frag" superior officers (Bond, 1976). Although details of these descriptions are beyond the scope of this discussion, some interesting phenomena should be mentioned. The methodology is clinical, the most commonly employed research tool being a clinical observation or interview, or a self-report questionnaire with a strong clinical flavor, devised by the investigator. The procedure makes comparisons of studies difficult.

The work in this area is of two kinds: single case studies (Bromberg, 1951; Rosenzwieg, 1956; Kahn, 1960; Rose, 1960; Beit-Hallahmi, 1971; Goldstein, 1972) and surveys of various violent population groups (Lander and Schulman, 1963; Hellman and Blackman, 1966; Anthony, 1968; Cormier and Siebert, 1969; Lachman and Gravens, 1969; Tanay, 1969; Toch, 1969; Bach-Y-Rita et al., 1971; Kahn, 1971; Rothenberg, 1971; Malmquist, 1971; Roth, 1972; Climent et al., 1973; Tupin et al., 1973; Bach-Y-Rita, 1974; Bey and Zecchinelli, 1974; Bach-Y-Rita and Verro, 1974; Yager, 1975; Stotland, 1976; Bond, 1976; Yochelson and Samenow, 1976; Lefkowitz et al., 1977). Furthermore, investigators of single case studies are inclined to write about intrapsychic conflicts while reports focusing on groups are likely to report similarities based on behavioral and social histories.

The large body of descriptive literature seems to define, at best, two subgroups of violent individuals whom we will term habitual and non-habitual. In the habitual group, violence is congruent with past behavior and a history of childhood problems; as adults, these persons show little evidence of psychopathology. Their violent behavior is often perpetrated against strangers, and is likely to be repeated. In the nonhabitual group, violence is more likely to be incongruent with past behavior, with no clear history of difficulty. As adults, persons in this second group evidence severe psychopathology; the violence, often perpetrated against intimates, is more severe than that of the habitual group.

CONCLUSION

It would be gratifying and valuable if this overview of the literature concerning the psychological etiology of violence could be summarized and integrated into one coherent explanation for the occurrence of violent behavior. The process of reviewing the literature involved makes it clear, however, that while it is possible to some extent to summarize descriptions of violent populations, explanations fall into the area of hypothesis and opinion and are not readily summarized. In addition, the review reinforces two truisms about violence: 1) Violence is not a unidimensional concept, and a better description of behavior is required than merely labeling it "violent." 2) Purely psychological theories are unlikely to provide the most parsimonious explanation for the occurrence of violence. The perpetrator and the victim, their relationship, and the situational determinants, including cultural context, all must be considered in an equation "explaining" violence. Of course, the ultimate reason for developing an adequate understanding of violence is its prediction and prevention.

Although those goals seem beyond our reach given the present state of knowledge, still it might be worthwhile to select those variables that can be controlled and begin to change them in the hope that the occurrence of violence may be lessened, if only to a minor degree. While we cannot totally "explain" violent behavior, it would seem foolish not to act on the components of violence that have been identified. In addition, an area ignored in the study of violence is that of individuals who have the history and apparently the psychological characteristics of violent individuals, but who are not violent. What does it take to inoculate a child from a high-risk background against violence? The discovery of that variable would rank with the polio vaccine or smallpox vaccinations in alleviating human suffering.

REFERENCES

ANDERSON, L. M. Personality characteristics of parents of neurotic, aggressive, and normal preadolescent boys. *J. Consult. Clin. Psychol.* 33(5):575-581, 1969.

AMIR, N. Victim precipitated forcible rape. *J. Crim. Law, Criminology and Police Science* 58:493-502, 1967.

ANTHONY, H. S. The association of violence and depression in a sample of young offenders. *Br. J. Criminol.* 8(4):346-365, 1968.

ARDREY, R. *The Territorial Imperative,* Atheneum, New York, 1966.

ARDREY, R. *The Social Contract: A Personal Inquiry into the Evolutionary Sources of Order and Disorder.* Atheneum, New York, 1970.

AUFREITER, J. The dilemma with aggression: Primary need or consequence of frustration. *Can. J. Psychol.* 14:493-496, 1969.

BACH-Y-RITA, G. Habitual violence and self-mutilation. *Am. J. Psychiatry* 131(9): 1018-1020, 1974.

BACH-Y-RITA, G., LION, J., CLIMENT, C., and ERVIN, F. Episodic dyscontrol: A study of 130 violent patients. *Am. J. Psychiatry* 127:1473-1478, 1971.

BACH-Y-RITA, E., and VERRO, A. Habitual violence: A profile of 62 men. *Am. J. Psychiatry* 131:1015-1017, 1974.

BALL-ROKEACH, S. J. Values and violence: A test of the subculture of violence thesis. *Am. Sociol. Rev.* 38:736-749, 1973.

BANDURA, A. *Aggression, a Social Learning Analysis,* Chapter 1. Prentice-Hall, Englewood Cliffs, N. J., 1973.

BANDURA, A., and WALTERS, R. H. *Social Learning and Personality Development.* Holt, Rinehart and Winston, New York, 1963.

BARCLAY, A. Linking sexual arousal and aggressive motives: Contributions of "irrelevant" arousals. *J. Pers.* 39:481-492, 1971.

BEATTIE, R. H., and KENNEY, J. P. Aggressive crimes. *American Academy of Political and Social Science* 364:73-95, 1966.

BENDER, L. Hostile aggression in children, in *Aggressive Behavior*. S. Garattini, Jr., and E. B. Sigg, eds. Wiley and Sons, New York, 1969.

BERNARD, V. W., OTTENBURG, P., and REDL, R. Dehumanization, in *Sanctions for Evil*. N. Sanford and C. Comstock, eds. Jossey-Bass, San Francisco, 1971.

BEIT-HALLAHMI, B. Motivation for murder: The case of G. *Corrective Psychiatry and J. Soc. Ther.* 17(1):25-30, 1971.

BERKOWITZ, L. Impulse, aggression and the gun. *Psychology Today* 2:19-22, 1968.

BERKOWITZ, L. Some factors affecting the reduction of overt hostility. *J. Abnorm. Soc. Psychol.* 60:14-21, 1960.

BERMAN, A. Neurological dysfunction in juvenile delinquents: Implication for early intervention. *Child Care Quarterly* 1:264-271, 1972.

BEY, D. R., and ZECCHINELLI, V. A. GI's against themselves: Factors resulting in explosive violence in Viet Nam. *Psychiatry* 37(3):221-228, 1974.

BLACKBURN, R. Personality types among abnormal homicides. *Br. J. Criminol.* 11(1): 14-31, 1971.

BLACKBURN, R. Personality in relation to extreme aggression in psychiatric offenders. *Br. J. Psychiatry* 114:821-828, 1968.

BOLMAN, W. M. Aggression and violence in children. *Curr. Prob. Pediat.* 4(9):1-32, 1974.

BOND, T. C. The why of fragging. *Am. J. Psychiatry* 133(11):1328-1331, 1976.

BROMBERG, W. A psychological study of murder. *Int. J. Psychoanalysis* 32:117-127, 1951.

BROWNMILLER, S. *Against Our Will*. Simon and Schuster, New York, 1975.

BUSS, A. *The Psychology of Aggression*. Wiley and Sons, New York, 1961, pp. 183-206.

BUSS, A. Physical aggression in relation to different frustrations. *J. Abnorm. Soc. Psychol.* 67:1-7, 1963.

CARROL, J. L., and FULLER, G. B. An MMPI comparison of three groups of criminals. *J. Clin. Psychol.* 27:240-242, 1971.

CLARK, K. The pathos of power: A psychological perspective. *Am. Psychol.* 26:1047-1051, 1971.

CLIMENT, C. E., ROLLINS, A., ERWIN, F., and PLUTCHIK, R. Epidemiological studies of women prisoners: Medical and psychiatric variables related to violent behavior. *Am. J. Psychiatry* 130(9):985-990, 1973.

CORMIER, B. M. Psychodynamics of homicide committed in a marital relationship. *Corrective Psychiatry and J. Soc. Ther.* 8(4):187-194, 1962.

CORMIER, B. M., and SIEBERT, P. S. The problems of the dangerous sexual offender. *Can. Psychiatric Assoc. J.* 14:329-334, 1969.

CROOK, J. H. The nature and function of territorial aggression, in *Man and Aggression*. A. Montagu, ed. Oxford University Press, New York, 1968, pp. 141-178.

CROWE, R. An adoption study of antisocial personality. *Arch. Gen. Psychiatry* 31: 785-791, 1974.

CURRAN, S. F., BLATCHLEY, R. J., and HANLON, T. E. The relationship between body buffer zone and violence. *Crime, Justice and Behavior* 5(1):53-62, 1978.

CURTIS, G. C. Violence breeds violence—perhaps? *Am. J. Psychiatry* 120:386-387, 1963.

CURTIS, L. A. Victim precipitation and violent crimes. *Social Problems* 21(4), 594-605.

DAVIS, K. R., and SINES, J. O. An antisocial behavior pattern associated with a specific MMPI profile. *J. Consult. Clin. Psychol.* 36(2):229-234, 1971.

DEIKER, T. E. WAIS characteristics of indicted male murders. *Psychol. Rep.* 32(3): 1066, 1973.

DE ROSIS, H. Violence: Where does it begin? *The Family Coordinat*or October, 1971.

EISEN, P. The infantile roots of adolescent violence. *Am. J. Psychol.* 36(3):211-218, 1976.

EISENBERG, D. The human nature of human nature. *Science* 176(4):123-128, 1972.

EVSIEFF, C. S., and WISNIEWSKI, E. M. A psychiatric study of a violent mass murder. *J. Forensic Sci.* 17(3):371-376, 1972.

FESHBACH, S. Dynamics and morality of violence and aggression: Some psychological considerations. *Amer. Psychol.* 26(3):281-292, 1971.

FISCHER, D. G., KELM, H., and ROSE, A. Knives as aggression-eliciting stimuli. *Psychol. Rep.* 24:755-760, 1969.

FROMM, E. *The Anatomy of Destructiveness.* Holt, Rinehart and Winston, New York, 1973.

GARDNER, G. E., Aggression and violence—the enemies of precision learning in children. *Am. J. Psychiatry* 128(4):77-82, 1971.

GARDNER, G. E. The aggressive-destructive impulses in the sex offender. *Mental Hygiene* 34:44-63, 1950.

GAULT, W. B. Some remarks on slaughter. *Am. J. Psychiatry* 128(4):82-86, 1971.

GAYFORD, J. J. Wife-battering: A preliminary survey of 100 cases. *Br. Med. J.* 1:194-197, 1975.

GELLES, R. Violence and pregnancy: A note on the extent of the problem and needed services. *The Family Coordinator* 24:81-86, 1975.

GOLD, L. H. Invitation to homicide. *J. Forensic Sciences* 10:415-421, 1965.

GOLDSTEIN, J. H. *Aggression and Crimes of Violence.* Oxford University Press, New York, 1975.

GOLDSTEIN, R. L. Those who kill without thinking. *Am. J. Psychiatry* 129(6):766-767, 1972.

GORNEY, R. Interpersonal intensity, competition, and synergy: Determinants of achievement, aggression, and mental illness. *Am. J. Psychiatry* 128(4):68-77, 1971.

GRUEN, A. On evil: Psychosis and conscience. *Review of Existential Psychology and Psychiatry* 13(1):88-97, 1974.

GUTTMACHER, M. S. *The Mind of Murderer.* Farrar, Straus, and Cudahy, New York, 1960.

HAMBURG, D. A. Psychiatry's potential contribution to behavioral and environmental health. Mid-winter meeting of American Association of Directors of Psychiatric Residency Training, 1977, pp. 5-11.

HAMBURG, D. A., and BRODIE, H. K. Psychological research on human aggressiveness. *Impact of Science on Society* 23:181-193, 1973.

HELLMAN, D. J., and BLACKMAN, N. Enuresis, firesetting and cruelty to animals: A triad predictive of adult crime. *Am. J. Psychiatry* 122:1431-1435, 1966.

HEPBURN, J. R. Violent behavior in interpersonal relationships. *Sociological Quarterly* 14(3):419-429, 1973.

HILDRETH, A. M., DEROGATIS, L. R., and MCCUSKER, K. Body buffer zone and violence: A reassessment and confirmation. *Am. J. Psychiatry* 127(12):1641-1645, 1971.

HOKANSEN, J. E. The effects of frustration and anxiety on overt aggression. *J. Abnorm. Soc. Psychol.* 62:346-351, 1961.

HOLMES, D. S. Effects of overt aggression on level of physiological arousal. *J. Pers. Soc. Psychol.* 4:190-194, 1966.

HOOVER, E. L. Far out: Violence and pleasure. *Human Behavior* 5(1):10-11, 1976.

HOTT, L. R. Individual and mass aggression—neo-Freudian point of view. *Behav. Neuropsychiatry* 2:15-16, 1970.

ILFELD, F. W., JR. Overview of the causes and prevention of violence. *Arch. Gen. Psychiatry* 20:675-689 (1969).

KAHN, M. W. Murderers who plead insanity: A descriptive factor-analytic study of personality, social, and history variables. *Genet. Psychol. Monogr.* 84:275-360, 1971.

KAHN, M. W. Psychological test study of mass murder. *J. Projective Techniques* 24: 148-160, 1960.

KAHN, R. L. The justification of violence: Social problems and social solutions. *J. Soc. Issues* 28(1):155-175, 1972.

KARDENER, S. H., and FULLER, M. Violence as a defense against intimacy. *Mental Hygiene* 54(2):310-315, 1970.

KELMON, H. C. Violence without moral restraint: Reflections on the dehumanization of victims and victimizers. *J. Soc. Issues* 29(4):25-61, 1973.

KINZEL, A. F. Body-buffer zone in violent prisoners. *Am. J. Psychiatry* 127:59-64, 1970.

KOPERNIK, L. The family as a breeding ground of violence. *Corrective Psychiatry and J. Soc. Ther.* 10:315-322, 1964.

KUNCE, J. T., RYAN J. J., and ECKELMAN, C. C. Violent behavior and different WAIS characteristics. *J. Consult. Clin. Psychol.* 44(1):42-45, 1976.

LACHMAN, J. H. The murders—before and after. *Psychiatric Quarterly* 43:1-11, 1969.

LANDER, J., and SCHULMAN, M. Homicide, acting out and impulse. *Am. J. Orthopsychiatry* 33:928-930, 1963.

LA TORRE, R. A. Sexual stimulation and displaced aggression. *Psychol. Rep.* 33:123-125, 1973.

LEFKOWITZ, M. M., ERON, L. D., WALDER, L. O., and HUESMAN, L. R. *Growing Up To Be Violent.* Pergamon Press, New York, 1977.

LESTER, D. Suicide, homicide, and the effects of socialization. *J. Pers. Soc. Psychol.* 5(4):466-468, 1967.

LACHMAN, J. and GRAVENS, J. The murderers . . . before and after. *Psychiatric Quarterly* 43:1-11, 1969.

LORENZ, K. *On Aggression.* Bantam Books, New York, 1966.

LOTHSTEIN, L. M., and JONES, P. Discriminating violent individuals by means of various psychological tests. *J. Pers. Assess.* 42(3):237-243, 1978.

LYSTAD, M. H. Violence at home: a review of the literature. *Am. J. Orthopsychiatry* 45(3):328-348, 1975.

MALMQUIST, C. P. Premonitory signs of homicidal aggression in juveniles. *Am. J. Psychiatry* 128(4):93-97, 1971.

MARTIN, C., and CHANNELL, L. H. Personality and social history characteristics of delinquents and their parents. *Corrective Psychiatry and J. Soc. Ther.* 10:93-107, 1964.

MATRANGA, J. T. The relationship between behavioral indices of aggression and hostile content on the TAT. *J. Pers. Assess.* 40(2):130-134, 1976.

MCCONAHAY, S. A., and MCCONAHAY, J. B. Sexual permissiveness, sex role rigidity and violence across cultures. *J. Soc. Issues* 33(2):134-143, 1977.

McCreary, C. P. Trait and type differences among male and female assaultive and non-assaultive offenders. *J. Pers. Assess.* 40(6):617-621, 1976.

McGrath, W. B. Cabin fever. *Arizona Medicine* 34(8):542, 1977.

Meade, M. Warfare is only an invention—not biological necessity, in *Peace and War.* C. R. Bertz and T. Herman, eds. Freeman, San Francisco, 1973.

Megargee, E. I. Undercontrolled and overcontrolled personality types in extreme antisocial aggression. *Psychological Monographs: General and Applied* 80(3): 1-29, 1966.

Megargee, E. I. The psychology of violence: A critical review of theories of violence, in *Crimes of Violence: A Staff Report to the National Commission on the Causes and Prevention of Violence,* Vol. 13. D. J. Mubihill and M. M. Tumin, eds. U.S. Government Printing Office, Washington, D.C., 1969.

Megargee, E. I., Cook, P. E., and Mendelsohn, G. A. Development and validation of an MMPI scale of assaultiveness in overcontrolled individuals. *J. Abnorm. Psychol.* 72(6): 1967.

Milgram, S. Behavioral study of obedience. *J. Abnorm. Soc. Psychol.* 67:317-378, 1963.

Miller, N., and Dollard J. *Social Learning and Imitation.* Yale University Press, New Haven, 1941.

Mohr, J. W., and McKnight, C. K. Violence as a function of age and relationship with special reference to matricide. *Can. Psychiatr. Assoc. J.* 16:29-32, 1971.

Monahan, J. The prediction of violence, in *Violence and Criminal Justice.* D. Chappel and J. Monahan, eds. Lexington Books, Lexington, Mass., 1975.

Montagu, A. Animal and man: divergent behavior. *Science* 161:963, 1968.

Montagu, A. *The Nature of Human Aggression.* Oxford University Press, New York, 1976.

Morgan, D. Early modern empiricism, in *A History of Philosophical Systems.* Philosophical Library, New York, 1950.

Nordlicht, S. Determinants of violence. *N.Y. State J. Med.* 72(17):2163-2165, 1972.

Owens, D. J., and Straus, M. A. The social structure of violence in childhood and approval of violence as an adult. *Aggressive Behavior* 3:193-211, 1975.

Paddock, J. Studies on antiviolent and "normal" communities. *Aggressive Behavior* 1(3):217-233, 1975.

Palmer, S. Frustration aggression and murder. *J. Abnorm. Soc. Psychol.* 60(3): 430-432, 1960.

Perdue, R. L., and Lester, D. Personality characteristics of rapists. *Percept. Motor Skills* 35(2):514, 1972.

Perdue, W. C., and Lester, D. Those who murder kin: A Rorschach study. *Percept. Motor Skills* 36(2):606, 1973.

Persons, R. W., and Monks, P. A. The violent 4-3 MMPI personality type. *J. Consult. Clin. Psychol.* 36(2):189-196, 1971.

Pinderhughes, C. A. Managing paranoia in violent relations, in *Perspective on Violence.* C. Usdin, ed. Brunner/Mazel, New York, 1972, p. 109.

Plutchik, R., Climent, C., and Erwin, F. Research strategies for study of human violence, in *Issues in Brain/Behavior Control.* W. L. Smith and A. Kleg, eds. Spectrum, New York, 1976, pp. 69-94.

Ramsperger, A. Early murder rationalism, in *A History of Philosophical Systems.* V. Ferm, ed. Philosophical Library, New York, 1950.

ROGER, D. B., and SCHALEKAMP, E. E. Body buffer zone violence: a cross-cultural study. *J. Soc. Psychol.* 98:153-158, 1976.

ROSE, G. J. Screen memories in homicidal action, out. *Psychoanal. Q.* 29:328-343, 1960.

ROSENZWIEG. S. Unconscious self-defense in an uxoricide. *J. Crim. Law, Criminology and Public Science* 46:791-795, 1956.

ROTH, M. Human violence as viewed from the psychiatric clinic. *Am. J. Psychiatry* 128(9):1043-1056, 1972.

ROTHENBERG, A. On anger, *Am. J. Psychiatry* 128(4):86-92, 1971.

ROTTER, J. *Social Learning and Clinical Psychology*. Prentice-Hall, Englewood Cliffs, N.J., 1954.

RUFF, C. F., TEMPLER, D. I., and AZER, J. L. The intelligence of rapists. *Arch. Sex. Behav.* 5(4):327-329, 1976.

RUOTOLO, A. D. Dynamics of sudden murder. *Am. J. Psychoanal.* 28:162-176, 1968.

RUOTOLO, A. K., Neurotic pride and homicide. *Am. J. Psychoanal.* 35(1):1-18, 1975.

SANFORD, N., and COUSTOCH, C. eds. *Sanctions for Evil.* Jossey-Bass, San Francisco, 1971.

SCOTT, J. Hostility and aggression in animals, in *Roots of Behavior.* E. L. Bless, ed. Harper, New York, 1962, pp. 167-178.

SERBAN, G. Aggression and mass aggression—the existential point of view. *Behav. Neuropsychiatry* 2(5-6):16-17, 1970.

SHAWVER, L., and JEW, C. Predicting violent behavior from WAIS characteristics: A replication failure. *J. Consult. Clin. Psychol.* 46(1):206, 1978.

SILVER, L. B., DUBLIN, C. C., and LOURIE, R. S. Does violence breed violence? *Am. J. Psychiatry* 126:404-407, 1969.

SOARES, L., and SOARES, A. Social learning and social violence. Proceedings of 77th Annual Convention, American Psychological Assn., 463-464, 1969.

STOTLAND, E. Self-esteem and violence by guards and state troopers at Attica. *Criminal Justice and Behavior* 3(1):85-96, 1976.

STRAUS, M. A. Sexual inequality, cultural norms, and wife beating. *Victimology* 1(1): 54-70, 1976.

STRAUS, M. A. Some social antecedents of physical punishment: A theory interpretation. *J. Marriage and the Family* 33:658-663, 1971.

TANAY, E. Psychiatric study of homicide. *Am. J. Psychiatry,* 125:1252-1258, 1969.

TAYLOR, S. P., and PISANO, R. Physical aggression as a function of frustration and physical attack. *J. Soc. Psychol.* 84:261-267, 1971.

TIDMARSH, M. Violence in marriage: the relevance of structural factors. *Social Work Today* 7(2):36-38, 1976.

TINBERGEN, M. On war and peace in animals and man. *Science* 160:1411-1418, 1968.

TOCH, H. *Violent Men.* Aldine, Chicago, 1969.

TOBY, J. Violence and the masculine ideal: Some qualitative data. *American Academy of Political and Social Science* 364:19-27, 1966.

TOMAY, E. Psychiatric study of homicide. *Am. J. Psychiatry* 125(9):1252-1258, 1969.

TUPIN, J. P., MAHAR, D., and SMITH, D. Two types of violent offenders with psychosocial descriptors. *Dis. Nerv. Syst.* 34:356-363, 1973.

WHITING, D. Sex identity conflict and physical violence: A comparative study. *American Anthropologist* 67:123-139, 1965.

WOLFGANG, M. E., and FERRACUTTI, F. *The Sub-Culture of Violence.* Tavistock, London, 1967.

YAGER, J. Personal violence in infantry combat. *Arch. Gen. Psychiatry* 32(2):257-261, 1975.

YOCHELSON, J., and SOMENOW, S. E. *The Animal Personality,* vol. 1, *A Profile for Change,* Aronson, New York, 1976.

ZEGANS, L. S., Towards a unified theory of human aggression. *Br. J. Med. Psychol.* 44:355-365, 1971.

CHAPTER 3

Moral Reasoning and Judgment in Hypothetical and Actual Dilemmas Involving the Police Officer's Use of Deadly Force in the Line of Duty

PETER SCHARF
DAVID MARRERO
RODNEY LININGER

This chapter describes the role of moral judgment in relation to a police officer's decision to shoot his gun. We will attempt to describe the existing research relevant to moral decision-making and violence in an effort to understand differences in police officer reasonings in terms of what constitutes the moral and legal right to use deadly force in the line of duty. Research dealing with officers' responses to hypothetical shooting situations as well as a case analysis of an actual "shooting decision" will be presented. We believe that our framework for interpreting moral decision-making in shooting provides insight into differences in what officers consider to be illegitimate and legitimate uses of deadly force.

THE PROBLEM

In April 1978 two young officers were on duty in a two-man car when they received a call indicating that a "recreational vehicle" had been stolen and was proceeding toward them on a crowded freeway. One of the officers described the event:

> I was on patrol with Officer S. We were advised to assist with a stolen motorhome involving a 245B (assault on a police officer) advising in that the motorhome was involved in numerous accidents. The assault clearly was intentional. . . . Approximately one minute later we saw suspects approaching on the median divider, which is 12 to 15 feet wide. We started gaining speed to coordinate pursuit. The motorhome was riding approximately six inches from fence. Suspects were approaching at 70 mph . . . we heard what appeared to be gunfire at this time. (Later investigation proved that these shots came from deputies.) Two sheriffs' deputies were in front of us in the pursuit. We were in the third car. Traffic slowed. Suspect was weaving between #1 and #3 lanes. As he went through lanes he was ramming several cars. When all three lanes became blocked he returned to the median divider lane and plowed through several cars on either side. We continued in this fashion going between #1 and #3 lanes. . . . The suspect at this time proceeded to ram citizens' cars. There were numerous traffic crashes . . . approximately 37 crashes in 4½ miles. . . . One of the deputies in front of us got blocked in a slow lane. The other deputy car attempted to get on his side. He immediately was rammed and forced to slam on brakes and was knocked onto the dirt on side of the road . . . and then we found ourselves as the lead car directly behind the suspect's.
>
> We went directly behind the suspect's car, going wherever he went. At this point we began to talk among ourselves. . . . "Watch out for this car, watch out for that one, oh, he hit another." At this point I suggested to Officer S that we shoot out the tires. Officer S removed the shotgun—at this point we were uncertain about where the gunshot had come from—and he fired approximately three rounds at the tires. We observed one shredded and flattened, but as this was a dual tire job on back, it hardly mattered. At this point we saw the motorhome ram a Honda Civic and literally demolished it. At this point we began discussing that the suspect was about to kill someone. We had seen numerous accidents, and there was no way to terminate pursuit. After seeing the Honda demolished, we saw him sideswipe a Cadillac and literally knock it into the dirt; we discussed shooting the driver. . . . Officer S said that he had been thinking about that and said was it necessary. . . . I said, he's going to kill someone or already has. We thought of sideswiping him but didn't have the angle or power (even though we had a large Dodge) to knock him off the freeway. Officer S agreed. . . . Officer S leaned out of car with the

shotgun. Suspect drew back. I was watching his hands. He leaned forward and shifted as if he was going to sideswipe us. At this point Officer S fired one round (the only one left), striking suspect in the head.

In this incident the officers faced what might be considered the most tortuous and irreversible decision faced by a police officer in the line of duty: when, if ever, is it right to shoot another human being? Unlike many shooting situations, the action represented in the minds of the officers and others a conscious, reasoned action, one which both officers would defend as both morally and legally right. How, we might ask, do officers reason about this issue of taking a human life?

One framework for analyzing moral reasoning in complex moral situations is Kohlberg's (1968) theory of moral reasoning. Kohlberg suggests that as the child matures in terms of moral development, there is a progressive reconsideration of what is right, as well as of the relationship between law and society. At stage 1 there is an orientation toward punishment and conscience. Law is conceived as the force of the powerful, to which the weaker submit. At stage 2, correct actions are those that satisfy one's own needs. Law is conceived in terms of the rules of experience or a naive rational hedonism ("In America, the law says everyone can get what he wants"). Stage 3 offers what is called the good boy/girl orientation. Law becomes associated with collective opinion. One obeys the law because that is what others expect. At stage 4, there is a shift toward fixed definitions of law and society. The law is justified in terms of its order-maintaining function. "Without law, the entire fabric of society would crumble." Stage 5 is a legalistic-contract orientation. Law becomes the agreed upon contract among social equals with duties of state and individual clearly defined and regulated. At stage 6, Kohlberg argues that there is a universal basis for ethical decision-making. The law here is a repository for broader social principles and is subordinate where law and justice conflict.

The theory suggests the importance of the social environment in stimulating moral reasoning. Social institutions play a critical role in determining both the rate of moral growth and the final stage of moral reasoning. Institutions that encourage open dialogue, moral conflict, and democratic interaction are associated with rapid sociolegal development (Kohlberg, 1968). Individuals, for example, placed in positions in which they are responsible for maintaining group and institutional norms tend to develop more quickly than do other people.

The empirical evidence for the validity of Kohlberg's stage sequence comes from two sources. First, he cites evidence from cross-sectional and longitudinal studies which suggest that people move through the stages in order. Cross-sectional data indicate that in seven different cultures (Turkey, Israel, Yucatan [Mexico], Taiwan, France, England) older children as a group are more mature in their thinking than are younger children (Kohlberg, 1977). In addition to making an empirical claim for the validity of his six stages, Kohlberg argues that each higher stage offers a philosophically more adequate means of resolving moral conflict. This claim, which obviously is one of normative ethics rather than science, is much more controversial. Using deductive ethical analysis, Kohlberg has attempted to demonstrate, at least through stage 5, how each higher stage resolves ethical contradictions evident at earlier stages. He argues, for example, that the stage 5 "legalistic" position offers rational and ethical perspective unavailable at the less mature, stage 4 law-and-order orientation (Kohlberg, 1977).

Kohlberg's work has been criticized. It is frequently argued that conduct in a particular society may be judged only by that society's values. From this relativistic perspective it follows that there are neither universally valid ethical principles nor moral or legal standards that might be said to bind all societies. An extreme example of this philosophic perspective is found in the argument of a Brazilian judge who freed three "backcountry Amazon men" who had mercilessly killed a group of travelers, arguing that for these people in their society, killing was deemed to be morally correct and decided that there should be no moral punishment. Also, while Kohlberg has argued that people tend to reason by using the principles of the highest stage they are capable of understanding, many critics have observed that a stage 5 person often may act more in accordance with stage 2 realities than with his or her highest principled ideals. The case of the European intelligentsia, who, when forced into Hitler's concentration camps, quickly regressed to childlike behavior and rather primitive moral reasoning and action, presents a striking case of apparent moral regression. Finally, Brown (1975) and Fraenkel (see Scharf, 1978) among others, have observed that the claims of Kohlberg and his associates regarding the *relationship between moral judgment and action* are greatly overstated. The few empirical studies relating judgment and action, according to these critics, allow only the most tentative hypotheses about the role of moral reasoning in determining behavior. They suggest that, while there may be a loose association between moral stage and moral action, this relationship should be considered only in conjuntion with other social and psychological variables.

MORAL REASONING AND ACTION IN MORAL ISSUES RELATED TO THE TAKING OF HUMAN LIFE

A few empirical studies have attempted to relate people's stage of moral reasoning to the way they resolve conflicts involving the possibility of taking human life. Scharf (1978) described the public moral statement of participants in the My Lai Massacre. One participant, Paul Meadlow, demonstrated moral thinking (as revealed in a television interview and subsequent testimony at the Calley trial) that was striking in that it appeared to have been primarily at the preconventional level of moral thought, stage 1 or 2. One obeys an officer not because one respects the authority he represents, but because one wishes to avoid the physical punishment that might result from disobedience. For example, Meadlow said: "During basic training if you disobeyed an order, if you were slow in obeying orders, they'd slap you on the head, drop-kick you in the chest and rinky-dink stuff like that." Meadlow similarly believes that it was right to "waste" the Vietnamese to get "satisfaction" and a morally primitive stage 1 revenge:

> Why did I do it. . . . We was supposed to get satisfaction from this village for the men we lost. They was all VC and VC sympathizers. I felt, at the time, I was doing the right thing, because, like I said, I lost buddies. I lost a damn good buddy, Bobby Wilson.

Lieutenant Calley, the officer charged with ordering Meadlow to shoot the civilians, provides a contrast in moral judgment to the younger private. Calley defines his obligations to prevent violence in terms of what he anticipates others will expect of a good officer. He attempts to win praise for fulfilling this role and is chagrined when he violates others' expectations. At conventional stages of moral thinking, one is only responsible for fulfilling the expectations of what the "higher ups" define as right and advantageous. Calley says: "If intelligent people say Communism is bad, it's going to engulf us [sic]. I was only a second lieutenant. I had to obey and hope that the people in Washington were smarter than me." If legitimate others define a group of people as the enemy and define a soldier's role as being to destroy them, the conventional moral thinker may reason that this expectation is valid and he may act upon it.

> Q: What was your intention in terms of operations?
>
> Calley: To go in the area and destroy the enemy that were designated there, and this is it. I went into the area to destroy the enemy. That was my job on that day. That was my mission I was given. I did not sit down and think in terms of men, women and children. They were all classified the same, and that was the classification,

> we dealt with them, enemy soldiers. . . . I felt, and still do, that I acted as I was directed . . . . and I do not feel wrong in doing so.

Michael Bernhardt, the only soldier to refuse to fire at My Lai, provides an interesting contrast in reasoning to Meadlow's and Calley's. Bernhardt agreed to submit to an extended formal moral-judgment interview in June, 1970. For Bernhardt, law is not the ultimate standard of justice; there are more general standards and principles that transcend the law:

> The law is only the law, and many times it's wrong. . . . It's not necessarily just, just because it's the law. . . . My kind of citizen would be guided by his own laws. These would be more strict than in a lot of cases, the actual laws. People must be guided by their own standards, by their self-discipline.

Faced with a dilemma like the one he faced at My Lai, Bernhardt is able to apply these moral principles in deciding whether a specific order was legitimate and should be obeyed:

> I was telling Captain Franklyn about an old woman that was shot. I couldn't understand why she was shot because she didn't halt. First of all, she is in her own country. We never found anything to indicate that she was anything but what she appeared to be—a non-combatant. It wasn't a case like we had been wiped out by an old woman with a fishbag full of grenades. I told him that she was shot at a distance. They said to shoot her was a brigade policy. They couldn't think of a better way of stopping her. I would have said, "No." I just wouldn't have stopped her at all. Nothing needs an excuse to live!

An analogous study of moral reasoning about the issue of capital punishment (Kohlberg and Elfenbein, 1975) found a striking (considering the controversial nature of the subject matter) relationship between one's position on capital punishment and moral stage. Young children at the preconventional stages (stages 2 and 3) tended to believe in the justice of capital punishment in terms of a stage 1 concept of retaliation. Later development reveals a series of "flip-flops" in orientation, closely related to moral stage. Most stage 3 subjects, for example, favored leniency, while stage 4 individuals supported the use of capital punishment; morally principled subjects (those beyond stage 4) were almost unanimously opposed to the use of the death penalty. The longitudinal transitions in the philosophy of punishment of one of Kohlberg and Elfenbein's longitudinal subjects (given the code name Jim) illustrates the way a position on a legal issue involving lethal force is related to moral reasoning and how this reasoning transforms itself over a period of years. The relationship of moral reasoning to choice on the issue of capital punishment is especially persuasive in the contrast between conventional (stages 3 and 4) and post-conventional (stages 4/5 and 5) subjects. Fully 36 percent (n = 11) of Kohlberg and Elfenbein's (1975) stage 4 subjects favored capital punishment while none of the eight postconventional subjects favored its use. While the issues posed in the case of capital punishment are quite different from those posed at My Lai, the study does support our hypothesis that, at different moral stages, individuals might perceive the issue of taking a life quite differently.

Gilligan (1977) found a similar stage sequence in a recent study of reasoning by women facing the personal dilemma of abortion. Women at preconventional stages faced the issue of abortion quite differently from more morally mature women. For example, one woman scored at stage 2 defined the abortion dilemma as primarily an issue of pragmatism: "I really didn't think anything except that I didn't want it." (Why was that?) "I didn't want it, I wasn't ready for it, and next year will be my last year and I want to go to school." More mature women, in contrast, saw the abortion decision as more than a conflict between the needs of the self and those of pragmatic necessity. Conventionally reasoning women saw the decision as a means of meeting the expectations of others (boyfriends, parents, etc.). At the postconventional level (stages 4 and above) the conflict was seen as a conscious choice to make a responsible adult decision. One woman explained:

> I am looking at myself differently in the way that I have had a really heavy decision put upon me, and I have never really had too many hard decisions in my life, and I have made it. It has taken some responsibility to do this. I have changed in that way, that I have made a hard decision. So I see myself as I'm becoming more mature in ways of making decisions and taking care of myself, doing something for myself.

In resolving the decision of whether or not to have an abortion, Gilligan suggests, the women's perception of choice seems closely related to their moral stage. Gilligan finds that women who failed to confront the moral issue involved in the abortion decision found the experience to be a devastating one (relationships often fell apart and some women became depressed or emotionally distant). For the women who actively confronted the abortion dilemma, the experience elicited moral and personal growth.

The My Lai, capital punishment and abortion studies, while investigating different types of social contexts, suggest in common that the issue of taking human life appears very different to people at different moral stages. Even when individuals agree with a specific choice in a dilemma, they may agree with the choice for different reasons. In the My Lai incident, for example, one soldier who did not obey Calley's order to shoot the civilians was a private who was later court-martialed for raping a Vietnamese girl during the time of the massacre. He and Michael Bernhardt did not shoot any civilians, but their choice was based on different reasoning processes. These three studies suggest also that at higher stages of moral reasoning the moral criteria for taking a human life become increasingly stringent and the justification for taking a life more precisely defined.

THE UNIQUE DEMANDS OF POLICE SHOOTING DECISIONS

A special case of the dilemma of lethal force is found in the police officer's decision to use deadly force in the line of duty. In most states police officers are allowed to use lethal force when:

1. The officer's life is in danger.
2. A civilian's life is in danger.
3. A dangerous felon is fleeing from arrest.

In many legal statutes the decision is posed as an explicit legal dilemma: the officer is required to weigh the "probable" danger of the suspect, the "probable" risk to civilians, and must define what might constitute "reasonable" force in the situation. Although many police departments have guidelines on shooting, there is still a wide range of discretion within which the officer must weigh the risk to self, fugitive, and others in the decision to shoot. Police shooting incidents often occur with great suddenness, most often under emotionally stressful conditions. In such circumstances, perceived facts are almost always ambiguous, and the decision to shoot is *at best* made with only a tentative definition of the situation. What is believed to be true may not in fact be true. The confusion as to what I. A. Thomas calls the "definition of the situation" is compounded by the fact that most officers in shooting situations are in a state of emotional agitation. One officer we interviewed, who had been in two different shooting situations, described one incident in which he had "pulled a Wyatt Earp" (i.e., shot the gun out of a suspect's hand):

> There were two "hypes" in town. Two of them came towards me about 15 feet apart with what looked like .22's. I instinctively fired. My heart was going crazy. I got a medal for shooting the gun out. I only told a few people that I was really shooting at the other guy. I couldn't hit a bus, feeling like that.

While "deadly force" situations inevitably involve ambiguous facts and heightened emotions, they also most always present tortuous moral issues.

One such issue is the possible danger to innocent bystanders. This dilemma is often posed in cases in which hostages are taken. Additionally (and unfortunately often), a life may be lost because the officer fails to exercise "deadly force" and the perpetrator either kills the officer, a hostage, or perhaps an innocent bystander. A related problem implicit in the police role pertains to the use of lethal force in the recapture of escaping felons and the protection of property. Although such actions are legally justifiable in many state penal codes, many officers perceive such actions as not being *morally* justified. At issue is the problem of taking a suspect's life as he flees from a felony arrest but is not armed nor in immediate danger of taking another's life.

THE MORAL REASONING OF POLICE OFFICERS IN RESPONDING TO HYPOTHETICAL DILEMMAS DEALING WITH THE USE OF "DEADLY FORCE"

To begin to explore the relationship between police officers' moral reasoning and the decision to use deadly force, we initiated a study in which hypothetical dilemmas were posed for police officers on duty. Twenty-four police officers were randomly selected from 2 police departments in western states. The sample included 18 patrolmen, 4 sergeants, and 2 lieutenants. The officers ranged in experience from 6 months to 27 years of duty. Half of the officers were college graduates, and the mean age was 30 years. A schedule of interviews on moral dilemmas in police and standard situations was developed for the study. The standard dilemmas (Kohlberg, 1968) were carefully rated, using issue-scoring procedures (Gibbs, 1977). A police dilemma was developed by the authors; it asked officers to decide whether or not it was right to shoot a suspect who was holding a hostage in a convenience store. Probabilities were 50 percent that he could kill the

Table 1

Association Between Moral Stage and Shooting Decision

	Shoot	Not Shoot
Postconventional (Stages 4-5 and 5)	0	5
Conventional (Stages 3 and 4)	5	9
Preconventional (Stage 2)	4	1
Total responses:	9	15

perpetrator without harm to the hostage, and 30 percent that, if he did not shoot, the perpetrator would shoot the hostage. Descriptive analysis revealed a qualitative association between moral stage and decision on the "shooting dilemma" (Table 1).

Most stage 2 officers in our sample tended to view the hostage dilemma as a problem of personal authority and control; many showed a strong concern with power and domination:

> I go into a situation and attempt to show control. I am king of this roost. I am going to show everyone who is boss. I first get control, then I decide what to do. . . . I try to get them to respect my uniform, to know that I am the law!

These stage 2 officers typically gave greater consideration to the risk of their own life than that of the hostage: What would you consider in deciding whether to shoot?:

> It would depend whether or not he fired at me. That's the first thing. . . . If he shoots at me and misses—he's a dead man.

The 14 stage 3 and 4 officers demonstrated quite different reasoning processes. While the stage 2 police officers were concerned with concrete consequences to themselves or others, the conventionally reasoning subjects showed a far greater concern with the procedural legality of particular actions. For example, one officer suggested that the penal code's sanctions defined his obligations in the shooting situation. What is right is defined by what is legally permissible rather than by a specifically moral assessment:

> I'd be more inclined to shoot than not shoot. Like, there was a guy who had 56 arrests. Given that kind of background, I think the law would back me up in shooting. . . .

The stage 5 officers (there were no stage 6 officers in our study) demonstrated a quite different perspective from that seen in either preconventionally or conventionally reasoning officers. These officers suggested that while taking a life would be justified under certain circumstances, it must be regarded as a last, *in extremis* strategy. One officer characteristically suggested:

> Taking a life must be the ultimate thing. It's like playing God. I would never shoot *unless* a life were in imminent danger. Shooting for property makes no sense at all. We don't have capital punishment for theft. The important thing is saving the life.

The analysis of the officer interviews tentatively supported earlier research which showed that the process of decision-making would be related to the outcome of the hypothetical deadly force decision. It was clear also that officers of different moral stages viewed the dilemma of taking a human life in distinct philosophic frames of reference. What was considered morally acceptable at stage 2 was thought both morally and legally wrong at higher stages.

MORAL DECISION-MAKING IN A LIVE SHOOTING EPISODE

Less than a year after we completed our hypothetical reasoning study, 2 officers in our sample found themselves involved in the shooting episode described earlier. They were pursuing a stolen motorhome on a crowded freeway and eventually shot one of the suspects in the car. This offered us a unique opportunity to study moral reasoning processes in a real-life rather than purely hypothetical context. The officers were interviewed extensively about their reasoning during the incident. Both agreed that the decision to shoot was in fact a deliberate decision on their part and not an instinctive reaction to the situation. One officer commented:

> The decision was made over a period of time as we watched approximately 37 accidents take place, and it was obvious that the driver had no regard for the lives or property of people who were there. . . . Initially, when we observed the serious nature of the crime, Officer S had the shotgun already out and asked me if we should shoot out the tires. I said *no* I didn't think we had quite enough. . . . If we shot it might endanger others . . . Things escalated as we went along . . . then we shot the tires . . . and finally it went to shooting the driver; it was all based on what we had in front of us. . . . It was made in stages as we watched his actions. . . . The severity of the one accident where he deliberately ran over a small car indicated to us that there were going to be deaths. . . . The only course of action was to shoot the driver. It was talked about and discussed. It was only reached after the conclusions we described. . . .

The officers found it possible to actively discuss with each other the facts of the incident and their possible options:

> Well, I remember discussing it with S. I remember saying we are going to have to shoot the driver. Officer S said, Yeah, I think so. This conversation took place yelling at the top of our lungs. We had the windows down and the siren on. Even though we were straining we could hear each other and communicate effectively. It was one of those rare times when two officers had enough time to talk about it. It wasn't a car stopping and somebody runs out shooting. It was a thing that, as it got worse, we had to use deadly force to terminate it. There was enough time to talk and plenty of things to base our decision on.

Possibly because of the time available to make the decision and the opportunity to discuss the issue, the officers felt certain that they had made the correct decision based on what they believed to be true. (This is surprising, considering that, except for the suspect shot by the officers, no other civilian in fact was killed, though the officers did not know this to be true at the time.) The driver commented:

> Since we had the time and based on the severity of the accidents, it was clear in my mind, and officer S said this was the only course of action available to us in order to save people's lives.

The two officers agreed that they made the decision to shoot even though they realized that this course of action would place them in great danger were they to miss. One officer suggested "that we didn't even think about missing." The second officer said:

> We were down to our last round of shotgun ammo and we did discuss that if I miss, it's going to get a little sticky. It would probably happen we would get rammed and get into a severe collision. . . . I remember I said, Hang on if we miss, and did think that if I rammed him I could control the accident to the point where we would not be severely injured.

Neither officer described in any personal detail any of the people in the motorhome, even though they were visible through the rear and side windows, rather referring to them as simply the "suspects" or "fugitives." One officer suggested that after he "shot out the windows, they weren't doing any looking out." It was additionally noted that neither officer saw the incident in terms of an irrational response to anger or other emotion. One said, "We weren't mad at them." Both officers, while obviously tense, described themselves as being emotionally controlled enough to consider the complex options and alternatives available to them. Both later concurred that the decision was only agreed upon *after* all other options were considered and found to be impossible, for example, slowing the vehicle by shooting out its tires. Also interesting was the ambiguity of certain key facts. For example, one officer said he was uncertain as to *who* was firing the shots they heard during the chase:

> We did hear several other shots fired, we didn't know where they were coming from, whether it was from the motorhome or other police units. We did hear these things, and they sort of formed another state of mind. . . . There were a bunch of shots . . . it was unmistakable, but we didn't know who was shooting.

Both officers described in detail some of the reasons they recalled thinking about before making their final decision to shoot. Officer S commented:

> He was still able to move that truck. Here he was running on three wheels, doing the same kind of stuff, still hurting people. A couple of the comments (the other officer) and I made were, Hey, he's hurting people. To us he was killing people, rolling over them just like a tank . . . after the last shot at the tires missed I said, Hey, what are we gonna do? . . .

The second officer responded similarly: "It was simply that if we didn't shoot there was going to be a lot of loss of life." Both officers felt themselves to be in a position of special moral responsibility. Officer S:

> Well I don't think that anybody else is going to shoot him, and it looks to me that there is only one thing that is going to happen. What are we going to do? Drive off the exit. . . . He is going to keep killing people . . . he's going to hit people . . . this thing has got to stop. . . . I told (other officer) we got to shoot him . . . if it was unfair to anybody, it was unfair to us, being there. . . .

Later on both officers seemed convinced of having done the right thing. Immediately after the shooting, the other officers on the scene told the officers not to look at the body. The officer who actually did the shooting insisted, however, on seeing the man he had just shot, commenting:

> I guess I should. I shot the guy. I just don't want to walk away from it. . . . I looked at him and I said that guy is dead. . . . People were concerned about how I felt. "How you feel; how you feel?" I didn't feel bad. Pretty soon I began to wonder—how am I supposed to feel. . . . I didn't feel bad because I had done my job. Some of the decisions were made because we were the only people there to do it. We couldn't shirk the responsibility. That was to me the reason we were doing it. It was the potential risk to the rest of the people on this freeway, not because we felt that we just wanted to kill someone, not because if we didn't kill him he was going to kill us. . . . There was that possibility, but that wasn't it. It was the fact that we were put in the position where we had already seen many people being hurt, with the potential of death to somebody. All of them who were innocent! That is what we are ready to do. That is what we are called upon to do. That's what we are ready to do. If we backed off we didn't know how far it was going!

Surprising was the sparse mention made by either officer about the legal issues in the case. This was considered interesting, given the long training officers have in looking at problems as legal problems. In this situation, law for the officers seemed of less importance than their sense of personal moral obligation in the situation. One officer noted:

> Of course in the back of your mind you have the legality of the thing. I had already pretty much run it down real quickly. You knew there was injuries, deaths, etc. (part of the penal code requirements for justifiable homicide by a police officer). But . . . to hell with legalities; this guy had to be stopped. It was here a responsibility we couldn't shirk.

The case indicated apparent parallels in reasoning in the response to the hypothetical situations and the shooting decision itself. In responding to a hypothetical dilemma about a fleeing fugitive, the officer demonstrated what was scored as both stage 4 and 5 moral reasoning:

> If the armed man didn't stop I might have to shoot. Chasing after a suspect is dangerous. If I was certain that he knew I was an officer and he was endangering others, then I would shoot. It's not the legal thing—recapturing a felon, rather it was the harm to others. . . . Of course there are other things you would try. It's a last-ditch thing.

In defining his reasons for shooting in the freeway incident, the officer suggested rather similar reasons for agreeing to shoot:

> The other officers at the scene thanked us and gave us congratulations. The decision was made in terms of the fact that this person had no regard for others and that there would be deaths if we didn't stop him. We had tried other things; this was the only way to save lives and people and property.

It should be pointed out that several things make this case a rather unusual one from several perspectives: First, there was an unusually long time interval (eight minutes) in which the officers could reach their decision to shoot. And because they were a two-man patrol, the officers could discuss the incident before shooting. It was only because one officer could drive and the other could shoot that shotgun fire could be effectively utilized. Finally, both officers involved were accurate shots as well as unusually high in moral stage. On hypothetical and police dilemmas, each officer scored at mixed stage 4 and 5 reasoning. That they both reasoned quite similarly about the incident was reflected in the fact that they agreed on the precise moment when lethal force was justified and required. One could only speculate on the outcome of the incident had they had radically different styles of moral reasoning.

These officers behaved somewhat atypically; officers from another police department were firing continuously throughout this incident from long range, using bullets that could have carried onto the streets below. In contrast, those who actually shot the suspect showed great restraint; they refused to use deadly force until it was clear to both of them that they had no alternative.

CONTRIBUTIONS OF MORAL-REASONING THEORY TO AN UNDERSTANDING OF POLICE VIOLENCE

The findings presented here have some implications for those interested in violence as a general area of scientific research, as well as those concerned with understanding the legal and psychological contexts of police violence.

Generally, there is a type of violence that is often misinterpreted by researchers. In defining violence as a pathological process, which society and the violent person himself want controlled or reedirected, there is a tendency to ignore human violence which the individual judges as legitimate and justified. The police officers described in the case study acted violently, but they regarded their actions as legitimate and correct. This type of violence cannot be explained by either "drive" or "situational" theories, for it is not considered to be a deviation from rational behavior, but rather what the actor believes to be morally right.

Moral development theory, in contrast, is extremely useful in interpreting this type of *rational violence* in that it describes the evolution of moral principles by defining under which circumstances taking a life is believed to be morally justified. In evaluating moral actions by universalistic criteria rather than relativistic ones, it allows the researcher to avoid the philosophic trap of judging violent acts by the norms of a particular society. For example, the attempted assassination of Hitler during World War II might be considered wrong by the standards of German society of that time, but it might be considered justifiable by Kohlberg's philosophic criteria. Clearly not all violent behavior can be interpreted by using the framework presented here. As we noted earlier, the situation presented in our case study was atypical of violence in general as well as of police shooting incidents in that there was time to make a moral judgment and the opportunity to discuss it in advance.

If our stage framework is accepted as valid, then some questions must be raised about officers' ability to understand and implement the complex moral demands of the law dealing with the use of deadly force by police officers. In California, for example, officers are required (as were the two officers in our case study) to decide what means were both "necessary" as well as "reasonable" to stop a fleeing felon "who is intent upon doing bodily harm to another" (Section 196—California Penal Code). This requires a type of moral assessment many officers might not be able to make. While the officers in the case described possessed at least the stage 4 or 5 reasoning required to make such complex judgments of context and intent, less mature officers might simply be incapable of reasonably and lawfully making such assessments. Our analysis of hypothetical police dilemmas indicates that some lower-stage officers, presented a case involving fleeing offenders, focus more on what they consider the badness of the offender than on weighing the danger the felon poses to the officer himself or others if the officer must use lethal force. One officer, scored at stage 2, responded as follows to the dilemma of dealing with a fleeing felon: "Well, I'd have to snuff him. He was obviously up to no good and deserved anything he got."

Our data on the variation of moral reasoning among police officers (limited as it is) tend to show that the law seriously "overexpects" the moral ability of many officers. As the trials following the My Lai Massacre indicated, many officers in the Calley platoon had no moral comprehension of the issues implied in the Geneva accords or the military codes dealing with the rightful refusal to obey orders that were against military or international law. So too do our studies show that the law dealing with justifiable homicide may not be morally comprehensible to many officers.

Our research further suggests that the decision to shoot represents a complex cognitive assessment on the part of the officer. This assessment requires that facts be isolated quickly and that probable truth be distinguished from what is really true. For example, the officers in the case presented here made a series of assumptions which turned out *later* to be false (for example, that the traffic crashes caused by the motorhome had killed people and that there were shots fired from the motorhome). What was critical in evaluating their actions was not that the officers established what actually had happened (this was impossible). Rather, it was imperative to establish that, given the facts available to them, the officers had sufficient factual grounds to shoot. In addition, the officers were required morally to evaluate the facts available to them. Although some officers clearly are able to make such judgments consistent with legally acceptable ethical criteria, there is some evidence that this might not be true of many or even most police officers.

POLICY QUESTIONS

Some tentative policy questions follow from our initial findings (obviously, a great deal of research must precede firm policy recommendations). If our contention is that some types of lethal force by police officers occur in a context that allows for rational moral dialogue, and that some officers may not be morally (or intellectually) capable of implementing the statutes dealing with use of deadly force, then several alternatives present themselves.

First, police departments might use some means of moral-reasoning evaluation to select officers entering police work. Although the methodology of available systems for evaluating moral reasoning is controversial, such data might be useful to police departments and be a legitimate requirement of those empowered to enforce complex legal statutes. The increased use of shooting guidelines might also be helpful.

Another strategy is the continuous moral and legal education of law enforcement personnel. We conducted a 12-week dilemma training course which briefly tested this approach. Dilemma situations involving, for example, the harassment of known felons, overreaction by officers to citizen provocation, as well as shooting situations, were discussed in a similar manner, focusing upon the legal as well as strategic issues relevant to the case.

Elaborate training simulations were created, with the officers placed into potential shooting situations analogous to those they might face in the line of duty. In one simulation, officers were ordered to report to a building where they met a neighbor, actually a plain-clothes officer, who reported a family disturbance. Entering the building, the officers found a psychotic husband with a knife at the throat of his panicked wife (both, in reality, police officers). During a debriefing session using videotapes of the simulation, the moral, legal and strategic elements of the case were discussed in small groups.

We hypothesized that it might be possible to stimulate moral maturity gains among the officers involved in both standard and police moral dilemmas. Interviews of 10 police officers selected at random were conducted and scored following procedures described by Gibbs (1977). Analysis of moral change during the course of the intervention revealed complex results. Nonsignificant change was found in the responses to the standard Kohlberg dilemma. This is understandable because of the high average age of the subjects and the short duration of the intervention, 36 contract hours. A significant shift was found in responses to the police dilemma ($t = 2.10$, $df = 9$, p .05). This was theoretically interesting, as it suggests a form of what Piaget calls *horizontal decalage*: a change in the application of existing cognitive or moral capacities. Thus, several of the officers who *did not* change in terms of moral judgment, as measured by standard interviews, did change in their responses to the police dilemmas. This implies that, although we were not able to alter the moral reasoning capacity of officers, we did encourage them to apply their available moral capacities to the police situations.

The approach suggests a new conception of law enforcement education. Instead of simply training in techniques and the rules of law enforcement, we have attempted to create a training program that focuses on the *process* of legal decision-making. If, in future replications, we find that it *is* possible to alter officers' moral reasoning through such a case-method program, it would seem possible to design a new form of law enforcement education which would focus on the process of legal reasoning rather than simply on legal roles and police strategy. Our approach seeks not only to encourage philosophic reflection by officers, but the application of philosophy to the practical problems of police work. Although our program is still in a pilot phase, we hope that it proved suggestive for those committed to the selection and training of a police force appropriate for a democratic society.

REFERENCES

BROWN, R. *Psychology*. Little, Brown, Boston, 1975.

GIBBS, J. Kohlberg's theory of moral judgement. *Harvard Educational Review* 47:43-61, April 1977.

GILLIGAN, C. In a different voice. *Harvard Educational Review* 47:481-517, Nov. 1977.

KOHLBERG, L. Stage and sequence, in *Handbook of Socialization*. D. Goslin, ed. Russell Sage, New York, 1968, pp. 286-367.

KOHLBERG, L. Cognitive-developmental approach to moral education, in *Readings in Moral Education*. P. Scharf, ed. Winston Press, Minneapolis, 1977.

KOHLBERG, L., and ELFENBEIN, D. Moral judgement on capital punishment, in *Collected Papers on Moral Education*. L. Kohlberg, ed. Harvard University, Cambridge, Mass. 1976.

SCHARF, P. *Moral Education*. Responsible Action, Davis, California, 1978.

SCHARF, P., and HICKEY, J. Inmates' conception of legal justice. *Criminal Justice and Behavior* 3(2), 1976.

CHAPTER 4

Psychopathy and Violence

ROBERT D. HARE

The extensive literature on psychopathy and violence makes it clear that any attempt to understand aggressive and violent behavior must take into account the interactions between a host of individual and situational variables. Accurate predictions of violence are notoriously difficult to make because the context in which violence occurs is so complex and in such a state of flux (Kozol et al., 1972; Wenk et al., 1972; Steadman and Cocozza, 1975; Geis and Monahan, 1976; Pasternack, 1976). I believe, however, that the violence of the psychopath may be more predictable.

DEFINITION OF PSYCHOPATHY

Cleckley's *The Mask of Sanity* (1976) provides the clinical basis for much of the North American research on psychopathy, and it contains extensive accounts of the disorder and its manifestations. Several shorter books have recently been published, including *The Menacing Stranger* (Grant, 1977) and *The Psychopath in Society* (Smith, 1978). Detailed discussions of the research literature can be found in two recent volumes, *The Psychopath: A Comprehensive Study of Antisocial Disorders and Behaviors* (Reid, 1978), and *Psychopathic Behavior: Approaches to Research* (Hare and Schalling, 1978). This last book contains a chapter in which I have outlined procedures for selecting subjects for research purposes. A checklist for the assessment of psychopathy is described in Hare (1980).

The term *psychopath* or *sociopath* is applied to individuals who exhibit a specific pattern or combination of personality traits and behaviors. Like most terms of this sort, "psychopath" serves as a convenient summary statement of the similarities between some individuals. It is true that some of these characteristics may exist in more normal individuals, but in the psychopath they are more pronounced and coordinated.

The term psychopathy and its synonyms have had a troubled history, and I believe that there would be advantages in replacing it with a term that does not evoke so many inferences. Until this is done, however, we should make certain that the term is used in a specific way. It is now used in so many ways that it is easy to lose sight of the underlying construct and to dismiss it as a meaningless, wastebasket category. The concept of psychopathy can be salient and well-defined, and the fact that many people abuse it does not mean that others cannot use it effectively, particularly for research purposes.

The belief is sometimes expressed that the putative cluster of characteristics does not exist, that is, that the concept itself is a myth. However, we should be certain that this view is based on an empirical foundation, and not on armchair psychology, psychiatry, or sociology, or on some preconceived belief about the way human behavior is organized. Many people have an aversion to using labels to pigeonhole others. But, at least for research purposes, the crucial question is whether it is possible to demonstrate empirically that the characteristics used to define psychopathy hang together; that is, does a cluster or syndrome actually exist. And if it exists, we may ask whether or not it can be measured reliably, and whether or not it is a valid construct, related in meaningful ways to other aspects of behavior. Although much more research is required, the literature clearly indicates that the answer to each of these questions is yes.

The behavior of the psychopath is directed almost entirely toward the satisfaction of personal needs, without any concern for the needs and welfare of others. This behavior apparently is not merely symptomatic of some underlying neurosis, psychosis, or lack of general intelligence, although Cleckley's term, "the mask of sanity," implies that there is something basically wrong somewhere. The psychopath is extremely impulsive, irresponsible, hedonistic, selfish, and intolerant of frustration. But perhaps his most important distinguishing features are an almost total lack of empathy and affection for others, coupled with an absence of any genuine indications of guilt, anxiety, or remorse for his persistent pattern of social and amoral behavior. At the same time, psychopaths are often quite charming, persuasive, fascinating, and fun to be around, for at least a while.

The characteristics of the psychopath will often give him/her a distinct advantage over the rest of us. Indeed, some observers go so far as to say that the psychopath, with his overriding concern for himself and his general lack of inhibitions about doing what he wants, is more rational than the rest of us. In some respects they may be right; perhaps it is the prosocial behavior of the ordinary person that presents the greater puzzle. If the behavior of the psychopath is rational, however, it is often only so in the short run; in the long run the psychopath's behavior can be self-defeating and extremely injurious to others, psychologically and physically.

Psychopathy and Crime

One might assume that the nature of the psychopath would routinely get him into trouble with the law, and that prisons would be full of these individuals. But most convicted criminals are not psychopaths, and many psychopaths manage to avoid incarceration, even though their behavior is persistently asocial. About this point Cleckley (1976) says that "most typical psychopaths, despite their continually repeated transgressions against the law and the rights of others and their apparent lack of moral compunction, seem to avoid murder and other grave felonies that remove them indefinitely from free activity in the social group. Most of these people carry out antisocial acts that would make it likely for them to be confined most of their lives in penal institutions, but often succeed, through the efforts of their families or through their equivocal medico-legal status, in escaping punishment altogether or in being released long before the expiration of ordinary terms of confinement" (pp. 265-266). Although I think that Cleckley underestimates the proportion of psychopaths who find their way into prison (probably because his practice involves many patients from the middle and upper classes), his main point is valid—many psychopaths do remain out of prison.

In this regard, I might comment that periodically I am foolish enough to give an interview to one of the local newspapers. Shortly after each report of my research I always receive several telephone calls from male criminals, some of them presumably psychopaths, who accuse me of giving them a bad name, and they occasionally threaten to do me in. (Presumably these are individuals with a Type 3 violence profile, described later, because, so far, the threats have not been carried out.)

Most of the letters and calls that come in are from women who have had the misfortune to be associated with men who they believe are psychopaths. The women's stories are invariably distressing, and they are usually about individuals who are seldom charged and convicted for their depredations. A recurrent theme is the woman's belief that the fault lies with her, and that she must deserve the emotional and physical abuse she experiences. This belief is often compounded by the good appearance that her husband or boyfriend is able to put on for friends and associates. Like battered wives and abused children, the victims of the psychopath learn to cope with or adapt to their situation in a variety of different ways. This is an area that warrants some intensive research.

In any case, it is clear that many psychopaths operate on the shady side of the law, or in situations which permit their behavior to be condoned, covered up, or even rewarded. Many, no doubt, get what they want by "bleeding" others, often appearing as helpless and in need of sympathy. Others may be what Arieti (1967) described as "complex" psychopaths, individuals whose behavior is guided not only by need gratification but also by how to get away with it. They peddle phony stocks, run home-repair rackets, flog worthless land, and generally wheel and deal. Some even find their way into the professions, politics, and academia. I am not sure to what extent these individuals engage in violent behavior, but on the basis of many informal reports, I suspect that they are quite capable of using violence when "required" to do so. And although I am concerned here only with physical aggression, any family counselor, social worker, or police officer can attest to the tremendous social damage and emotional abuse that any psychopath is capable of, including the more successful ones. For the present, since there is no simple way of studying these individuals, any conclusions to be drawn from the research I am reporting should be restricted to psychopaths whose behavior is too grossly and persistently antisocial to avoid incarceration.

INCIDENCE OF PSYCHOPATHY IN PRISON POPULATIONS

The incidence of psychopathy in prison populations is a matter of considerable practical importance, since many decisions about treatment programs, parole, probation, etc., are influenced by assessments of the inmates involved (Hare, 1978). For example, it is extremely difficult to modify the behavior of psychopaths, and if the majority of inmates are considered to be psychopaths, the prisons could not be expected to provide much more than a custodial function. There is a real problem here; while different investigators may agree on what they mean by psychopathy, they may not agree on the best way of actually making a diagnosis. The result is that estimates of the incidence of psychopaths in prison populations range from 10 or 15 percent to 75 or 80 percent. Guze (1976) has recently presented data showing that about 78 percent of a group of 223 male felons were sociopaths. Although the conception of sociopathy was similar to that used in this chapter, the actual diagnosis was made if an inmate had a history of trouble with the police and if two of the following were present: a history of excessive fighting, school delinquency, a poor job record, and a period of wanderlust. In this case, the diagnosis of sociopathy is more or less synonymous with criminality, and as such, is not useful. Unfortunately, it is likely that the same sort of problem will occur when the American Psychiatric Association (APA) begins to use its new criteria for the diagnosis of psychopathy. The 1968 version of the APA's *Diagnostic and Statistical Manual of Mental Disorders* (DSM-II) category for psychopaths was 301.7, *antisocial personality,* described as unsocialized, incapable of loyalty, selfish, callous, irresponsible, impulsive, intolerant of frustration, and incapable of feeling guilt and learning from experience. In DSM-III (1980), the category name has been changed to *antisocial personality disorder*. The description of this category is greatly expanded and elaborated, and is consistent with the classic conception of psychopathy. The diagnostic criteria for inclusion in this category have gone through several revisions, but are still very stringent.

It is quite clear that anyone who meets these criteria is antisocial, but is he also a psychopath in the strict (and useful) sense of the term? To answer this question we compared diagnoses made using the DSM-III criteria with those based on global clinical assessments. My colleagues and I have used the latter procedure extensively, and it has proven to be valid and highly reliable. It involves having two researchers independently rate each inmate on a seven-point scale of psychopathy, the ratings being based on interviews and detailed analyses of case history data (Hare and Cox, 1978). Typically, the two sets of ratings are added together; thus, the rating score for each inmate may range from 2 to 14, psychopaths being defined as inmates with a score of 12 to 14. Our experience with comparisons between ratings of psychopathy and early versions of the DSM-III criteria is reported elsewhere (Hare, 1978). For example, in one study we found that 79 percent of a sample of 75 prison inmates satisfied the December, 1977 DSM-III criteria for antisocial personality disorder, while we considered only 27 percent to be psychopaths. In a more recent study with the latest revision of DSM-III, we found that 76 percent of a sample of 145 prison inmates met the criteria for antisocial personality disorder, while we considered 33 percent to be psychopaths. It is obvious from these results that either our rating system is failing to identify psychopaths or the DSM-III is still too liberal in its approach to diagnosis. I believe that the latter is more likely, and that there is a great deal of slippage between the DSM-III conception of psychopathy and the criteria used for diagnosis.

I should note that my data on the incidence of psychopathy are based on research with white, male inmates in a variety of Canadian penal institutions. In some cases, the estimates are derived from groups of volunteers, and in other cases from a random selection of inmates. It seems that in maximum-security institutions most of the psychopaths are highly aggressive, while medium- and minimum-security institutions contain a greater proportion of psychopaths who are more manipulative and adept at using the system to their own advantage. But in each case somewhere around 30 percent of the inmates seem to be psychopaths by our criteria. The incidence among individuals with less extensive criminal histories is no doubt lower than this. Schuckit et al. (1977) found that about 16 percent of 199 white males arrested for their first felony crime warranted the diagnosis of antisocial personality.

My reason for belaboring this point about the prevalence of psychopaths in criminal populations is that it bears heavily upon the sort of conclusions that are drawn about the relationship of psychopathy, crime, and violence. For example, Guze (1976) concluded that once a man has been convicted of a felony, psychiatric diagnosis plays only a limited role in predicting criminal behavior. Many investigators would agree with this position, particularly as it applies to violence and dangerousness. And they could point to the extensive literature that indicates that violent behavior is extremely difficult to predict. More generally, they would argue that there is no such thing as a "dangerous" person, since, as Shah (1977) has put it, "physical violence or other dangerous acts are usually rather infrequent, occur in specific situational contexts, and may not be representative of the individual's customary behavior" (p. 105). He later suggests, however, that the study of dangerous behavior "should not concentrate *solely* (italics in original) upon discovering or uncovering aspects of an individual's personality and psychodynamics" (p. 106). Although I agree with this caveat, I also believe that some people are persistently and predictably dangerous, and that many of these people are psychopaths.

LACK OF INHIBITIONS AGAINST VIOLENCE

The nature of the person-situation interaction as a determinant of violent behavior is not the same for psychopaths as it is for others. Most of the factors that help to inhibit antisocial and aggressive behavior in normal persons—empathy, fear of punishment, etc.—are more or less missing in the psychopath. As a result, he has a larger repertory of actual behaviors than does the normal person. While most of us have strong inhibitions about inflicting physical damage upon others, the psychopath does not. Aggression and violence are simply ordinary forms of behavior, to be called upon when needed, and seldom associated with strong emotional coloring. And following such behavior, there is none of the concern, guilt, or remorse that prevents most people from placing themselves in the same sort of situation again. What this means is that the psychopath's behavior is not influenced by personal inhibitions, and that it is of little emotional consequence to him whether he satisfies his needs aggressively or otherwise. In terms of low cortical-arousal models of psychopathy (Eysenck, 1977; Hare and Schalling, 1978) or Moyer's (1976) physiological model of aggression, we might assume that the neural systems that inhibit aggressive and impulsive behavior are relatively ineffective in psychopaths. This may be particularly true when such cortical depressants as alcohol are used.

Research on the neurology of violence (e.g., Mark and Ervin, 1970; Monroe, 1970; Fields and Sweet, 1975; Smith and Kling, 1976; Elliott, 1978) has greatly increased understanding of the dynamics of some forms of violent behavior, but little of the violent and aggressive behavior of the classical psychopath can be attributed to a specific form of brain damage or neurological disorder. Most psychopaths seem to be neurologically normal, although there have been frequent reports of excessive amounts of slow-wave activity in their electroencephalographic (EEG) records. Even here, we do not know whether the slow-wave activity reflects an underlying cerebral dysfunction, a general tendency toward low cortical arousal (and a reduction in the efficiency of cortical inhibitory control of behavior), or simply drowsiness and boredom during routine EEG examinations (Hare and Schalling, 1978; Syndulko, 1978). Although patients with frontal lobe damage may exhibit some of the characteristics of the psychopath, they do not show the complete psychopathic syndrome (Elliott, 1978). Some of our recent research, involving neuropsychological tests and the presentation of verbal material to the left and right hemispheres via a tachistoscope, does not provide much support for the hypothesis of cerebral dysfunction in psychopaths (e.g., Hare, 1979).

In some respects, the psychopath is like the "undercontrolled aggressive type" described several years ago by Megargee (1966). The individuals fitting this type, however, seem to be much more heterogeneous in behavior and dynamics than do those defined as psychopaths. In any case, even though we would expect psychopaths to engage in a wide variety of antisocial and aggressive activities, there is some evidence that they may differ among themselves in the type of aggressive activity most often exhibited.

SOME EMPIRICAL DATA

Some of our findings have been presented elsewhere and will only be summarized here (Hare, 1978). The rest are still being analyzed and puzzled over, and only some preliminary results will be presented.

Study I

The first set of data is based on a follow-up of inmates who took part in at least one of our psychophysiological studies during 1964 to 1974 (Hare, 1978). About 100 psychopathic (Group P) and 100 nonpsychopathic (Group NP) individuals were involved in the study, although the actual numbers varied somewhat for different analyses. The two groups differed considerably in their criminal history before taking part in our research. Compared with the other inmates, the psychopaths were first convicted in adult court at an earlier age ($\bar{x} = 18.1$ for Group P and 20.0 for Group NP), spent more of their time in prison (42 percent versus 30 percent), were convicted of far more crimes including violent crimes ($\bar{x} = 5.46$ per year free versus 3.65), used more aliases, and broke out of prison more often. In spite of their generally horrendous record, the psychopaths were also more successful at obtaining parole.

During the follow-up period, which ranged from 15 months to 11 years after our initial assessment, the same sort of pattern emerged; the psychopaths committed more crimes and were imprisoned more often than the other inmates. Again, however, the psychopaths were more successful at obtaining parole, in spite of the fact that a relatively high proportion of their crimes contained elements of aggression and violence.

Some additional data are of interest here. For example, in the years following their first adult conviction, the psychopaths were convicted of a greater variety of crimes than were the other inmates—a mean of 4.62 different types for inmates in Group P, and 4.10 for inmates in Group NP ($t = 2.17$, $df = 200$, $p < .05$). The incidence of violent crimes was also considerably greater among the psychopaths than among the other inmates; compared to the other inmates the psychopaths were more likely, at some point in their criminal career, to have been convicted of assault, possession of a weapon, and robbery.

Several investigators have shown that age is related to subsequent criminal activity, particularly when combined with information on previous criminal history. Cocozza and Steadman (1974), Robins (1966), and Suedfeld and Landon (1978) have shown that after age 30 or 35 there is often a reduction in the severity of the antisocial behavior of some sociopaths. Therefore, we divided our subjects into subgroups based on age at the time we first assessed them. These age groups were 18 to 25, 26 to 30, and over 30. After assessment, the mean number of criminal convictions for each subject during each year he was free was calculated. The results clearly indicated that the psychopaths who were between 18 and 25 years old when we evaluated them had a higher conviction rate ($p < .05$) during the postassessment period (an average of just over four years) than did the other inmates of similar age. The most dramatic finding was that psychopaths who were between 26 and 30 years old when assessed had by far the highest conviction rate during the postassessment period, while those who were over 30 years old at the time of assessment had a subsequent conviction rate that was as low as that of the other inmates. The data suggest that the criminal activity of the psychopaths, as inferred from conviction rates, reached a peak when they were around 30 to 35 years old, and that it dropped off sharply when they were over 35. The conviction rate of the other inmates remained relatively constant over the time periods involved. These conclusions also apply to crimes of violence. Thus, although the psychopaths were generally more violent, they were far more likely to be convicted of robbery and assault when they were around 30 to 35 years old than when they were younger or older. However, it is important to note that even though the psychopaths showed a decrease with age in the incidence of aggressive crimes, the older psychopaths were still considerably more aggressive than were other inmates of similar age.

Study II

Recently we began a research program on the relationship between psychopathy and violence. We have a considerable amount of information on 243 white male inmates, about two-thirds of them from a provincial prison where sentences of less than two years are served, and the rest from a federal medium-security institution near Vancouver. We had hoped to include inmates from a maximum-security institution, but recent hostage-taking incidents and tight security arrangements made this impossible. Each inmate received a global rating of psychopathy from two investigators, using a seven-point scale. Seventy-five inmates (30.9 percent) received a combined rating of 12 to 14 and were defined as psychopaths (Group P); 64 received a rating of 8 to 11 (Group M), and 104 received a rating of 2 to 7 (Group NP).

The first analyses began with tabulations of convictions for different kinds of violent crime and assessments of aggressive and violent behavior. In general, the assessments, made by two researchers from case-history

Table 1

Percentage of Inmates in Each Group That Engaged in Various Types of Violent and Aggressive Behavior

Activity	P	M	NP	(P vs. NP)*
Convictions				
Murder or manslaughter	4	4	4	
Armed robbery	19	8	9	<.05
Robbery	20	16	16	
Assault	24	14	7	<.01
Forcible seizure	9	0	1	<.01
Rape	4	0	1	
Behavior				
Use of gun	11	4	1	<.01
Use of other weapon	7	0	3	
Fights	56	46	20	<.001
Aggressive homosexuality	6	6	0	<.01
N	75	64	104	

* Based on χ^2, $df = 1$.

information, were very reliable. Some of the data, presented in Table 1, show that, compared to the other inmates, the psychopaths were more likely to have been convicted of armed robbery, assault, forcible seizure, and rape. They were also more likely to have used a weapon, to have been involved in fights, and to have engaged in aggressive homosexual behavior in prison.

Forty-one of the 243 inmates (17 percent) had no recorded history of violence, and since we were mainly interested in patterns of violence, these inmates were excluded from most of the following analyses. Scarcely any of these nonviolent inmates were psychopaths. Thus, 97 percent (73 of 75) of the psychopaths had at least one conviction for a crime of violence, while 78 percent (58 of 74) of the inmates in Group M, and 75 percent (71 of 94) of those in Group NP had been convicted of violent crime; the difference between groups was significant ($\chi^2 = 15.8$, $df = 2$, $p < .001$) and for Groups P versus NP ($\chi^2 = 15.7$, $df = 1$, $p < .001$).

Factor analysis of violence variables. For the remaining 202 inmates, 21 violence variables were subjected to factor analysis. (Murder, attempted murder, aggressive homosexuality, and attempted suicide were not included in the analysis because of their rarity.) Two factoring procedures were used (Hakstian and Bay, 1973). First, a principal components analysis was performed to examine the eigenvalues of the 21 × 21 correlation matrix for an indication of the number of factors to extract. The Kaiser-Guttman rule (eigenvalues greater than one) and Cattell's (1966) scree test suggested that four factors were appropriate. A maximum-likelihood common-factor analysis was then performed, and four factors were extracted. The unrotated factor pattern was transformed to oblique simple structure by the Harris-Kaiser (1964) procedure. Overall, 56 percent of the coefficients fell in the factor hyperplanes (i.e., in the ± .10 region).

The four factors and their loadings are presented in Table 2. It seems reasonable to label Factor 1 as *intimidation with weapons* (threatens others with weapons, convicted of armed robbery); Factor 2 as *verbal aggression and hostility* (verbally abusive to others, belligerent, irritable, threatens others, temper tantrums); Factor 3 as *extreme physical aggression* (uses

Table 2

Oblique Factor Pattern for 21 Violence and Aggression Variables*

	Factor				
Variable	1	2	3	4	$h2$
Convictions					
Possession of weapon	09	–06	07	16	05
Robbery	16	02	08	28	13
Armed robbery	*39*	–19	11	–06	19
Roberry with violence	–02	–09	27	09	09
Assault	–07	–04	01	22	05
Assault causing bodily harm	–12	07	*45*	16	25
Escape	04	03	01	–14	02
Vandalism	–06	15	–03	*44*	19
Causing a disturbance by fighting	–08	01	07	*44*	19
Behaviors					
Attempted suicide	03	17	00	15	05
Temper tantrums	00	*57*	00	05	32
Verbally abusive	03	*74*	02	–10	58
Verbal threats	19	*58*	16	–20	49
Critical of others	03	17	–12	–11	06
Irritable	05	*61*	–05	07	36
Belligerent	–02	*62*	–08	13	37
Impaired driving	04	–29	00	09	10
Aggressive use of auto	00	–14	–07	10	04
Physical fights	15	–13	*50*	04	33
Threatens with weapons	*99*	00	00	00	99
Uses weapons on others	00	–07	*52*	–14	27

* Decimal points omitted. $N = 202$.

weapons on others, threatens others with weapons, convicted of assault causing bodily harm); and Factor 4 as *minor, diffuse physical aggression* (convicted of causing a disturbance by fighting, convicted of vandalism).

Profiles of violence. Although it is of theoretical interest that 21 aggression and violence variables may be reduced to four factors, we were more interested in a means of describing patterns of violence. Accordingly, the regression procedure was used to obtain each inmate's score on each of the four factors. Mean factor scores were then computed for each of the three inmate groups. (Because of a programming error, 52 subjects were not included in the analysis, and it was not possible to redo it in time for this paper. The proportion of subjects in each group was unchanged, however, and the reduced N of 150 should not have had any effect on the results.) The results are shown in Figure 1; the difference between groups was significant on Factor 2 ($F = 12.37$, $df = 2/147$, $p < .001$) and Factor 3 ($F = 4.53$, $df = 2/147$, $p < .05$). The psychopaths were clearly more hostile and physically aggressive than the other inmates, confirming

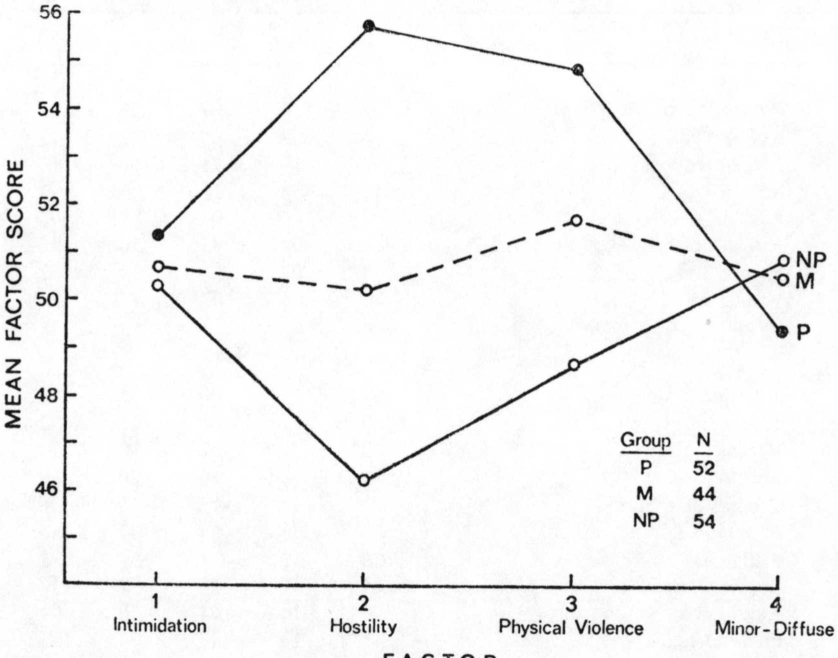

FIGURE 1. Mean scores obtained on each violence factor by inmates with high (P), medium (M), and low (NP) ratings of psychopathy.

much of what I have said about the criminal psychopath. In this regard, several clinicians and investigators have commented that psychopaths whose behavior does not include much blatant violence and who have the appropriate intellectual, personality, or family resources, often manage to stay out of prisons. Those without these resources and whose behavior is persistently aggressive and violent may spend a lot of time incarcerated. I believe that this is the case with the psychopaths in the present study; many were from the lower socioeconomic levels and did not have the family resources to be routinely bailed out of difficulty.

The data presented in Figure 1 are mean factor scores, and they tell us little about the individual differences that might exist within each group, particularly Group P, the psychopaths. For this reason, the factor profiles of the 52 psychopaths were grouped on the basis of their similarity to one another, using the CGROUP program developed at the University of British Columbia Computing Center (Osterlin et al., 1978). This program employs a clustering technique to organize profiles into "natural" clusters or groups (Veldman, 1967, pp. 308-317). Four groups or types of profile emerged as the optimal number for Group P; these are plotted in Figure 2.

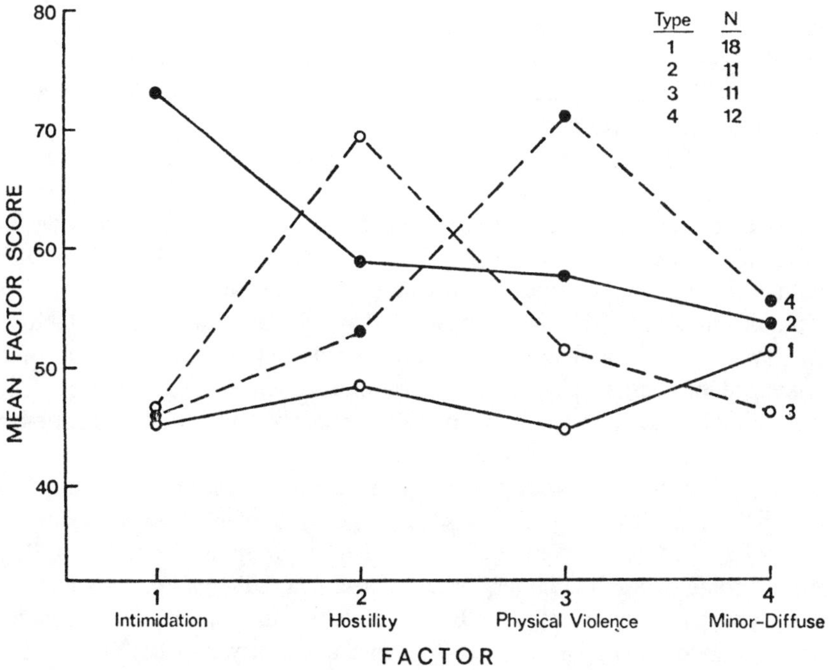

FIGURE 2. Four types of violence profile obtained by clustering the individual profiles of 52 psychopaths (Group P) on the basis of similarity to one another.

We are still gathering data on the correlates of each of these profile types. Analyses completed so far, however, clearly indicate that the factor profiles accurately reflect individual criminal records and case histories. The Type 1 profile contains 18 psychopaths who received about average scores on each of the violence factors. Most of the inmates in this group had convictions for simple assault, theft, escape, and possession of drugs. In general, they were moderately aggressive on occasion but were not characterized by any particular displays of persistent or extreme aggression.

The Type 2 profile is made up of 11 psychopaths who scored above the mean on each violence factor, with a particularly high score on Factor 1. *intimidation with weapons.* The inmates in this group were persistently aggressive and hostile, and had many convictions for assault, armed robbery, robbery with violence, and possession of weapons. Weapons seemed to be one of the tools of their trade, and they didn't worry about the possibility of having to use them on a victim or about the stern view of the courts on the use of weapons in the commission of a crime.

The Type 3 profile contains 11 psychopaths with a high score on Factor 3, *verbal aggression and hostility,* and a low score on Factor 4, *minor, diffuse physical aggression.* Most of their convictions were for theft, fraud, false pretenses, and escape, with occasional displays of physical violence, mostly assault and fighting. Their files contained many reports of belligerence, hostility, and threatening behavior, although their aggressive behavior was more verbal than physical.

The Type 4 profile consists of 12 psychopaths who were extremely violent. Unlike Type 3, these inmates were far more likely to engage in physical rather than verbal aggression. Most of them had many convictions for assault, assault causing bodily harm, armed robbery, robbery with violence, etc. In spite of the fact that murder and attempted murder were not included in the factor analysis that generated the violence factors, the Type 4 profile managed to include the only psychopaths who had been convicted of murder (3 inmates) or attempted murder (2 inmates). The violence of these Type 4 psychopaths was clearly severe and was, in most cases, an integral part of their behavior.

CGROUP analyses were also done on the factor profiles of Groups M and NP. In each case, the same three types of profile emerged; therefore the two groups were combined into a single group of 98 inmates. The three profile types that emerged from a CGROUP analysis of these 98 nonpsychopaths are plotted in Figure 3. In some respects, these profiles are similar to the Type 1, 2, and 3 profiles of the psychopaths (Figure 2). For example, both the psychopaths and the nonpsychopaths include (a) a relatively large group of inmates who received low scores on each of the

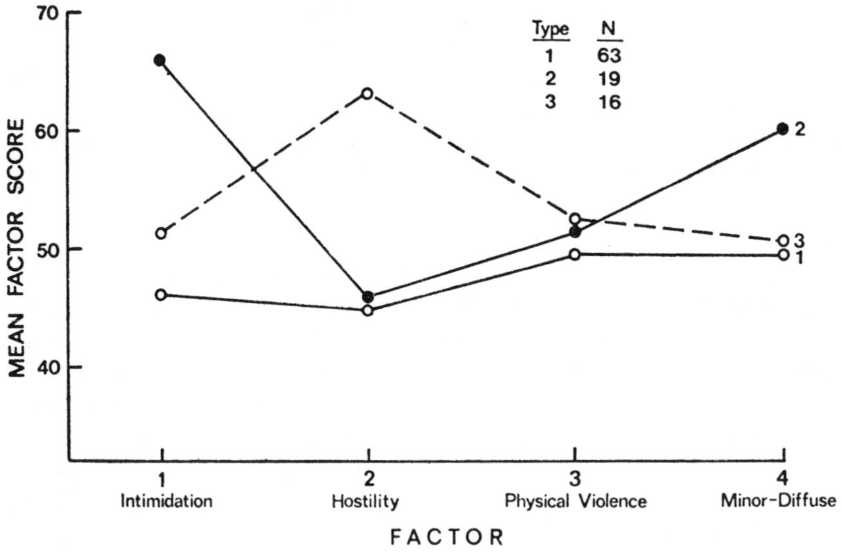

FIGURE 3. Three types of violence profile obtained by clustering the individual profiles of 98 nonpsychopaths (Groups M and NP) on the basis of similarity to one another.

violence factors (the Type 1 profiles in Figures 2 and 3), and (b) a group of inmates who are much more verbally aggressive and hostile than physically violent (the Type 3 profiles in Figures 2 and 3). There are, however, some important differences between the psychopaths and the other inmates. The psychopaths who use weapons to intimidate others are also rather hostile and violent (Type 2 profile in Figure 2), while the nonpsychopaths who use weapons to intimidate others are more likely to engage in minor-diffuse aggression than in verbal hostility and serious physical violence (Type 2 profile in Figure 3). Many of these Type 2 nonpsychopaths seem to use weapons to protect themselves or because they feel inadequate without them. The severe violence (Type 4 profile in Figure 2) that was so prominent in the psychopaths was not present in the nonpsychopathic group. What this means is that the psychopaths (especially the 23 with a Type 2 or Type 4 profile) were responsible for most of the serious violent and aggressive behavior in our sample of 202 criminals.

It could be argued, of course, that there is a certain degree of circularity involved in these analyses and the conclusions drawn from them That is, perhaps criminals who are aggressive and violent tend to be diagnosed as psychopaths in the first place. However, the presence or absence of serious violence is not an important consideration in our diagnosis of psychopathy. In fact, over half (56 percent) of the psychopaths in our sample (those with Type 1 and Type 3 profiles) received relatively low scores on the physical violence factor. Nevertheless, it is clear that the majority of the criminal psychopaths we study do engage in some form of aggressive behavior.

It is also clear that they differ in the type and severity of aggressive and violent behavior typically exhibited. Given that this is so, and that the profiles in Figure 2 adequately represent the different patterns of violence among psychopaths, it is logical to ask about the correlates of these profile types. That is, in addition to criminal behavior, how does a Type 1 profile differ from a Type 2 profile, and so on? So far we don't have much information to answer this question. However, some data are available. We have found that the four profile types displayed in Figure 2 do not differ in mean age of first juvenile conviction (overall $\bar{x} = 12.8$), age of first conviction in adult court ($\bar{x} = 17.5$), education ($\bar{x} = 9.0$), occupational level (31 unskilled, 17 semiskilled, 3 skilled, 1 professional), alcohol use (4 alcoholics, 28 problem drinkers, 17 moderate drinkers, 3 abstainers), drug use (12 addicts, 35 users, 6 nonusers, or IQ ($\bar{x} = 103$). There were also no differences in a variety of psychological test scores.

Factor analysis of precursors of violence. Some of our other data suggest, however, that there may be identifiable precursors of several of the four types of violent behavior engaged in by adult psychopaths. These are based on results of a factor analysis involving variables considered to be precursors of antisocial and aggressive behavior. A survey of the literature led us to select 16 variables that deal with family background and childhood behavior and for which we could make reasonably good assessments. Two raters were used for these assessments, and the interrater reliability was quite good, though it could be improved in subsequent research. Ratings on each of these variables were made for 202 inmates and were subjected to the same kind of factor analysis described earlier. Briefly, a principal-components analysis was followed by a maximum-likelihood common-factor analysis, and four factors were extracted. The unrotated factor pattern was then transformed to oblique simple structure, with 47 percent of the coefficients falling in the factor hyperplanes (in the $\pm$ .10 region).

The four factors and their loadings are presented in Table 3. Factor 1 was labeled as *physical child abuse* (violent father, parental brutality); Factor 2 as *poor home life* (broken home, unstable family, parental drinking, parental promiscuity), Factor 3 as *early behavior problems* (school

Table 3

Oblique Factor Pattern for 16 Variables Considered to Be Precursors of Aggressive and Violent Behavior*

Variable	Factor 1	2	3	4	h^2
Parental alcohol problems	*30*	*37*	–02	02	25
Parental promiscuity	15	*35*	08	–04	19
Parental instability	24	02	30	–12	18
Parental brutality	*63*	11	14	17	53
Parental nagging and criticisms	04	–01	01	*95*	92
Parental rejection	–07	24	20	21	17
Broken home	–13	*68*	–06	01	43
Unstable family	05	*57*	18	–01	42
Parental quarreling	23	27	21	–11	25
Violent father	*82*	03	–02	–08	67
Childhood fighting	–02	07	*53*	–06	31
Childhood temper tantrums	13	03	29	–10	13
Childhood peer problems	19	01	*34*	14	20
Childhood school problems	07	02	*54*	09	33
Childhood enuresis	–06	08	*40*	07	18
Childhood fire-setting	–04	17	*46*	03	28

* Decimal points omitted. $N = 202$.

problems, fighting, fire-setting, enuresis, peer problems). Factor 4 might be labeled *emotional abuse,* but since it is defined by only one variable (and not a highly reliable one), it is not considered in any detail.

Factor scores were computed for each of the 202 inmates, and the resulting profiles were grouped in terms of their similarity, using the CGROUP program described above. Four groups emerged as the optimal number, and these are plotted in Figure 4.

Compared with the other types of profile, Type A inmates generally had better family backgrounds and the fewest early behavior problems. The primary feature of Type B was evidence of early behavior problems. Type C inmates appeared to have experienced a great deal of physical abuse as children while Type D inmates had a particularly poor home life. These four patterns of early experience tended to be related to the type of violent adult behavior exhibited. As Table 4 indicates, inmates with the Type A profile (relatively little evidence of early problems) had lower ratings of psychopathy and lower scores on each of the violence factors (especially *physical aggression*) than did the other groups. The Type B

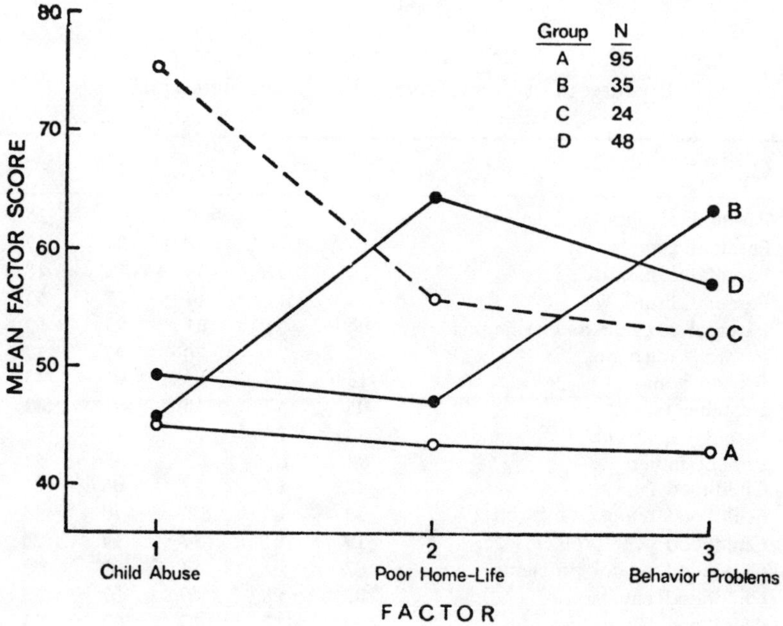

FIGURE 4. Four types of "precursors of violence" profile obtained by clustering the individual profiles of 202 criminals on the basis of similarity to one another.

profile (early behavior problems) was associated with the highest ratings of psychopathy and with above-average scores on each of the violence factors. The Type C profile (child abuse) was associated with slightly above-average degrees of physical violence, while Type D (poor home life) was

Table 4

Mean Rating of Psychopathy and Violence Factor Scores Obtained by Inmates with Each Type of Precursor Profile

Variable	Type of Precursor Profile A	B	C	D	F ($df = 3/198$)	p
$\bar{X}$ Rating of Psychopathy	2.9	4.9	3.9	4.3	11.69	<.001
$\bar{X}$ Violence Scores						
Factor 1 (intimidation)	47.9	51.7	51.4	51.9	2.42	<.10
Factor 2 (hostility)	48.9	42.8	49.3	50.4	1.43	—
Factor 3 (physical aggression)	46.8	52.3	51.2	53.9	6.85	<.001
Factor 4 (minor, diffuse)	48.2	42.3	42.0	50.7	2.05	—

related to extreme physical violence. Social-learning theories of violence would, of course, have little trouble accounting for these findings, particularly for Types A, C, and D, for whom the pattern of adult violence seemed to have been modeled after the sort of experiences they were exposed to as children.

The Type B profile is somewhat more problematical since it seemed to include inmates whose most distinguishing early feature was general acting-out-behavior—school problems, fighting, fire-setting, enuresis, etc. As several investigators have argued that adult psychopathy does not stem from any particular family or environmental background (Cleckley, 1976), it is noteworthy that this type also had the highest mean rating of psychopathy. This may very well be true, but it is possible that the sort of early environment a potential psychopath is exposed to has an influence on the pattern of aggressive behavior he or she will exhibit as an adult. Since only 43 percent (15 of 35) of the inmates in Type B were actually psychopaths, we carried out another analysis in which the scores on each of the precursor factors of psychopaths and nonpsychopaths were compared directly.

There were no significant differences between Groups P, M, and NP on the *physical child abuse* or *poor home life* factors. However, Group P (the psychopaths) had the highest score on the *early behavior problems* factor ($\bar{x} = 54.4$), Group NP had the lowest score ($\bar{x} = 49.0$), and Group M fell in between ($\bar{x} = 52.9$); the difference between groups was significant ($F = 4.92$, $df = 2/147$, $p < .05$). Thus, adult criminal psychopathy was associated with early conduct and behavior problems, but not with any particular type of family or environmental experiences. But, as suggested above, the family life of psychopaths apparently bore some relationship to the kind of aggressive behavior pattern they typically engaged in. Psychopaths who were extremely violent and physically aggressive (Type 4 violence profile; Figure 2) received high scores on the poor home life factor (unstable family, broken home, parental drinking and promiscuity); presumably their behavior was at least in part modeled after the behavior patterns they were constantly exposed to. There was also a tendency for psychopaths who were verbally aggressive and hostile (Type 3 violence profile) to have been subjected to a considerable amount of verbal and emotional abuse as children.

Similar analyses were carried out with the nonpsychopathic inmates in Groups M and NP. A general finding was that nonpsychopaths who made frequent use of weapons to intimidate others scored high on the poor home life factor.

CONCLUSIONS

The clinical concept of psychopathy, in its strict sense, should be taken into account when attempts are made to assess dangerousness or to predict violence.

Many psychopaths are not persistently aggressive and violent, and they manage to satisfy their needs with wit, charm, and manipulation. Most of the psychopaths who end up in prison, however, have some history of violent behavior. This is not too surprising, since the characteristics that define psychopathy (impulsivity, lack of empathy, etc.) are not generally associated with strong inhibitions against the expression of aggressive, asocial behavior.

Psychopathy is probably not associated with any particular type of family background or early experiences. Nevertheless, it is possible that a psychopath's preferred mode of dealing with others may be partly the result of shaping by early experiences and early modeling processes.

Among the many reasons violence is difficult to predict is the low base rate for violence that exists in most populations, including criminal ones. There are some groups for whom the base rates are much higher, however, and these include well-diagnosed psychopaths with a history of aggressive and violent behavior (e.g., those with Type 2 or Type 4 violence profiles). Predictions of subsequent violent behavior by these individuals are easier to make than is usually the case, at least until they reach middle age.

As a final point, it could be argued that the concept of psychopathy is superfluous in attempting to understand dangerous and aggressive behavior, and that it would be sufficient to consider specific behaviors and criminal-history data when making predictions about future behavior. There is considerable merit in this argument, since it should be possible to perform multivariate analyses to work out the best combination and weightings of predictive variables. Procedures of this sort have not been successful. As I have reported elsewhere (1978), the predictive value of these variables is better when used in combination with clinical assessments of psychopathy than when used by themselves. Clinical judgment and inference are required to capture the salient nature of psychopathy, and something of importance is lost when only highly objective and easily measured variables are considered. On the basis of a considerable amount of research, Kozol et al., (1972) concluded that the best predictor of violence is the intuitive feeling of the clinician that the individual is cold, aloof, emotionally distant, and without regard for others. They also concluded that the dangerous person is "nearly identical with the classical stereotype of the criminal or antisocial psychopath."

Most dangerous and aggressive people, however, are not psychopaths, and it would be more accurate, perhaps, to put it the other way around; that is, most criminal psychopaths are dangerous, while some are exceedingly so.

ACKNOWLEDGMENTS

Preparation of this paper and the research reported herein were supported by Grant MA-4511 from the Medical Research Council of Canada. The advice and assistance of Janice Frazelle, John Lind, and Ralph Hakstian are gratefully acknowledged.

REFERENCES

AMERICAN PSYCHIATRIC ASSOCIATION. *Diagnostic and Statistical Manual of Mental Disorders*. Washington, D. C., 1968, 1980.

ARIETI, S. *The Intrapsychic Self*. Basic Books, New York, 1967.

CATTELL, R. B. The scree test for the number of factors. *Multivariate Behavioral Research*, 1:245-275, 1966.

CLECKLEY, H. *The Mask of Sanity*, 5th ed. Mosby, St. Louis, Missouri, 1976.

COCOZZA, J., and STEADMAN, H. Some refinements in the measurement and prediction of dangerous behavior. *Am. J. Psychiatry*, 131:1012-1014, 1974.

ELLIOTT, F. Neurological aspects of psychopathic behaviors, in *The Psychopath: A Comprehensive Study of Antisocial Disorders and Behaviors*. W. Reid, ed., Brunner/Mazel, New York, 1978.

EYSENCK, H. J. *Crime and Personality*, 3rd. ed. Routledge & Kegan Paul, London, 1977.

FIELDS, W. S., and SWEET, W. H. *Neural Bases of Violence and Aggression*. Warren H. Green, St. Louis, Missouri, 1975.

FLOR-HENRY, P. Lateralized temporal-limbic dysfunction and psychopathology. *Ann. N. Y. Acad. Sci.* 280:777-797, 1976.

GEIS, G., and MONAHAN, J. The social ecology of violence, in *Moral Development and Behavior*. T. Lickona, ed. Holt, Rinehart and Winston, 1976, pp. 342-356.

GRANT, V. W. *The Menacing Stranger*. Dabor Science Publications, Oceanside, New York, 1977.

GUZE, S. *Criminality and Psychiatric Disorders*. Oxford University Press, New York, 1976.

HAKSTIAN, A. R., and BAY, K. S. The Alberta General Factor Analysis Program. Division of Educational Research Services, University of Alberta, Edmonton, Canada, 1973.

HARE, R. D. Psychopathy and crime, in *Colloquium on the Correlates of Crime and the Determinants of Criminal Behavior: Invited Papers*. L. Otten, ed. The Mitre Corporation, McLean, Virginia, 1978, pp. 95-132.

HARE, R. D. Psychopathy and laterality of cerebral function. *Journal of Abnormal Behavior* 88:605-610, 1979.

HARE, R. D. A research scale for the assessment of psychopathy in criminal populations. *Personality and Individual Differences* 1:1-9, 1980.

HARE, R. D., and COX, D. N. Clinical and empirical conceptions of psychopathy, and the selection of subjects for research, in *Psychopathic Behavior: Approaches to Research*. R. D. Hare and D. Schalling, eds. Wiley, New York, 1978, pp. 1-21.

HARE, R. D., and SCHALLING, D., eds. *Psychopathic Behavior: Approaches to Research*. Wiley, New York, 1978.

HARRIS, C. W., and KAISER, H. F. Oblique factor analytic solutions by orthogonal transformations. *Psychometrika* 29:347-362, 1964.

KOZOL, H., BOUCHER, R. J., and GAROFALO, R. F. The diagnosis and treatment of dangerousness. *Crime and Delinquency* 18:371-392, 1972.

MARK, V. H., and ERVIN, F. R. *Violence and the Brain*. Harper & Row, New York, 1970.

MEGARGEE, E. I. Undercontrolled and overcontrolled personality types in extreme antisocial aggression. *Psychological Monographs* 80, (Whole No. 611), No. 3, 1966.

MONROE, R. R. *Episodic Behavioral Disorders*. Harvard University Press, Cambridge, Massachusetts, 1970.

MOYER, K. E. *The Psychobiology of Aggression*. Harper & Row, New York, 1976.

OSTERLIN, D., PATTERSON, J. M., and WHITAKER, R. A. *Hierarchical Grouping Analysis with Optional Contiguity Constraint*. University of British Columbia Computing Center, Vancouver, Canada, 1978.

PASTERNACK, S. A., ed. *Violence and Victims*, Spectrum, New York, 1976.

REID, W. H., ed. *The Psychopath: A Comprehensive Study of Antisocial Disorders and Behaviors*. Brunner/Mazel, New York, 1978.

ROBINS, L. N. *Deviant Children Grown Up*. Williams & Wilkins, Baltimore, 1966.

SHAH, S. A. Dangerousness, in *The Criminal Justice System*. B. D. Sales, ed. Plenum Press, New York, 1977.

SCHUCKIT, M. A., HERRMAN, G., and SCHUCKIT, J. J. The importance of psychiatric illness in newly arrested prisoners. *J. Nerv. Ment. Dis.* 165:118-125, 1977.

SMITH, R. *The Psychopath in Society*. Academic Press, New York, 1978.

SMITH, W. L., and KLING, A. *Issues in Brain Behavior Control*. Spectrum, New York, 1976.

STEADMAN, H. J., and COCOZZA, J. Violence, mental illness and preventive detention: We can't predict who is dangerous. *Psychology Today* 84:32-35, 1975.

SUEDFELD, P., and LANDON, B. Approaches to treatment, in *Psychopathic Behavior: Approaches to Research*. R. D. Hare and D. Schalling, eds. Wiley, New York, 1978, pp. 347-376.

SYNDULKO, K. Electrocortical investigations of sociopathy, in *Psychopathic Behavior: Approaches to Research*. R. D. Hare and D. Schalling, eds. Wiley, New York. 1978, pp. 145-156.

VELDMAN, D. *Fortran Programming for the Behavioral Sciences*. Holt, Rinehart, and Winston, New York, 1967.

WENT, E. A., ROBINSON, J. O., and SMITH, G. B. Can violence be predicted? *Crime and Delinquency* 18:393-402, 1972.

CHAPTER 5

Brain Dysfunction in Prisoners

RUSSELL R. MONROE

Prisoners represent a heterogeneous population which undoubtedly demands diverse dispositional and rehabilitative strategies. My interest, hence my focus in this chapter, is limited to recidivist aggressive criminals who, though a diverse subgroup, have been most resistant to rehabilitation. As few as 6 percent of offenders contribute to more than half of all criminal acts (Wolfgang, 1975; Mednick and Christiansen, 1977). Thus, an effective therapeutic regime for these few individuals would have considerable impact on crime rates.

Recent advances in pharmacologic treatment of the psychoses have shown that the medical model is an effective research strategy; it has dramatically reduced the cost of psychiatric care and the need for prolonged institutionalization of psychotic individuals. The medical model should be pursued in the investigation of the aggressive criminal as well. This model assumes that there is a genetic metabolic defect that predisposes the individual to criminal behavior, which becomes manifest when it interacts with such other factors as perinatal trauma, trauma in early childhood, central nervous system insult, learning disabilities, and family and social deprivation.

There is a further assumption that the social-cultural aspects of this multidimensional causality account for only a small amount of the variance; hence pharmacologic modification of the metabolic defect becomes the crucial, although not the only, ingredient of the therapeutic strategy.

Testing a pharmacologic regimen undoubtedly demands a therapeutically meaningful phenomenologic subclassification of the group we usually refer to as psychopaths. Such an analysis in turn depends on theory. The fact that the earliest medical model used to understand criminal behavior, that of epilepsy, has failed, should not deter investigators from exploring other medical models. There are new theories that invite exploration. These include limbic system dysfunction, adult versions of childhood attentional disorders, adult consequences of certain childhood learning disabilities, adult consequences of minimal brain dysfunction, and problems of cerebral dominance. All of these theories have implications for specific but as yet untried psychopharmacologic regimes.

Testing these models is feasible because diagnoses require only psychodiagnostic and physiologic laboratories in the prison setting. Tape-recorded data can be analyzed by laboratory computers available at most universities and medical centers. The procedures are nonintrusive and offer the prisoner the possibility of specific help for his or her problems.

I shall summarize briefly the findings presented in our recent monograph, *Brain Dysfunction in Aggressive Criminals* (Monroe, 1978). One of our strategies in that study was a two-dimensional analysis of aggressive criminal behavior. The episodic behavioral disorders have been defined as any precipitously appearing maladaptive behavior, usually intermittent and recurrent, which interrupts the life style and life flow of the individual. A subcategory, the dyscontrol syndrome, is characterized by an abrupt single act or short series of acts with a common intention carried through to completion with at least partial relief of tension or direct or indirect gratification of specific needs. Such behavior is loosely referred to in the psychiatric literature as "acting on impulse," "irresistible impulse," or "acting out."

As criterion variables we used a self-reporting dyscontrol scale (Table 1) which included 18 statements selected by Plutchik et al. (1976), from my earlier monograph on episodic behavioral disorders, as representative comments by individuals suffering from the dyscontrol syndrome (Monroe, 1970). The second criterion variable included drug-activated generalized theta activity (Figure 1) which we reported as correlating significantly with subcortical seizural activity and/or central nervous system (CNS) instability as the result of a maturational lag (Monroe, 1970, 1974).

Ninety-three relatively unselected aggressive criminal subjects were as-

Table 1

MONROE SCALE

Instructions:

Here are statements that describe the way some people feel or act. Please read each statement carefully and place a check-mark (√) on the appropriate line to indicate how often you have felt or acted that way.

	Never	*Rarely*	*Sometimes*	*Often*
1. I have acted on a whim or impulse.	—	—	—	—
2. I have had sudden changes in my moods.	—	—	—	—
3. I have had the experience of feeling confused even in a familiar place.	—	—	—	—
4. I do not feel totally responsible for what I do.	—	—	—	—
5. I have lost control of myself even though I did not want to.	—	—	—	—
6. I have been surprised by my actions.	—	—	—	—
7. I have lost control of myself and hurt other people.	—	—	—	—
8. My speech has been slurred.	—	—	—	—
9. I have had "blackouts."	—	—	—	—
10. I have become wild and uncontrollable after one or two drinks.	—	—	—	—
11. I have become so angry that I smashed things.	—	—	—	—
12. I have frightened other people with my temper.	—	—	—	—
13. I have "come to" without knowing where I was or how I got there.	—	—	—	—
14. I have had indescribable frightening feelings.	—	—	—	—
15. I have been so tense I would like to scream.	—	—	—	—
16. I have had the impulse to kill myself.	—	—	—	—
17. I have been angry enough to kill somebody.	—	—	—	—
18. I have physically attacked and hurt another person.	—	—	—	—

(Scoring is on basis of never = 0, rarely = 1, sometimes = 2, and often = 3 to arrive at a sum for the total score.)

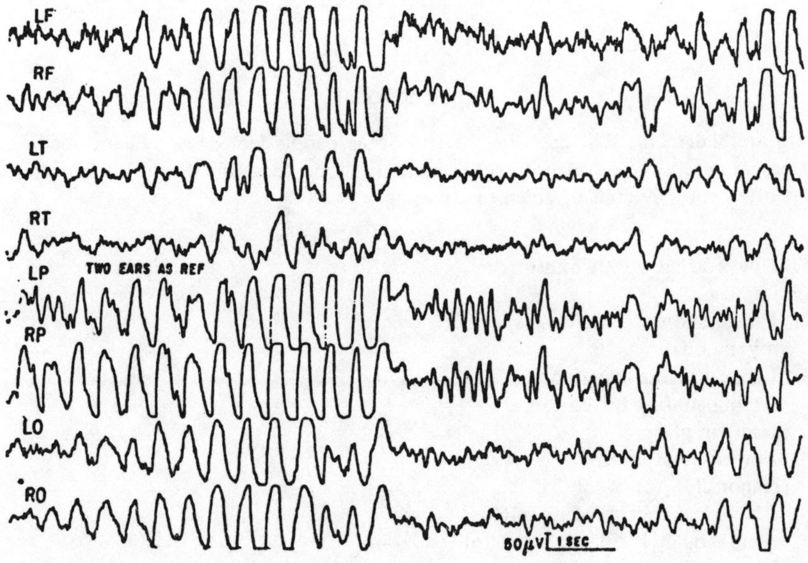

FIGURE 1. A specific chloralose activation pattern (Monroe and Mickle, 1967).

signed to four groups (Figure 2). Group 1 with high theta and high dyscontrol symptoms was ultimately labeled the "epileptoid" dyscontrol group for reasons that will be explained. Group 2, with equally high dyscontrol symptoms but low theta activity, was labeled "hysteroid" dyscontrol because it seemed probable that the impulsive behavior of these individuals was influenced more by psychodynamic than neurophysiologic mechanisms. Group 3's theta activity was as high as that of group 1 but was rated low on the dyscontrol scale. An analysis of symptoms suggested the label "inadequate" psychopath for group 3, and it was felt that the electroencephalographic (EEG) abnormality more likely reflected a maturational lag than a subcortical epileptoid mechanism. Finally, group 4 with low theta and low dyscontrol symptoms, which in a random population would have been the "normal" group, was in our population of criminals as psychopathic as the other groups and thus labeled the "pure" psychopathic group. The criterion variables of theta waves and dyscontrol symptoms were sufficiently powerful to separate four unique clinical entities, although we needed to apply psychometric, psychiatric, and neurologic measures to define these groups.

The neurological scale was the most powerful in identifying epileptoid

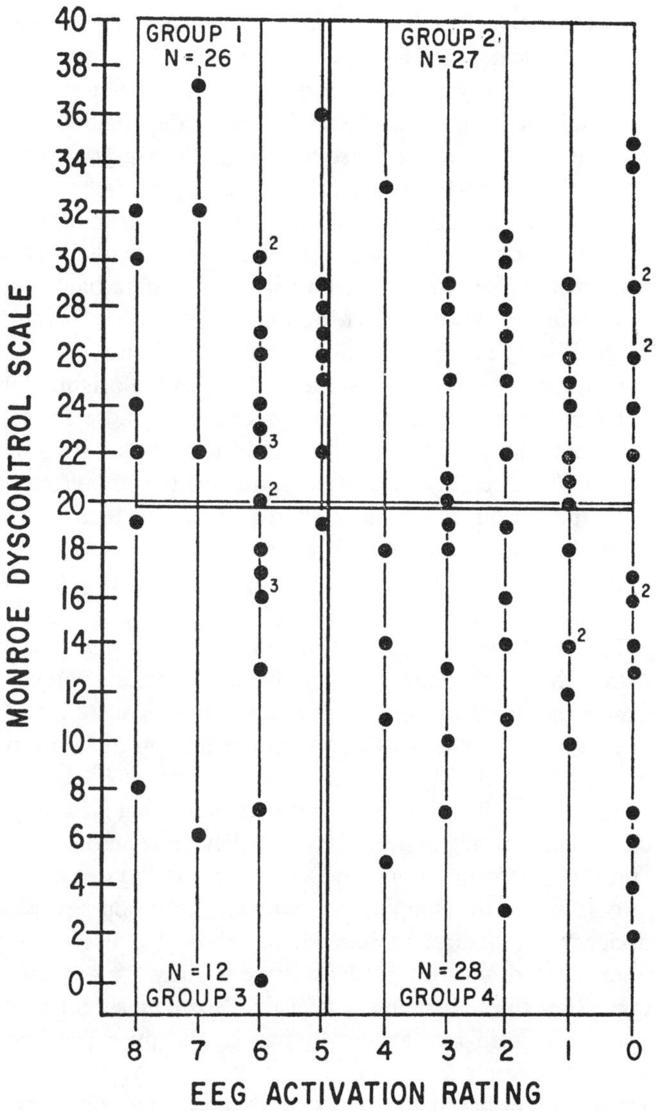

FIGURE 2. Scattergram of the four-group system.

dyscontrol, and the neurologic history items seemed more powerful than the neurologic examination in making this discrimination. The positive findings were those that might be expected in minimal brain dysfunction in adults or individuals with *formes frustes* of epilepsy. The important items on the neurologic scale were congenital abnormalities, hyperacusis, photophobia, apraxia, and asymmetries in motor strength. On the other hand, compared to the other groups, the epileptoid group demonstrated better gross coordination and sensory discrimination. The psychiatrist's as well as the neurologist's global suspicions of an epileptoid mechanism behind the patient's symptoms proved to be a powerful discriminating factor in identifying the epileptoid dyscontrol subjects. This global estimation of an epileptoid mechanism was based on two distinct data banks, psychiatric symptoms of primary dyscontrol (Monroe, 1970) for the psychiatrist and the neurologic history and examination for the neurologist.

Unexpected, that is, not predicted on the basis of the original hypotheses, was that the epileptoid dyscontrol group appeared more sexually active and perverse both in the prison setting and in their past lives and tended to be more active and energetic. It was impressive that the group therapists employed by the prison, functioning blind with regard to their "patients'" label and for that matter with regard to the hypothesis being tested, found the epileptoid subjects more impulsive and aggressive during the therapeutic sessions.

Group 2, the hysteroid dyscontrol prisoners, showed no distinctive characteristics that differentiated them from all other groups, but they could be differentiated from one or the other groups in terms of passive-aggressive personality traits; less overt guilt regarding their behavior; and, as was predicted by the hypothesis, they were more likely amnesic for their dyscontrol acts. It is important to remember that in this population the dyscontrol act was aggressive criminal behavior which led to incarceration. We predicted that the psychodynamic factor in "hysteroid" dyscontrol behavior would be, to oversimplify, an explosive rebellion against an overly strict conscience mechanism in individuals whose behavior was generally overly inhibited, and who would deny responsibility for an explosive dyscontrol aggression through repression. Table 2 summarizes the absence of pathological findings in our group 4, that is, the pure psychopaths that would represent normals in a random sample. We actually found that this group showed somewhat better abstract thinking and planning than the other groups, even though their behavior was equally psychopathic.

Table 2 illustrates that, except for group 1, group 3 showed the most outstanding deviations and was differentiated from all other groups in terms of irresponsibility and poor judgment. These evaluations, plus indications of social ineptness, aimlessness, poor interpersonal relations, and alcohol abuse, suggest that the label inadequate personality or inadequate psychopath was appropriate for this group.

Table 2

Summary of Four Group Characteristics

	Group 1	Group 2	Group 3	Group 4
Suspicion of epilepsy	+			
Neurologic dysfunction	+			
Excessive motor activity	+			
Unrealistic thinking	+			
Sexual aggression	+			
Hostility	+			
Poor academic performance	+			
Passive-aggressive		+		
Amnesia		+		
Less overt guilt		+		
Socially inept			+	
Irresponsible			+	
Poor judgment			+	
Aimless			+	
Poor interpersonal relations			+	
Alcohol abuse			+	
Better abstract thinking				+

A discriminant function analysis of our data revealed that if the two psychodynamic-socially determined groups (hysteroid and pure psychopaths) were collapsed, we could predict group membership in this three-group schema with 89 percent accuracy on the basis of psychiatric and psychometric data alone. The first function included fatigue, inertia, and level of tension on the mood and affect scales. The second function included social-sexual relations, scholastic performance, and scores on the WAIS (Wechsler Adult Intelligence Scale) Subtest of Similarities and Block Design. The fact that possible differences between the hysteroid dyscontrol subjects and the pure psychopaths were not clarified can be rationalized in that our research design did not emphasize the collection of psychodynamic and social data.

The necessity of multiple measurements for identifying these clinically distinct groups is illustrated by the following: Figure 3 shows the MMPI (Minnesota Multiphasic Personality Inventory) profiles for the four groups, illustrating that the high dyscontrol groups (epileptoid and hysteroid dyscontrol subjects) have similar profiles that are quite distinct from the low dyscontrol groups (inadequate and pure psychopaths). Both sets of groups, not surprisingly, show elevated psychopathic deviant (Pd) scores, but the former two groups show elevation in the psychotic tetrad of paranoia (Pa), psychasthenia (Pt), schizophrenia (Sc), and hypomania (Ma) scores, al-

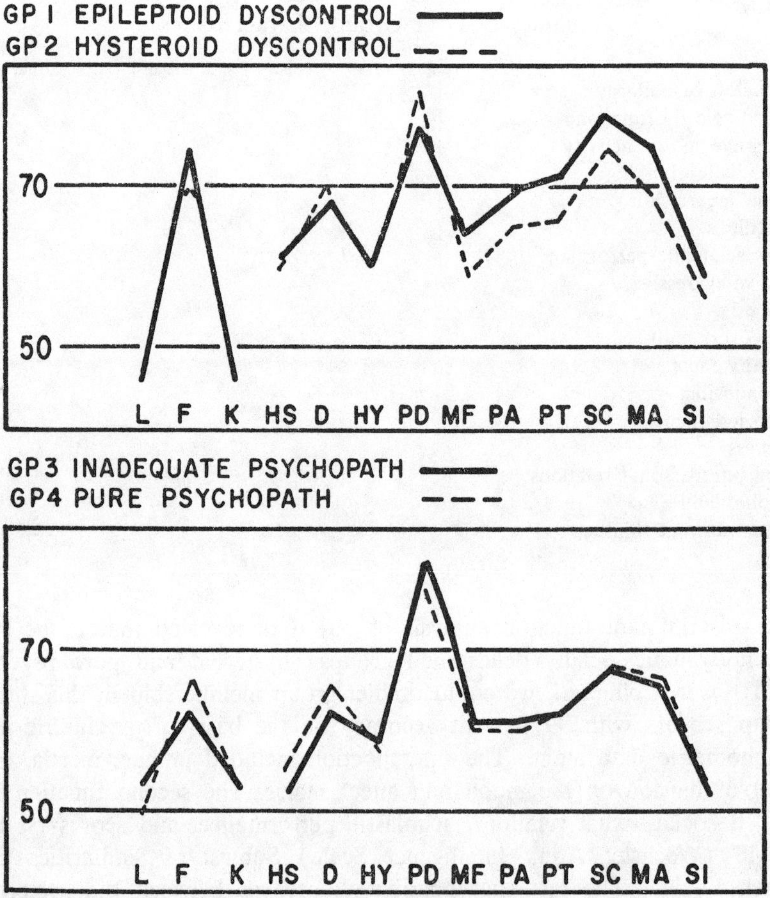

FIGURE 3. Mean Minnesota Multiphasic Personality Inventory (MMPI) profile scales for the four-group system.

though none of these subjects had any symptoms suggestive of psychotic thought disorders. The standard MMPI profile, then, does not differentiate between the central nervous system instability as reflected in the high versus low theta activity. On the other hand, systematically scored psychiatric data on the Current and Past Psychiatric Scales (CAPPS, Endicott and Spitzer, 1972) does differentiate between these groups (Figures 4 and 5). For example, group 1 was differentiated from group 2 on the CAPPS item

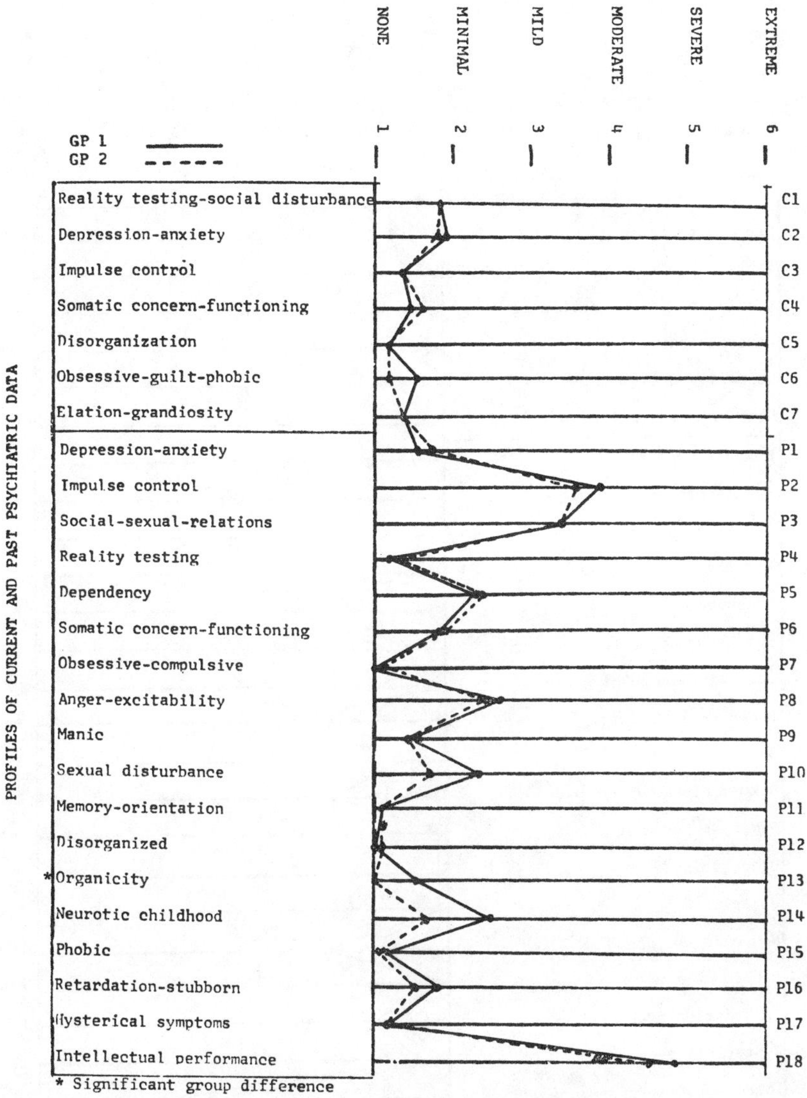

FIGURE 4. Comparison of "epileptoid" dyscontrol and "hysteroid" dyscontrol groups. Group 1, continuous line; group 2, broken line.

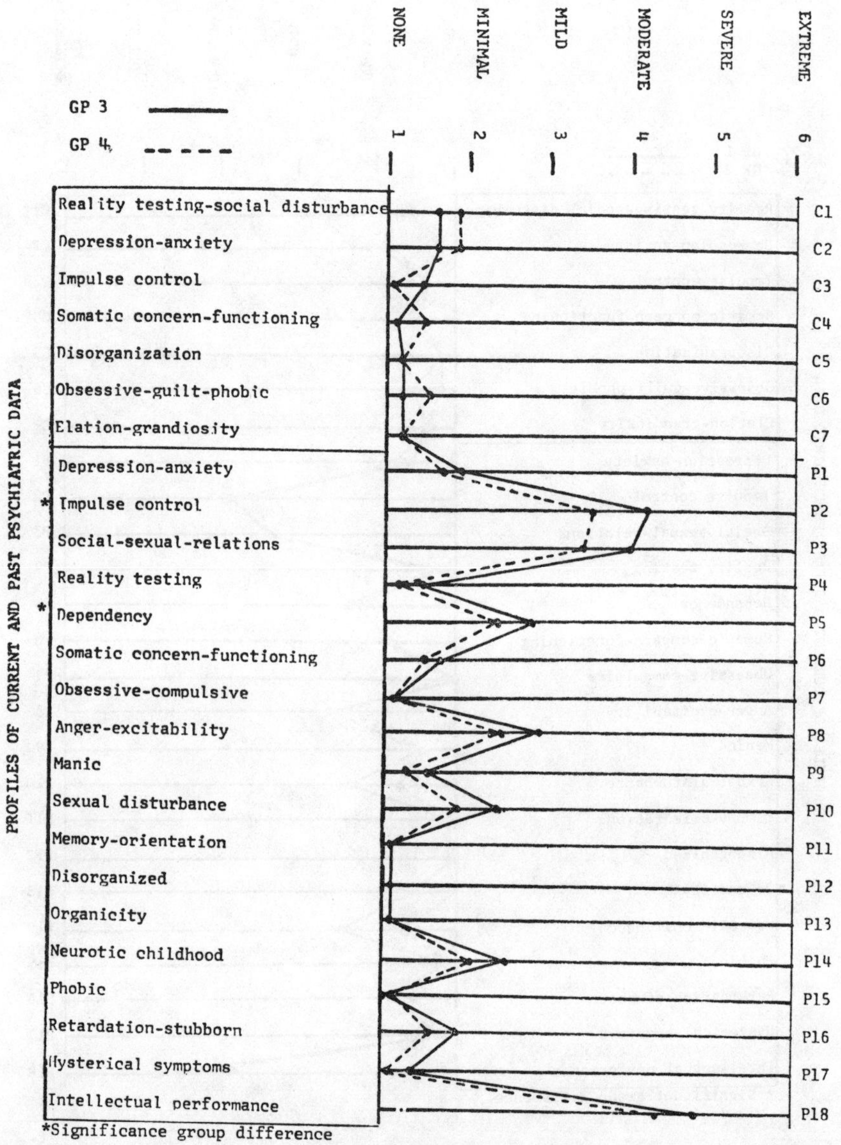

FIGURE 5. Comparison of "inadequate" psychopaths and psychopaths. Group 3, continuous line; group 4, broken line.

labeled CNS impairment (Figure 4), while group 3 was significantly higher than group 4 (Figure 5) on the scale labeled poor impulse control, which included such factors as no occupational goals and plans, narcotics and alcohol abuse, antisocial traits, impulsiveness, poor judgment, self-defeating behavior, lack of responsibility, ineffectual adaptation to stress, hypersensitivity, fluctuation in interpersonal feelings, clinging behavior, passive-aggressive behavior, and blaming others.

The clinical validity of this study will ultimately be determined by the therapeutic effectiveness of a regimen based on the data. Thus, our target group, the epileptoid dyscontrol patients, theoretically should respond to an anticonvulsant regimen. Our study investigated this possibility, using the anticonvulsant drug primidone (Mysoline). The results of this double-blind crossover study are suggestive, but they need further confirmation. We found that the stringent external controls provided by the prison setting inhibit dyscontrol acts, even among predisposed individuals. Our data were confounded by strong order effects and the possibility that the anticonvulsant medication had a more general effect than was predicted. Patients who "liked" the drug and were able to distinguish between placebo-active phases described the improvement in terms we did not predict and so did not rate, namely, that they were "thinking more clearly." When asked for specific details about what this meant, they reported that they were more aware of the consequences of impulsive acts and better able to inhibit the act despite intense urges. One group, the hysteroid subjects, seemed to respond negatively to the therapeutic regimen, objecting strongly and exaggerating the known disagreeable side effects of primidone. The target epileptoid group responded better than the others in terms of the Porteus Maze Quality Score which suggests better control of impulsivity, but this was true only in the placebo-active sequence. It is obvious that a rigorous test of the therapeutic usefulness of these concepts will have to be tried in other than prison settings, namely when the prisoners are back in society or, as they say, "on the street," or among more psychotic patients who seem less inclined to inhibit their dyscontrol actions regardless of the setting (Monroe and Wise, 1965).

REFERENCES

ENDICOTT, J., and SPITZER, R. L. Current and past psychopathology scales (CAPPS): Rationale, reliability, and validity. *Arch. Gen. Psychiatry* 27:678-687, 1972.

MEDNICK, S., and CHRISTIANSEN, K. O. *Biosocial Bases of Criminal Behavior.* Garden Press, New York, 1977.

MONROE, R. R. *Episodic Behavioral Disorders.* Harvard University Press, Cambridge, Mass., 1970.

MONROE, R. R. Maturational lag in central nervous system development as a partial explanation of episodic violent behavior, in *Determinants and Origins of Aggressive Behavior,* J. de Wit and W. W. Hartup, eds. Mouton Publishers, The Hague, Netherlands, 1974.

MONROE, R. R. *Brain Dysfunction in Aggressive Criminals.* Lexington Books, D. C. Heath & Company, Lexington, Mass., 1978.

MONROE, R. R., and MICKLE, W. A. Alpha chloralose activated electroencephalograms in psychiatric patients. *J. Nerv. Ment. Dis.* 144:64, 1967.

MONROE, R. R., and WISE, S. Combined phenothiazine, chlordiazepoxide and primidone therapy for uncontrolled psychotic patients. *Am. J. Psychiatry* 122:694, 1965.

PLUTCHIK, R., CLIMENT, C., and ERVIN, F. Research strategies for the study of human violence, in *Brain Behavioral Control,* W. L. Smith and A. Kling, eds. Spectrum, New York, 1976.

WOLFGANG, M. E. Delinquency and violence from the viewpoint of criminology, in *Neural Bases of Violence and Aggression,* W. S. Field and W. A. Sweet, eds. Warren H. Green, St. Louis, 1975.

CHAPTER 6

Time Perception, Cortical Evoked Potentials, and Impulsiveness Among Three Groups of Adolescents

ERNEST S. BARRATT

The research reported herein is part of an extensive study of the neurobiology of impulse control (Barratt, 1958, 1959a, b, 1965a, b, 1967, 1968; Barratt and White, 1969; Barratt, 1971, 1972; White, 1978). Our current research emphasis is on a better understanding of the etiology of impulsiveness as a personality trait. This work has focused for the past several years on the definition and role of impulsiveness during the adolescent period of development (Barratt, 1977; Barratt et al., 1977; Barratt and Adams, 1978; Barratt et al., 1978; Barratt, 1979). The purpose of the study described here was to compare time perception, cortical evoked potentials, and impulsiveness among three groups of male adolescents: psychiatric patients, delinquents, and "normal" controls. We hypothesized that the delinquents would be more impulsive than the patients and that both of these groups would be more impulsive than the control subjects. Further, in line with our past research that related time perception and cortical evoked potentials to measures of impulsiveness (Barratt, 1977; Barratt et al., 1977; Barratt and Adams, 1978; Barratt et al., 1978), we expected the delinquents to be visual evoked-potential augmentors and to "underproduce" time intervals. There is general agreement in the literature (Callaway, 1975, p. 128) that personality measures that correlate significantly with impulsiveness relate positively to augmenting of visual evoked cortical potentials. The study was restricted to males because of gender differences in impulsivity at this age (Barratt, 1979).

METHODS AND PROCEDURES

Subjects

The control subjects were 15 male adolescent students, ages 13 to 16 years, who were randomly selected from a larger population of high school students. They were Caucasians of middle to upper middle-class socioeconomic status. They were reported by their parents and teachers to have no serious interpersonal problems and were doing well in school.

The delinquents were 15 male Caucasians, ages 13 to 16 years, who were being detained until a court trial because of a crime they had allegedly committed. The alleged crimes involved homicide, stealing cars, breaking and entering businesses and residences, and assault. The delinquents were from families of lower-middle and upper-lower status based on the father's occupation and level of education.

The 15 psychiatric patients were chosen from a larger sample of patients. They had been diagnosed as having unsocialized aggressive reactions of adolescence according to DSM II criteria. None had ever been apprehended for any violation of the law. They were all hospital patients and had been medication-free for at least two weeks before testing. They were from middle to upper middle-class families.

Techniques

Impulsiveness was measured by two tests: the Matching Familiar Figures Test (MFFT) (Kagan et al., 1966), and the Barratt Impulsiveness Scale (BIS) (Barratt, 1965b). Intelligence was measured, using the WISC-R (Wechsler, 1974), because of differences frequently found between the ability levels of delinquents and controls.

Time perception was measured by the "method of production" (Carlson and Feinberg, 1968). The adolescents were asked to produce one- to ten-second time intervals, three times. The intervals to be produced were randomized. The subject started to "produce" a time interval when he heard a click through ear phones he was wearing, and he said "aye" when the time interval had passed. A voice key was used to close a timing circuit;

the elapsed time for the subjects' time interval productions was recorded automatically.

It has been well documented that as the stimulus intensity for eliciting visual evoked potentials (VEP) is increased, the amplitude of the P100-N140 component of the VEP decreases for some individuals (reducers) and increases for others (augmentors) (Callaway, 1975, pp. 125-128). VEPs were recorded at three light intensity levels: 4-, 8-, and 16-ft. candles at settings of 1, 2, and 4 on a Grass Photostimulator (Model PS1). The subjects were presented 64 light flashes at each intensity level with a 2-second interstimulus interval. The light flashes lasted 10 μsec. The subjects' eyes were closed during the presentation of the light flashes; their heads rested on a chin rest at the opening of a globe of 40-cm inside diameter (Gouras, 1970). The inside of the dome was illuminated constantly with a background light level of 0.24-ft. candles. The bulb of the photostimulator was located 20 to 22 cm. from a subject's face. Lower intensity levels for visual stimuli were used in this research than in that of others (e.g., Buchsbaum and Silverman, 1968) because we did not want to risk retinal damage.

Evoked potential signals were amplified using a Beckman Type R Dynagraph. The signals were stored and averaged using a Fabritek Model 1620 signal analyzer with a dwell time of 2 ms/point and a sweep window of 512 ms. Cortical electrodes were Ag/Ag C1 with a diameter of 10 mm. Beckman electrode paste was used to prepare the scalp; electrodes were secured with bentonite paste. Electrodes were placed at the vertex (C_z) and referenced to the left and right mastoid region of the temporal bone. The subjects were grounded at the forehead.

Data analyses

Augmenting and reducing were measured by the slope of the P100-N140 component of the vertex VEP at the three intensity levels. For the subject to be classified as an augmentor or reducer, the change in amplitude from intensity level 2 to 3 had to exceed 1 μV.

The MFFT was scored using a procedure suggested by Shipe (1971). Although this is not a popular method, we believe that it yields a better measure of conceptual tempo (impulsivity-reflectivity) than do most others. The technique involves obtaining a ratio of the total errors to the mean latency of the first response for each subject. The lower the ratio, the less impulsive (more reflective) is the subject.

The differences among the three groups on these were tested for significance using analysis of variance, analysis of covariance, *t*-tests, and the Kruskal-Wallis analysis of variance procedure.

RESULTS

There were significant differences among the groups on WISC-R Full Scale IQs ($F = 8.95$, $df = 2/42$, $p < .01$) and Verbal IQs ($F = 10.54$, $df = 2/42$, $p < .01$). Performance IQs were not significantly different among the three groups. The most significant group differences in Full Scale and Verbal IQs were between the controls and each of the other two groups (Table 1).

Table 1

Comparison of WISC-R Intelligence Scores Among Three Groups of Male Adolescents

	Full Scale		Verbal		Performance	
	Mean	S.D.	Mean	S.D.	Mean	S.D.
Controls (N = 15)	104.1	5.4	106.0	7.6	103.0	5.2
Psychiatric Patients (N = 15)	96.1	9.6	96.1	9.8	97.2	9.9
Delinquents (N = 15)	93.8	6.4	92.1	7.5	97.5	10.6

There were no significant differences among the three groups on the Barratt Impulsiveness Test; means were 53 for controls, 55 for patients, and 55 for delinquents. Significant differences were found among the groups on the MFFT ($F = 4.7$, $df = 2/42$, $p < .05$). Using analysis of covariance to control for the Full Scale and Verbal IQ differences, these MFFT differences were still significant. The *t*-tests between individual groups showed, however, that the significant differences were between control subjects and each of the other two groups. The control group was significantly less impulsive than the two other groups, which did not differ significantly between each other on the MFFT. The controls' MFFT $\bar{x}$ ratio was 0.38; the patients' MFFT $\bar{x}$ was 0.67; the delinquents' MFFT $\bar{x}$ ratio was 0.64. Results of the MFFT and the Barratt Impulsiveness Scale were not significantly correlated ($r = 0.12$).

Time perception among the three groups differed significantly (Figure 1) as shown by a repeated-measures analysis of variance ($F = 4.7$, $df = 2/42$, $p < .05$). The differences were also significant when Full Scale IQ scores ($F = 3.81$; $p < .05$) were used in an analysis of covariance. The differences between controls and each of the other two groups were significant, but patients and delinquents did not differ significantly on time

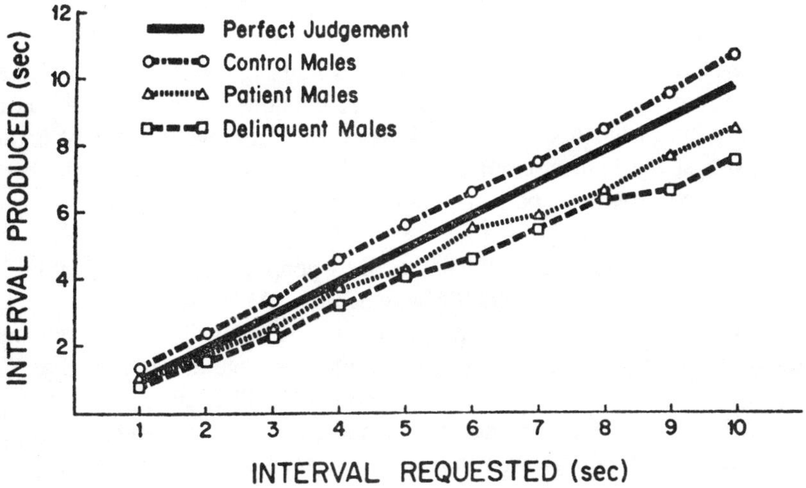

FIGURE 1. Comparison of three groups of adolescent males on production of time intervals.

perception. As may be seen in Figure 1, the control subjects were more accurate and consistently overproduced time intervals. For the delinquents and patients, time seemed to pass more slowly, i.e., they underproduced, than it did for the control subjects.

The evoked-potential comparisons among groups were limited to the five most extreme augmentors and reducers in each group (Table 2). The most significant differences among groups were found among the aug-

Table 2

Visual Evoked Potential Amplitudes (P100-N140) at Three Stimulation Levels for Three Groups of Male Adolescents

		Flash Intensity		
		1 (low)	2	3
Controls	A	9.2	11.8	18.3
	R	14.2	13.3	7.0
Psychiatric Patients	A	5.6	13.9	20.7
	R	14.7	7.2	5.1
Delinquents	A	12.0	19.1	23.8
	R	13.4	11.0	9.7

A = augmentor, R = reducer. Cell entries are in μVolts.
Results are for five most extreme augmentors and reducers in each group.

mentors; here VEP amplitude for the delinquents was clearly different from that of the other groups. At the two highest intensity levels, in both delinquents and patients, evoked potentials had higher average amplitudes than in the controls. In the comparison of delinquents and controls, however, amplitudes did not overlap—those of the delinquents were all higher than those of the highest controls at both high intensity levels. In the comparison of controls and patients, there were two overlaps, one at each of the two higher levels.

Group differences among visual evoked-potential reducers (Table 2) were not as marked as among the augmentors. At no intensity level were differences significant between any two groups. At intensity level 3, reducers among the delinquents responded with higher average amplitudes than did the reducers in the other two groups. Although the differences among groups at each intensity level were not significant among the reducers, the slope of the delinquents' curve was more gradual than that of the patients and controls.

MFFT scores were significantly correlated ($r = .34$; $p < .05$) with the slope of time perception measures for all subjects. As the Kruskal-Wallis analysis of variance showed, the augmentors significantly underproduced time intervals compared to the reducers ($H = 3.9$, $df\,1$, $p < .05$). The difference in time perception (cognitive tempo) between delinquent and patient augmentors and reducers was statistically significant; among the controls, this difference approached significance.

DISCUSSION

Although there were significant differences between controls and both patients and delinquents on the MFFT, the Barratt Impulsiveness Scale showed no significant group differences. One could speculate that since adolescence is a difficult period of adjustment, and learning to control impulses is especially difficult for everyone at this developmental level, one would not expect groups differences on a questionnaire measure of impulsiveness. Or, one could speculate that the Barratt Impulsiveness Scale is not sensitive to differences in impulsiveness at this level. Obviously, the MFFT and the BIS are not measuring the same construct; this is a common finding not only between the BIS and MFFT but also between the MFFT and other questionnaire measures of impulsiveness (Saunders et al., 1973).

On the WISC-R and the MFFT, the control group was significantly different from both delinquents and patients. The latter two groups did not differ significantly on these measures. On time-perception measures, the delinquents and patients were also not significantly different from each other, but they were different from the controls. The MFFT scores across groups were significantly correlated with the slope of the time-perception measures. Augmenting and reducing were also significantly related to time perception. These overall results indicate that augmenting and reducing, conceptual tempo as measured by the MFFT and time perception are not only related to each other, but also are significantly different between adolescent controls and both adolescent psychiatric patients and delinquents. The latter two groups do not differ significantly from each other on these measures.

These data are consistent with a more comprehensive study recently completed in our laboratory (Barratt, 1979). In this study, even though differences on a wide range of neuropsychological measures were sufficient to significantly discriminate among normal adolescents, delinquents, and adolescent psychiatric patients, the differences between delinquents and patients were minimal compared to differences between these two groups and controls. The data in the larger study and in this study confirm the hypothesis that both juvenile delinquents and selected adolescent psychiatric patients were part of a "population at risk" at a younger age. Whether or not a child at risk becomes a delinquent, a psychiatric patient, or a "normal" adolescent may depend on fortuitous environmental circumstances. Shah and Roth (1974), among others, have emphasized the pitfalls in dichotomized thinking about the nature-nurture bases of antisocial behavior. Conceptual tempo, time perception, and cortical functioning were shown to be interrelated in the current study. Further, the controls were significantly different from the patients and delinquents on these measures. The evoked-potential data, the MFFT, and the time-perception data suggest immature cortical functioning among the patients and delinquents compared with the controls. These three measures have been related to learning and learning disabilities, which are increasingly seen to be related to delinquency. For example, in a study currently being conducted by the Educational Testing Service, results indicate that 16 percent of the public school students have a learning disability while this is true of 32 percent of the juvenile delinquents (ETS Developments, 1978). We propose that these learning-disabled children are a population at risk who could be identified at an early age with techniques similar to those used in our research.

ACKNOWLEDGMENT

This research was supported by the Office of Naval Research, Environmental Physiology, and by a grant from the Criminal Justice Division, Office of the Governor, Austin, Texas.

REFERENCES

BARRATT, E. S. Psychomotor efficiency in a conflict situation related to anxiety and impulsiveness. *Am. Psychol.* 13:358, 1958.

BARRATT, E. S. Relationships of psychomotor tests and EEG variables at three developmental levels. *Percept. Motor Skills* 9:63-66, 1959a.

BARRATT, E. S. Anxiety and impulsiveness related to psychomotor efficiency. *Percept. Motor Skills* 9:191-198, 1959b.

BARRATT, E. S. The amygdalae related to release of a suppressed response. *Electroencephalogr. Clin. Neurophysiol.* 18:709, 1965a.

BARRATT, E. S. Factor analysis of some psychometric measures of impulsiveness and anxiety. *Psychol. Rep.* 16:547-554, 1965b.

BARRATT, E. S. Perceptual-motor performance related to impulsiveness and anxiety. *Percept. Motor Skills* 25:485-492, 1967.

BARRATT, E. S. Orienting reflex related to impulsiveness and anxiety. *Psychophysiology* 4:501-502, 1968.

BARRATT, E. S. Psychophysiological correlates of classical differential eyelid conditioning among subjects selected on the basis of impulsiveness and anxiety. *J. Biol .Psychiatry* 3:339-346, 1971.

BARRATT, E. S. Impulsiveness and anxiety: Toward a neuropsychological model, in *Anxiety: Current Trends in Theory and Research.* C. Spielberger, ed. Academic Press, New York, 1972, pp. 195-222.

BARRATT, E. S. Time estimation related to measures of distraction and impulsivity among adolescent psychiatry patients. Presented to International Neuropsychological Society, Santa Fe, New Mexico, 1977.

BARRATT, E. S. *Multivariate Diagnostic Assessment of Juvenile Delinquents.* Final Report, Grant #EA-78-CO1-4900, Criminal Justice Division, Office of the Governor, Austin, Texas, 1979.

BARRATT, E. S., ADAMS, P. M., and WHITE, J. H. The relationship of evoked potential characteristics to time perception judgment. Presented to Society for Neuroscience, Anaheim, California, 1977.

BARRATT, E. S., and ADAMS, P. Psychopathy: Impulsiveness, time perception, and cortical evoked potential correlates. Presented to International Congress of Applied Psychology, Munich, Germany, 1978.

BARRATT, E. S., and WHITE, R. Impulsiveness and anxiety related to medical students' performance and attitudes. *J. Med. Educ.* 7:604-607, 1969.

BARRATT, E. S., WHITE, J. H., and ADAMS, P. Evoked potential correlates of conceptual tempo in adolescence. Presented to Society for Neuroscience, St. Louis, Missouri, 1978.

BUCHSBAUM, M., and SILVERMAN, J. Stimulus intensity control and the cortical evoked response. *Psychosom. Med.* 30:21-22, 1968.

CALLAWAY, E. *Brain Electrical Potentials and Individual Psychological Differences.* Grune & Stratton, New York, 1975.

CARLSON, V., and FEINBERG, I. Individual variations in time judgment and the concept of an internal clock. *J. Exp. Psychol.* 77:631-640, 1968.

ETS Developments. Study links learning disabilities with delinquency. Educational Testing Service, Berkeley, California 25:6-7, 1978.

GOURAS, P. Electroretinography: Some basic principles. *Invest. Opthalmol.* 9:557-569, 1970.

KAGAN, J., PEARSON, L., and WELCH, L. Conceptual impulsivity and inductive reasoning. *Child Dev.* 37:583-594, 1966.

SAUNDERS, J. T., REPUCCI, N. D., and SARATA, B. P. V. An examination of impulsivity as a trait characterizing delinquent youth. *Am. J. Orthopsychiatry* 43:789-795, 1973.

SHAH, S. A., and ROTH, L. H. Biological and psychophysiological factors in criminality, in *Handbook of Criminology*. D. Glaser, ed. Chicago, Rand McNally College Publishers, 1974.

SHIPE, D. Impulsivity and locus of control as predictors of achievement and adjustment in mildly retarded and borderline youth. *Am. J. Ment. Defic.* 76:12-22, 1961.

WECHSLER, D. *Wechsler Intelligence Scale for Children-Revised.* Psychological Corp., New York, 1974.

WHITE, J., BARRATT, E., and ADAMS, P. The hyperactive child in adolescence. *J. Am. Acad. Child Psychiatry* 18:154-169, 1978.

CHAPTER 7

Sociocultural Overview of Criminal Violence

MARVIN E. WOLFGANG

In the sociology of crime and criminality, emphasis is placed on cultural and group forces that produce individuals who represent forms of deviance from the dominant value, or moral demand, system. The individual offender is not ignored; he or she is simply clustered with other individuals alike in attributes deemed theoretically or statistically meaningful. Individual "uniqueness" is retained by the improbability that on several attributes or variables he or she will appear identical to everyone else. Hence, the researchers resort to means, medians, modes, to probability theory, inferential statistics, and mathematical models for analyzing predominant patterns and regularities of behavior. Biological and psychological factors are not ignored, but when a monodisciplinary perspective is used by sociologists, the biopsychological is suspended. Biological needs and psychological drives may be declared uniformly distributed and hence of no utility in explaining one form of behavior relative to another. They may be seen as differential endowments of personalities that help to assign, for example, a label of mental incapacity to a group of individuals, some of whom have also violated the criminal codes. But neither the biology of many biographies nor the psychology of many personalities helps to explain the overwhelming involvement in crime of men over women, slums over suburbs, youth over age, urban over rural life. It is this latter set of macroscopic regularities to which the sociological perspective addresses itself.

DEFINITION AND CULTURAL DIMENSIONS

Violence should be distinguished from aggression in general. The 13 task force volumes of the National Commission on the Causes and Prevention of Violence struggled with these terms in 1968 and 1969. I shall use the term violence to refer to the intentional use of physical force on another person, or noxious physical stimuli invoked by one person on another. The physical force may be viewed as assaultive and designed to cause pain or injury as an end in itself, sometimes referred to as "expressive violence," or as the use of pain or injury or physical restraint as a coercive threat or punishment to induce another person or persons to carry out some act, commonly called "instrumental violence." Violence may also be legitimate (a parent spanking a child, a police officer forcefully arresting a suspect, a soldier killing during war) or illegitimate (criminal homicide, rape, aggravated assault). In general, I shall concentrate on illegitimate violence, but behind illegitimate violence are cultural dimensions that involve the acceptance of violence.

Every society contains in its normative system some elements of acceptable limits to violence in some form (Wolfgang, 1970). Thus, the use of physical force by parents to restrain and punish children is permissible, tolerated, encouraged, and is thereby part of the normative process by which every society regulates its child-rearing. There are, of course, varying degrees of parental force expected and used in different cultures and times, and there are upper limits vaguely defined as excessive and brutal. The battered-child syndrome is an increasingly recorded phenomenon in American society.

Our norms approve or permit parents to apply force for their own ends against the child. The application of force is a form of violence, and it may be used consciously to discipline the child to the limits of permitted behavior, to reduce the domestic noise level, to express parental disapproval, and even unconsciously as a displacement for aggression actually meant for others. This model of parent-child interaction is a universal feature of all human societies. The model is one that the child comes to ingest; that is, that superior force is power permitting manipulation of others and can be a functional tool for securing a superordinate position over others, for obtaining desires and ends.

The violence in which the child engages is but an expressed extension of this basic model. The use of physical restraint and force is not a feature only in lower-class families, although studies have shown that its persistent use, and use in greater frequency over a longer span of childhood, is more common in that socioeconomic class. The substitutions, by middle-class parents, of withdrawal of rights and affection, of deprivation of liberty, and of other techniques are designed to replace the need for force. And by these substitutions an effort is made to get the child to respect other forms of social control. They are also ways of masking the supreme means of control, namely physical force.

Violence and the threat of violence form the ultimate weapons of any society for maintaining itself against external and internal attacks. All societies finally resort to violence to solve problems that arise from such attacks. War is aggressive force between nations and is legitimized within each. The recognition of relativity in moral judgments about violence is quite clear in the case of war. When our colonies collected themselves together in the eighteenth century to sever ties, we called the action revolution and, in historical retrospect, good despite the violence it engendered. When some states in the nineteenth century sought to divide the nation, we called the action civil war and bad, and lamented the bloodshed. The Nazis gave justice to our bombs and enlisted the world's generation of youth to react violently to violence. There are other international conflicts in which nations have been involved and for which the label of legitimacy has been seriously questioned by substantial numbers within their own territories. And when this happens a society becomes more conscious of the process of socializing its own youth to accept violence as a mode of response, as a collective problem-solving mechanism. When war is glorified in a nation's history and included as part of the child's educational materials, *a moral judgment about the legitimacy of violence is firmly made.*

Socialization means changing the individual into a personality; it is the process of cultural transmission, of relaying through the social funnel of family and friends a set of values, beliefs, attitudes, and habits, and speech. When the front-line instruments of war become part of the physical features of a child's life space, when cannons, rifles, grenades, and soldiers are moved from real battlefields to the mind of the child and the plastic world of the playroom and are among the relatively few objects touched and manipulated by the child in the process of becoming, then a set of values associated with the legitimacy and recognition of the superiority of violent activity is transmitted. What is not empirically clear is the extent to which such transmission is later translated into violence by the child, as a child, youth, or adult. As a legislator, parent, police officer, or any other role-actor, the individual is still the carrier of attitudes related to that play activity, unless contrary values have intervened.

There are many areas of social life that witness the protection of order by representatives of control. In their roles and in their persons, agents embody the actual or potential use of legitimized violence. The police and national guard are the most patent examples of these agents, but there are also the less visible and more silent cadres of guards in prisons, mental institutions, banks, parks, and museums. Even less visible and of questionable legality, but surely subjectively self-legitimized, are unofficial groups like the lynching mobs of yesteryear, the Minutemen, vigilantes of the rural South and the urban North, and certain black militants who have armed their members for assault.

The presence of all these groups, ranging from the culturally prescribed to the societally disruptive, has diffusive effects that are part of the socializing experience of youth in the acceptance of violence as a means of control. Each agent has his own circle of family and friends sharing his stand of legitimate availability to use violence. As these personalized radii spread and overlap throughout a society, they collectively represent another substratum of the culture which is in part committed by requirement to an expression that fundamentally means violence. The more these agents of real or potential aggression are used, the more impact such use has in socializing others, particularly children and youth, to the functional utility of violence. If the official legitimacy of the violence is stressed in the transfer of values, many of the young exposed to such values will have heightened acceptance of its use. On the other hand, many who are ethnically or otherwise aligned with the targets of officially legitimized violence will, with its more common and intensified use, respond in like manner, thereby confirming the need to use violence to combat violence. And this message is passed on to yet another group of the younger generation who learn to attack the guardian executors of the larger society with their own contrived version of legitimate violence.

Social scientists, psychologists, and psychiatrists have often stressed the importance of the theme of *masculinity* in American culture and the effect this image of the strong masculine role has had on child-rearing and the general socialization process. The middle-class child today has some difficulty if he seeks to match himself to the old masculine model, and he may become neurotic and insecure. Among the lower classes, says W. B. Miller (1958), the continuity of the physically assertive male is still one of the "focal concerns." The desire to prove one's masculinity, added to the desire to become a successful male adult member of the lower-class culture, requires adolescent rehearsal of the toughness, heavy drinking, and quick aggressive response to certain stimuli that are characteristic of the lower-class adult male. Such rehearsal involves activities not necessarily delinquent but often involving participation in conduct that is defined as delinquent by the representatives of the dominant middle-class culture.

We have claimed elsewhere that the strong masculine emphasis may be starting on its way out in our culture (Wolfgang and Ferracuti, 1967). What remains, however, is undeniable, and evidence of it is still available as part of the socializing experience of many males who engage in violence. The role that females have had in consciously promoting the strong male image has often been overlooked. In their own search for identity as females, they have, in the past, driven the male to notable distinctions of difference by encouraging the myth of medieval chivalry; they have sought his strong arms of security, buttressed his aggressivity against other suitors, and passed on this male model to their progeny.

A culture in which parents direct their small boys to "act like little men" and refrain from crying when hurt may be preparing them in the customary fashion for strength against adversity and for stalwart stoicism in the face of more severe pain ahead. It may also promote a greater desensitization to noxious assaults performed on or by him. Males commonly carry the role of committing the required deeds of assault, of investigating homicides and suicides, being mortician assistants, handling the injuries of highways; in short, men are required to assume responsibility for the physical public injuries and tragedies of humanity. Women are often protected, faces turned, from such displays. It is also the male who is expected to use violence in prescribed ways and at prescribed times, during which he must be sufficiently desensitized to the pain he inflicts, whether in the street or on a battlefield. It should not be unexpected, therefore, that most delinquent acts of physical injury are also committed by males.

Many other cultural items contribute to a general aura of violence. Violence in the mass media, automobile advertising that promotes aggressive driving—"Drive it like you hate it—it's cheaper than psychiatry"—and the possession of 100 million guns in our population with a higher gun-to-population ratio than any other country in the world must make a difference. Research gives evidence to these claims (Wolfgang, 1970).

EXTENT AND CHARACTER OF FAMILY CRIMINAL VIOLENCE

Crimes of violence ordinarily found in official police statistics offer baseline data. Despite limitations, the *Uniform Crime Reports*, police reports from all over the country submitted to the FBI and annually reported in *Crime in the United States* (the latest of which is 1974), offer some information. The only family information offered concerns criminal homicide, which has an amazing stability of frequency distributions since 1930, when police statistics were first collected on a national basis.

Of the 15,910 homicides in 1970, for example, 12.1 percent were spouse killing spouse; and of the 20,600 homicides in 1974, 12.1 percent were again in this category. In this latter year, in addition, 2.7 percent involved a parent killing a child, 8 percent "other relative killings," and 6.2 percent "romantic triangle and lovers' quarrels." Murder within the family made up about one-fourth of all the murder offenses, and half of the family killings involved spouse killing spouse. In these murders, the wife was the victim in 52 percent of the incidents and the husband in the remaining 48 percent. Fifty percent of the victims were black, 48 percent white, and the remaining were of other races (*Uniform Crime Reports,* 1974, p. 19).

In an earlier study entitled *Patterns in Criminal Homicide* (1958), 588 homicides in Philadelphia were examined to obtain more detailed information about family criminal violence. Of the 136 victims who had a familial relationship to their slayers, there were 100 husbands or wives, 9 sons, 8 daughters, 3 mothers, 3 brothers, 2 fathers, 1 sister, and 10 other types of associations. Of the 100 marital relationships, 53 wives were slain by their husbands and 47 husbands by their wives. Significantly, the number of wives homicidally assaulted by their husbands constituted 41 percent of all women who were killed, whereas husbands homicidally assaulted by their wives made up only 11 percent of all men who were killed.

When a man *was* killed by a woman, he was most likely to be killed by his wife. Of 75 black men slain by black women, 40, or 53 percent, were husbands slain by their mates; and of 9 white men killed by white women, 7 were slain by their mates.

When a woman committed homicide, she was more likely than a man to kill her mate. Of 89 black female offenders (for whom a victim-offender relationship has been identified), 40, or 45 percent, killed their husbands; and of 15 white female offenders, 7 killed their husbands. On the other hand, of 321 black male offenders, only 40, or 12 percent, killed their wives; and of 118 white male offenders, only 13, or 11 percent, killed their wives.

Aggravated assault is a *Uniform Crime Report* category that refers to physical injury of a grievous character, with a gun, knife, or similar dangerous weapon, causing serious injury. In the 17-city survey (Mulvihill et al., 1969), 14 percent of all aggravated assaults were between family members, half of which were again husband-wife assaults. Sex-race relationships similar to homicide occur in aggravated assaults. When the victim is a woman, the relationship is more likely to be between husband and wife than when a man is a victim of aggravated assault. When a mate is assaulted, the husband is the offender in about three-fourths of the cases. Additionally the difference between an aggravated assault and a homicide may be little more than speedy communication to the police in an assault offense, rapid transportation to a hospital, or the degree and speed of medical technology applied to a serious injury.

Finally, from the National Commission survey, the weapons used in spouse slayings and assaults were noted. Guns were used in half the cases of homicide, but knives, blunt instruments, and beatings were more common in assaults not ending in death. The weapon, rather than the intention or motive, makes more of a difference between serious injury and death. The rates and proportions of family assaults and slayings in cross-cultural studies (Curtis, 1974) from primitive African societies to comparisons between Jews and non-Jews in Israel, the Soviet Union, Canada, England, Denmark, and Japan reveal similar or slightly higher intrafamilial violence.

Even so, the incidence of homicide in the family is highest in the lower socioeconomic class. And it is in this lower-class structure that the use of physical assaultive behavior is a more common reaction to social interaction.

EXTENT OF CHILD AND YOUTH VIOLENCE

The true extent of child violence is little known if not unknowable. Neither official public records of the police and juvenile courts, nor the individual files of child guidance clinics and private physicians yield adequate or valid indexes of the total amount of violence among children. Individual research projects may give us hints about racial, sexual, age, and other differentials, but these studies do not inform us about the volume of violence in this age group in our population.

Studies in criminology refer to what is known as 'hidden delinquency' or the 'dark figures' of crime. Most of these studies ask junior and high school children in anonymous questionnaires whether they have committed a variety of offenses, how often, and approximately when.

The increasingly methodologically refined studies of hidden delinquency have not clearly or consistently reported a significant reduction in the disparity of social classes for crimes of violence. The incidence and frequency of crimes of violence seem to remain considerably higher among boys from lower social classes when the appropriate questions are asked about these offenses over specific periods of time. In their recent study of delinquents, Fannin and Clinard (1965) reported:

One of the more important of the tests was a comparison of the frequency with which reported and unreported robberies and assaults were committed by members of the two class levels (middle and lower). The vast majority of all lower class deliquents, 84 percent, had committed at least one such offense compared to 28 percent of the middle class (probability less than 0.01); 28 percent of the lower and 8 percent of the middle class had committed 10 or more violent offenses. Class level was also related to the frequency of fighting with other boys. Lower class delinquents fought singly and in groups significantly more often (probability less than 0.05) than middle class delinquents, with 20 percent of them averaging five or more fights per month compared to 4.0 percent.

Official data on child violence may be found in the *Uniform Crime Reports* published by the Department of Justice. These are police statistics reported voluntarily to the FBI about crimes known to the police and about persons arrested. It must he kept in mind that we know something about offenders only when there are arrests and that of the more serious known crimes only about 20 percent result in arrest; of the crimes of violence—homicide, robbery, aggravated assault—about 45 percent result in arrest. Whether it is easier for the police to arrest juvenile than adult suspects is still debatable but generally believed to be true (Sellin and Wolfgang, 1964).

The latest annual police statistics are available for 1976 and show a continuing increase in juvenile violence. For index crimes (violence and theft), 16 percent of all persons arrested were under the age of 15 and 42 percent were under 18 years of age (Uniform Crime Reports, 1976). Juveniles are arrested three times more often for property than assault crimes, but still comprise 12.5 percent of all persons arrested for violent criminality. Increases in violent crime have been greatest for this young age group. Between 1960 and 1974 national arrests for violence among persons 18 years and *older* have increased 126 percent, but among persons under 18 years of age have increased twice that amount, or 254 percent (Uniform Crime Reports, 1974).

The National Commission on the Causes and Prevention of Violence presented data on crimes of violence in 1969 that covered ten years, based on a national sample from 17 major cities. Combining the crimes of homicide, rape, robbery and aggravated assault, the rate for all ages 10 and over was 189, but for ages 15 to 17 the rate was as high as 408, and even for children aged 10 to 14 the rate was 123, nearly as high as the rate for all ages 25 and over (127). In fact, the greatest percentage increase in all crimes of violence was for children aged 10 to 14. For this group, the increase from 1958 to 1967 was 222 percent, compared to 103 percent for ages 15 to 17 and 66 percent for all ages. In short, violent crimes committed by children have been increasing between three and four times faster than violence in general (Mulvihill et al., 1969).

It should be pointed out that the general rise in crimes of violence in the United States has been to a considerable extent the result of the sheer increase in the number of children and youth in the general population, a function of the high fertility rates after World War II in the late 1940s and the 1950s. There has been since 1964 a rapid rise in the 10 to 24 age group, and probably as much as 20 percent of the rise in violent crime can be attributed to the youth bulge in the age pyramid. The National Violence Commission carefully documented a 12 percent attribution to this young group for the rise in violent crime between 1950 and 1965 (Mulvihill et al., 1969).

We should witness, however, a reduction in overall rates of violent crime between 1975 and 1990, if for no reason other than a population diminution in the violence-prone ages of children and youth (unpublished projections from Hudson Institute, New York). Youth aged 14 to 24 represented 27 million or only 15 percent of the total United States population in 1960, 19.7 percent in 1970, 21 percent in 1975, but should drop to 16 percent by 1990. Even with continued higher rates of fertility among black families, black children and youth were 6 million or 3 percent of the nation's population in 1973 but will drop slightly to 5.8 million or 2.4 percent in 1990.

VIOLENT CRIME IN A BIRTH COHORT

New kinds of evidence about juvenile crime are being analyzed by the Center for Studies in Criminology and Criminal Law at the University of Pennsylvania (Wolfgang et al., 1972). The data constitute a unique collection of information in the United States about a birth cohort of boys born in 1945. About 10,000 males born in that year and who resided in Philadelphia at least from ages 10 to 18 have been analyzed in a variety of ways. Using school records, offense reports from the police and some Selective Service information, the center has, among other things, followed the delinquency careers of those boys in the cohort who *ever* had any contact with the police. Comparisons have been made between delinquents and nondelinquents on a wide variety of variables, thus yielding findings that are not tied to a single calendar year. The entire group of cases is under review, not merely one that happened to be processed at a given time by a juvenile court or some other agency. It was possible to compute a birth-cohort rate of delinquency as well as providing analyses of the dynamic flow of boys through their juvenile court years. The time analysis uses a stochastic model for tracing delinquency of the cohort and includes such factors as time intervals between offenses, offense type, race, social class, degree of seriousness of the offenses.

Some of the findings from this Philadelphia study are particularly pertinent for more understanding about youth and crimes of violence. Of the total birth cohort of 9946 boys born in 1945, about 85 percent were born in Philadelphia, and about 95 percent went through the Philadelphia school system from first grade. From the entire cohort, 3475 or 35 percent were delinquent, meaning that they had at least one contact with the police. Of the 7043 white subjects, 2017 or 28.64 percent were delinquent. It is a dramatic and disturbing fact that just slightly more than half of all black boys in the same year were delinquent, more than were nondelinquent. This higher proportion of nonwhite delinquents constitutes one of the major statistical dichotomies running throughout the analysis of the cohort, and particularly of the delinquent subset.

Of special significance is the fact that only 627 boys were classified as chronic offenders, or heavy repeaters, meaning that they committed five or more offenses during their juvenile court ages. These chronic offenders represent only 6.3 percent of the entire birth cohort and 18 percent of the delinquent cohort. Yet these 627 boys were responsible for 5305 delinquencies, which is 52 percent of all the delinquencies committed by the entire birth cohort.

Chronic offenders are heavily represented among those who commit violent offenses. Of the 815 personal attacks (homicide, rape, aggravated and simple assaults), 450 or 53 percent were committed by chronic offenders; of the 2257 property offenses, 1397 or 62 percent were from chronic offenders; and of 193 robberies, 135 or 71 percent were from chronic offenders. Of all violent offenses committed by nonwhites, 70 percent were committed by young male chronic offenders; of all violent acts committed by whites, 45 percent were performed by boys with a chronic history of arrests. Clearly, these chronic offenders represent what is often referred to as the "hard core" delinquents. That such a high proportion of offenses —particularly serious acts of violence—is funnelled through a relatively small number of offenders is a fact that loudly claims attention for a social action policy of intervention.

Besides crude rates of delinquency, the birth cohort study also scores seriousness of offenses. Derived from an earlier study of psychophysical scaling by Sellin and Wolfgang, *The Measurement of Delinquency* (1964), these scores denote relative mathematical weights of the gravity of different crimes. The scores represent a ratio scale such that a murder is generally more than twice as serious as rape; aggravated assault, depending on the medical treatment necessary, may be two or three times more serious than theft of an automobile, and so on. The scale has been replicated in over a dozen cities and countries and proved useful in the cohort analysis. Each offense from the penal code committed by members of the cohort was scored. This process permitted us to assign cumulative scores to the biography of each offender, to average seriousness by race, socioeconomic status (SES), age, and other variables.

A further refinement shows the types of physical injury committed by each racial group. The frequency distributions as well as the weighted rates show that more *serious* forms of harm are committed by nonwhites. No whites were responsible for the 14 homicides. The modal weighted rate for nonwhites is to cause victims to be hospitalized (although the modal number is in the "minor harm" category). The modal weighted rate (WR) and number for white offenders is for minor harm. By using the weighted rate, based on the judgmental scale of the gravity of crime, the 14 homicides represent more social harm to the community during the juvenile life span (WR = 125.4) of nonwhite boys than all the combined 456 acts of physical injury committed by white boys during their juvenile years (WR = 119.3). The same can be said about the 59 acts of violence committed by nonwhites that resulted in hospitalization of the victims (WR = 142.3).

In short, if juveniles are to be delinquent, a major thrust of social action programs might be able to cause a change in the *character* rather than in the absolute reduction of delinquent behavior. It could also be argued that concentration of social action programs on a 10 percent reduction of white *index* offenses (N = 1400; WR = 483.63) would have a greater social payoff than a 10 percent reduction of nonwhite *nonindex* offenses (N = 3343; WR = 382.45). To inculcate values against harm to body or property of others is obviously the major means to reduce the seriousness of delinquency, both among whites and nonwhites. We are simply faced with the fact that more social harm is committed by nonwhites, and the resources and energies of social harm reduction efforts should be employed among *nonwhite* youth, especially the very young.

An examination of age-specific rates, especially weighted rates, by race, clearly reveals that the incidence of nonwhite offenses at young ages is equal to or more serious than that of whites at later ages. For example, the average crude rate per 1000 nonwhites aged seven to ten (83.32) is higher than the rate for whites between 14 and 15 years of age (72.24). In fact, for the single year when nonwhites in this cohort were 16 years old, their weighted rate of delinquency (633.49) was higher than the rates for whites accumulated over their entire juvenile careers (587.84). It may be said that nonwhites in their sixteenth year inflict more social harm, through delinquency, on the community than do all whites from age seven to age 18. The incidence (weighted) of nonwhites at age 11 (112.80) is just slightly less than that for whites at age 15 (120.79) or 17 (122.50), a striking indication of the relatively high rate of delinquency at a very youthful age among nonwhites.

Our studies provide age-specific index offense estimates for ages 14 to 30 (Collins, 1977). (We have given estimates of self-reported offenses from ages 26 to 30 by using the mean number of index offenses reported between 18 and 25.) The means refer to index offenses committed by offenders who have come into contact with the juvenile or adult criminal justice system for *any* offense. Officially reported injury offenses are low in the juvenile years, increase in the early adult years, and then remain stable and relatively high. Self-reported injury offenses, however, are high in juvenile years and lower and stable in adult years. Officially reported property offenses are relatively stable over all ages, but self-reported property offenses are highest in the juvenile years and decrease in adult years. The ratios between self-reported and officially reported acts are highest in the juvenile years, or about eight to 11 index offenses committed for every one officially recorded. The ratio for males 18 to 25 ranges between three and six self-reported offenses for each officially recorded act.

Using our birth cohort data up to age 30, James Collins of the criminology center at the University of Pennsylvania worked on a report concerned with an incapacitation or restraint model. His study indicates that for each index offender incarcerated in the 14-to-17-year age span, four to five index offenses would be prevented. For each adult offender incarcerated for a year between ages 18 and 25, about three to three and one-half index offenses would be prevented. The general model shows that restraint of the chronic offender would have the greatest per capita impact. The probability that an offender, after his fourth offense, will recidivate is about 0.80, and the likelihood that his next offense will be an index one, over the next 16 offense transitions, is, on the average, 0.426, ranging from 0.300 to 0.722.

SOME IMPLICATIONS FROM THE COHORT STUDY

Serious offenses are committed frequently by a relatively small number of offenders: up to age 30 in a birth cohort, about 14 percent. Serious offenses, officially known and self-reported, committed by juveniles, have a higher probability of being committed by these same persons as adults.

Race is significantly associated with this finding, which is to say that proportionately many more nonwhites than whites will be involved in this serious juvenile/serious adult offender status grouping. But the transition stability also occurs among the proportionately smaller number of whites. The chronic offender continues to be the most important category with which the criminal justice system should deal in its concern about serious, particularly personal injury, offenses.

Perhaps as meaningful as anything to emerge from this longitudinal study thus far is that, with respect to chronicity of offenders, the juvenile/adult statutory dichotomy has little justification. At whatever age the chronic offender begins his fourth or fifth offense, the probabilities are very high that he will commit further offenses, and, on the average, the next offense will be an index offense nearly half the time. It may be, therefore, that if the severity of the sanction is proportionate to the gravity of the crime and to the cumulative history of serious crime, the sanction should be similar for chronic serious offenders whatever their age.

SUBCULTURE OF VIOLENCE

Within our broader cultural context there is what I have called elsewhere a "subculture of violence." By this I mean a set of values, attitudes, and beliefs congealed in pockets of populations characterized by residential propinquity and shared commitment to the use of physical aggression as a major mode of personal interaction and a device for solving problems (Wolfgang and Ferracuti, 1967). In this subculture, generated primarily in a lower socioeconomic class disadvantaged in all the traditionally known ways, the use of violence is either tolerated and permitted or specifically encouraged from infancy through adulthood. From child-rearing practices that commonly use physical punishment and that contain many elements of abuse, to childhood and adolescent play, street gang and group behavior, domestic quarrels and barroom brawls, physically assaultive conduct is condoned and even an expected response to many interpersonal relationships. Machismo, but more than this, is involved in the value system that promotes the ready resort to violence upon the appearance of relatively weak provoking stimuli. The repertoire of response to frustration or to certain kinds of stimuli (including name-calling, challenges to the ego) is limited often to a physically aggressive one, and the capacity to withdraw or to articulate a verbal response is minimal.

Within the subculture of violence the cues and clues of this stimulus-response mechanism are well known to the culture carriers and thus promote social situations that quickly escalate arguments to altercations and apparently quick-tempered aggression to seemingly trivial encounters. This subculture of violence is culturally transmitted from generation to generation and is shared across cohorts of youth who will fight instead of flee, assault instead of articulate, and kill rather than control their aggression.

The proposition of a subculture of violence suggests that violence is learned behavior and that if violence is not a way of life it nonetheless is normal, not individual pathological behavior. And the greater the degree of commitment to the subcultural values, the less freedom, the fewer the alternative responses the individual has with which to cope with social encounters. Homicide, rape, aggravated assault have historically been crimes predominantly intragroup, within the family, among friends and acquaintances, neighbors, and the intimate social network. More physical mobility and intergroup interactions have increased the number of victims outside the subculture, the number of victims who are strangers to the offenders, and these factors have promoted wide public fear of random assaults and victimization.

IMPORTANCE OF DOMESTIC DISTURBANCE CALLS

The usual caveat about domestic homicides and the incapacity of the police to do much about them appears in almost every annual report from the FBI.

> . . . police are powerless to prevent a large number of these crimes. . . . The significant fact emerges that most murders are committed by relatives of the victim or persons acquainted with the victim. It follows, therefore, that criminal homicide is, to a major extent, a national social problem beyond police prevention (Uniform Crime Reports, 1971).

But new rationales and new empirical evidence suggest rejection of this assertion. About ten years ago I wrote about this issue:

> A particularly intriguing innovation suggested as a special function of community centers is the "emergency domestic quarrel team" of specialists. With a staff of sufficient size and training to provide twenty-four hour service on call, the team is viewed as capable of offering rapid social intervention, quick decisions and accelerated resolutions to families caught in a conflict crisis. Traditionally, the police are called into service when domestic quarrels erupt into public complaints. The police are trained principally to interrupt fights in verbal or physical form. Their chief function is to prevent assault and battery at the moment of arrival, to arrest assaulters on complaint, and then to go about the business of patrolling their sector. It is well known that some of the most potentially

dangerous calls police officers act upon are reports of domestic quarrels. About one-fifth of all policemen killed on duty are those who responded to "disturbance" calls which include family quarrels.

The suggestion of an emergency domestic quarrel team is meant to include the police as part of the group, primarily to protect the team itself from violent attack. After the initial danger has subsided, the police could withdraw, leaving the team of psychological and social work specialists to talk with the family, to suggest the best solution to the immediate problem, and work out a program for a more enduring resolution.

It should be kept in mind that a relatively high proportion of criminal homicides is classified as emerging from domestic quarrels. These are acts usually committed indoors, not normally subject to observation by patrolmen on the street, and therefore considered virtually unpredictable and unpreventable. An emergency domestic quarrel team might, therefore, function from a community center as an effective homicide-prevention measure. Intervening in earlier stages of physically aggressive strife in the family, the team could conceivably thwart the progression of family violence to the point of homicidal attack. The strategies for resolving domestic conflict are details too specific to pursue further here, but, clearly, experience would accumulate to provide increasing sophistication. In addition to information shared in an adequate referral system, these teams would soon develop expertise in handling many difficult family situations. It should be further noted that twice as many homicides among blacks as among whites are known to develop from quarrels within the family, usually between husbands and wives. These are almost invariably lower class, poor black families. The emergency teams to which we refer would operate out of centers often located in areas with high concentrations of the black poor.

Various indices to measure the success of these teams can easily be imagined. Keeping in mind our focus on crimes of violence, one index of the value of emergency intervention could be changing rates of domestic homicides and aggravated assaults. Perhaps even rate changes in general throughout an ecological area would be influenced. After all, an unresolved family conflict may cause some family members to displace their cumulative aggressivity on close friends, neighborhood acquaintances, or even strangers. For we do not know the number of homicides and aggravated assaults recorded by the police as due to altercations which may have had their genesis in a hostile exchange in the family (Wolfgang and Ferracuti, 1967, pp. 301-302).

Stimulated by the work of Bard (1969), a family crisis intervention unit was established in New York City some years ago, but the research design and findings were inconclusive, although Bard did report that training police officers for handling family disputes appeared to be related to the fact that no homicides occurred in any of the 962 families previously seen by the family crisis intervention unit, that family assaults were fewer, and there were no injuries to any officer in the intervention unit (Bard and Berkowitz, 1969; Bard and Zacker, 1971).

New and as yet unpublished data yield empirical support for the hypothesis that family homicides might be reduced if more intensive, focal attention were given to domestic emergency disturbance police calls. Data were collected, with support from the Police Foundation, on homicides and aggravated assaults occurring in Kansas City, Missouri during 1970 and 1971.* In one-fourth of the homicides and one-third of the aggravated assaults either the victim or the suspect had an arrest for a disturbance or assault within two years previous to the homicide or assault in question. Even more striking is the fact that about 90 percent of the homicide victims and suspects had previous disturbance calls to their address, with about 50 percent of them having 5 or more calls. The same was true for assault victims and suspects. Unfortunately, in most of these previous disturbance calls, the police did nothing more than prevent immediate physical injury and there were few arrests or court convictions. When asked, if charges were not brought, whether the family members expected to repeat their disturbance behavior, two-thirds said yes. And apparently future disturbances often result in family homicide. The best set of variables to predict a future domestic killing or aggravated assault includes the presence of a gun, a history of previous disturbance calls, and the presence of alcohol. Moreover, when physical force was used in a family disturbance, known threats to do so had preceded it in 8 of 10 cases.

The study in Kansas City is a complex and elaborate one and I hope it will soon be published. My major reason for mentioning it is to suggest that with appropriate intervening counseling, referral, and treatment of family disturbances, there is a probability of reducing not only domestic homicide but family violence in general.

CONCLUSION

Violence in the family is partly a reflection of violent expressions in the culture generally. But serious crimes within the family are most commonly related to subcultural values that, at best, do not much inhibit physical responses or, at worst, condone and encourage them.

---

* *Conflict Management: Analysis Resolution.* Submitted by Northeast Patrol Divission Task Force, project director Captain Robert Sawtell. See also Wilt, G. M., and Bannon, J. *A Comprehensive Analysis of Conflict-Motivated Homicides and Assaults, Detroit, 1972-1973.* Submitted to Police Foundation, Washington, D. C., May 1974, unpublished.

The residential propinquity of the individuals in a subculture of violence has been noted. Breaking up this propinquity, dispersing the members who share intense commitment to the violence value, could also cause a break in the intergenerational and intragenerational communication of this value system. Dispersion can be done in many ways and does not necessarily imply massive population shifts, although urban renewal, slum clearance, and housing projects suggest feasible methods. Renewal programs that simply shift the location of the subculture from one part of a city to another do not destroy the subculture. In order to distribute the subculture so that it dissipates, the scattered units should be small. Housing projects and neighborhood areas should be small microcosms of the social hierarchy and value system of the central dominant culture. It is in homogeneity that the subculture has strength and durability.

Before one set of values can replace another, before the subculture of violence can be replaced by the establishment of nonviolence, the first must be disrupted, dispersed, disorganized. The resocializing, relearning process best takes place when the old socialization and old learning are forgotten or denied their validity. Once the subculture is disintegrated by dispersion of its members, aggressive attitudes are not supported by likeminded companions, and violent behavior is not regularly on display to encourage imitation and repetition.

Murray Straus (1974) has written eloquently about aggression in families, especially about the notion of "leveling" in the sense of giving free expression to one's aggressive feelings in the natural family setting and in therapy, referred to as the ventilationist approach. He argues compellingly and convincingly against it and suggests instead that "the greater the degree of intellectualization the lesser the amount of physical aggression. The "rationality of middle-class life" and the "rules of civility" which have evolved through the ages in the name of humanism are viewed as significant elements in the reduction of family violence.

Violence among children, adolescents, and young adults has been steadily and rapidly increasing, and increasing more significantly than in any other age grouping, thus contributing to the overall increase of crimes of violence in society. But reduced fertility in recent years should result in a corresponding decrease in violence in the 1990s. Child violence among blacks is dramatically high and exceeds by as much as twelve times the rate among similarly aged whites. Sociologically, a subculture of violence thesis may be used to explain much of this violence that is generated by a value system geared to a ready response of physical assault or ritually acknowledged cues. When the repertoire of response is limited to relatively inarticulate capacities, when physical punishment of children is common practice, when the rational civility of middle-class values of respect for person and property are undeveloped or missing, when parental affection and caring supervision of children are absent, the major modal categories of the violent child are more likely to emerge in behavioral expressions that violate both codified law and dominant communal norms.

Parental affection and firm supervision cannot be legislated. Teachers and significant others cannot, by administrative fiat, become kind and gentle. But activities can be promoted in the home and schools to socialize children—even those from a subculture of violence—into nonviolence, to desensitize them to linguistic and behavioral cues that evoke violence. Pleasurable rewards and lucid, certain, but milder sanctions promote the greatest probability of nonviolent conformity to social rules of conduct. If, as Prescott (1975) claims, pleasure and violence are antitheses, the message is as old as it is clear and is buttressed by evidence from all the healing arts and behavioral sciences:

Give the infant, child, and adolescent affection, recognition and reward for being alive and unharming to others; freedom from excessive restraints; pleasures for the body; and a broad repertoire of verbally articulating ways to respond to stimuli in all dramas of social interaction.

REFERENCES

BARD, M. Family intervention police teams as a community mental health resource. *J. Crim. Law, Criminology and Police Science* 60(2):247-250, 1969.

BARD, M., and BERKOWITZ, B. Family disturbance as a police function, in *Law Enforcement, Science and Technology II*, S. Cohn, ed. I. I. T. Research Institute, Chicago, 1969.

BARD, M., and ZACKER, J. The prevention of family violence: Dilemmas of community intervention. *J. Marriage and the Family* 33(4):677-682, 1971.

COLLINS, J. J. JR. *Offender careers and restraint: The probabilities and policy implications*. Dissertation supported by grant from National Institute of Law Enforcement and Criminal Justice, Law Enforcement Assistance Administration, U.S. Department of Justice, Grant Number 76N1-99-0089, 1977.

CURTIS, L. A. *Criminal Violence*. Lexington Books, Heath, Lexington, Mass., 1974, pp. 51-56.

FANNIN, L. F., and CLINARD, M. B. Differences in the conception of self as a male among lower and middle class delinquents. *Social Problems* 13:205-214, 1965.

MILLER, W. B. Lower class culture as a generating milieu of gang delinquency. *J. Soc. Issues* 14:5-19, 1958.

MULVIHILL, D. J., TUMIN, M. M., and CURTIS, L. A. *Crimes of Violence*, vol. II, National Commission on the Causes and Prevention of Violence. U.S. Government Printing Office, Washington, D.C., 1969, pp. 145-152, 169, 298-299.

PRESCOTT, J. W. Body pleasure and the origins of violence. *Bulletin of the Atomic Scientists* 75, pp. 10-20, November 1975.

SELLIN, T., and WOLFGANG, M. E. *The Measurement of Delinquency*. Wiley, New York, 1964.

STRAUS, M. A. Leveling, civility, and violence in the family. *J. Marriage and the Family* 36:13-29, 1974.

Uniform Crime Reports 1970. U.S. Department of Justice. U.S. Government Printing Office, Washington, D.C., 1971, p. 9.

Uniform Crime Reports 1974. U.S. Department of Justice. U.S. Government Printing Office, Washington, D.C., 1975.

Uniform Crime Reports 1976. U.S. Department of Justice. U.S. Government Printing Office, Washington, D.C., 1977.

WOLFGANG, M. E. *Patterns in Criminal Homicide*. University of Pennsylvania Press, Philadelphia, 1958, pp. 213-217.

WOLFGANG, M. E., and FERRACUTI, F. *The Subculture of Violence*. Barnes and Noble, New York, 1967, pp. 301-302, 305-306.

WOLFGANG, M. E., *Youth and Violence*. U.S. Department of Health, Education, and Welfare, Washington, D.C., 1970, pp. 12-19.

WOLFGANG, M. E., FIGLIO, R. M., and SELLIN, T. *Delinquency in a Birth Cohort*. University of Chicago Press, Chicago, 1972.

CHAPTER 8

Effects of Television on Violent Behavior

ELI A. RUBINSTEIN

In January, 1972, the Surgeon General's Scientific Advisory Committee on Television and Social Behavior issued its formal report on the impact of televised violence (Surgeon General's Committee, 1972). The Surgeon General had been requested, in 1969, by Senator John Pastore, chairman of the Senate Subcommittee on Communications, to examine the effects of TV violence on the behavior of children. The National Institute of Mental Health was authorized by the Surgeon General to organize a program of research, and one million dollars was allocated for the purpose. The final committee report in 1972 was based on the results published in five volumes of technical reports containing the evidence collected in that research.

Now, seven years after publication of those technical papers and much analysis of the report, disagreement continues about the committee's conclusions and about the relationship between televised violence and later aggressive behavior. Despite the use of some cautious qualifiers in its statement, the advisory committee, composed of 12 senior behavioral scientists, found a causal relationship between viewing violence on television and later aggressive behavior.

That conclusion, although shared by many researchers in the field, was not unanimously endorsed. According to one recent evaluation of the evidence, "This paper should not be interpreted as stating that TV fantasy violence can not cause aggression; rather we have argued that no such link has been demonstrated to date. . . . We are not contending that the null hypothesis is true, but that the no-effect view is currently the most plausible one given" (Kaplan and Singer, 1976, p. 63).

Almost simultaneously, another comprehensive review of much the same evidence came to the opposite conclusion, finding that the cumulative results of 67 studies revealed "at least a weak positive relationship between watching violence on television and the subsequent aggression displayed by viewers of that violence" (Andison, 1977, p. 323).

Two extensive studies reported in 1977 also reach opposite conclusions. Addressing the convention of the American Psychological Association in San Francisco, Milavsky (1977), reported preliminary results of a portion of a major longitudinal study of the effects of televised violence. Having examined 800 elementary school children in grades 2 to 6, Milavsky and his colleagues found no detectable effect of exposure to televised violence. The study itself, funded by the National Broadcasting Company where Milavsky is director of social research, is a carefully designed and sophisticated panel study in which six waves of data were collected between 1970 and 1973. The data analysis was rigorous. It should be noted, however, that the findings were only one part of the study and the full report has not yet been published.

A week after Milavsky reported on the NBC study, a major research project funded by the Columbia Broadcasting System was described by Belson (1977) to the British Association for the Advancement of Science in London. Using a complex process of statistical analysis, Belson had examined the effects on 1565 teenaged London boys of long-term exposure to television violence. The statistical analysis involved an iterative search procedure in which a series of matching variables (presumed predictors of violent behavior) were selected for a control group with low scores on TV violence exposure and an experimental group with high scores on TV violence exposure. According to Belson's argument, the matching of correlates of violent behavior should eliminate any differences in terms of violent behavior, and any residual differences should be considered an estimate of the effect of viewing TV violence on actual violent behavior. Belson found a significant residual difference (11 percent), and he concludes that long-term exposure to TV violence increases the degree to which boys engage in serious violence.

With these contradictory evaluations and research conclusions, it is no surprise that there is still no overwhelming consensus on the effects of

TV violence on later aggressive behavior, although many more experts endorse the causal relationship than deny it.

The crucial question is not whether the viewer, especially the young viewer, is affected by what he or she sees on television. Most likely, the pervasive viewing of television by millions of youngsters has some effect on their behavior. The real question is still what kinds of violent behavior are induced under what circumstances with what kinds of children watching what kinds of programs. Unfortunately there are no definitive answers to that question at this time.

At least two controversial circumstances are present in this complex issue. One is the definition of violence on television. The other is the measurement of aggressive behavior induced by watching such violence, however defined. The definition of violence most often cited is that by Gerbner (1972), "the overt expression of physical force against others or self, or compelling action against one's will on pain of being hurt or killed, or actually hurting or killing." Despite criticism from various sources, including television executives, this definition has been widely accepted by other scientists. Among other problems, however, this definition does not take into account such aspects as motivation, justification, or level of violence used. While recognizing these and other weaknesses, a special committee of the Social Science Research Council (SSRC), examining the entire matter, ended up essentially endorsing Gerbner's definition (SSRC, 1975).

The actual measurement of aggressive behavior that follows the viewing of TV violence is another problem. Most measures in published research involve aggressive behavior, either observed or from ratings, that are far short of the level of serious crime. Quite obviously, no studies have been done in which efforts were made to actually induce subjects to do serious harm to others. Belson (1977) reports that his measures of violence committed included some serious crimes such as personal injury and property damage and even attempted rape. But these were retrospective self-reports and not actual observations directly related to the TV viewing.

Despite these problems, the consensus among researchers is that TV violence has a weak positive effect on subsequent aggressive behavior. That general conclusion does not seem destined to be effectively contradicted by new evidence.

A more interesting inquiry can and should be made into some circumscribed aspects of this general question. What, for example, are the effects on subpopulations of viewers? An important relevant issue was raised in the Surgeon General's Committee report, which has never been adequately explored. Despite the fact that the advisory committee found a causal relationship between viewing violence on television and later aggressive behavior, the language used in reaching that conclusion was qualified in many respects. One such qualifier, the use of the word "predisposed," was the source of much public debate.

The committee, in attempting to characterize those children to whom the causal sequence seemed most applicable, identified them as children who are "predisposed" to aggressive behavior. That term was widely misinterpreted by critics of the report to mean that the committee was singling out children with some emotional problems of which excessive aggressive behavior was one manifestation. While the committee did not mean to exclude such children from the category of "predisposed," the term was intended to include all children whose psychological makeup somehow made them more prone to engage in aggressive behavior.

Indeed, the findings in many studies suggest, as one would expect, that not all children react similarly to the violence on television. Perhaps the most common difference is gender-related; in many instances girls are less likely to respond with aggressive behavior than boys. In fact, since there were no samples of disturbed children included in the many research projects undertaken for the Surgeon General's program, the committee had no basis on which to assume that "predisposition" was a function of emotional disability.

The larger question remains, however, about the television viewing behaviors of disturbed children and how televised violence affects such children. This question was brought to dramatic public attention last year when a defense attorney in a murder trial in Florida claimed that his client, a 15-year-old boy, was suffering from "involuntary subliminal television intoxication." Although that condition has no scientific foundation and cannot be found in any psychiatric glossary, it has intriguing implications. It certainly is in keeping with a common belief by the layperson that too much television viewing has an almost hypnotic effect and reduces children to passive, if not mindless, victims of the images on the television screen.

The defense attorney claimed that his adolescent client was compelled to act as he did (it was admitted that the murder of an elderly woman did take place) as a result of a mental disease "by which he lacked substantial capacity to appreciate the criminality of his conduct and rendered him unable to conform his conduct to the requirements of the law."

At the trial, one expert on television research was queried initially, with the jury sequestered, to establish whether or not such research was relevant to the case. When the prosecuting attorney asked specifically if any published research established a direct link between TV violence and the commission of a serious crime, the scientist correctly replied, No. The fact that, statistically, a causal relationship had been established between TV violence and later aggressive behavior was not considered pertinent to the case by the judge, and no such scientific evidence was presented to the jury. The jury found the defendant guilty of murder and rejected the plea of "involuntary subliminal television intoxication."

It is significant that no extensive scientific evidence is available, not only on the single case issue of severe crimes, but on the general population of mentally disturbed children. Some data are relevant, however. In addition to the general statistical finding that viewing televised violence relates to later aggressive behavior, there are findings that the social realities of life may be modified in the mind of the viewer by the images portrayed on the television screen. It follows that differences between the real world and the television world—and there are many such differences—influence the perception of the viewer about the world in which he or she lives. Dean Gerbner of the Annenberg School of Communication, who has explored this problem, has found that heavy viewers see the world in a much more sinister light than do individuals who do not watch as much television (Gerbner et al., 1977).

While there are no data at present on this difference between heavy and light viewers among psychologically disturbed children, it would seem that their perceptions of reality—already disturbed by emotional problems —may be even more affected by the excesses that exist in the television world. Perhaps of even more importance is Gerbner's argument that excessive portrayals of violence on television foster feelings of fear among heavy viewers. Again, these emotionally disturbed children may be even more affected by this influence than those who are emotionally stable.

To examine some of these questions and to explore more systematically the role of television in the lives of emotionally disturbed children, my colleagues and I at the Long Island Research Institute initiated a survey of the television viewing behaviors of mental patients in psychiatric centers in New York State in 1976 (Rubinstein et al., 1977).

All 23 major psychiatric centers under the purview of the New York State Department of Mental Hygiene were sent two sets of survey forms, one for the directors of the institutions and one for ward personnel. The directors' survey forms requested general information on the impact of television on the institutionalized patients, its value as a leisure-time activity, its effect on patients' behavior, and its potential as a therapeutic procedure.

The ward staff survey was designed to gather data describing where and how television was watched, what its impact was on the patients and information on unusual television-related incidents.

The centers that completed our forms serve about 80 percent of New York State's mental hospital population. Our sample of respondents included 2181 patients. Of these, about 7 percent were adolescents, 23 percent were acutely disturbed adults, 36 percent were chronic adult patients, and 34 percent geriatric patients. The male/female ratio was 55/45 percent.

The directors indicated that television viewing has a generally beneficial influence on geriatric and chronic patients. For acute schizophrenic patients, the directors believed television had a more negative than positive effect. For disturbed adolescents, only about half the respondents believed television was beneficial for this group. Almost all the directors of these institutions saw television as a primarily valuable leisure-time activity, and almost two-thirds of them saw television as having some potential as a therapeutic procedure.

Our survey of the ward personnel confirmed both the positive potential for television viewing and its extensive use as a leisure-time activity. In general, the ward staff felt that television was more beneficial for the geriatric patients than the adolescent patients, although television was seen as having a positive effect on institutionalized patients as a whole.

In another part of our survey, we examined the television viewing behaviors of 94 emotionally disturbed children in a state-operated inpatient facility for children on Long Island. Most of the children, aged 6 to 14, were diagnosed as psychotic or with severe behavior disorders. About one-third of the children, identified as autistic, were housed in separate living units. Only 21 of the children were girls.

The television sets, one in each unit for 8 or fewer children, were on for an average of nine hours per day. For the 34 children on the autistic units, the average viewing time per child was about one hour per day. Children on the other units averaged about 3½ hours of television viewing per day. Therapy aides on the autistic units generally imposed more restrictions on type of program, usually selecting cartoons or "Sesame Street" or programs with music. On the other units, the children themselves were more likely to select the program to be viewed. Therapy aides noted that certain programs or types of programs were more often viewed and/or discussed by these children. These included action/adventure shows, crime dramas, cartoons, situation comedies and some noncommercial programs like "Mr. Rogers' Neighborhood" and "Sesame Street."

It was noted that patients newly admitted to the children's facility typically went through an initial period of heavy television viewing. As the children became more familiar with the institutional setting, they tended to reduce the amount of TV watching.

Nearly all therapy aides observed a variety of behaviors by the children that seemed to be related to what they had seen on television. These included imitating aggressive behavior and pretending to be one of the major characters on a favorite program. On the autistic units some unusual behaviors seemed to have been provoked by what was seen on television, for examples, hallucinating in response to televised violence, acting out in response to commercials, or repeating commercial jingles. For children who otherwise communicate little, this behavior can properly be classified as unusual.

For these children, both those in autistic units as well as in the less severely disturbed groups, the staff reported that heavy viewers tend to be more stable and less troublesome than the average patient. Almost 60 percent of the aides reported that television made their job easier. It kept the children occupied, tended to quiet them, and sometimes stimulated helpful behavior.

In a more recent examination of this same population of institutionalized children, my colleagues and I examined more closely some of the previous home TV-viewing behaviors of inpatient and outpatient samples in the facility (Kochnower et al., 1978). The data involve the children's use of television and their reactions to it. Twenty-five inpatients and 25 outpatients were interviewed. Data were also collected on the parents' viewing habits and preferences, their control over the children's TV viewing, and their perception of their chidren's viewing behaviors.

The mean age of the hospitalized children was 11.7 years while that of the outpatient children was 10.2 years. The diagnoses of the inpatient group were either psychoses or severe behavior disorders. For the outpatient group the diagnoses were primarily transient situational disturbances or less severe behavior disorders. Many of the fathers in both groups were either skilled workers or managers and were high school graduates. Compared to the general population in this geographic region, fewer fathers in these two groups were professionals or had college degrees. Thus, the sample of patients' parents seems to have a slightly lower socioeconomic status than a sample of "normal" school children's parents.

Many aspects of the viewing habits and practices of the two study groups were similar to those of normal populations, with the greatest degree of similarity found in the data pertaining to characteristics of the TV-viewing environment. In particular, the number and location of sets available, restrictions placed on television viewing in the home, parental encouragement or discouragement of programs, and the presence of various co-viewers were fairly comparable among groups.

There were more differences between the patient groups and normal populations on the quantitative and qualitative aspects of viewing. Inpatients seem to watch somewhat less television than has been reported for samples of normal children, and outpatients seem to view somewhat more. The prevalent preferences for cartoon programs and identification with cartoon characters by the inpatients indicate that, in some ways, they are more similar to younger children than they are to children of the same chronological age.

The greatest difference among the groups appears to be in the impact of television on the children. More inpatients than either outpatients or normals dream frequently about what they see on television, and many of those dreams are frightening to them. A majority of both patient groups wish to imitate something seen on television, but more inpatients have attempted to do so. Four-fifths of both patient groups indicated that watching television was associated with positive mood states, but more inpatients than outpatients reported negative mood states while not viewing.

On the whole, the findings strongly suggest that television viewing influences some aspects of the children's behavior while awake or asleep, the magnitude of these effects being somewhat greater in the inpatient sample.

The data from the two surveys, demonstrating that television has an impact on institutionalized children, have important implications for future research. Research on normal children has moved from documenting television's general influence on behavior to focusing on its positive potential. Much the same shift in emphasis should be attempted in research with disturbed children.

Encouraged by the findings that television is an important part of the daily life of these children, we are now developing a more rigorous study to explore the implications of our surveys.

In the survey described above, children newly admitted to that facility were more constant TV viewers than children who had been in the institution for some time. Given the considerable amount of home TV-viewing by most children, coupled with the fact that television viewing is one of the few activities in the institution familiar to the child, it is understandable ther children would turn to that activity in the early transition phase of their hospitalization.

More important, the early findings with this at-risk population suggest the possibility that television viewing might be used as a modest form of therapeutic intervention. It is not far-fetched to make comparison with such approaches as recreational therapy and dance therapy, in which otherwise recreational activities have been structured to have some therapeutic utility. What is still not known is how this therapeutic value may be achieved.

As a first step in this direction, we are developing a field study in the state children's psychiatric center in which we conducted our earlier survey. The study will explore the assumption that a diet of prosocial television programming selected from existing commercial television may induce positive or prosocial behavior. As an added intervention, postprogram discussions will be conducted with the children by trained personnel as a means of labeling and encouraging prosocial attitudes and behaviors.

The primary objectives of the study are to examine in depth the impact of television viewing on the daily lives of a sample of institutionalized children who have psychiatric problems and to assess the effects of increasing the amount of prosocial TV programming presented to these institutionalized children. The study will allow the assessment of the effects of a postprogram intervention designed to mitigate negative effects of violent programming and enhance positive effects of prosocial programming.

The subjects will be about 120 of the higher-functioning children at the children's center. They will participate in a four-week experimental intervention during which their TV viewing will be controlled. The other independent variable will be the absence or presence of postprogram discussion.

The TV diet will be either: a) one consisting of programs that are typically watched on the wards, or b) an experimental one consisting of specially selected programs from a videotape library of recently aired commercial shows which are high in prosocial content and low in aggressive content. All presentations will consist of programs popular with members of this population.

Thus, there will be essentially four conditions: "normal" TV diet with no postprogram discussion (essentially the present condition of TV viewing), normal diet with discussion, prosocial diet with no discussion, and prosocial diet with discussion.

Baseline information will be obtained during a week of pretreatment observation, followed by two weeks of treatment/observation using one of the four conditions. A final week of posttreatment observation will complete the four-week experiment. The pretreatment and posttreatment phases in each instance are identical: children watching normal programming without structured discussions. Behavioral observations and ratings will be collected. The same observations and ratings will be made during the middle two weeks of experimental treatment conditions. In addition to behavioral observations, the dependent measures will include ward staff ratings and a variety of specially developed structured situations. Appropriate statistical procedures, primarily analysis of co-variance, should tell us the respective treatment effects.

This brief description does not, of course, cover all the complexities of the research design. Not the least of the methodological problems derive from doing this study in a clinical setting. The rigor of the design must in some instances yield to the needs and demands of clinical care. Nevertheless, this approach seems a useful way to begin to see whether or not television viewing can be modified to serve as a positive influence in the daily lives of these children. The study is intended as the first in a series to attempt to transform the potentially harmful effects of TV viewing into a more constructive influence on this at risk population. If the anticipated results occur, the approach may have useful long-range implications for the care and treatment of institutionalized children. Further, since the role of television in other institutional settings, for example, homes for the aged, prisons, and detention centers, is unknown, the approach may have implications for explorations in these settings as well.

REFERENCES

ANDISON, F. S. TV violence and viewer aggression: A cumulation of study results, 1956-76. *Public Opinion Quarterly* 41:314-331, 1977.

BELSON, W. Television violence and the adolescent boy. Paper delivered at meeting of British Association for the Advancement of Science, London, England, September 6, 1977.

GERBNER, G. Violence in television drama: Trends and symbolic functions. In *Television and Social Behavior, vol. 1, Media Content and Control.* G. A. Comstock and E. A. Rubinstein, eds. U.S. Government Printing Office, Washington, D.C., 1972.

GERBNER, G., GROSS, L., ELEEY, M. F., JACKSON-BEECK, M., JEFFRIES-FOX, A., and SIGNORIELLI, N. TV violence profile No. 8: The highlights. *J. Commun.* 27: 171-180, 1977.

KAPLAN, R. M., and SINGER, R. D. Television violence and viewer aggression: A reexamination of the evidence. *J. Soc. Issues* 32:35-70, 1976.

KOCHNOWER, J. M., FRACCHIA, J. F., RUBINSTEIN, E. A., and SPRAFKIN, J. N. *Television Viewing Behaviors of Emotionally Disturbed Children: An Interview Study.* Brookdale International Institute, New York, 1978.

MILAVSKY, W. R. TV and aggressive behavior of elementary school boys. Paper delivered at meeting of American Psychological Association, San Francisco, California, August 19, 1977.

RUBINSTEIN, E. A., FRACCHIA, J. F., KOCHNOWER, J. M., and SPRAFKIN, J. N. *Television Viewing Behaviors of Mental Patients: A Survey of Psychiatric Centers in New York State.* Brookdale International Institute, 1977.

Social Science Research Council. *A Profile of Televised Violence.* New York, 1975.

Surgeon General's Scientific Advisory Committee on Television and Social Behavior. *Television and Growing Up: The Impact of Televised Violence.* U.S. Government Printing Office, Washington, D.C., 1972.

CHAPTER 9

Comparison of Trends for Suicide and Homicide in the United States, 1900-1976

A. JOAN KLEBBA

This examination of death certificates filed during this century for the people who took their own lives or who died at the hands of other persons may tell us something about their times of crisis that will help to prevent such tragedies in the future. Trends for these violent deaths are presented by age, color, and sex; and by year, month, and day of death.

GROWTH OF DEATH REGISTRATION AREA

This report is not based on the complete count of suicides and homicides for 1900-1976 in what are now the 50 states and the District of Columbia, but only on the "death registration area" established for the census year 1880. For that year, and for 1890 and 1900, transcripts of death certificates were received from the states and cities included in the area, in addition to the enumerators' returns. The annual collection of mortality statistics for the part of the United States known as the registration area began in 1900. By 1933, the area had expanded from 10 states and the District of Columbia to the entire United States. The year in which each state entered the death registration system is shown in Table 1.

Table 1

Year in Which Each State Was Admitted to the Death-Registration System

Year	State	Year	State	Year	State
1880–	Massachusetts	1908–	Washington	1919–	Florida
	New Jersey		Wisconsin		Mississippi
	District of	1909–	Ohio	1920–	Nebraska
	Columbia*	1910–	Minnesota	1922–	Georgia§
1890–	Connecticut		Montana		Idaho
	Delaware**		Utah		Wyoming
	New Hampshire	1911–	Kentucky	1923–	Iowa
	New York		Missouri	1924–	North Dakota
	Rhode Island	1913–	Virginia	1925–	Alabama
	Vermont	1914–	Kansas		West Virginia
1900–	Maine	1916–	South Carolina	1926–	Arizona
	Michigan		North Carolina‡	1927–	Arkansas
	Indiana	1917–	Tennessee	1928–	Oklahoma
1906–	California	1918–	Illinois	1929–	Nevada
	Colorado		Louisiana		New Mexico
	Maryland		Oregon	1933–	Texas
	Pennsylvania			1959–	Alaska
	South Dakota†			1960–	Hawaii

* Included as a state.
** Dropped from registration system in 1900, readmitted in 1919.
† Dropped from registration system in 1910, readmitted in 1930.
‡ Included only municipalities with populations of 1,000 or more in 1900 (about 16 percent of total population); remainder of state was added to system in 1916.
§ Dropped from registration system in 1925, readmitted in 1928.

More specifically, for 1900-1932, the data shown in this report include only those for the expanding number of registration states and the District of Columbia. For 1933-1958, the data are for the first 48 states and the District of Columbia. Data from Alaska have been included since 1959, and from Hawaii since 1960, the years that these states were admitted to the Union.

UNDERCOUNT OF SUICIDES AND HOMICIDES

The number of suicides recorded in this expanding area was 1,156,784 for 1900-1976; homicides, 639,203. But large as these numbers are, they are lower than the actual number of suicides and homicides. As early as the report on national mortality statistics for the years 1900-1904 this straightforward complaint (U.S. Bureau of the Census, 1906) is found:

> It would seem that in this class of deaths more than any other there should be no difficulty whatever in securing a proper classification, to the extent specified, at least, since it is the only class in which there are practically universal provisions for an official inquiry into the circumstances attending each death, by a coroner, medical examiner, or other official, for the precise purpose of determining whether the death was due to homicide or suicide, or to purely accidental causes; but instead of this being true the returns in this class of cases are the most unsatisfactory.
>
> It may be that the inquests or investigations of the coroners and medical examiners do develop the facts upon the points specified, but if so there is a very large proportion of the cases in which these facts do not appear in connection with the statements of the causes of death contained in the certificates filed with the registration officials.
>
> While the coroners or other officials exercising the same functions usually state the *manner* of death as "gunshot wound," "carbolic acid poisoning," "fracture of skull," "asphyxia by gas," etc., very many of them give no further information, and when the causes of death are stated in these or similar terms, without qualification, they can only be construed as *accidental* and compiled accordingly, notwithstanding the strong probability that most of them were due actually to either suicide or homicide.

Over the years, efforts to correct this overassignment of deaths to accidents and underassignment to suicide and homicide have met with considerable success. But, as late as 1976, medical examiners and coroners were unable to determine whether the injuries resulting in the known deaths of 4744 persons were accidentally or purposely inflicted. There are still unregistered homicides. As is well known, sometimes the bodies of victims are found long after their deaths. It is also likely that some persons listed as "missing" are unregistered homicide victims.

The changing composition of the death-registration states makes it impossible to obtain comparable mortality data for the entire United States, especially before 1933. In a constant death-registration area before 1933, the year in which the process of admitting the first 48 states was completed, the suicide and homicide rates did not change as much during a decade as the rates for the expanding area would indicate. This was true for homicides because some of the newly admitted states had higher homicide rates than the group of states that had been admitted earlier to the registration area (Table 2). Conversely, it was true for suicides because some newly admitted states had lower suicide rates than the group of states already in the area.

Table 2

Suicide and Homicide Rates Within Groups of Death-Registration States for Specific Years: United States, 1900-1940

Death-registration states of:	1900	1910	1920	1930	1940
	Suicide rate per 100,000 population				
Expanding area	10.2	15.3	10.2	15.6	14.4
1900	10.2	15.4	11.0	16.9	15.9
1910		15.3	11.4	17.7	16.7
1920			10.2	16.3	15.1
	Homicide rate per 100,000 population				
Expanding area	1.2	4.6	6.8	8.8	6.2
1900	1.2	3.9	4.2	5.1	2.7
1910		4.6	4.9	5.7	3.2
1920			6.8	8.2	5.4

GROUPS EXCLUDED AND DEFINITIONS OF RACE

Deaths among armed forces overseas and among U.S. nationals living abroad are excluded for all years. Deaths among nonresident aliens are excluded for 1970 and later years.

The category "white" includes, in addition to persons reported as white, persons reported to be Mexican or Puerto Rican. The categories "races other than white" and "all other" consist of persons reported as Negro, American Indian, Chinese, and Japanese; other numerically small racial groups; and persons of mixed white and other races.

The Bureau of the Census reports that in 1976 about 28,424,000 of the 214,649,000 people in the United States (or 13.2 percent) belonged to "races other than white." Of these 28,424,000 people, about 24,763,000 (or 87.1 percent) were black (U.S. Bureau of the Census, 1977).

MEDICAL EXAMINER'S OR CORONER'S RESPONSIBILITY

It is the responsibility of the medical examiner or coroner to complete and sign the medical certification section of the death certificate and enter the date of death for all "subject deaths." The definition of a subject death is set forth in each jurisdiction by statute, varying in detail from a multitude of particularized situations to merely any suspicious, unnatural, or unattended death (DHEW, 1978). In general all violent deaths (accident, suicide, or homicide) and all deaths due to natural disease processes where the death occurred suddenly and without warning or where the decedent was not being treated by a physician must be investigated. When a death is discovered to have occurred unattended by a physician, it is to be reported to a law enforcement officer who in turn is to notify the legal authorities exercising jurisdiction in the place where the body is found.

As of January 31, 1977, 15 states still did not require medical degrees of medical-legal officers mandated with responsibility for death investigation at the state and territorial level. On the other hand, 21 of the 41 state and territorial jurisdictions that require the medical examiner to be a licensed physician require in addition that the physician have training or experience in pathology and other medicolegal sciences.

Present instructions for filling out certificates provide that for reporting on deaths due to violence one of the following terms should be used: accident, suicide, homicide, undetermined, or pending investigation. If "pending investigation" is used, it should subsequently be changed to suicide, homicide, or accident when the mode has been determined; or, if after completing the investigation, the mode remains unknown, to "undetermined."

DISCONTINUITIES OF STATISTICS AND INCLUSIONS UNDER SUICIDE AND HOMICIDE

During 1900-1976, causes of death were classified according to 8 revisions of the International Classification of Diseases. These revisions are made about every 10 years to reflect progress in medical knowledge. The revision in use in the United States since 1968 is the *Eighth Revision of the International Classification of Diseases,* adapted for use in the United States, 1965—hereinafter denoted by ICDA.

These eight revisions did not result in severe discontinuity in mortality statistics for homicide. But considerable discontinuity was introduced for suicide by the Eighth Revision. The comparability ratio for suicide (ICDA Nos. E950-E959) between the Seventh and Eighth Revisions was 0.9472 (National Center for Health Statistics [NCHS], COMP. 8th/7th, 1975). About 31 percent of the 3059 deaths in the comparability study based on deaths in 1966 assigned by the Eighth Revision to the new category "injury undetermined whether accidentally or purposely inflicted" (ICDA Nos. E980-E989) had been assigned by the Seventh Revision to suicide. Despite the fact that about 5 percent fewer deaths were assigned to suicide by the Eighth Revision, the suicide rate continued to rise during 1967-1976, except for the year 1968, for which the rate (10.7 per 100,000) was about the same as that for 1967 (10.8 per 100,000).

The Eighth Revision specifies that deaths from suicide (category numbers E950-E959) include deaths from injuries in suicide and attempted suicide, and self-inflicted injuries specified as intentional. Deaths from homicide (category numbers E960-E969) are defined as injuries inflicted by another person with intent to injure or kill, by any means. The ICDA provides a distinct title for injuries due to legal intervention and operations of war. In the present report, however, the term "homicide" includes deaths due to legal intervention.

The Eighth Revision of the International Classification of Diseases provides that the title "legal intervention" (category numbers E970-E978) includes "injuries inflicted by the police or other law-enforcing agents, including military on duty, in the course of arresting or attempting to arrest lawbreakers, suppressing disturbances, maintaining order, and other legal action." The title also includes "legal execution," but excludes "injuries caused by civil insurrections," which are assigned to injury resulting from operations of war (ICDA Nos. E990-E999).

Throughout the century, deaths from legal intervention constituted only a small part of the total number of deaths attributed to homicide. For example, in 1976 there were 294 deaths attributed to legal intervention among a total of 19,260 homicides. Unless otherwise stated, the numbers and death rates shown are measures obtained by taking together both deaths resulting from legal intervention and other deaths resulting from injuries inflicted by another person with intent to injure or kill.

The definition of homicide in this report differs from that of "murder and nonnegligent manslaughter" used by the Uniform Crime Reporting Program of the Federal Bureau of Investigation (UCRP-FBI). For one thing, the assignment of a death to homicide in the vital-statistics system is based solely on the determination of the medical examiner or coroner

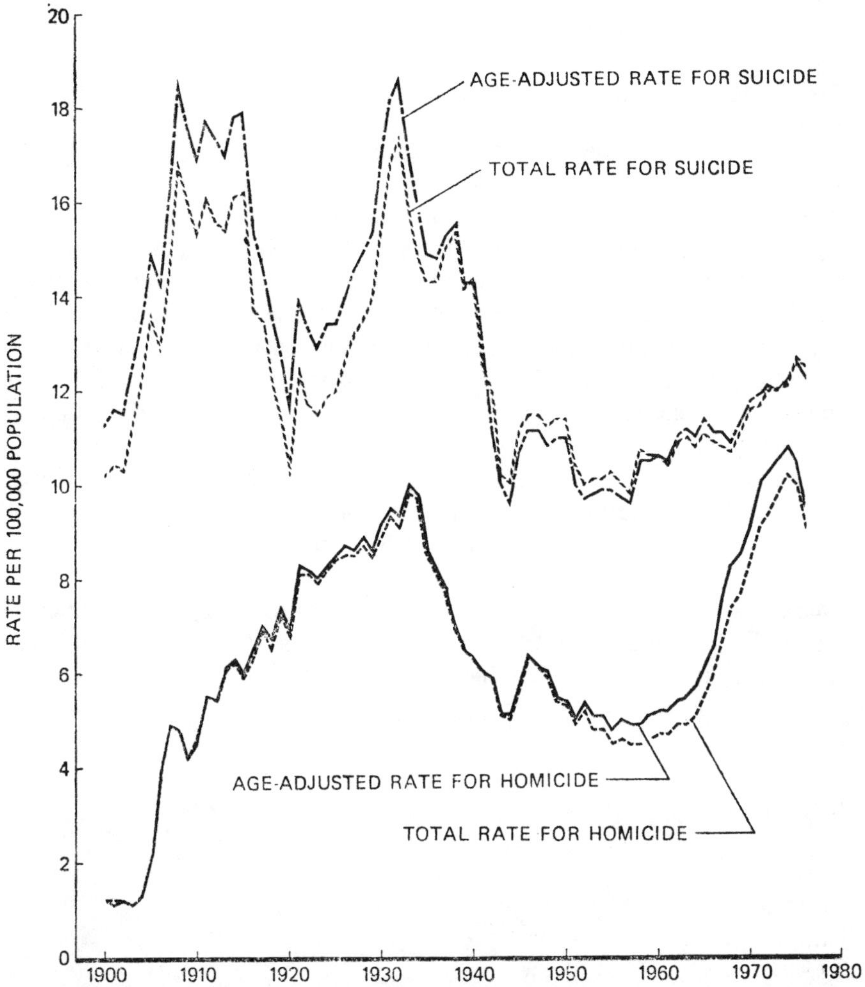

FIGURE 1. Death Rates for Suiucide and Homicide (Total and Age-adjusted): United States, 1900-76.

who completed the medical section of the death certificate, whereas the assignment by the UCRP-FBI is based solely on police investigation. Moreover, as noted above, justifiable homicide is included in this report under homicide, but is excluded by the UCRP-FBI under "murder and nonnegligent manslaughter."

PERSONAL PARTICULARS FROM THE DEATH CERTIFICATE

Present Magnitude of the Problem

In 1976, 26,832 men, women, and children ended their lives by self-inflicted injuries and an additional 19,260 lost their lives from injuries inflicted by another person or persons with intent to injure or kill. These figures give a suicide rate of 12.5 deaths per 100,000 population for 1976, and a homicide rate of 9.1 deaths per 100,000. Provisional data for 1977, based on a 10 percent sample of all deaths in the United States for that year, indicate that the suicide rate is still rising—reaching 13.4 suicides per 100,000 population for 1977. This is the highest suicide rate recorded for this nation since 1940, when the rate was 14.4 suicides per 100,000 (Figure 1).

The fluctuation in the homicide rate between 1973 and 1977 makes it unclear whether the direction of the rate for this cause is still upward, or whether it reached a peak in 1974 (with a rate of 10.2 per 100,000) and is now turning downward. In any event, the estimated rate for 1977 (9.7 homicides per 100,000) is higher than the rate for 1976 (9.1 homicides per 100,000), and the rates for the years in the period 1971-1977 are higher than those since 1933 (Figure 1).

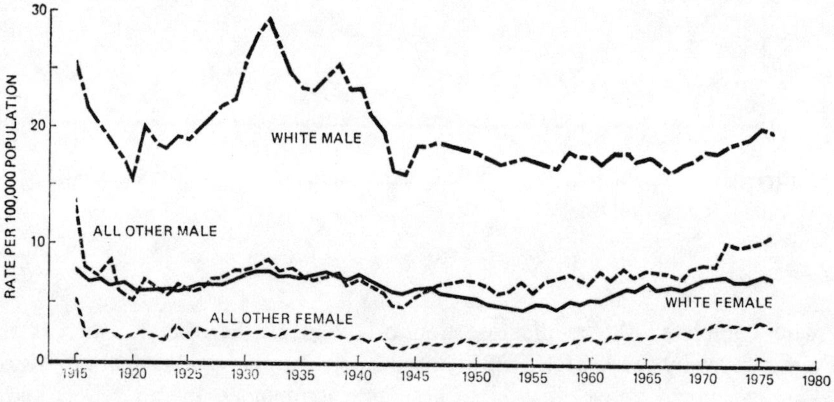

FIGURE 2. Suicide Rates, by Color and Sex: United States, 1915-76.

Trends by Color and Sex

Figures for the United States by race, age, and cause of death were tabulated for the first time for 1914. They are shown in this report for the white and all other racial groups for each year of the period 1915-1976. Throughout these years, the white male population had the highest death rate for suicide (Figure 2). Since World War II, the male population of races other than white has rates that are somewhat higher than those for the white female population, and considerably higher than those for the female population of races other than white.

In contrast, the male population of races other than white was relatively

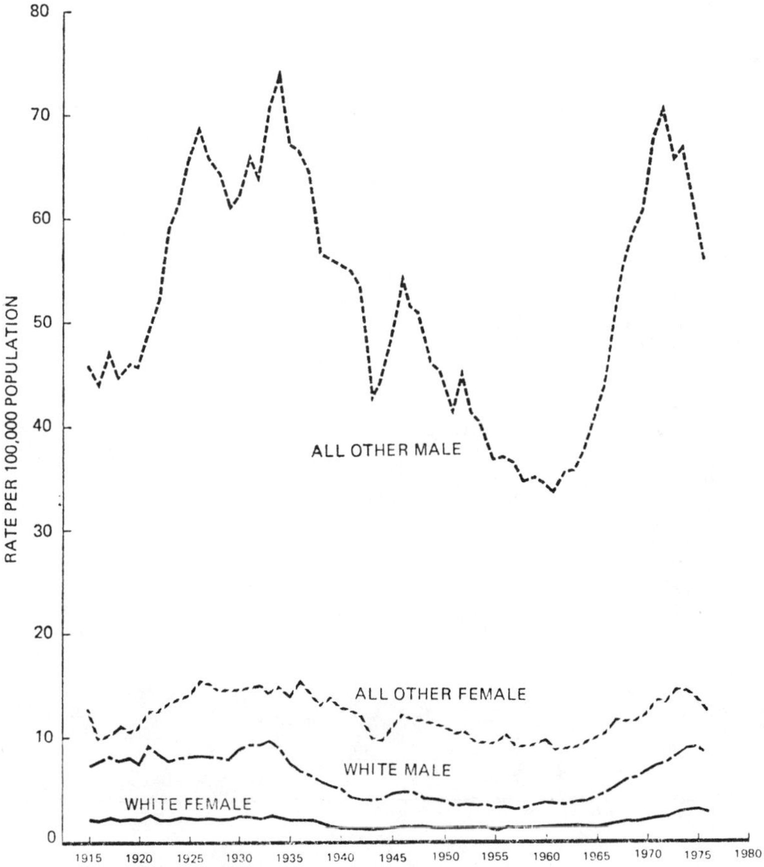

FIGURE 3. Homicide Rates, by Color and Sex: United States, 1915-76.

more frequently the victim of homicide than the other three color-sex groups (Figure 3). The sex differential in this rate increased in recent years for both the white and other populations as a result of the accelerated rise in the rates for both the white and all other male populations.

Age Patterns by Color and Sex

Patterns for white male population. Age-specific rates exhibit different patterns by color and sex (Figure 4). In 1976 the suicide rate for the white male population rose sharply from 1.3 at ages 10 to 14 years to 27.0 deaths

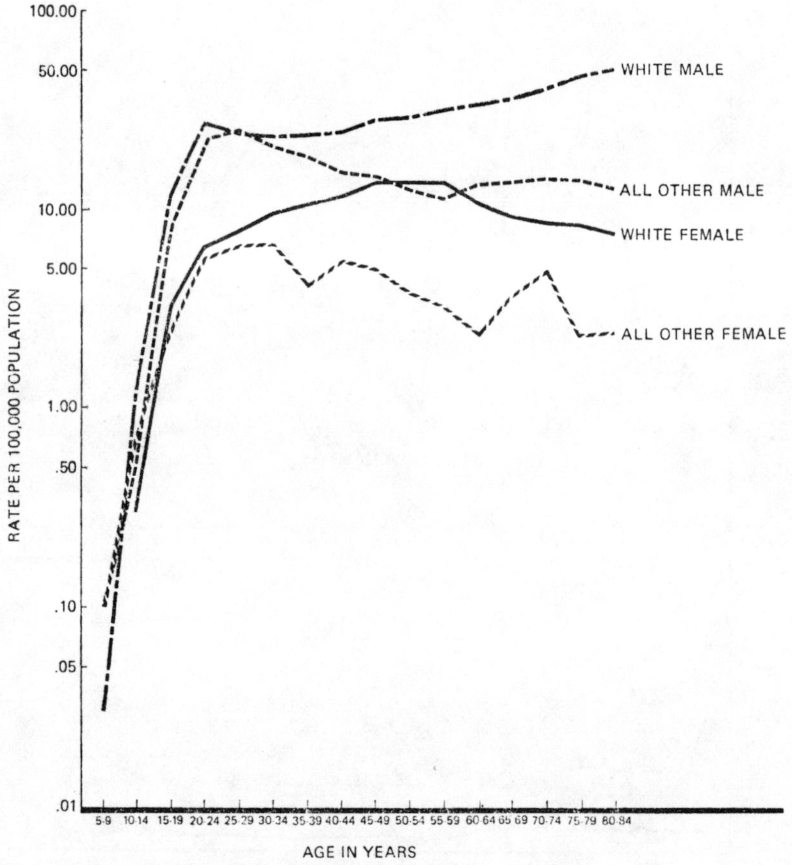

FIGURE 4. Suicide Rates, by Age, Color, and Sex: United States, 1976.

per 100,000 at ages 20 to 24 years. Then after falling to 23.1 at ages 30 to 34 years, the rate increased to 47.8 deaths per 100,000 at ages 80 to 84 years. The relative stability in the suicide rate for this group during the 27-year period 1950-1976 (with a death rate of 19.0 per 100,000 population for 1950 and a rate of 19.8 for 1976) results from the offsetting of substantial decreases in the death rate for white men 45 years of age and over by steady increases in the rate for those under 45. The decline in the suicide rate for older white men started in the mid-1930s, concomitant with the establishment of broad social security programs for the nation; the upturn in this rate for younger persons began about 1956.

For white male teenagers and young adults the suicide rate was in general downward between 1930 and 1955-56; but between 1955-56 and 1976 the rate for these young people more than doubled. Actually, at ages 15 to 19 years the rate more than tripled, rising from 3.9 in 1955 to 11.9 suicides per 100,000 for 1976. In 1976 alone, 1200 white boys and teenagers ages 10 to 19 years and 2268 white men ages 20 to 24 years committed suicide. For older white men the suicide rate was markedly downward between 1930 and 1976. For every 5-year age group in the span 50 to 75 years of age the suicide rate dropped 50 percent or more.

Age-specific homicide rates for the white male population show that for most years during 1930-1976 they had the highest death rate for this cause at ages 25 to 29 years. In fact, for 16 of the 17 years in the period 1960-1975, when homicide rates were rising most markedly, their rates at ages 25 to 29 years were higher than those for any other age group.

Although at an increasingly higher level, the shape of the age-specific mortality curve was about the same during 1960-1975 as during 1976—with a relatively high rate for infants, then a decline to a low for children at ages 5 to 9 years, followed by a sharp increase until the peak ages, usually 25 to 29 years, and finally a gradual decline with some fluctuation during the remainder of the life span (Figure 5). The age-specific mortality curves for the 1970s, however, are increasingly higher at both ends of the life span than are the curves for earlier years. This upturn reflects the increase in the number of victims among the most defenseless in our midst—infants and children, and older Americans. In 1976, 288 white male victims were under 15 years of age; 483 victims were 65 and older. Between 1960 and 1976, the victim rate more than doubled for white men at ages 75 to 79 years—from 2.5 to 6.0 deaths per 100,000.

Patterns for the white female population. The age-specific mortality curve for suicide for the white female population differs from that for the white male population (Figure 4). Instead of increasing gradually to the end of the life span after reaching a high rate in early adulthood, the curve for

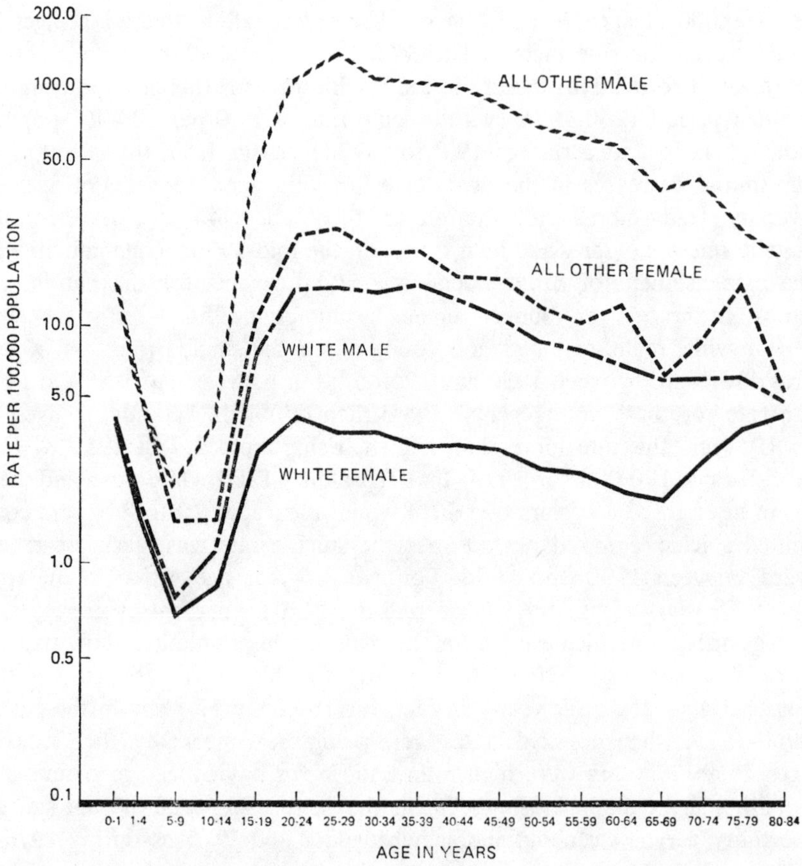

FIGURE 5. Homicide Rates, by Age, Color, and Sex: United States, 1976.

the white female population peaks during the middle years of life, and then turns downward with advancing age. For example, for 1976, the rate rose from 0.3 per 100,000 at ages 10 to 14 years to 13.7 at ages 45 to 49 years, and to 13.9 per 100,000 at ages 50 to 54 years. Then the rate declined to 7.4 per 100,000 for the group 80 to 84 years old. A similar relationship was observed for most years in the 1930-1975 period.

A study based on data for 1959-1961 shows that the suicide rate did not increase for any of the marital classes of white women with advance in age (NCHS, 1970). Instead, the death rate for this cause peaked at ages 45 to 54 years for married and widowed white women, and at ages 35 to 44 years for single and divorced white women, and then generally declined during the remainder of the life span.

As measured by standardized mortality ratios, for 1959-1961 suicide among divorced white women was about three times the level among married white women, and that among widowed white women was about 1.7 times the level among married white women. In this marital status study it was also found that the suicide rate for white men in each marital class was higher than the corresponding rate for white women, and that the rates for white women were higher than the rates for women of other races.

For every 5-year age group in the span 10 to 14 to 55 to 59 years, the suicide rate for white girls and women was higher for 1976 than for 1960; for every 5-year age group at ages 60 to 64 to 80 to 84 (except 70 to 74), the suicide rate for white women for 1976 was lower than that for 1960. This variation by age indicates that the moderateness of the increase in the total suicide rate for the white female population during 1960-1976 (from 5.3 for 1960 to only 7.2 per 100,000 for 1976) results from the offsetting of decreases in their rate at ages 60 years and over by substantial increases in the rate at ages under 60 years.

Age-specific homicide rates for the white female population show several shifts in pattern between 1930 and 1976. For the years 1930-1936 and 1970-1976 (except for 1971) white women had the highest death rate for this cause at ages 20 to 24 years. In the intervening years (1937-1969) their highest rates occurred at somewhat older ages.

The shape of the age-specific mortality curve for homicide for the white female population, although at an increasingly higher level, was about the same during 1970-1975 as during 1976. For 1976, the most vulnerable age groups (under one year of age, with a rate of 4.0 deaths per 100,000, and 80 to 84 years, with a rate of 4.1 deaths per 100,000) are the victims of homicide at about the same rate as are white women at ages 20 to 24 years (with a rate of 4.2 deaths per 100,000). In 1976, 233 white female victims were under 15 years of age; 356 were 65 years and older. Between 1960 and 1976 the victim rate more than quadrupled for white women at ages 80 to 84 years—from 1.0 to 4.1 per 100,000.

Patterns for the male population of races other than white. In 1976 the suicide rate for this group rose from 0.1 at ages 10 to 14 years to 24.4 deaths per 100,000 at ages 25 to 29 years, a rate for this age group that was even higher than the corresponding rate for white men (24.1 deaths per 100,000). Then after the rate for these men fell at ages 55 to 59 years to 11.2 per 100,000, it rose again and remained above 13 per 100,000 for every 5-year age group in the span 60-64 to 75-79 years.

The marked upturn in the total suicide rate for the male population of races other than white between 1960 and 1976 (from 6.1 to 11.0 deaths per 100,000) reflects increases in suicide for almost every age group, but the greatest increases were for young men. The rate rose rapidly between 1960 and 1976 for the age groups 20 to 24 years, 25 to 29 years, and 30 to 34 years, with the greatest absolute increase in the rate for the age group 25 to 29 years. At these ages, the rate almost tripled, rising from 8.4 for 1955 to 24.4 per 100,000 for 1976.

In 1976 the homicide rate for men other than white at ages 25 to 29 years (132.7 deaths per 100,000 population) was 9.2 times the corresponding rate for white men (14.5 deaths per 100,000) (Figure 5). The color differential in the homicide rate for men at these ages has been even larger in the past. In 1966 this ratio was 11.7; in 1956, 15.1.

The shape of the age-specific mortality curve for homicide for this group, although at an increasingly higher level, was also about the same during 1960-1975 as during 1976—with a very high rate for infants (14.7 per 100,000 in 1976), a decline to a low for children at ages 5 to 9 years, followed by a marked increase until the peak at ages 25 to 29 years (except for 1961 and 1962 when the peak ages were 30 to 34 years), and then a decline with some fluctuation during the remaining years.

The victim rate for male infants of this group increased from 10.1 for 1960 to 14.7 per 100,000 for 1976. This rate for 1976 was 5.1 times the corresponding rate for white male infants. During the 10 years 1967-1976, the number of homicide victims among all other male children was 336 at ages under 1 year, 583 at ages 1 to 4 years, and 966 at ages 5 to 14 years. Thus, 1885 children under 15 years of age lost their lives through homicide during 1967-1976. During this period 2360 men 65 years and older were the victims of homicide.

Patterns for the female population of races other than white. There is some fluctuation in the age-specific mortality curve for suicide for this group (Figure 4). A review of these curves for 1960-1976 shows clearly, however, that in early childhood their suicide experience is about the same as that of their male counterparts. After ages 10 to 14, their suicide rate remains much lower than the male rate. One characteristic of the suicide curves for this group that does not appear in the curves for the white female population is the upturn at older ages.

The 1976 suicide rate was higher than that for 1960 for every 5-year age group in the span 10 to 50 years, and lower than that for 1960 for every 5-year age group in the span 50 to 65 years. But for the age groups

70 to 74 and 75 to 79 years, the rate for 1976 was higher than that for 1960.

Age-specific homicide rates for this group show little change over the years in the age range for their highest rates. Throughout 1930-1976, peak rates usually occurred at ages 25 to 29 or 30 to 34 years. For almost every age group their homicide rate was higher for 1976 than for 1960. Large increases in the rate have occurred for older women. For example, their rate at ages 70 to 74 years increased from 1.7 for 1960 to 8.3 per 100,000 for 1976; their rate at ages 75 to 79 years increased from 2.6 for 1960 to 14.4 for 1976.

The number of victims of homicide among the female population of races other than white during 1960-1976 totaled 1365 at ages under 15 years, and 665 at ages 65 years and over.

YEAR, MONTH, AND DAY OF DEATH

Times of Crisis for the Nation

The peaks and low points in the mortality curves for suicide and homicide during 1900-1976 divide the curves into the following 5 sections: the 1900 to 1915 upturn in the rates for both suicide and homicide; the brief 1915 to 1920 downturn in the suicide rate and continuing upturn in the homicide rate; the 1921 to 1932-33 upturn in both rates; the 1932-33 to 1957 downturn in both rates—with one interruption related to the more than 7 million men who served overseas during World War II; and the 1957 to 1977 upturn in both rates, with the rate for 1977 based on provisional figures (Figure 1).

Both the suicide and homicide rates rose swiftly during 1900-1914. During this decade and a half many Americans were fearful of the challenge to democracy by the misery of millions of its people. Woodrow Wilson in his inaugural address of 1912 said:

> . . . We have been proud of our industrial achievements, but we have not hitherto stopped thoughtfully enough to count the cost, the cost of lives snuffed out, of energies overtaxed and broken, the fearful physical and spiritual cost to the men and women and children upon whom the dead weight and burden of it all has fallen pitilessly the years through . . .

During these years, 1900-1914, millions were plunged into actual want; unemployment and child labor went hand in hand; industrial accidents from unsafe working conditions soared; the treatment of the aged, the poor, the incapacitated, the defective, the insane, the criminal, and prostitutes was frightful. Lynching of Negroes continued in all its ferocity (Morrison and Commager, 1951).

The upheavals in the world in the next 5 years seem to have had a marked downward effect on the total suicide rate in the United States, which fell from 16.2 for 1915 to 10.2 for 1920. The drop in the suicide rate for the white male population was even more pronounced; it plunged from 24.8 per 100,000 for 1915 to 15.4 for 1920. But the total homicide rate appears to have been little affected by these world-shaking events, primarily because the high homicide rate for males of races other than white failed to decrease (45.4 per 100,000 in 1915 and 45.9 in 1920). Part of this persistent high level in their homicide rate during 1915-1920 is artifactual—resulting from the admission to the death registration area of states whose homicide rates were higher than the rate for the states already in the area (Table 2). Among the states admitted between 1915 and 1920, whose rates continued through 1976 to be higher than that for the nation as a whole were South Carolina, North Carolina, Tennessee, Illinois, Louisiana, Florida, and Mississippi.

In August 1914, Germany declared war on Russia and then on France. Great Britain declared war on Germany three days later. But it was not until April 6, 1917, that the Congress of the United States declared war on the German Empire. In the meantime American neutrality afforded the profits of war without the sacrifices and taxation that participation would have demanded. The nation enjoyed unprecedented prosperity—with many new millionaires and prosperous workers.

During the 19 months the United States participated in World War I, 2,086,000 men were sent overseas. Of these, 50,000 died in battle and 206,000 were wounded. The impact on the suicide and homicide rates of the removal of these men (mostly young) to the battleground overseas is discernible in the fall in the total rates for these causes between 1917 and 1918. The suicide rate fell from 13.0 to 12.3 deaths per 100,000 and the homicide rate fell from 6.9 to 6.5 per 100,000. The homicide rate for the white male population fell 6.1 percent (from 8.2 to 7.7 per 100,000), and that for the male population of races other than white 5.5 percent (from 47.2 in 1917 to 44.6 per 100,000 in 1918) (Figures 2 and 3).

Between 1921 and 1932-33, both the suicide and homicide rates again climbed swiftly upward. This was the period in which the nation experienced the terrible aftermath of World War I. Debts and disappointments harassed both the government and the people. The farmer's purchasing power was severely reduced. Unemployment kept spiraling upward. Much of the wealth generated during World War I had gone to the privileged few.

Between 1923 and 1928 the index of wages rose only from 100 to 112, while the index of speculative profits went from 100 to 410. The stock market crash came in October, 1929. By 1930 there were about 3 million unemployed, and by 1933 this number had grown to an estimated 12 to 15 million.

The difficulties encountered in the unsuccessful attempt to enforce the Eighteenth Amendment undoubtedly accounts for some of the rise in homicides as the gang wars escalated for control of the illicit liquor market. But white men, who were most frequently involved in the gang wars, continued to have a much lower rate than men of other races.

Then came long downturns in homicide and suicide rates between 1932-33 to 1957. These downturns lasted throughout the years of recovery from the Depression, through World War II, and through the postwar baby boom that ended in 1957. During the early years of this period the Social Security Act and other legislation brought relief to the unemployed victims of the Depression and to farmers and labor.

Part of the explanation for the precipitous drop in the number of suicides and homicides between 1941 and 1945 is that about seven million men were serving overseas. As mentioned, any suicides or homicides that may have occurred among these men while stationed abroad are not included in the statistics in this report. Most of these men were in the age groups 20 to 24 and 25 to 29 years, when the risk of homicide is highest. In 1944 white men in this country at ages 25 to 34 already had a suicide rate of 14.0 per 100,000, and all other men a rate of 6.1 per 100,000.

The ongoing upturn in suicide and homicide rates that began in 1957 may still be too much with us to assess the impact of all recent events on these rates. But there can be little doubt that the growing divorce rate—over one million a year for the past several years—the struggle for civil rights, the Vietnam war, high unemployment, and the growing drug culture all were factors in the upturn in suicide and homicide rates.

In addition, this country did not prepare for the new citizens born in the baby boom. When these children reached school age, many of them were put into overcrowded and poorly taught classes. Now between the ages of 21 and 35, many of them cannot find employment because they do not have the skills needed in the labor force. All about us we see society reaping the whirlwind from this lack of preparation, but it is possible that the young people born into the period are suffering most of all.

White men who were 15 to 24 years of age in 1976 had suicide and homicides rates in that year (19.2 and 10.6 per 100,000) that were more than double the corresponding rates for white men at these ages in 1957 (6.5 and 3.9 per 100,000). The absolute increase in the homicide rate for

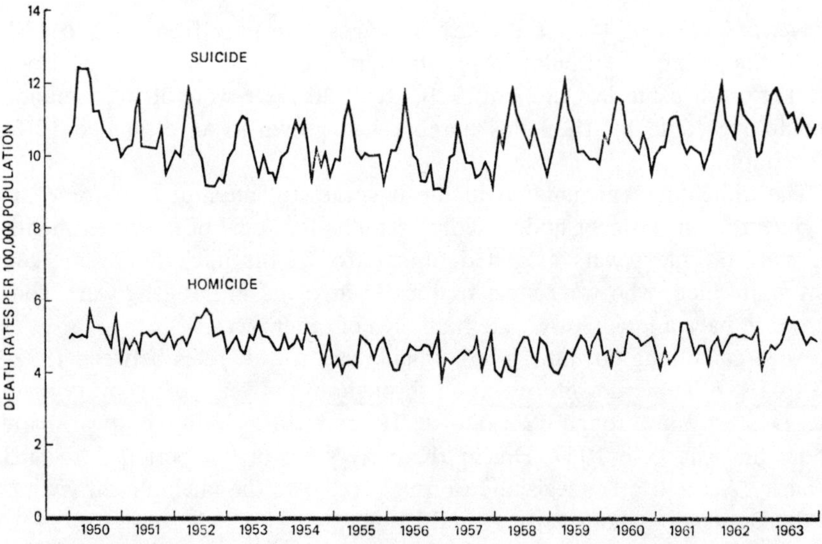

FIGURE 6. Death Rates for Suicide and Homicide, by Month: United States, 1950-63.

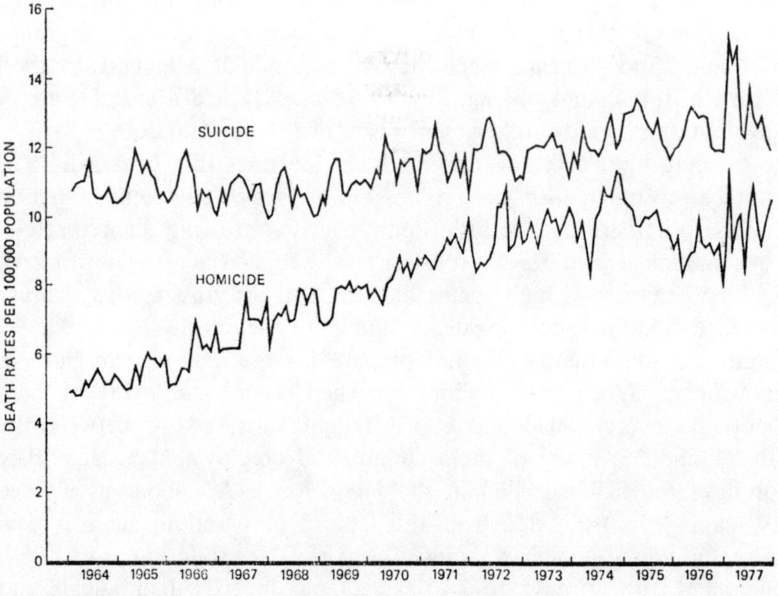

FIGURE 7. Death Rates for Suicide and Homicide, by Month: United States, 1964-77.

all other men at ages 15 to 24 between 1957 and 1976 was even greater—from 45.8 to 70.2 per 100,000; their suicide rate more than doubled, increasing from 5.6 for 1957 to 14.7 per 100,000 for 1976.

White men who were 25 to 34 years old in 1976 also experienced much higher suicide and homicide rates than did the white men at these ages in 1957. The suicide rate for men at these ages increased from 12.7 for 1957 to 23.7 per 100,000 for 1976 and their homicide rate from 5.6 to 14.2 per 100,000. Again the homicide death rate at ages 25 to 34 for their male counterparts of other races had an even greater absolute increase—from 86.7 for 1957 to 122.3 per 100,000 for 1976. The suicide rate at these ages for these men increased from 13.0 for 1957 to 22.8 per 100,000 for 1976.

Times of Crisis for the Individual

Superimposed on these great fluctuations in the suicide and homicide rates during 1900-1976 are seasonal patterns that persisted for the periods in which the rates were rising and for periods in which they were falling (Figures 6 and 7).

The National Center for Health Statistics and its predecessor offices have computed suicide and homicide rates on an annual basis for each month in the period 1933-1976. Almost without exception the suicide rate peaks in the spring—usually in April—and falls in the winter; the homicide rate peaks in the summer, and most often falls in the winter.

These results must be interpreted with care. Perhaps the increase in homicide in summer is not associated with the warm temperature itself, but with the fact that people spend more time outdoors and thereby increase their risk of being victimized.

Tabulations by the National Center for Health Statistics of the average number of suicides and homicides per day for days of the week for each year of 1974-1976 show an increase in suicides on Monday and an increase in homicides on Saturday (Tables 3 and 4).

SUMMARY

The United States now has mortality data for suicide and homicide for the expanding death registration states for each year in the period 1900-1932, and for the entire United States for each year beginning with 1933.

Over the years these data have been useful to health planners and other research workers who need an overall view of mortality from these causes and are interested in identifying, not individuals, but subgroups of the population at high risk from violence. The reason these data do not serve those

Table 3

Average Number of Suicides per Day for Days of Week: United States, 1974-1976*

Day of week	1976	1975	1974
All days**	73	74	70
Sunday†	72	72	70
Monday†	78	78	76
Tuesday†	75	75	72
Wednesday†	72	75	71
Thursday†	73	74	68
Friday†	73	73	69
Saturday†	72	72	66

* Deaths are those assigned to category numbers E950-E959 of *Eighth Revision of the International Classification of Diseases, Adapted for Use in the United States,* adopted 1965. Deaths include those of nonresidents of United States.
** Number of homicides in specified year divided by number of days in year.
† Number of homicides on specified day of week in specified year divided by number of times specified day of week occurred in specified year.

Table 4

Average Number of Homicides per Day for Days of Week: United States, 1974-1976*

Day of week	1976	1975	1974
All days†	54	58	59
Sunday†	65	69	71
Monday†	48	50	52
Tuesday†	43	48	52
Wednesday†	43	50	45
Thursday†	48	50	49
Friday†	53	60	58
Saturday†	74	82	84

* Deaths are those assigned to category numbers E960-E978 of *Eighth Revision of the International Classification of Diseases, Adapted for Use in the United States,* adopted 1965. Deaths include those of nonresidents of United States.
** Number of homicides in specified year divided by number of days in year.
† Number of homicides on specified day of week in specified year divided by number of times specified day of week occurred in specified year.

who want to investigate violent deaths as products of individual pathology is that the National Center for Health Statistics is required by laws and regulations to maintain the confidentiality of the death records.

Already the vital statistics system has been in existence long enough to serve an additional group of program planners and researchers in the country—namely, that group who believes that violent behavior is a product not only of individual pathology but of social pathology (Cloward and Ohlin, 1960). The value of the data for them will increase with the passage of time.

The data for the first 77 years for which annual tabulations of deaths have been made show the closeness with which the upturns in suicide and homicide rates throughout the century have paralleled the upturns in great national distress (with rises in unemployment, racial hostility, inhuman use of the labor force, unconcern for the weak and aged, etc.), and the closeness with which the downturns in the rates have paralleled the periods of national prosperity and humaneness (with provisions for some financial security for old age, unemployment and illness, fair labor practices, lessening of racial tension, etc.).

The trends make clear that in both good and bad years for the nation, more individuals commit suicide in the spring than in any other season, on Monday than on any other day of the week, and that the suicide rate for white women constantly peaks during the middle years of life—at ages 45 to 49 and 50 to 54.

The data also reveal a new homicide pattern, the slaying of the most vulnerable people in our society. The victim rate for white women at ages 80 to 84 years quadrupled between 1960 and 1976. Among the white male population the number of victims during this period totalled 288 for children under age 15 and 483 for white men 65 and older. The homicide rate for male infants of races other than white increased from 10.1 for 1960 to 14.7 por 1976, in which year the rate was more than 5 times the corresponding rate for white male infants. In this same period 2360 older men and 665 older women of races other than white were victims of homicide.

An examination of the suicide trends also focuses on a number of disturbing new components, especially for young people who were born in the baby boom of 1943-1957. The 1976 suicide rate for men of races other than white at ages 25 to 29 (24.4 per 100,000) was almost three times the corresponding rate for men at these ages in 1955 (8.4 per 100,000). The rate for white male teenagers more than tripled between 1955 and 1976, in which year 1200 white boys and teenagers 10 to 19 years of age and 2268 white men at ages 20 to 24 committed suicide.

On the other hand, the examination of suicide trends reveals the one bright pattern that has emerged in this whole picture of violence—the downturn in the suicide rate for older people that began in the 1930s, concomitant with establishment of broad social security programs. This downturn in suicide for older people continued through the long upturn in suicide for other age groups, and in homicide for all age groups that began in the latter part of the 1950s.

REFERENCES

CLOWARD, R. A., and OHLIN, L. E. *Delinquency and Opportunity: A Theory of Delinquent Gangs.* Free Press, New York, 1960.

National Center for Health Statistics. *Mortality from Selected Causes by Marital Status, United States,* Part A. Vital and Health Statistics—Series 20, no. 8a. U.S. Government Printing Office, Washington, D.C., 1970.

National Center for Health Statistics. *Comparability of Mortality Statistics for the Seventh and Eighth Revisions of the International Classification of Diseases, United States.* Vital and Health Statistics—Series 2, no. 66. U.S. Government Printing Office, Washington, D.C., 1975.

MORRISON, S. E., and COMMAGER, H. S. *The Growth of the American Republic,* vol. 2, 4th ed. Oxford University Press, New York, 1951.

U.S. Bureau of the Census. *Mortality Statistics, 1900 to 1904.* U.S. Government Printing Office, Washington, D.C., 1906.

U.S. Bureau of the Census. Estimates of the population of the United States, by age, sex, and race: July 1, 1974 to July 1, 1976. *Current Population Reports,* Series P-25, no. 643. U.S. Government Printing Office, Washington, D.C., 1977.

U.S. Department of Health, Education, and Welfare, Health Services Administration. *Death Investigation: An Analysis of Laws and Policies of the United States, Each State and Jurisdiction* (as of January 31, 1977). DHEW Publication No. (HSA) 78-5252. U.S. Government Printing Office, Washington, D.C., 1978.

Part II

MEASUREMENT AND PREDICTION OF VIOLENCE

CHAPTER 10

Dangerousness: Conceptual, Prediction and Public Policy Issues

SALEEM A. SHAH

My concern here is with some issues pertaining to the phenomena of dangerous behaviors. And, although such behaviors may be directed at oneself as well as at others, this discussion will deal only with behaviors that are dangerous to others.

Acts that threaten and actually inflict serious harm on the lives and physical welfare of other members of a community have been of long-standing concern to all societies. Clearly, the criminal justice system is not the only system in our society concerned with the regulation and control of dangerous behaviors; the mental health, health, social welfare, and other systems are also involved in various ways and to varying degrees. This discussion will focus upon a number of issues and problems as they pertain to and have major implications for criminal justice and mental health systems, as well as for other social agencies and institutions.

After defining the term "dangerousness," I shall focus on some important considerations about how behavior should be conceptualized. This will lead to a discussion of controversies and dilemmas dealing with the prediction of dangerousness. Finally, I will address some questions and problems pertaining to public policies concerned with the handling of dangerous and violent behaviors in our society.

The topic of "dangerousness" seems often to be associated with strong beliefs and ideologies and, understandably, such feelings and explicit or implicit value systems tend very much to influence how we define and study such phenomena and also how we wish to deal with them. It seems desirable, at least initially, to distinguish certain essentially empirical and technical questions from the normative, ideological, and policy concerns that also have to be considered.

I am using the word dangerousness despite my awareness of certain problems associated with the term. Certainly it is a rather vague term and one which is often used with numerous different meanings. Another problem is that the term seems to imply that there is a trait of dangerousness that constitutes a relatively enduring and stable characteristic of persons so designated. But, as I will indicate later in discussing some conceptual issues, this particular connotation of the term (as necessarily suggesting an enduring characteristic) requires clarification and correction. Despite such problems, however, there are two main reasons why I still prefer to use the term "dangerousness." First, the term is widely used in both criminal and civil law and thus has broad reference and recognition. Second, "dangerousness" serves better to illustrate a broad range of programmatic and policy concerns than do terms like aggression and violence.

DEFINITION

As used here, *dangerousness* refers to a propensity, i.e., an increased probability as compared to others, to engage in dangerous behavior. *Dangerous behaviors* refer to acts that are characterized by the application or overt threat of force and are likely to result in injury to other persons. This definition also applies to the term violent behaviors. Thus, as used here, dangerous behaviors are considered to be synonymous with violent behaviors.

Acts that commonly are defined as *crimes of violence* exemplify the behaviors of major concern; the core offenses of concern to the criminal law are probably represented in the Uniform Crime Reports (UCR) of the FBI (Webster, 1978). The category of violent crimes includes murder, aggravated assault, rape, and robbery. Along with these major offense categories would also be included the so-called inchoate crimes or attempts.

Of course, one could go well beyond this category of violent crimes and include such other criminal acts as assault and battery, arson, kidnapping, extortion, and other offenses (Goldstein and Katz, 1960). The range of dangerous acts to be included under formal legal and other societal responses is basically a matter of public policy that is determined by the political processes of a society. And, as I shall discuss later, considerations of values and power are inextricably involved in the political process and in matters affecting public policy.

An individual's dangerousness is considered at many decision points in the criminal justice and mental health systems. Indeed, with respect to the mental health system, there has been a marked increase in the past few years in the number of jurisdictions that have begun to use the criterion of dangerousness (and/or the closely related notion of "likelihood of serious harm") for purposes of involuntary commitment of the mentally ill. A survey of civil commitment statutes published in the *Harvard Law Review* (1974) indicated that only four state laws were explicity phrased in terms of "dangerousness" as a commitment criterion, and ten laws used the criterion of "likelihood of serious harm." A survey done as of September, 1977 (Schwitzgebel, 1978), indicates, however, that fully 20 commitment laws included the "dangerousness" criterion, either alone or in conjunction with other criteria, and the phrase "likelihood of serious harm" was used in 28.

Following is a list of some decision points that involve considerations of an individual's dangerousness:

1. Decisions concerning the granting of bail (or release on personal recognizance) to persons accused of crimes, and the level at which bail is to be set.
2. Decisions concerning the waiver of juveniles charged with serious crimes to adult courts.
3. Sentencing decisions following criminal convictions, including those about release on conditions of probation.
4. Decisions pertaining to work-release and furlough programs for incarcerated offenders.
5. Parole and other conditional release decisions for offenders.
6. Decisions pertaining to removal of a child from the home in cases of child abuse or battery.
7. Decisions pertaining to the commitment and release of persons handled via a number of quasicriminal statutes concerned with "sexual psychopaths," "sexually dangerous persons," "mentally disordered sex offenders," and the like.
8. For criminal defendants who have been civilly committed after adjudication as incompetent to stand trial or as not guilty by reason of insanity and who have been sent to maximum security hospitals or units, a transfer to a nonsecurity unit is based on

a determination that the individuals are not "manifestly dangerous."[1]

9. Decisions regarding the special handling (including transfer to special prisons) of offenders who are disruptive and dangerous in regular penal settings.
10. Decisions regarding the transfer to security hospitals of mental patients found to be too difficult or dangerous to be handled in regular civil hospitals.
11. Commitment of drug addicts because of fears that they will commit violent crimes to support their drug habits.
12. Decisions concerning the emergency and longer-term involuntary commitment of mentally ill persons considered to pose a "danger to self or others."
13. Decisions concerning the "conditional" and "unconditional" release of involuntarily confined mental patients.
14. Decisions concerning the hospitalization (on grounds of continuing mental disorder and dangerousness) of criminal defendants acquitted by reason of insanity.
15. Decisions concerning the invocation of special legal proceedings or sentencing provisions for "habitual" and "dangerous" offenders.
16. Decisions concerning the likelihood of continued dangerousness of persons convicted of capital crimes as a basis for determinations regarding the imposition of the death penalty.[2]

Despite the serious consequences that may follow for persons officially designated as dangerous, it is astonishing to note the frequent absence of clear and specific definitions and criteria as bases for the key terms in relevant laws. Moreover, even though "dangerousness" as used in various laws and regulations is clearly a *legal* term that requires determinations by courts and other designated triers of fact, often such crucial determinations actually tend to be made by various mental health experts. This situation has been critiziced with regard to the apparent arrogation by psychiatrists and other mental health professionals of roles and determinations that are fundamentally legal. In fairness it must be noted, however, that the problem is much more a reflection of judicial default than of the arrogance of mental health experts (Shah, 1974).

---

[1] Texas Code of Criminal Procedure (1975), Art. 46.02, Sec. 608; Art. 46.03, Sec. 8.

[2] Texas Code of Criminal Procedure (1975), Art. 37.071, "Procedure in capital case." Section (b) refers to three issues that the jury has to address; subsection 2 requires a determination "whether there is a probability that the defendant would commit criminal acts of violence that would constitute a continuing threat to society."

SOME CONCEPTUAL ISSUES

A major consideration in efforts to assess, predict, prevent, and change dangerous behavior pertains to the manner in which behavior is conceptualized. Behavior—whether defined as dangerous, friendly, constructive, or antisocial—is often viewed as stemming largely if not entirely from within the person, that is, as being a stable and fairly consistent characteristic of the person. In a traditional trait perspective, behavior is viewed as being determined largely by the individual's personality.

The trait model of behavior seems to have been a dominant force in personality research, theory, and clinical practice. According to the classic personality-trait model, traits were considered to be the prime determinants of behavior and helped to explain the apparent consistencies of behavior over time and in different situations. And, even though the trait model recognizes the impact of situational factors, there has tended to be an assumption that persons described as "friendly," or "dependable," or "honest," or "aggressive" tend to display such behaviors across a variety of situations. That is, such personality traits are believed to reflect fairly general and enduring personality and behavioral characteristics (Endler and Magnusson, 1976). In contrast to such notions of personality traits, more recent uses of the trait concept indicate only that there are indeed individual differences in certain personality and behavioral characteristics, that such differences are often quite stable over time and across settings, that individuals do have certain stylistic consistencies in interpersonal behaviors, and also discernibly different probabilities of displaying certain behaviors (Gough, 1969; Hogan et al., 1977).

Psychodynamic theories of personality are much like the trait model in that they also assume a basic personality core which is believed to serve as a predispositional base for behavior in various situations. In the stress upon person-related factors as major determinants of behavior, the psychodynamic model is analogous to the traditional trait model (Endler and Magnusson, 1976).

In contrast, a *situation-focused* model places much emphasis on external stimuli and variables in the setting and situation as the basic determinants of individual behavior. Although recognizing individual differences, *situationism* is basically a stimulus-response (S-R) approach that focuses major attention on the stimulus factors that influence subsequent responses (Endler and Magnusson, 1976). The weakness of this model is that it tends to ignore, or at least underemphasize, person-related consistencies in interpersonal behaviors.

Much theoretical and empirical work has been done in recent years with respect to an *interactional* model of behavior. This model emphasizes the importance of person-situation interactions in efforts to understand both personality and behavior. The view is that behavior involves an indispensable and continuous interaction between individuals and the various situations they encounter (Shah, 1966). As Endler and Magnusson (1976) recently noted:

> Not only is the individual's behavior influenced by significant features of the situations he or she encounters, but the person also selects the situations in which he or she performs, and subsequently affects the character of these situations (p. 958).

During the past decade the interactionist perspective has gained many followers in the field of personality and social psychology. After some earlier debates among those emphasizing person-related and others emphasizing situation-related factors, the accumulating empirical evidence has demonstrated rather clearly that individual-situation interactions are much more helpful in understanding and predicting behavior than either set of variables alone (Endler and Magnusson, 1976). Thus, the field has moved ahead and there is now general recognition that questions about the relative importance of one or the other set of factors are futile—both are unquestionably important, especially the particular ways in which they interact (Bowers, 1973; Bem and Allen, 1974; Ekehammer, 1974; Mischel, 1973, 1977; Moos, 1969, 1973).

The available evidence does not imply, however, that different persons will not indeed act differently and also with some degree of consistency across situations and with some stability over time. Rather, the evidence strongly indicates that particular classes of settings and situations must be taken into account far more carefully than they have in the past (Mischel, 1973). Just as individuals vary in range and types of behaviors likely in particular situations and also across situations, social settings of life also vary in the degree to which they prescribe and limit the range of expected and acceptable behaviors for persons in particular roles and situations. Mischel (1973), for example, described a number of cognitive social-learning person-related variables that help in understanding how the individual will tend to perceive, construct, and respond to various environmental situations. Similarly, Bowers (1973) points out that ". . . situations are as much a function of the person as the person's behavior is a function of the situation" (p. 327). Pervin (1977) notes that personality is coming to be seen as expressing both stability and change, and that it is the *pattern* of stability and change in relation to specific situations that needs to be better understood.

The point was demonstrated by J. Douglas Grant and Hans Toch (Toch, 1969) in a study of violence-prone men. The study involved 128 men (police officers, men who had assaulted police officers, prison inmates, and parolees) who had shown patterns of repeated violent encounters. Attention was focused on the chain of interactions between aggressors and victims and on the sequential developments as the encounters resulting in violence unfolded. As Toch points out: ". . . consistencies in a person's approach to others can produce situations in which violence always results —sometimes without the person being aware of the fact that he is the instigator of destructive (or self-destructive) games" (p. 6).

From detailed interviews with aggressors and their victims, as well as intensive study of relevant reports of the violent incidents, Toch developed a ten-category typology of violence-prone men. These categories were given rather descriptive titles such as "rep defending," "norm enforcing," "self-image defending," and "self-image promoting."

> The *rep defending* . . . person commits violence because his social position, physical size, or group status obligates him to do so—a matter of 'noblesse oblige,' so to speak. This sort of person is expected to have violent involvements, and he has therefore come to expect the same himself; he is aware of his role and of the need to defend it or to sustain it or to live by it (Toch, 1969: p. 149).

> A *self-image promoter* is a man who works hard at manufacturing the impression that he is not to be trifled with—that he is formidable and fearless. He goes out of his way to make sure that people understand how important he is and how important it is to him that he is important (p. 137).

Toch's study of violence-prone men provides a vivid illustration of the point that some individuals have rather consistent interpersonal orientations and styles which enable them to perceive, construct, and respond to a variety of interpersonal situations in a manner that produces high probabilities of violent interactions. These individuals respond aggressively to certain interpersonal stimuli which arouse no such response from other individuals. In a very real sense, therefore, such "violence-prone" individuals manage to *create* their own situations with minimal external cues or provocation.

The foregoing conceptual issues with regard to personality and behavior have been discussed at some length because the implicit or explicit conceptualization that one uses has implications for the manner in which the tasks of assessment, prediction, and handling of dangerous behaviors will be approached. Thus, traditional practice (following trait and psychodynamic perspectives) is to focus attention primarily on the individual's major personality and behavioral traits and inferred psychodynamics. Relatively little attention seems to be focused on the particular setting and situational factors, and on the pattern of individual-specific interactions which may differentially affect the occurrence of certain behaviors of concern. It is essential, however, that greater attention be focused on the particular setting and situational conditions which have in the past and are likely in the future to elicit, provoke, and maintain certain violent, criminal, and other related behaviors. More attention also needs to be paid to social settings and contexts in the community in which the person will live; similarly, assessments of likely functioning and problems must consider the availability and nature of supportive, stressful, and other relevant factors likely to affect the person's functioning in the community. It has been shown, for example, that accurate predictions of posthospital adjustment of mental patients in the community hinged on knowledge of the environment in which the ex-patients would be living, the availability of jobs, family and related support systems—rather than on any measured characteristic of the individual's personality or his in-hospital behavior (Fairweather, 1967; Fairweather et al., 1974).

SOME ISSUES PERTAINING TO PREDICTIONS OF DANGEROUSNESS

Earlier in this chapter the term dangerousness was defined as referring to a propensity (i.e., an *increased probability* as compared to others) to engage in dangerous or violent behavior. The words emphasized above indicate that what is to be predicted is the *probability* that certain persons are likely to engage in violent behaviors. Such predictions need to be distinguished from those in which some specific dangerous or violent behavior is to be predicted, for example, that Mr. Smith is very likely in the next 12 months to commit an armed robbery or a rape.

Given the admittedly vague and overly broad uses—and misuses—of the term "dangerousness," it has often been suggested that what should be predicted is the specific dangerous behavior and not some vague propensity. Such a view is common and understandable. To require mental health professionals and others to make definite predictions of some specific behaviors reduces the opportunity for them to encompass their own particularistic notions of what constitute harmful and violent acts under the term "dangerousness." There is much evidence that for a variety of reasons, and especially when dealing with behaviors that have very low frequency of occurrence (i.e., low base rates), mental health professionals display poor predictive accuracy and tend to markedly overpredict dangerousness (Steadman and Cocozza, 1974; Monahan, 1975; Cocozza and Steadman, 1974, 1976).

However, to require a yes/no type of prediction of a specific act that has a low base rate poses a number of problems. Yes/no type predictions do not reflect the considerable range of variability and probability that are actually involved and that will be reflected in the predictions. Such predictions are also expected to ignore the aleatory factors commonly involved in determining whether or not a criminal act will actually take place. A variety of factors, such as those pertaining to situational events, targets of opportunity, and presence or absence of pressure from companions, will typically be involved.

Thus, the predictions to be made should refer to the *probability* that certain individuals with particular characteristics (as reflected mainly in past behavioral patterns), and functioning in particular social settings, may engage in certain types of behaviors (e.g., serious criminal acts) over a given period of time such as 12 or 24 months. Given the many problems associated with the clinical predictions typically provided to courts and other related agencies (Monahan, 1978b; Shah, 1978a, b; Steadman and Cocozza, 1978b) and in order that the probabilities may be determined reliably and precisely, actuarial and statistical approaches should be relied on in predicting dangerousness. The use of such statistical approaches (e.g., base expectancy tables and other related devices) combined with more systematically derived and periodically tested clinical indicators, would markedly reduce the problems inherent in relying on the vague clinical judgments, hunches, and intuitions of mental health professionals. Moreover, although some clinicians may well have good predictive skills, quite typically the predictive expertise of mental health professionals is assumed or ascribed—it has *not* been tested and demonstrated empirically. Thus, it is understandable when clinicians cite their clinical experiences as the basis for their predictive judgments and still come to widely differing conclusions. It is difficult to make systematic assessments to predictive validity (accuracy) when the reliability (consistency) of such judgments varies markedly across cases and is generally poor.

In essence, then, I suggest that what is very much needed are predictions that are more systematically and empirically related to probability statements. Various actuarial and statistical methods may be used to develop such probability estimates. Reliable and relevant clinical information about the individual could be used to modify the actuarially derived probabilities within some specified range. The reliability and validity of the clinical information should be determined empirically. Such an approach would, I believe, make it easier to separate the essentially empirical and technical questions pertaining to predictive accuracy from the normative, legal, and public policy decisions that must eventually be made. It might be stated, for example, that Mr. Smith seems to have a 75-percent probability of engaging in further serious criminal behavior within a 12-month period; however, were his drinking problem to be controlled and other community supports provided, this probability might be markedly lowered. It would then be the responsibility of the sentencing judge to determine whether (given the nature and seriousness of the instant offense, the past criminal record, the likelihood of adequate probation supervision, and other pertinent factors) the above probability estimate justifies probation, probation with a variety of specific conditions, or some period of incarceration. In short, predictions of dangerousness will seldom point *directly* to the ultimate legal or policy decision. Such predictions constitute only one of the many considerations that must be weighed and balanced by the ultimate decision-makers.

Can Dangerousness Be Predicted?

Given the considerable literature that has developed on the topic, many, if not most, persons may well respond to such a question with a flat, No! Such a response to the general question may be accompanied by a comment like, We know from social science research that dangerous or violent behavior cannot be predicted. This seems to have become the common wisdom, and several empirical studies (of varying relevance to the specific predictive situation) could be cited in support of such a view (Wenk et al., 1972; Steadman and Cocozza, 1974, 1978b; Monahan, 1975; Cocozza and Steadman, 1976). It must be noted, however, that the answer to the question as it was posed in the heading of this section cannot be given in any clear or definite fashion.

The question was posed in a very general and vague fashion. No reference was made to particular groups or subgroups for whom future dangerousness was to be predicted, nor was there any mention of the prediction methods to be used (clinical or actuarial) or the level of accuracy to be expected or even desired in such predictions. In view of these considerations, we might wonder whether a flat response to such a question would have been made had the reference been to another aspect of behavior. Suppose, for example, the question were, Can generosity be predicted? Can friendliness be predicted? Can trustworthiness be predicted? Or, to turn the issue around completely, Can public safety be predicted?

The point is simply that such questions cannot be answered with a flat yes or no. To say that something is difficult to do (namely, to achieve high levels of accuracy in predicting events with very low base rates) is *not* the same as asserting that the task is impossible and simply cannot be done. As Monahan (1978a) recently noted, ". . . a careful reading of the prediction research to date does not support the unqualified conclusion that the accurate prediction of violence is imposible under all circumstances or that psychiatrists, psychologists, and others will invariably overpredict its occurrence by several orders of magnitude" (p. 198).

Of course, as a matter of public policy, certain levels of predictive accuracy may well be needed—even required—before particular decisions could be based upon such predictions. The basic issue, therefore, is the degree of reliability and accuracy that should be expected before a variety of important legal, social, and public-policy decisions can properly be made.

Events that have low base rates are very difficult to predict with high levels of accuracy. Moreover, even the accuracy that is achieved comes at the cost of high rates of "false positives," that is, persons who are predicted to be dangerous but who will not actually display such behavior. The relevant literature on this point goes back more than 20 years (Meehl, 1954; Meehl and Rosen, 1955), but many of the "experts" who appear regularly in courts to testify on the issue of "dangerousness" seem not to be familiar with this work and its implications for their clinical predictions.

It must also be noted, however, that the level of reliability and accuracy that is needed is not absolute. It will vary with the nature and importance of the decisions to be made. Likewise, the specific decision situation will involve differing sets of competing objectives and trade-offs; thus, differing rates of "error" will be acceptable as long as certain other objectives can be met. For example, different rates of "false positive" errors will be accepted depending on whether we are dealing with discretionary release decisions for an offender with several previous felony convictions, with protecting the president from certain would-be assassins, or with a probation-versus-incarceration decision involving a check passer. In short, the fundamental public-policy decision will not hinge simply or only on the empirical or technical state of the predictive information.

PREDICTIONS INVOLVING RECIDIVISTIC OFFENDERS

In situations related to events with very low base rates, there are typically rather high rates of "false positive" errors. When dealing with a group that has much higher base rates for dangerous behaviors (e.g., offenders with three or more previous convictions for serious misdemeanors and felonies), however, the predictive task is easier. Nevertheless, since one is still predicting "dangerousness" (the *probability* of engaging in further serious and violent crimes), higher levels of accuracy, but not absolute accuracy, will be obtained. Much recent research evidence points clearly to certain groups of delinquents and criminals who have high rates of committing serious and violent offenses.

Wolfgang et al. (1972), for example, in a birth cohort study involving almost 10,000 boys born in Philadelphia, found that about one-third (3475) of the boys had had at least one officially recorded police contact; but almost half of these youngsters showed no further police contacts. A very small proportion of the total cohort (6 percent), however, and a small proportion of those who had had a single police contact (18 percent), had been charged with five or more offenses. This group of 627 chronic offenders accounted for fully *71 percent* of all the homicides committed by the cohort, *77 percent* of the rapes, *70 percent* of the robberies, and *69 percent* of the aggravated assaults. Wolfgang and his associates have followed a 10-percent random sample of the original cohort since 1968, and official and self-reported offenses through age 26 and arrests and dispositions to age 30 have been analyzed further (Wolfgang, 1977). The followup shows that while 18 percent of all the offenders in the cohort were chronic offenders (with five or more crimes) by age 18, by age 30 fully 31.4 percent were chronic offenders. Using the birth cohort data up to age 30, Wolfgang found that, after the fourth offense, the probability that the offender will recidivate was about 0.80, and the likelihood that the next offense would be an index crime averaged 0.426 (ranging from 0.300 to 0.722).

Similarly, a study in New York City (Shinnar and Shinnar, 1975) found that while only two percent of all persons arrested had been previously arrested for homicide, 40 percent of all those arrested for homicide had previous arrests for a violent crime and 30.5 percent for felonious assaults.

The Rand Corporation has conducted a series of studies of career criminals. One of these (Petersilia et al., 1977; Petersilia, 1978) involved 49 felons in a medium-security prison who had at least one conviction of armed robbery, and who had served at least one previous prison term. In contrast to research that uses official police statistics or relies on victimization surveys, the data in this study were derived from detailed personal interviews with the felons and from checks of official criminal justice records. Obviously, given the selected nature of this sample, no broad generalizations can be made, but some interesting and potentially useful information was obtained by these investigators.

The 49 offenders reported a total of 10,500 crimes, or an average of 214 per offender. In a criminal career averaging about 20 years (with about half the time spent in prison), each offender committed an average of about 20 major felonies per year (about 4 violent and 16 property crimes). When the self-reported crimes were compared with the official data, *only 12 percent* of the reported crimes were found to have resulted in a recorded arrest. (These and similar findings have obvious implications with respect to relying only on officially recorded arrests, let alone criminal convictions, for accurate estimations of the nature and extent of an individual's actual criminal behavior.)

Petersilia (1978) reports that criminal careers typically had begun as early as age 14, had tended to peak in the early twenties, and then begun to decline around and after age 30. For instance, in the age group of 14 to 21 years, the offense rates averaged between 20 to 40 crimes per year; for those 22 to 25 years old, the rate was about 12 crimes per year; and by the time the offenders were 26 to 30 years old, the number of offenses had dropped to 7 per year.

In addition, two broad categories of offenders emerged from this study sample: the *intensives,* who saw themselves as criminals and went about their crimes in a rather purposeful manner, and the *intermittents,* who were less likely to see themselves as criminals and whose crimes were less frequently but more recklessly committed. The *intensives* tended to commit several crimes a month but were arrested for only about 5 percent of their crimes. In contrast, even though the *intermittents* had generally lower rates of crimes, they were much more likely to be arrested (Petersilia et al., 1977).

As interesting and informative as these findings are with respect to career offenders and the pattern of their offensive behavior, there are limitations to the wider generalization of the findings in view of the small size and selected nature of the sample. Similar findings, however, have been obtained by the Institute for Law and Social Research (INSLAW) in Washington, D. C., based on information from PROMIS (Prosecutor's Management Information System) Research Project. PROMIS (1977a, b) analyzed data pertaining to all arrests for nonfederal crimes in the District of Columbia between January 1, 1971 and August 31, 1975. Information was available on 72,610 arrests which involved 45,575 defendants; the data file provided information about the frequency with which individuals were rearrested, reprosecuted, and reconvicted during the 56-month period of the study.

This major study found that persons who were repeatedly arrested, prosecuted, and convicted accounted for a disproportionately large share of street crime. For example, persons who had been arrested four or more times in the 56-month period represented only 7 percent of the arrestees but they accounted for fully 24 percent of all the arrests. Thus, the extensiveness of the criminal history (regardless of whether it is expressed in terms of arrests, prosecutions, or convictions) seems to be a good predictor of future criminality. In essence, the PROMIS project found that if a defendant had 5 or more arrests before the current arrest, the probability of subsequent arrest approached certainty. It was also found that a significant percentage of these repeat offenders switched between felonies and misdemeanors: today's petty larceny defendant may have been involved in a past robbery and might possibly be involved in a future aggravated assault or even homicide. Similarly, 30 percent of defendants who had been arrested at least twice during the 56-month period accounted for the majority of arrests (felonies and serious misdemeanors) during this period. With respect to crimes of violence, it was found that 18 percent of the persons arrested for crimes of violence accounted for 35 percent of the arrests. Moreover, fully 26 percent of all felony cases—31 percent of robbery cases and 28 percent of the murder cases—involved defendants who had been arrested while on conditional release (pretrial release or probation or parole).

Given this type of empirical data about career and recidivistic criminals, especially the findings from the PROMIS project that involved 45,575 defendants and Wolfgang's longitudinal study of a birth cohort, is it really accurate to say that dangerousness cannot be predicted? Although there will certainly be public policy and moral dilemmas pertaining to the actual uses of such predictive judgments, the technical predictive task is not as difficult for groups who have high base rates for serious and violent criminal behavior.

Improving Clinical Predictions

Elsewhere (Shah, 1978a, b) I have discussed some systematic sources of error in clinical assessments and predictions, namely, errors associated with illusory correlations and those caused by ignoring certain statistical rules in making predictive judgments. Some of these were not simply the result of careless clinical practices but appeared to be inherent in the nature and social context of the judgmental tasks. Moreover, the errors were very much influenced by powerful social contingencies which, in particular situations, implicitly or even explicitly direct that "false positive" errors are much to be preferred to "false negative" errors. Nevertheless, as I noted, greater awareness of and sensitivity to these systematic errors, and related training efforts, should help to distinguish the technical difficulties of the predictive task from certain social and political pressures and to develop procedures that make more effective use of normative statistical principles in efforts to reduce errors in predictions.

Another problem associated with the use of clinical predictions is that we have not developed effective means for evaluating their reliability and accuracy. The usual error-rate method (whether the particular prediction was right or wrong) is simple, but not very useful. It is insensitive to some important aspects of the predictive task. For example, the error-rate method does not take into account the magnitude of the error; it fails to distinguish a decision from the particular evidence on which the decision was based; and it does not penalize the judge who chooses to forecast dire outcomes (i.e., overpredicts dangerousness) rather than to attempt accurate predictions. Thus, as noted earlier, while case outcome decisions can be considered right or wrong, probabilities are not. They are best considered as being more or less accurate.

These aspects of evaluating clinical predictions have been demonstrated by Shapiro (1967) in his effort to evaluate the predictive skills of physicians in managing particular medical cases and problems. The error-rate method failed to detect meaningful differences between faculty and students, since the range was between 23 and 27. In contrast, when an accuracy coefficient was used, these measures ranged from 0.039 to 0.323, and they not only revealed important differences among the physicians with respect to predictive accuracy, but the method helped to pinpoint various sources of inaccurate judgments.

The work by Shapiro (1977) has not been cited to suggest that predictions of dangerousness are much like the medical predictions he studied. Rather, this work points to the critical importance of developing more systematic and meaningful methods for evaluating the reliability and the accuracy of clinical predictions of dangerousness. Only when such assessments have been undertaken can meaningful distinctions be made between clinicians who tend to be fairly good predictors and those lacking such skills. Such systematic assessments of clinical predictions could also allow clinical indicators to be combined with various actuarial data in efforts to further improve the accuracy of predictions of dangerousness.

SOME PUBLIC POLICY CONCERNS

In any pluralistic society there are numerous values, ideologies, goals and interests, as well as proponents and advocates of these interests who seek to influence public policies. Rarely is there a single value or societal goal involved with respect to issues of broad public concern, and seldom are such issues simple or clear-cut. Typically, the decisions regarding formulation and implementation of policies involve the weighing and balancing of several competing, and at times even conflicting, values and objectives. The primary responsibility for balancing competing claims and interests rests with specially designated decision-makers who are expected to be aware of a broad range of perspectives relevant to public concerns. In arriving at determinations of public policy, legislatures, courts, and other policymakers attempt to weigh competing interests, to consider their respective social value, and to articulate a balance that is compatible with the perceived interests and welfare of society at large. Following are a few of the many public policy concerns that pertain to the definition, assessment, prediction, and handling of dangerousness.

Societal Values and Dangerous Behaviors

There are markedly different societal and governmental responses to various types and sources of danger to the community. Clearly, societies are not equally concerned about all forms of behaviors, social conditions and practices that are likely to result in serious injury and/or loss of life. The basic problem is not simply whether or not a person is viewed as dangerous; much appears to depend upon *who* the person is, in *what ways* he is dangerous, the *social contexts* in which the behavior occurs, and the *value judgments* of influential and powerful groups in society with respect to the perceived harms that are officially to be designated as "dangerous." In essence, the defining, labeling, and handling of dangerous behaviors and situations are very much influenced by the dominant values, power structures, and associated political processes that exist in a society. For example, social deviants labeled as mentally ill have for several hundred years in the Anglo-American experience aroused much societal apprehension and have been major targets for preventive confinement (Dershowitz, 1974a, b). Yet many other categories of persons and groups who have quite glaringly demonstrated their dangerousness to society (e.g., repeatedly drunken drivers and offenders with 3 or more convictions for serious and violent crimes) do not seem to evoke similar concerns, nor are they as readily subjected to preventive confinement as are the mentally ill (Shah, 1974).

It is also ironic that our society tends to focus attention more readily on the dangerous acts of particular individuals but appears less concerned about certain social conditions and practices that pose serious hazards to the health, safety, and physical well-being of literally millions of citizens each year. For example, the *President's Report on Occupational Safety and Health* (1972) estimated that total deaths annually from job-related injuries amounted to over 14,000, with an estimated 2.2 million disabling injuries. The incidence of occupational diseases is less well-known, but estimates have pointed to "at least 390,000 new cases of disabling occupational diseases each year" (*President's Report on Occupational Safety and Health,* 1972, p. 111). It was also estimated in this report that there may be as many as 100,000 deaths per year from occupationally caused diseases (see also Hunter, 1970; Greene, 1974; Schanche, 1974).

Obviously, not all nor perhaps even the majority of these industrial and occupation-related deaths, diseases, and disabling injuries can be avoided. It is important to note, however, the remarkably different societal and governmental response to different types and sources of danger to the community. It seems very difficult for lawmakers and other governmental agencies to establish effective controls when powerful groups are involved. And even when regulations and established standards do exist for occupational safety and health, enforcement practices and sanctions reflect marked tolerance and "kid-glove" treatment of these powerful interests (Franklin, 1969; Page and O'Brien, 1973; Brodeur, 1974; Scott, 1974).

Thus in testifying before the House Select Subcommittee on Labor, Paul Brodeur (author of *Expendable Americans,* 1974) said:

> I submit that if a million people in the so-called middle class or professional class were dying each decade of preventable occupational disease, and if nearly four million were being disabled, there would long ago have been such a hue and cry for remedial action that if the Congress had not heeded it vast numbers of its members would have been turned out of office (Brodeur, 1974, p. 274).

Why Does "Dangerousness" Get Linked with Mental Illness?

One troublesome aspect of involuntary civil commitment of the mentally ill pertains to general beliefs and presumptions about the dangerousness of such persons. The concept of dangerousness (or the related notion of "likelihood of serious harm") is considered both in reference to danger to oneself and danger to others. I have argued (Shah, 1977) that many problems are created when the *parens patriae* responsibilities of the state (the benevolent functions of providing care for persons who are unable to care for themselves) are confused and confounded with the state's duty to protect the community from danger and harm (the police-power functions). As noted at the beginning of this discussion, the major concern here is with dangerous acts that are directed toward others.

The police-power concerns of the state involve the social control of criminal behavior and also the control of dangerous acts by persons considered to be mentally ill. With respect to the use of preventive confinement measures designed to protect the community, however, our society seems primarily to have singled out the mentally ill. There is the implicit, sometimes even explicit, assumption that by virtue of being mentally ill a person is more likely to engage in dangerous and violent behaviors. Yet, despite the presence of extensive and serious criminal records and the possibility of fairly accurate predictions of further criminal recidivism, in our criminal justice system such considerations are not the bases for continued incarceration once a prisoner's sentence has expired. In short, commitment laws for the mentally ill seem to be premised on the assumption (actually a belief) that, as a group, the mentally ill constitute one of the most dangerous groups in our society. Yet there is no sound or convincing empirical evidence to support such belief.

Many empirical studies over the past several decades have compared the arrest rates of hospitalized mental patients after their release with the arrest rates for the general population. The earlier studies indicated fairly consistently that released mental patients had lower arrest rates than the general population (Ashley, 1922; Pollock, 1938; Cohen and Freeman, 1945; Brill and Malzberg, 1954), while more recent studies rather consistently found higher arrest rates for the mental patients (Rappeport and Lassen, 1965, 1966; Giovannoni and Gurel, 1967; Zitrin et al., 1976; Durbin et al., 1977). Given the different jurisdictions and time periods involved, as well as methodological variations among these studies, it is not possible to make precise comparisons. There are clear suggestions however, about variations over time with respect to policies and practices for the hospitalization and release of mental patients. The studies, by and large, did not undertake more refined analyses to ascertain the reasons for the variations in arrest rates among mental patients. Moreover, all the comparisons were between released mental patients and the general population. Oddly, no comparisons were done with a sample of offenders released from penal institutions—if in fact one of the concerns was to determine the dangerousness of certain population groups.

Steadman and his associates (Steadman et al., 1978a, b) have recently undertaken some research that provides a much-needed clarification and explication of the basic policy-relevant questions. These investigators also have compared, in a New York jurisdiction, the arrest rates of released mental patients and the general population with similar rates for released criminal offenders. Two samples were used, patients released (during a 12-month period) in 1968, and another sample released in 1975. Summarized briefly, Steadman et al. (1978a) indicate that it is patients with arrest records before their hospitalization who account for the subsequently higher arrest rates for the released mental patients. Hospitalized mental patients without previous arrest records had later arrest rates generally *lower* than those of the general population. What seems to account for the higher arrest rates of the mental patients (as compared with the general population) in more recent years (namely, the 1975 sample), is the fact that there were more persons in state mental hospitals who had previous arrest records.

More importantly, when comparisons were made between patients released from state mental hospitals and offenders released from penal institutions in the same jurisdiction and during the same period of time, it was glaringly evident that the ex-prisoners had subsequent arrest rates *three to six times higher* than those of the patients. And, with respect to *violent crimes* the arrest rates (per 1000) for the 1968 sample for the general population, the ex-patients, and the ex-prisoners were 2.2, 2.05, and 22.63, respectively. Similarly, the arrest rates for *violent crimes* for the 1975 group, and in the same sequence, were 3.62, 12.35, and 87.50, respectively (Steadman et al., 1978b).

These findings support what is well-known to criminologists. For both the 1968 and the 1975 groups, those persons (mental patients and offenders) who had one arrest before their confinement were rearrested substantially more often than the general population, and those with multiple prior arrests had exceedingly high rates for arrests following their release. The ex-offenders had rearrest rates for violent crimes that were *six to ten times higher* than those of the mental patients.

As is evident from the research cited earlier (PROMIS Research Project, 1977a, b; Wolfgang et al., 1972; Wolfgang, 1977) persons who have displayed repeated and serious criminal conduct constitute one of the most dangerous groups in our society. Yet the mentally ill have been the group most affected by preventive confinement measures. This situation may be explained, perhaps in large measure, by the considerable research that has shown that strongly negative and rejecting public attitudes typify societal reactions to the mentally ill (Nunnally, 1961; Phillips, 1963, 1964; Bord, 1971; Rabkin, 1972). Selective reporting by the media of criminal and violent acts by mental patients may also have helped to foster and maintain public attitudes and policies that are discriminatory and stigmatizing (Steadman and Cocozza, 1978a).

In recent years there has been much reform in laws and practices concerning the commitment and release of mental patients, and a wide range of procedural due process protections has been extended to these citizens.

Nevertheless, there continues to be a noteworthy absence of judicial scrutiny of the more basic *substantive* due process problems inherent in such policies. Stated simply, one aspect of substantive due process demands that all state actions be reasonably related to a reasonable and valid goal. Further, when such actions involve infringements of other "fundamental interests," e.g., depriving citizens of their right to liberty, these actions must be shown to promote not only a reasonable or valid but a *compelling* state goal. Although one would not dispute the validity of the state's interest in protecting the community from harm, very serious constitutional problems pertaining to equal protection and fundamental fairness are raised by the fact that the mentally ill have in large measure been singled out for preventive confinement, even though recidivistic offenders are clearly and demonstrably a far more dangerous group (Note, 1974; Shah, 1977).

The Rule of Law and the Role of "Experts."

When such key terms as "mental illness" and "dangerous" appear in various laws, they are meant to have precise legal meaning and should be defined carefully in the statutes. When these terms are used in such legal contexts they have a legal, and not a medical, psychiatric or psychological meaning. And, since these statutory definitions pertain to broad public policy concerns and objectives, the definition and interpretation of such key terms should not devolve exclusively, nor even primarily, upon mental health experts. However, as a result of vagueness in statutory language, the lack of clear definitions, and also because of judicial default, in practice the "experts" often seem to end up making such crucial public policy determinations (Shah, 1974, 1977).

The Texas Code of Criminal Procedure provides, for example, that criminal defendants who have been committed following adjudication, as incompetent to stand trial and as not guilty by reason of insanity, to a maximum security hospital or unit, cannot be transferred to nonsecurity units *unless* they are determined not to be "manifestly dangerous" (see footnote 1). It seems, however, that when the legislature revised this statute in 1975) and mandated the establishment of a review board, it failed to define "manifestly dangerous" (Dudley, 1978). Thus, even though the Texas Department of Mental Health and Mental Retardation set about establishing criteria and standards for the review board to determine manifest dangerousness, it must obviously be difficult to determine something that the legislature did not see fit to define.

Situations of this type place mental health experts in roles that are specifically designated for legislative and judicial policymakers, since the relevant decisions involve not only narrow technical questions but ultimate legal and public policy determinations. The blurring and confusing of such roles and responsibilities means that experts may be placed in positions of bringing their own particularistic and personal views to the determination of issues that involve normative judgments and require careful balancing of competing societal objectives, for example, the rights of the individual and the protection of the community.

Legislative and judicial bodies as well as mental health and related experts may need to consider Freidson's admonition on the role of professionals in making essentially normative and policy decisions:

> (T)he profession's role in a free society should be limited to contributing the technical information men need to make their own decisions on the basis of their own values. When he preempts the authority to direct, even constrain men's decisions on the basis of his own values, the professional is no longer an expert but rather a member of a new privileged class disguised as expert (Freidson, 1970: p. 382).

Death-Penalty Decisions and the Role of Mental Health Professionals

The foregoing discussion about the role of "experts" is relevant to some recent developments in the use of mental health expertise in decisions on the imposition of the death penalty. The relevant law in Texas illustrates the manner in which the use of mental health professionals may blur fundamentally legal and moral judgments with considerations of technical expertise.

After finding a defendant guilty of a capital offense, courts in Texas are required to conduct a separate sentencing proceeding to determine whether the defendant shall be sentenced to death or to life imprisonment. Article 37.071 of the Texas Code of Criminal Procedure (footnote 2) spells out the sentencing procedures and decision criteria to be used in capital cases. At the conclusion of the presentation of the evidence, the court submits the following three issues to the jury:

> (1) whether the conduct of the defendant that caused the death of the deceased was committed deliberately and with the reasonable expectation that the death of the deceased or another would result;
> (2) whether there is a probability that the defendant would commit criminal acts of violence that would constitute a continuing threat to society; and
> (3) if raised by the evidence, whether the conduct of the defendant in killing the deceased was unreasonable in response to the provocation, if any, by the deceased (Art. 37.071).

If the jury returns an affirmative finding on each of these three questions, the court is required to impose the death penalty. If a negative finding is returned on any one of the issues, the court is required to give a sentence of confinement for life by the Texas Department of Corrections.

Expert testimony by mental health professionals has been used in reference to the second issue. Hence, it is this particular issue that will be the subject of this brief discussion. (Readers interested in a more detailed discussion of the legal questions and problems raised by Texas procedure in capital cases should see Dix, 1977a, b.)

As noted, mental health professionals who appear as expert witnesses in various legal and related proceedings should be knowledgeable about and sensitive to the relevant legal issues and questions. Moreover, when testifying as experts they should also reflect good awareness and understanding of the existing scientific and professional literature, and particularly of the empirical research evidence that points to the limitations associated with various technical tasks, for example, the prediction of events with low base rates. Indeed, it has been urged that since the statements and recommendations of the experts may well be accepted with undue deference, and since such statements can have very serious consequences for the persons affected, being knowledgeable about the specific legal and technical issue should be viewed as a professional and ethical obligation by mental health professionals (Shah, 1969).

Yet, in light of some of the published reports concerning the expert testimony given by mental health professionals in capital sentencing procedures in Texas (Dix, 1977a, 1978), serious questions arise about the role and function of the expert witnesses. Questions are also raised about the level and nature of the expertise that seems to have been displayed in some of these cases.

My particular concern here, however, relates to the broader implications of the role of mental health professionals with regard to the second issue cited above, "whether there is a probability that the defendant would commit criminal acts of violence that would constitute a continuing threat to society." Clearly, in these sentencing decisions, the alternative to imposition of the death penalty after conviction of a capital offense is penal confinement for life.[3] Thus, it seems that two major questions are raised by the concern about the defendant's posing a "continuing threat to society":

---

[3] The Texas Code of Criminal Procedure (1975), Art. 12.32, provides that an individual adjudged guilty of a first degree felony "shall be punished by confinement in the Texas Department of Corrections for life or for any term of not more than 99 years or less than 5 years" (p. 410).

whether the person is likely to display violent behavior toward other inmates and staff while serving a life sentence; and whether, following release to the community *after* serving a life sentence, the person would engage in further "criminal acts of violence."

It would typically be difficult to answer the first question without knowing about the specific penal setting in which the defendant is likely to be confined and the particular situations in which opportunities for violent behavior may be available. Penal authorities could address this concern by providing the necessary degrees of security and supervision during the confinement—as they doubtless do in the case of other inmates who pose such threats during their incarceration. As for the second question, given the numerous problems associated with even shorter-range predictions of behavior (e.g., for periods of 12 and 24 months), the prospects of reliable and accurate predictions *following* completion of a life sentence in prison boggle the mind. If the defendant is a young male with an extensive and serious record of criminal violence, and if a life sentence may in fact allow release on parole in 10 to 15 years, it may be that such a defendant released in his late twenties or early thirties could still pose some risk of further dangerousness. However, even though an individual might reasonably be considered to pose a "continuing threat" at the time of sentencing, the so-called burning-out phenomenon as a function of aging makes it rather unlikely that a person returned to the community in his late forties or early fifties will still pose a "continuing threat to society."

In light of what has been discussed about the problems associated with clinical predictions and the relative advantages of actuarial and statistical approaches, the most relevant and reliable information about future dangerousness could be obtained by triers of fact, weighing the nature and extensiveness of the defendant's previous criminal behavior. Since predictions of dangerousness always involve probabilities, even a very high probability (e.g., 90 percent) of further dangerous behavior would reduce—but not eliminate—the likelihood of error. The defendant could still be in that 10 percent that is *not* likely to present a continuing threat of violence either during or following a life sentence in prison. Thus, the ultimate decision-makers must still face awesome legal and moral judgments. If imposition of the death penalty serves primarily to express society's sense of condemnation, revulsion, and retribution for crimes regarded as especially brutal and horrifying, then the question arises whether there is *any* role for mental health professionals making such decisions.

In essence, it seems that mental health expertise may possibly be used, or even misused, in these situations to cloak and launder the vexing moral judgments that must be made by the triers of fact.

CONCLUSION

This discussion has noted several decision points in the criminal justice and mental health systems where the issues of an individual's dangerousness and of various dispositional options are considered. Yet, despite the extensive uses of the notion of dangerousness and the serious consequences that may follow such determinations, clear and precise definitions are overdue, and much clarification and improvement are needed. The vagueness of a concept that is so critical for a variety of decisions can and indeed does lead to many problems because the notion can be pulled and stretched to fit dispositional and ideological preferences. Similarly, the manner in which behavior is commonly conceptualized and various predictive assessments made gives insufficient attention to the setting and situational variables that influence behavior. It has been suggested that an interactional perspective, one which considers both individual and situational variables, offers many improvements over traditional personality-trait, psychodynamic, and situationistic approaches.

Even though major decisions about people are based on assessments and predictions about their future dangerousness, there are many technical difficulties inherent in predicting events with very low base rates. Although such predictive tasks remain difficult, greater use of actuarial and statistical approaches could lead to several improvements. Predictive accuracy may be increased only modestly and false-positive errors reduced to some degree, but the major gain would be in markedly improved consistency and reliability of such assessments. Improvements in consistency should enhance the equity and fairness of the decisions.

The manner in which therapeutic and social-control objectives tend to become confused and confounded, to the detriment of the individual affected, was noted. Even though the value placed on individual liberty leads to the use of demanding rules in the criminal process before conviction and incarceration can result, the values associated with coercive confinement undergo a major shift when the person is labeled as mentally ill and the purpose of the confinement is couched in the idiom of remediation and treatment. The application of the label mentally ill and the invocation of therapeutic objectives have long had the effect of neutralizing the values and decision rules that would otherwise require our society to let nine guilty persons go free rather than risk the erroneous confinement of a single individual. Although courts have in recent years given much attention to these sources of unfairness and significant improvements have been made, constitutional issues of substantive due process (namely, in singling out the mentally ill for preventive confinement) still remain to be addressed. The discriminatory practices vis-à-vis the mentally ill tend to reinforce and maintain longstanding social prejudices. Thus, to the extent that policy-makers concentrate their concerns with "dangerous" behaviors largely on the mentally ill, they help to perpetuate the myth that the mentally ill, as a group, are the most dangerous persons in our society. Yet there is abundant empirical evidence to demonstrate that certain other groups (e.g., drunken drivers and serious recidivistic criminals) are clearly and convincingly more dangerous to the community.

Mental health professionals who function as experts in interactions with the criminal justice and legal systems must be knowledgeable about and sensitive to the relevant legal issues and questions. If indeed such professionals are to function as experts, they should also be knowledgeable about the relevant professional and scientific literature—especially the empirical research that points to the limitations of assessment, predictive, and therapeutic skills. Indeed, when the lives and welfare of people are seriously to be affected, the acquisition of this knowledge and understanding should be viewed as a professional and ethical obligation.

Finally, mental health professionals and others who interact with the legal system should take care to ensure that their limited technical contributions and expertise are not blurred and confounded with the ultimate legal, moral, and public policy judgments that are the proper responsibility of other societal decision makers.

REFERENCES

ASHLEY, M. C. Outcome of 1000 cases paroled from the Middletown State Homeopathic Hospital. *State Hospital Quarterly* 8:64-70, 1922.

BEM, D., and ALLEN, A. On predicting some of the people some of the time: the search from cross-situational consistencies in behavior. *Psychol. Rev.* 81:506-520, 1974.

BORD, R. J. Rejection of the mentally ill: continuities and further developments. *Social Problems* 18:496-509, 1971.

BOWERS, K. S. Situationism in psychology: an analysis and critique. *Psychol. Rev.* 80:307-336, 1973.

BRILL, H., and MALZBERG, B. Statistical Report of the Arrest Record of Male Ex-Patients, Age 16 and Over, Released from New York State Mental Hospitals During the Period 1946-48. Albany: New York State Department of Mental Hygiene, Albany, 1954. (American Psychiatric Association, Mental Hospital Service Supplementary Mailing 153. August 1962).

BRODEUR, P. *Expendable Americans.* Viking Press, New York, 1974.

COHEN, L. H., and FREEMAN, H. How dangerous to the community are state hospital patients? *Connecticut State Medicine Journal* 9:697-700, 1945.

COCOZZA, J. J., and STEADMAN, H. J. Some refinements in the measurement and prediction of dangerous behavior. *Am. J. Psychiatry* 131:1012-1020, 1974.

COCOZZA, J. J., and STEADMAN, H. J. The failure of psychiatric predictions of dangerousness: clear and convincing evidence. *Rutgers Law Review* 29:1084-1101, 1976.

DERSHOWITZ, A. M. The origins of preventive confinement in Anglo-American law. Part I. *University of Cincinnati Law Review* 43:1-60, 1974a.

DERSHOWITZ, A. M. The origins of preventive confinement in Anglo-American law. Part II. *University of Cincinnati Law Review* 43:781-846, 1974b.

DIX, G. E. The death penalty, "dangerousness," psychiatric testimony, and professional ethics. *American Journal of Criminal Law* 5:151-214, 1977a.

DIX. G. E. Administration of the Texas death penalty statute: constitutional infirmities related to the prediction of dangerousness. *Texas Law Review* 55:1343-1414, 1977b.

DIX, G. E. Participation by mental health professionals in capital murder sentencing. *International Journal of Law and Psychiatry* 1:283-308, 1978.

DUDLEY, H. K. A review board for determining the dangerousness of mentally ill offenders. *Hosp. Community Psychiatry* 29:453-456, 1978.

DURBIN, J. R., PASEWARK, R. A., and ALBERS, D. Criminality and mental illness: a study of arrest rates in a rural state. *Am. J. Psychiatry* 134:80-83, 1977.

EKEHAMMER, B. Interactionism in personality from a historical perspective. *Psychol. Bull.* 81:1026-1048, 1974.

ENDLER, N. S., and MAGNUSSON, D. Toward an interactional psychology of personality. *Psychol. Bull.* 83:956-974, 1976.

FAIRWEATHER, G. W. *Methods in Experimental Social Innovation.* Wiley, New York, 1967.

FAIRWEATHER, G. W., SANDERS, D., and TORNATZKY, L. *Creating Change in Mental Health Organizations.* Pergamon Press, New York, 1974.

FRANKLIN, B. A. The scandal of death and injury in the mines. *N.Y. Times Magazine,* March 30, 1969.

FREIDSON, E. *Profession of Medicine.* Dodd, Mead, New York, 1970.

GIOVANNONI, J. M., and GUREL, L. Socially disruptive behavior of ex-mental patients. *Arch. Gen. Psychiatry* 17:146-153, 1967.

GOLDSTEIN, J., and KATZ, J. Dangerousness and mental illness. *Yale Law Journal* 70:225-239, 1960.

GOUGH, H. G. *Manual for the California Psychological Inventory* (rev. Ed.). Consulting Psychologists Press, Palo Alto, California, 1969.

GREENE, W. Life vs. livelihood. *N.Y. Times Magazine,* Nov. 24, 1974, pp. 95-98, 104-105.

HOGAN, R., DESOTO, C. B., and SOLANO, C. Traits, tests, and personality research. *Am. Psychol.* 32:255-264, 1977.

HUNTER, D. *The Diseases of Occupation.* English Universities Press, London, 1970.

MEEHL, P. E. *Clinical vs. Statistical Prediction.* University of Minnesota Press, Minneapolis, 1954.

MEEHL, P. E., and ROSEN, A. Antecedent probability and the efficiency of psychometric signs, patterns, or cutting scores. *Psychol. Bull.* 52:194-216, 1955.

MISCHEL, W. Toward a cognitive social learning reconceptualization of personality. *Psychol. Rev.* 80:252-283, 1973.

MISCHEL, W. On the future of personality measurement. *Am. Psychol.* 32:246-254, 1977.

MONAHAN, J. The prediction of violence, in *Violence and Criminal Justice.* D. Chappell and J. Monahan, eds. Lexington Books, Lexington, Mass., 1975, pp. 15-35.

MONAHAN, J. The prevention of violence, in *Community Mental Health and the*

Criminal Justice System. J. Monahan, ed. Pergamon Press, New York, 1976, pp. 13-34.

MONAHAN, J. Prediction research and the emergency commitment of dangerous mentally ill persons: a reconsideration. *Am. J. Psychiat.* 135:198-201, 1978a.

MONAHAN, J. The prediction of violent criminal behavior: a methodological critique and prospectus, in *Deterrence and Incapacitation: Estimating the Effects of Criminal Sanctions on Crime Rates*. A. Blumstein, J. Cohen, and D. Nagin, eds. National Academy of Science, Washington, D.C., 1978b, pp. 244-269.

MOOS, R. H. Sources of variance in responses to questionnaire and in behavior. *J. Abnorm. Psychol.* 74:405-412, 1969.

MOOS, R. H. Conceptualizations of human environments. *Am. Psychol.* 28:652-665, 1973.

Note. Developments in the law—civil commitment of the mentally ill. *Harvard Law Review* 87:1190-1406, 1974.

Note. Mental illness: a suspect classification. *Yale Law Journal* 83:1237-1270, 1974.

NUNNALLY, J. D. *Popular Conceptions of Mental Health*. Holt, Rinehart & Winston, New York, 1961.

PAGE, J. A., and O'BRIEN, M. *Bitter Wages*. Grossman, New York, 1973.

PERVIN, L. The representative design of person-situation research, in *Personality at the Crossroads: Current Issues in Interactional Psychology*. D. Magnusson and N. S. Endler, eds. Erlbaum, Hillsdale, N. J., 1977.

PETERSILIA, J. Career criminal prosecution: an idea whose time has come. *Prosecutor's Brief, July-August*, 24-27, 1978.

PETERSILIA, J., GREENWOOD, P. W., and LAVIN, M. *Criminal Careers of Habitual Offenders*. Rand Corp., Santa Monica, California, 1977.

PHILLIPS, D. L. Rejection: a possible consequence of seeking help for mental disorders. *Am. Sociol. Rev.* 28:963-972, 1963.

PHILLIPS, D. L. Rejection of the mentally ill: the influence of behavior and sex. *Am. Sociol. Rev.* 29:679-687, 1964.

POLLOCK, H. M. Is the paroled patient a menace to the community? *Psychiat. Quart.* 12:236-244, 1938.

President's Report on Occupational Safety and Health. U.S. Govt. Printing Office, Washington, D.C., 1972.

PROMIS Research Project. *Highlights of Interim Findings and Implications*. (Publ. 1) Institute for Law and Social Research, Washington, D.C., 1977a.

PROMIS Research Project. *Curbing the Repeat Offender: A Strategy for Prosecutors*. (Publ. 3) Institute for Law and Social Research, Washington, D.C., 1977b.

RABKIN, J. G. Opinions about mental illness: a review of the literature. *Psychol. Bull.* 77:153-171, 1972.

RAPPEPORT, J. R., and LASSEN, G. Dangerousness—arrest rate comparisons of discharged mental patients and the general population. *Am. J. Psychiatry* 121:776-783, 1965.

RAPPEPORT, J. R., and LASSEN, G. The dangerousness of female patients: a comparison of arrest rates of discharged psychiatric patients and the general population. *Am. J. Psychiatry* 123:413-419, 1966.

SCHANCHE, D. A. Vinyl chloride: time bomb on the production line. *Today's Health* 52:16-19, 70-72, 1974.

SCHWITZGEBEL, R. K. Survey of state civil commitment statutes, in *Civil Commitment and Social Policy*. A. L. McGarry, R. K. Schwitzgebel, P. D. Lipsett, and D.

Lelos, eds. (Final Report on NIMH grant MH25955) Laboratory of Community Psychiatry, Harvard Medical School, Boston, Massachusetts, 1978, pp. 70-104.

SCOTT, R. *Muscle and Blood*. Dutton, New York, 1974.

SHAH, S. A. Treatment of offenders: some behavioral concepts, principles, and approaches. *Federal Probation* 30:1-9, 1966.

SHAH, S. A. Crime and mental illness: some problems in defining and labeling deviant behavior. *Mental Hygiene* 53:21-33, 1969.

SHAH, S. A. Some interactions of law and mental health in the handling of social deviance. *Catholic Univ. Law Rev.* 23:674-719, 1974.

SHAH, S. A. Dangerousness: some definitional, conceptual, and public policy issues, in *Perspectives in Law and Psychology*, vol. 1. B. D. Sales, ed. Plenum, New York, 1977, pp. 91-119.

SHAH, S. A. Dangerousness: a paradigm for exploring some issues in law and psychology. *Am. Psychol.* 33:224-238, 1978a.

SHAH, S. A. Dangerousness and mental illness: some conceptual, prediction, and policy dilemmas, in *Dangerous Behavior: A Problem in Law and Mental Health*. C. J. Frederick, ed. U.S. Govt. Printing Office, Washington, D.C., 1978b, pp. 153-191.

SHAPIRO, A. R. The evaluation of clinical predictions. *N. Engl. J. Med.* 296:1509-1514, 1977.

SHINNAR, R., and SHINNAR, S. The effects of the criminal justice system on the control of crime: a quantitative approach. *Law & Society Rev.* 9:581-611, 1975.

STEADMAN, H. J., and COCOZZA, J. J. *Careers of the Criminally Insane*. Lexington Books, Lexington, Massachusetts, 1974.

STEADMAN, H. J., and COCOZZA, J. J. Selective reporting and the public's misconceptions of the criminally insane. *The Public Opinion Quarterly* 41:523-533, 1978a.

STEADMAN, H. J., and COCOZZA, J. J. Psychiatry, dangerousness and the repetitively violent offender. *J. Criminal Law & Criminology*, 69:226-231, 1978b.

STEADMAN, H. J., COCOZZA, J. J., and MELICK, M. E. Explaining the increased arrest rate among mental patients: the changing clientele of state hospitals. *Am. J. Psychiatry* 135:816-820, 1978a.

STEADMAN, H. J., VANDERWYST, D., and RIBNER, S. Comparing arrest rates of mental patients and criminal offenders. *Am. J. Psychiatry* 135:1218-1220, 1978b.

TOCH, H. *Violent Men: An Inquiry into the Psychology of Violence*. Aldine, Chicago, 1969.

WEBSTER, W. H. *Crime in the United States—1977*. (Uniform Crime Reports) U.S. Govt. Printing Office, Washington, D.C. 1978.

WENK, E. A., ROBISON, J. O., and SMITH, G. W. Can violence be predicted? *Crime and Delinquency* 18:393-402, 1972.

WOLFGANG, M. E. From boy to man—from delinquency to crime. Paper delivered at the National Symposium on the Serious Juvenile Offender, Dept. of Corrections, State of Minn., Minneapolis, Sept., 1977.

WOLFGANG, M. E., FIGLIO, R. M., and SELLIN, T. *Delinquency in a Birth Cohort*. University of Chicago Press, Chicago, 1972.

ZITRIN, A., HARDESTY, A. S., and BURDOCK, E. T. Crime and violence among mental patients. *Am. J. Psychiatry* 133:142-149, 1976.

CHAPTER 11

Methodological Problems in the Prediction of Violence

EDWIN I. MEGARGEE

The prediction of violent behavior has occupied a major portion of my professional career since I first faced the problem of attempting to identify potentially assaultive criminals when I worked in a probation setting some twenty years ago. Can we predict violence? In the beginning of my career I would have replied, of course. Twenty years later, my answer is, no. It is fortunate that I am a scientist, because science is the only profession in which one can achieve a good reputation by being a failure.

I have been involved recently in a comprehensive psychological study of a rapist and multiple murderer. Mr. *X*, hoping that his case will be of scientific value in helping to predict violence, has cooperated in extensive videotaped testing and interviewing. Of particular interest is a videotaped recording of his confession of the brutal murder of a mother and daughter who were hacked to death in the presence of younger siblings. This recorded confession, which was introduced in evidence at the trial, was no doubt instrumental in the speed with which the jury returned a verdict of guilty to two counts of murder in the first degree. This decision took them exactly 26 minutes, and the bulk of that time was spent in walking between the courtroom and the jury room and in electing a foreman.

After the verdict was returned, Mr. *X* took the stand in the penalty portion of the trial and told the jury that if released he would doubtlessly kill again. Moreover, he maintained that if sentenced to life in prison he would kill fellow inmates or be killed by them. This time it took the jury only 8 minutes to recommend the death penalty.

Two days later, when my associates, Drs. Joyce Carbonnel and Tom Tondo, and I interviewed and tested Mr. *X* and examined the photographs of the crime scene and the autopsy material, we concurred with his self-diagnosis. If called on to testify, I, too, would have classified him as a dangerous individual and stated that in my expert opinion, at this time, he is likely to engage in further violence if given the opportunity. Twenty or 30 years from now is another story.

Despite all these data, and despite my absolute certainty, shared by Mr. *X,* that he has been and continues to be extremely dangerous, the research evidence indicates that the odds are 2 to 1 against my prediction being correct. The best data we have been able to accumulate indicate that the state of the art when it comes to predicting violence is that for every 100 people we classify as dangerous, no more than a third subsequently engage in violent behavior. This is the state of the art; most studies indicate an even poorer prediction rate.

Is this a fair estimate of the accuracy of my expert opinion? After all, I am absolutely certain that Mr. *X,* if released now, would continue the violent ways that have already left at least three people—possibly more—dead, and would probably have resulted in the deaths of the younger children in that family had he not been promptly apprehended.

Obviously, the only way to test my prediction empirically would be to release Mr. *X* and observe his subsequent behavior. Although the sheriff's department had been extraordinarily cooperative and helpful to us in our study of Mr. *X,* their dedication to the scientific process did not extend quite that far. In fact, they got rather surly when I suggested it. Mr. *X* has done his best to help us, not only by cooperating in our extensive assessment procedures, but also by doing his best to escape from the county jail. Unfortunately for science, his efforts were detected while he still had one lock left to circumvent.

So the first methodological problem in the study of predicting dangerous behavior is that there is no systematic scientific way to test our predictions. Then how did I come up with the statement that the state of the art is such that we really can only accurately predict violence in one out of every three times we try? To determine our predictive rate, we are forced to rely on so-called "experiments of nature"—cases in which individuals who have been classified as potentially dangerous have been nevertheless released. Obviously, there are drawbacks to such procedures. Steadman followed up patients who were transferred or released from Matteawan, a facility for dangerous criminals, after the statutes providing for their confinement were held to be defective (Steadman and Halatyn, 1971). Many of these individuals had been confined for years after the original psychiatric diagnosis of dangerousness had been made, and Steadman is the first to point out that this could have influenced the results. Harry Kozol was forced to rely on a subsample of cases in which, for various reasons, staff recommendations for continued confinement were over-ridden (Kozol et al., 1972). That group of cases is undoubtedly biased in a number of ways. J. S. McGuire (1976) and I were able to use an entire population, but the generalizability of our finding was limited because we were only attempting to predict violence in prison, a highly structured and limited milieu.

But even if it were possible to do more rigorous and sophisticated predictive research, I doubt that we would find a success rate notably better than that of the three reported studies. In examining the process of clinical appraisal closely, I will show that the identification of the potentially violent individual with sufficient accuracy to warrant preventive detention or, as in Texas, execution, is an impossible quest.

Twenty years ago, when I was frequently asked to determine which applicants for probation were likely to engage in violence, I naively felt that all we had to do was to cross-validate the many tests and measures of hostility and aggressiveness available in our clinical armamentarium and select the best device. This led to a series of studies in which some of our most trusted and proved clinical instruments—the Rorschach, the Thematic Apperception Test (TAT), the Minnesota Multiphasic Personality Inventory (MMPI), and others—were evaluated with respect to their ability to discriminate violent from nonviolent criminals. In 1968, after ten years of such research, I summarized the results of my findings and those of other investigators for the President's Commission on the Causes and Prevention of Violence as follows:

> Thus far no structured or projective test scale has been derived which, when used alone, will predict violence in the individual case in a satisfactory manner. Indeed, none has been developed which will adequately *post*dict, let alone *pre*dict, violent behavior (Megargee, 1970: p. 145).

Mr. *X* is a case in point. His MMPI profile is not the profile one would expect from an individual who, by his own admission, would stab a mother and her daughter to death and open up the daughter's chest cavity to inspect and possibly extract her heart to keep for a souvenir. Of course, we do not have adequate MMPI norms for people who engage in such behavior. We are forced to rely on clinical judgment, and in my judgment his is not an MMPI profile that would lead me to suspect Mr. *X* had engaged in such bizarre acts of violence.

This was true also of the other tests we administered. The TAT and the Rorschach were relatively benign. My hackles did rise when Mr. *X,* after reporting that a small yellow detail on Card X looked like a lion, singled out a red spot as representing the heart, but without knowing the bizarre behavior in which he had engaged this response would not have attracted more than passing attention. Certainly, if everyone who ever perceives a heart on the Rorschach were assessed as having a propensity for amateur cardiac surgery, we would overpredict violence even more than we do now.

Is Mr. *X* simply a test miss? No. The test data accurately reflect his current psychological status. The problem is that he does not fit our conception of the "normal" multiple murderer. We simply have an inadequate understanding of human violence.

One of the basic difficulties in attempting to do research on human violence is that although everyone supposedly knows what violence is, there is no generally agreed-upon semantic or operational definition of the term. In my annual seminar on aggression and violence, I always start the first session by listing a dozen or so behavioral incidents and asking the class whether or not they would regard them as constituting aggressive behavior. No class has yet reached a consensus.

Whatever our individual definitions of violence, I am sure all of us would agree that Mr. *X*'s behavior would be included. Yet, this agreement would break down as we examined other cases. For example, most of the authors in this volume, myself included, have been acting as if the Mr. *X*s of this world were the only ones who are violent and dangerous. Despite the fact that in my work with the police I probably expose myself to somewhat more dangers than the average person, I submit that my life and well-being have been jeopardized more by the behavior of men and women in corporate boardrooms than by the individuals I have encountered in prisons, jails, and on the street. More people are killed, injured, and maimed annually by drunken drivers than by any other group of offenders (Stone, 1975). Yet drunken drivers and corporate executives are not the focus of our discussion in this book of violence. Why? Perhaps it is because of implicit differences in our definitions of dangerousness.

People disagree on whether legal as well as illegal injuries inflicted on others constitute violence. If Mr. *X* gets his professed wish and becomes the first person in his state to go to the electric chair in recent years, should we classify the executioner who pulls the switch or the governor who signs the death warrant as violent?

Intentionality is another point of dissension. Is the person who unintentionally causes injury or death to another violent? What of the individuals who plan acts of violence but are thwarted before they can carry them out, like the band of men who conspired to capture a nuclear submarine and fire a rocket at New London? They hurt no one. Are they violent?

Definitional problems like these are of more than academic interest because such differences in semantic definitions pave the way for differences in operational definitions. As a result, different theorists and investigators who are all ostensibly studying the same phenomenon, may in fact focus on quite different sorts of behavior, using a diverse array of subjects. It is not surprising that different theories on the etiology and dynamics of violence have emerged, and, given such diversity, that clinicians should differ on the diagnostic signs they believe are indicative of violence.

In science, we generally settle such differences of opinion by empirical investigation. However, rigorous studies of the psychology of human violence are difficult to perform. The experimental approach is impossible. It would be easy to make definitive causal statements if we could expose two matched groups to two sets of conditions—one calculated to arouse violence and the other not, and then observe whether the violence resulted. However, experiments inciting people to violence are unethical and illegal as well.

Unable to use the experimental method in the investigation of human violence, behavioral scientists have had to resort to different strategies, none of which is entirely adequate. One method is to apply the experimental method to milder forms of aggressive behavior in the hope that the principles derived can be extrapolated to violence without too much distortion or error. This method was used extensively in the 1950s, particularly in investigations of the frustration-aggression hypothesis. Our research has clearly shown, however, that the dynamics involved in potentially lethal aggression differ considerably from the milder forms of aggressive behavior that are amenable to laboratory study.

Naturalistic observations of human violence or attempts to reconstruct violent incidents by interviewing people who observed or took part in such events is also unsatisfactory. The disturbances in Chicago during the 1968 Democratic Convention were probably witnessed by more people, including members of the press who are trained to observe and report the facts, than any similar confrontation in our history. The multitude of differing accounts of what took place exemplifies the unreliability of this form of evidence for scientific purposes.

The tactic I have followed, as illustrated by the case of Mr. *X,* has been to investigate the personality structure of violent individuals. There are obvious drawbacks to this approach. It is questionable how representative people who have been apprehended and convicted for violent behavior are of the population of those who have engaged in such behavior. The violent incidents themselves, as well as the subsequent judicial and correctional experiences, inevitably leave their mark. Mr. *X* had experienced a religious conversion while in jail and had also been reconciled with his mother, changes which no doubt contributed to his desire to assist us in our investigation. These changes made the personality test pattern considerably more benign than one would expect in an individual who had been sentenced to death two days previously.

Another strategy that avoids some of the ethical dilemmas involved in the investigation of human violence is the study of extremely aggressive behavior in other species. Although Konrad Lorenz and Robert Ardrey comfortably extrapolate data obtained on greylag geese and three-prong sticklebacks to *homo sapiens,* most psychologists have serious reservations about the generality of the formulation derived from the study of other species.

Because of these difficulties in doing rigorous research on human violence, there is as yet no way of adequately testing the competing theories of violence to determine which formulations are correct and which are in error. This naturally makes it difficult for the clinician who would attempt to predict individual potential for violent behavior. Lacking a well established theory of the personality and situational factors resulting in violence, he must fall back on clinical experience, hunches, and intuition, all of which are notoriously fallible.

PERSONALITY FACTORS LEADING TO VIOLENCE

Despite the diversity of theories of violence, there is at least some agreement on the personality factors that interact to determine whether or not an individual will engage in violent behavior. These three personality factors can be labeled "instigation to aggression," "inhibitions against aggression," and "habit strength."

Instigation to aggression refers to all the motivational factors that lead an individual toward violent behavior. The first type of motivation is the conscious or unconscious desire to hurt or injure the victim; such behavior is reinforced by the victim's pain. When this motivation is a relatively enduring trait, we call it hostility or hatred; when it is a relevantly transient state, we refer to it as anger, or, if it is particularly intense, rage. The more enduring traits, hostility or hatred, are more easily assessed than are the highly transient, situation-specific emotions of anger or rage. It is particularly difficult to assess the latter in an institutional setting in which an individual is removed from the irritations and daily frustrations that will confront him in the community. Moreover, in an institutional setting, a person may be taking medication that is designed to minimize such feelings, thus compounding the difficulty of the assessment task.

In addition to instigation to aggression stemming from the conscious or unconscious desire to injure the victim, we must also deal with instrumental motivation to aggression. Aggression may be a means to some other end, such as status in a delinquent gang, mastery in a marital conflict, or material gain in robbery. Shooting someone in self-defense, in the line of duty, as part of a campaign of political terrorism, or to fulfill an underworld contract are all examples of instrumental aggression. Like anger, instrumental motivation may vary considerably according to the circumstances of which the person finds himself. Most of our clinical assessment devices are designed to assess hostility, but anger, rage, and instrumental motivation must also be appraised if instigation to aggression is to be assessed accurately.

The second factor is inhibitions against violent or aggressive behavior. Inhibitory factors have received less attention than motivation, but they are equally important because, whenever inhibitions against a response exceed the instigation, the response will be suppressed or repressed. Unfortunately for those who would predict violence, inhibitions are even more specific and changeable than is instigation. They differ markedly from target to target. In his book, *Working,* Studs Terkel quoted a steelworker who said, "All day I want to tell my foreman to go fuck himself, but I can't. So I find a guy in a tavern. To tell him that. And he tells me too . . . he's punching me and I'm punching him because we actually want to punch someone else" (Terkel, 1974: p. xxxiii).

Inhibitions also vary as a function of the specific act. Terkel's steelworker had few compunctions about hitting another man in a tavern, but he refrained from using a knife. Mr. *X* always used a knife but apparently never used a gun. (Speaking of Mr. *X,* it was fascinating to learn that he had been stabbed near the heart as a child and had also been raped several times in prison. It seems reasonable to us that the fact that these crimes had been inflicted on him lowered his inhibitions against stabbing and raping others.)

Like instigation, inhibitions may vary over time. Moreover, they can be influenced chemically. The association between alcohol and violence seems to stem from alcohol's anesthetic effect on the brain areas that mediate inhibitions. Chronic as well as acute brain syndromes may have similar effects. These variations in inhibitions over time and as a function of target, specific act, and intoxication all complicate the assessment process.

The third basic personality factor that must be assessed is what Spence referred to as habit strength, the degree to which the individual has been rewarded for engaging in aggressive behavior in the past. This is particularly relevant in the prediction of instrumental aggression. If the individual has grown up in a setting in which the most aggressive person got the largest portion of food, the warmest corner of the room, the sexual favors of the neighborhood girls, and the most respect from his peers, then it is more likely that he will use aggression to satisfy his desires in the future.

The situation is further complicated by the fact that different combinations of these three basic variables, instigation, inhibitions, and habit strength, may be associated with assaultive behavior. Violence is not limited to the individual with high instigation, low inhibitions, and a long history of repetitive assaultive behavior. Other patterns may also lead to violence, as in the case of the chronically overcontrolled assaultive type that I delineated in the early 1960s. The chronically overcontrolled person has extremely high inhibitions and minimal habit strength. When exposed to extreme or recurrent frustration or provocation, the excessive inhibitions of these mild-mannered and unassertive people prevent them from expressing their anger. As a result, instigation accumulates to a point where even their inhibitions are overcome, so they explode into an uncharacteristic outburst of extreme violence. Such individuals may be even more dangerous than the chronically undercontrolled type who engages in repetitive aggressive behavior. Nor do the overcontrolled and undercontrolled exhaust the types of violent individuals whom we encounter. This multiplicity of patterns associated with acts of violence further hinders those who attempt to predict violence in the individual case.

SITUATIONAL FACTORS

Thus far, we, like most behavioral scientists, have devoted all our attention to examining the personality characteristics that may be associated with violent behavior. Indeed, the very title of this book, *Violence and the Violent Individual,* exemplifies this preoccupation with personality factors. As we learned in our first psychology class, however, behavior is a function of the interaction of personality factors with situational variables. Even if we could assess perfectly the personality factors I have mentioned and calculate their interaction precisely, our prediction of violence would go astray without a consideration of the situational aspects.

I doubt many of us regard ourselves as violent. Yet, who can honestly say that he or she is absolutely incapable of violence, given the proper circumstances? This demonstrates the power of situational factors. Situational factors may also operate to inhibit or deter aggressive behavior. The steelworker mentioned earlier does his fighting in a tavern rather than a church. An increasingly important topic in rape research is the investigation of strategies a potential victim can use to deter her would-be assailant, and police officers are being trained in ways of defusing potentially violent confrontations.

Despite the overriding importance of situational circumstances, it is difficult if not impossible for behavioral scientists, particularly in institutional settings, to assess adequately the circumstances in which their clients are likely to find themselves. At present, I am involved in a law suit in which the plaintiffs are suing a certain mental institution for negligence for releasing a patient who subsequently shot and killed another individual. One possible reconstruction of this event suggests that the eventual victim first shot the former patient in the leg and was killed in the ensuing struggle for the gun. Assuming for the sake of argument that this was, in fact, what occurred, does this mean hospitals are obliged to confine for preventive detention any patient who would respond with violence after being shot? If so, we may anticipate vastly increased appropriations being required for mental institutions.

THE PREDICTION OF VIOLENCE

Clinical assessment involves taking small samples of behavior to estimate future behavior. Just as in political polling, such a process inevitably involves error. Even in predictive situations in which the relevant variables are much better understood and the situational factors relatively well controlled, such as predicting who will succeed in college, errors inevitably result. Given all the complexities and uncertainties associated with violent behavior and the problems involved in attempting to assess the relevant variables, it would be surprising if even more errors did not occur.

Unfortunately, once any errors are made, they are magnified greatly by another factor that is peculiar to such infrequent forms of behavior as violence. This is the base rate or false-positive problem. As Meehl and Rosen demonstrated in their classic 1955 article, whenever we attempt to predict infrequent events, it is inevitable that many people will be incorrectly diagnosed as exhibiting that rare behavior. Let me explain.

In predicting dangerous behavior, we can make two kinds of errors: false-positives are those people we erroneously predict will engage in dangerous behavior, whereas false-negatives are those we erroneously predict will not engage in dangerous behavior. The public is primarily concerned with false-negatives, people who, after being classified as not being dangerous, are returned to the community, and attack someone. I can share that view. I was pinned down for 90 minutes once by a sniper at the University of Texas who was a false-negative. However, Monahan has demonstrated that mental health personnel are much more inclined to overpredict dangerous behavior; that is, we are more likely to be conservative and classify doubtful cases as dangerous, thereby increasing our false-positive rates. The infrequency of violent behavior greatly magnifies the effects of this tendency.

Let us suppose that someone devised a method of predicting dangerous behavior that is far better than any currently available technique, and that a validation study showed that the new technique correctly identified 90 percent of the people who later engaged in dangerous behavior and 90 percent of those who did not subsequently behave dangerously; that is, the false-positive rate and the false-negative rate were both 10 percent.

Table 1

Hypothetical Prediction with False-Negative Rate of 10 Percent and False Positive Rate of 10 Percent Applied to Sample with Base Rate of 50 Percent

Predicted Behavior	Actual Behavior: Violent	Actual Behavior: Not Violent	Total
Violent	900 (true positive)	100 (false positive)	1000
Not violent	100 (false negative)	900 (true negative)	1000
Total	1000	1000	2000

This paragon of predictors is demonstrated in Table 1. Here we have a hypothetical sample of 2000 people, 1000 of whom are violent and 1000 of whom are not violent. The base rate for violence in this sample is 50 percent, and with a 50 percent base rate any test device can make its maximum contribution to prediction. In this example, the test correctly identifies 900 of the subsequently violent individuals and 900 of those who did not become violent. Thus, the test classifies 1000 as potentially violent, 900 of whom actually engage in violence.

What would happen if we applied this test to a sample with a lower base rate? For the past 10 years I have engaged in a major program of research at the Federal Correctional Institution (FCI) at Tallahassee, Florida. We have followed throughout their incarceration all inmates admitted during a two-year period. Among other things, we learned that the base rate for violence in the institution is about 14 percent. Table 2 shows what occurs when we apply this hypothetical predictive device to 2000 consecutive FCI admissions. The base rate for violence at the FCI is 14 percent, so 255 of the 2000 individuals would actually be violent. The test would correctly identify 80 percent or 230 of the 255 violent inmates. Similarly, of the 1745 not violent, 1570 would be correctly classified. Because of the base rates, however, the actual number of individuals erroneously classified as violent would be much higher. Of the 405 people the test would predict as being violent, 175 would be misclassified.

Table 2

Hypothetical Predictor with False-Negative Rate of 10 Percent and False-Positive Rate of 10 Percent Applied to 2000 Prison Admissions (Base Rate = 0.14 Percent)

Predicted Behavior	Actual Behavior: Violent	Actual Behavior: Not Violent	Total
Violent	230 (true positive)	175 (false positive)	405
Not violent	25 (false negative)	1570 (true negative)	1595
Total	255	1745	2000

In some situations, this many errors would still be acceptable. If the only consequence of being labeled potentially violent were perhaps being placed in a dormitory with greater staff coverage or being subjected to further evaluation, then the results would not be distressing. If, however, those labeled potentially violent were kept for the duration of their sentence rather than being paroled, this many errors would indeed be cause for concern.

However, as I have stated, we have no assessment device that correctly identifies 90 percent of our cases. Dr. Judith McGuire (1976) recently completed a dissertation in which she used actuarial methods in an attempt to derive an equation combining psychological tests and case history variables in an effort to identify potentially violent FCI inmates. McGuire (1976) derived and cross-validated several such equations. Table 3 shows the best of these equations applied to 2000 consecutive inmates. McGuire's best equation had a false-negative rate of 11 percent, almost the same as that in our hypothetical example, but the false-positive rate was 62 percent. As you can see, applying this equation to the Federal Correctional Institution at Tallahassee would result in 1308 inmates being labeled potentially violent, of whom only 226 would subsequently engage in assaultive behavior. I want to emphasize that McGuire's study is one of the most successful, perhaps *the* most successful, predictive equation yet reported. But for all practical purposes the equation is useless. (The other follow-up

Table 3

Actual Best Predictor with False-Negative Rate of 11 Percent and False-Positive Rate of 62 Percent Applied to 2000 Prison Admissions* (Base Rate = 14 Percent)

Predicted Behavior	Actual Behavior: Violent	Actual Behavior: Not Violent	Total
Violent	226 (true positive)	1082 (false positive)	1308
Not violent	29 (false negative)	663 (true negative)	692
Total	255	1745	2000

* Data from McGuire (1976).

studies that I have mentioned variously show false-positive rates ranging from 65 percent to as high as 90 percent.)

The social-policy implications of this finding are frightening. As Alan Stone, professor of law and psychiatry of Harvard University, has stated, "If dangerousness is the sole criterion for civil commitment or other preventive detention, and if an empirical study demonstrates that violence is a rare event . . . then even if we have a very good predictive technique or device, we would end up confining many more false than true-positives" (Stone, 1975).

What have we learned thus far? Because of the problems in defining and studying violence empirically, we at present have no adequate, scientifically validated theories of violence. It is clear, however, that a number of different personality patterns interacting with a vast array of situational factors may result in individual acts of violence. But the limitations of assessment techniques make it impossible to predict with perfect accuracy. Once errors occur, the rarity of violent behavior inevitably inflates the number of false-positives that will result. Unless the rate of violence increases vastly within society, the identification of the violent individual with any degree of precision appears to be an impossible task, and the prospects are dim for any marked improvement in the immediate future.

ACKNOWLEDGMENT

Preparation of this paper was supported in part by National Institute of Mental Health Grant No. MH-29911.

REFERENCES

KOZOL, H., BOUCHER, R., and GAROFALO, R. The diagnosis and treatment of dangerousness. *Crime and Delinquency,* 18,371-372, 1972.

MCGUIRE, J. S. *Prediction of Dangerous Behavior in a Federal Correctional Institution.* Unpublished doctoral dissertation, Florida State University, 1976.

MEGARGEE, E. I. The prediction of violence with psychological tests, in *Current Topics in Clinical and Community Psychology,* vol. 2. C. D. Spielberger, ed. Academic Press, New York, 1970.

MEEHL, P. E., and ROSEN, A. Antecedent probability and the efficiency of psychometric signs, patterns, or cutting scores. *Psychol. Bull.* 9:37-50, 1955.

STEADMAN, H., and HALATYN, A. The Baxstrom patients: Backgrounds and outcomes. *Seminars in Psychiatry* 3:376-386, 1971.

STONE, A. A. *Mental Health and Law: A System in Transition.* Washington, D. C., U. S. Government Printing Office, 1975.

TERKEL, S. *Working.* Pantheon, New York, 1974.

CHAPTER 12

Adolescent Murderers: Literature Review and Preliminary Research Findings

KENNETH S. SOLWAY
LINDA RICHARDSON
J. RAY HAYS
VICTOR H. ELION

Researchers and scientists were noticeably upset by Senator William Proxmire's critical comments on the social relevance of behavioral research as reflected in his Golden Fleece awards. Our review of the literature on adolescent violence—more specifically, adolescent murderers—revealed, however, that Senator Proxmire had hit the proverbial nail squarely on the head. At a time when violence by youth is regarded as a major, escalating social problem, it is surprising that so little scientific research has been done on its prediction and control. Among about 45 studies of young murderers reviewed, we found fewer than 5 that even alluded to a previous body of literature, let alone empirically based research, that might have guided our own investigation. We found only one literature review on child murderers (Adams, 1974) and even that was less than complete. Only four studies provided information on the ethnicity of the murderer. All studies in this area were retrospective and none were predictive except in the most general way.

The research program to be described is at an early stage. It began with a review of the literature on adolescent murderers, combined with a systematic collection of psychological test data and demographic variables on all adolescent murderers in a large metropolitan county in the southwestern United States. We contacted professionals in other metropolitan areas of Texas to expand our subject pool. At present, we have collected data on 18 adolescent murderers. With one exception, they represented a group of murderers referred consecutively through the juvenile authorities in the last 18 months. We know of no previous study of adolescent murderers in which psychological test data were systematically collected. We will focus first on a review of the literature on adolescent murderers, and second, on the description of data thus collected. A report on some intragroup analysis of the data will also be made, with a view to developing a typology of adolescent murderers.

EMPIRICAL STUDIES OF ADOLESCENT MURDERS

As indicated, the literature on adolescent murderers is disappointingly sparse in view of the apparent concern about teenage violence. Only two empirical studies that attempted to differentiate among murderers, or between murderers and other youths on broad or inferred psychological dimensions were found. Petti and Davidman (1977), using the Children's Locus of Control Scale (Bialer, 1961) to compare children who were matched for severity of illness, sex, age, and IQ, found that 9 homicidal children, ages 6 to 11, perceived themselves as more externally controlled than did the comparison group of children hospitalized for psychiatric disorders. Of the nine homicidal children in this study only one child's attempt to perform the act resulted in death to the victim. The authors reasoned that an external locus of control could be associated either with depression and suicidal ideation, or with hostility and homicidal preoccupation. In spite of the study's overall thoughtful methodology, the small sample renders this conclusion speculative.

Sendi and Blomgren (1975) compared 10 adolescent patients who committed murder with 10 adolescents who attempted homicide unsuccessfully and 10 adolescents randomly selected from among hospitalized patients. The first two groups differed from each other on clinical variables. The group who had committed murder was labeled by the authors as the psychotic-regressive group and reflected a long history of schizoid adjustment, maternal deprivation, and sexual inhibitions. The group who had attempted or threatened homicide was labeled the organic-impulsive group, its members characterized by organic brain syndrome or minimal brain damage, abnormal EEG, intellectual and educational deficiencies, and episodic dyscontrol. By contrast, the murderers in the psychotic-regressive group had average or above-average IQs and normal EEGs. The authors stated the "hostile, destructive nature of the environment of adolescents who committed homicides appears more detrimental to their premurder disposition than the less intense but hostile rejecting environment of adolescents who threatened or attempted homicide" (Sendi and Blomgren, 1975). Thus, even though clinical differences between groups were discovered, the researchers emphasized the importance of environmental factors.

CLINICAL STUDIES OF ADOLESCENT MURDERERS

Examination of the remaining investigations of youth who committed murder revealed only clinical and theoretical treatises usually based on a sample of fewer than 10 and frequently fewer than 3 or 4. The vast majority of the studies on adolescent murderers are based on descriptions of young people who were emotionally disturbed. These included youths who have killed someone in their family (parricides) or close acquaintances. A much smaller number of studies described youths who had a definite pattern of criminal activity or who, in addition to having committed murder, were diagnosed as psychopathic. A few studies deal with what were paradoxically referred to as "accidental murderers" (Foodman and Estrada, 1977). Thus, a typology of three conceptually distinct groups of adolescent murderers emerged or seemed implicit from the clinical literature; these groups were: the psychiatrically disturbed and/or intrafamilial murderers; the criminal or psychopathic-like murderers; and the innocent killers. The clinical literature on adolescent murderers will be reviewed using these three groupings.

Emotionally Disturbed Youths

There seemed to be a consensus on the family variables and personality characteristics of the young murderers who were considered emotionally or psychiatrically disturbed. The most frequently mentioned characteristic was an unusual relationship between the offender and his or her special, seductive, overprotective, or dominant mother (Easson and Steinhilber, 1961; Russell, 1965; Scherl and Mack, 1966; Smith, 1965; Walsh-Brennan, 1974; Offer et al., 1975; Sendi and Blomgren, 1975; Thornton and Pray, 1975; Walsh-Brennan, 1975; Evseeff, 1976; Corder et al., 1976). This maternal relationship often seemed to be associated with a father figure who was absent, distant, or passive (Easson and Steinhilber, 1961; Russell, 1965; Hellsten and Katila, 1965; Zients and Zenoff, 1977). The presence of violence in the family of the disturbed homicidal offender, often directly expressed against her or him, was also frequently mentioned in the literature (Bender, 1959; Easson and Steinhilber, 1961; Silver et al., 1969; Sadoff, 1971; Tanay, 1973; Bolman, 1974; Miller and Looney, 1974; McCarthy, 1974; King, 1975; Sendi and Blomgren, 1975; Corder et al., 1976; Mann et al., 1976; Evseef, 1976). Perhaps it is not surprising that this family constellation and interaction might produce a child with a paranoid or schizoid orientation to life, and this result has been well supported in clinical reports (Smith, 1965; Sadoff, 1971; Russell, 1965, 1973; McCarthy, 1974; Thornton and Pray, 1975; McCleary, 1975; Sendi and Blomgren, 1975).

The combination of an overly involved relationship to a mother figure and a distant relationship to a father figure has led many of the clinicians to conclude that homicidal youths have boundary problems between themselves and others, and that perhaps the act of homicide was an attempt by the adolescent to preserve a sense of self (Malmquist, 1971; Tanay, 1973). Another interpretation of the homicide was that it represented the adolescent's attempt to break out of a symbiotic relationship with the mother and, directly or indirectly, kill the mother (Russell, 1965). Other adjectives or characteristics used to describe young murderers included: poor role models, poor or no identifications, early oral deprivation, fear of object loss, disturbed psychosexual development, omnipotence, ambivalence, powerlessness, temporary suspension of a strict and punitive superego, and ego dyscontrol.

Smith (1965), in his study of eight murderers aged 14 to 21, provided perhaps the most integrative and meaningful clinical description of the prototypical young, disturbed murderer. His investigation of adolescent murderers revealed that each of the young men grew up in a family that was disintegrating, making normal processes of identification difficult. Even when the parents were still together, these families contained or expressed so much primitive violence that the effect on the adolescent was the same. Smith held the relationship between the adolescent and his mother to be primarily responsible for the youth's problems, and Smith conjectured that in every instance a parent or parent symbol became the murder victim. The adolescents were not psychotic or schizophrenic, but Smith perceived each of them "a person of considerable ego weakness, frustrated by severe object loss and crippled capacity for identification or a weak identification with poor ego models, coupled with potential for lapsing into episodes of destructive violence of psychotic proportions in which ordinary control is overturned" (p. 317). Smith believed the young murderers had in common a sense of abandonment, with a consequent angry distrust of lasting relationships and a hypersensitivity to the experience of loss.

At a time when family therapy and social-systems theory is popular, it is worthwhile to mention a number of studies that have implicated the total family system as an instigator of homicide, particularly in cases in which a family member was a victim (Bromberg, 1949; Easson and Steinhilber, 1961; Sargent, 1962; Russell, 1965; Hellsten et al., 1965; Tanay, 1973; Tooley, 1975; Corder et al., 1976; Haizlip et al., 1976). These studies advance the notion that families or parents unconsciously provoked and endorsed their offspring's crime. The homicidal youths experienced little remorse or guilt, and if one parent was a victim, the other parent often remarried quickly after the death of the spouse.

The psychological dynamics of the parricidal and psychologically disturbed young murderer seemed reasonably well defined in the clinical literature. The clinical picture provided is still not significantly different from the picture of many youths who, although disturbed, have not committed homicide. It is impossible, therefore, to predict which pathological youths are likely to commit homicide. Some consideration must be given to situational cues and the interaction of situational and personality cues (Megargee, 1976; Monahan, 1975) before prediction becomes possible.

The Psychopathic-like Murderer

A much smaller body of literature describes the family backgrounds and psychological characteristics of adolescent murderers who were seen as delinquent, criminal, or psychopathic, the second group in our derived typology (Russell, 1965, 1973; Tanay, 1969; Miller and Looney, 1974; Walsh-Brennan, 1974; King, 1975; Sendi and Blomgren, 1975; Zients and Zenoff, 1977). Descriptions of the youths involved were remarkably similar and generally fit the organic-impulsive type described by Sendi and Blomgren. Two of the studies on this topic will be reviewed because we consider them the most important and representative of the group.

King (1975) examined nine adolescents (8 boys and 1 girl) whose average age was 14 and who had committed an explosive, brutal homicide. Their families were generally intact. Father figures were either present or had spent a significant amount of time in the home. The homes were full of turmoil; the parents fought violently and the children were physically abused. The homicidal adolescents were usually singled out for mistreatment. On the one side, they experienced their father's unpredictable mood swings, often embellished by drinking and expressed physical violence, while on the other, they perceived their mothers as often afraid of their children. These adolescents were described as confused in personality orientation and disturbed in psychosexual development; they all had paranoid views of life and other people, they functioned in the dull-normal to average intellectual range but had considerable difficulty in an academic setting. All but one of the children were completely without remorse or awareness of what they had done, and all but one admitted the act.

In explaining why these adolescents became violent and committed murder, King cited the combination of deficits in the mastery of language and cognitive skills with the resultant absolute reliance on feelings to guide behavior. King's premise was that the initial level of coping with the world requires comprehension of society's code of verbal and written communication. Unable to relate through symbols, these violent youths reduced linguistic communication to terse speech and ultimately to terse action. Action became their basic method of communication, and language, when used, was usually action-loaded (Make me! Get off me! Knock it off!) and intended to cut off the possibility of more meaningful interaction. Therefore interpersonal exchanges were reduced to power struggles in which depersonalization and indiscriminate assessment of people occurred. In this context people may not be differentiated from inanimate objects. King found an inevitable shift toward absolute reliance on feeling as the "primary coin of interchange" for these young people, given their paucity of language and cognitive skills:

> "A naked raw-edged sensitivity to abuse of feeling was evident in all. The biggest threat to recommit homicide was that someone would make them mad, cause them to lose face, or hurt their feelings. Although they responded to people liked, the baffling thing about it was that this liking was transitory. A person liked in one incident may not even have been recognized during another" (King, 1975, p. 703).

In summary, King stated that the combination of cognitive deficit and overreliance on feeling leads to an inability of these homicidal youths to cope. Because of this inability, the youths became alienated, reactive, violent, and even homicidal.

Zients and Zenoff (1977) described a group of 7 adolescents charged with murder, who were interviewed by Zients, a psychiatrist in Washington, D.C. Zients and Zenoff refer to the group as primitive, nonempathic murderers, that is, youths who killed strangers either in the course of a robbery or for no discernible reason. Each had a history of previous assaultive behavior and many property offenses; the adolescents were educationally underachieving, their IQs ranged from borderline-retarded to low-average, and they evidenced perceptual-motor difficulties and minor neurological impairments. The youths were diagnosed as having borderline, sociopathic, or antisocial personality disorders. They had spent the first year of their lives in an overcrowded, poorly staffed institution or with an inadequate maternal figure. They displayed little guilt or conflict.

The Innocent Murderer

The literature on accidental or innocent murderers, the last group in the inferred typology, is quite sparse. Probably few of these youths are referred for psychological or psychiatric examination by police agencies because legal charges are not filed against them. Only two studies of these young people were available and they provided little information. In the study cited above, Zients and Zenoff (1977) reported 6 innocent murderers, 5 males and 1 female. The deaths in these cases resulted from self-defense or accidents; one of the youths involved was believed to be neurotic, one a primitive nonempathic murderer, and four were believed to be normal. Foodman and Estrada (1977), reporting on 4 adolescents who committed accidental homicides, concluded that the closer the accidental homicides approximated an impulsive act, the more features were found that are characteristic of high-risk groups. The authors defined high-risk groups as consisting of adolescents raised in a family or sociocultural environment that condoned violence. In a somewhat different vein, Bender (1959) reported that the children she studied neither anticipated nor expected their activities to result in the death of another person. The victim happened to block an activity initiated by the child. Bender concluded that the murderer was always innocent or the murder accidental, regardless of the child's behavior in carrying out the act.

The clinical literature reviewed above is primarily psychoanalytically oriented; therefore, it is often elegant and psychodynamically rich. The authors rarely, however, considered other ways of conceptualizing their clinical data and resorted to classic analytic theory to account for their findings. Unfortunately, no case study could be found in which the problem was seen from a different theoretical perspective, although ample social-learning, behavioral, and other theoretical viewpoints might have fostered more useful interpretations. The analytic case studies are of greatest value in treatment considerations for violent youth; their value for predictive purposes has not been established.

The Texas Research Institute of Mental Sciences Research Project

The first objective of our research was to examine sociodemographic, contextual, criminal-history, and psychological test data on as large and consecutive a sample of juvenile homicides as possible. Included in the sample were juveniles accused of either homicide or involuntary manslaughter. We will describe the sample obtained and then report within-group analyses conducted for the purpose of empirical testing of the inferred typology based on our literature review. Where possible, we will compare the sociodemographic information on our adolescent sample with samples of adults who have committed homicide, and compare the test data from the adolescent sample with normative adolescent responses.

Eighteen youths charged with murder or involuntary manslaughter were tested by one of two women examiners. The adolescents were given a battery of psychological tests before their court appearances. The tests from which data were used are the Wechsler Intelligence Scale for Children—Revised (WISC-R), Peabody Picture Vocabulary Test, Culture-Fair intelligence Test, Wide Range Achievement Test (WRAT), Bender-Gestalt Visual-Motor Test, Human Figure Drawings, Rorschach, Minnesota Multiphasic Personality Inventory (MMPI), and Interpersonal Checklist. We were reasonably certain that our sample was consecutive, with one exception. Statistics reported in the *Houston Post* (October 27, 1978) indicated that 10 juveniles were investigated for homicide in 1977; 16 juveniles have been investigated this year. Our data collection began in mid-1977.

The mean age of our subjects was 15.1 years; the age range was 11 through 17. There were 14 boys and four girls. Twelve are black, four white, and two are Mexican-American. The victims included 12 black persons, four whites, and two Mexican-Americans; the victims' mean age was 27.4 years, the age range between 12 and 64 years. Seven of the victims were teenagers, 8 were in their twenties or thirties. Three of the victims were the murderer's family members, 11 were friends or acquaintances, and four were not known by the murderers. All except one of the homicides were intraracial; in 14 of the 18 murders, males were the victims. These data are basically consistent with those reported on adult homicides (Wolfgang and Ferracuti, 1967; Ferracuti and Newman, 1974).

The murder weapons were a knife in 9 cases, a gun in 6. Assorted blunt objects were used in the remaining cases. Eight of the murders took place in the homes of either the murderer or the victim, five in the murderer's neighborhood, and five occurred outside the murderer's normal surroundings. Therefore, two-thirds of the incidents leading to murder took place in environments familiar to the murderer.

Ten of the 18 adolescent murderers had natural parents who were divorced. Only five of the youths were living at home with both their natural parents at the time of the offense. All the adolescents were living with an adult female, usually the natural mother, but at least five were living in a family without an adult male. None was the oldest of the siblings; seven were the youngest children, and three were the second youngest. The average family size of the latter ten youths was five, which is the average family size of the total sample. All but one of the youths came from a family of at least three siblings, and none were only children.

Three of the adolescents had no previous police referrals, three had one, three had two, one had three previous referrals, and eight had four or more. At first referral, the mean age of the children was 12.9 years. None had previously committed offenses that involved violence directed against people. These characteristics support Strasburg's (1978) recent findings that violent acts seem to be occasional events in a random pattern of delinquent behavior, rather than a specialty of juveniles, that recidivists are responsible for the vast majority of violent offenses by juveniles, and that it is not possible to predict violent behavior simply on the basis of previous offense records.

While Strasburg also reported that most violent juvenile acts (64 percent) were committed with co-actors, the present sample of adolescents tended to effect their homicide alone (30 percent). Thus, adolescent murder may differ from other juvenile violence in this respect.

The average level of intellectual functioning exhibited by the total sample, measured by the WISC-R, was 82 (range, 59 to 107); average verbal-scale IQ on the WISC-R was 78 (range, 50 to 96); average performance-scale IQ was 88 (range, 65 to 121). The youths scored somewhat higher on the Culture-Fair test of intelligence (mean = 92; range, 76 to 127). This finding is consistent with our previous studies (Smith et al., 1977a, 1977b), which demonstrated that delinquent youths score higher on the Culture-Fair Intelligence Test than on the WISC-R. The homicidal adolescents in this study also performed slightly better on the Peabody Picture-Vocabulary Test (mean = 84; range, 58 to 143). Although there were significant variations within and between individuals' intellectual functioning, the group may be characterized as being of low-normal intelligence.

The mean attained grade level of the group was 8.5. It was surprising, therefore, that the grade levels the youths achieved on the WRAT were oral reading, grade 5.4; spelling, grade 4.2; arithmetic, grade 4.5. Obviously, the adolescents had received social promotions in school.

Bender-Gestalt test reproductions were evaluated for each of the adolescents with the Watkins system (Watkins, 1976) which scores for items that distinguish learning-disabled youngsters from normal ones. Only three of the 18 youths scored in the learning-disabled range. Human-figure drawings by each youth were scored for emotional disturbance with the Koppitz system (Koppitz, 1967). On this dimension only two scored in the range that would indicate emotional problems.

The Rorschach test was administered and scored objectively, using the Exner system (Exner, 1976). The tests were administered by one of two examiners who scored their own protocols. A third rater scored all protocols independently, and a reliability check between his scoring and that of the examiners was made. The rate of agreement was more than 86 percent in both cases—statistically, greater than chance. Rorschach responses on each subject were compared to age-appropriate norms for nonpatients devised by Exner (1976). The number of responses in each scoring category that fell at least one standard deviation above on some variables and below on others was totaled, and only those on which there was a strong tendency in one direction or the other were considered. The total number of responses on the Rorschach was generally low. This finding, in addition to interpretations of the differences on other variables, indicated that the adolescents seemed to constrict and control their responses particularly to affective stimuli. The youths scored higher also on a variable related to oppositionality. Their Rorschach responses indicated that they viewed things unconventionally. Their tendencies to emotional and interpersonal constriction and oppositionality were shown also in their performance on the Leary Interpersonal Diagnostic System (Leary, 1957). The Leary system involves the MMPI and Interpersonal Check List; it may prove useful in future research.

The mean MMPI scale scores of the total group of juveniles, using adult norms, revealed two major elevations on the psychopathic deviate (Pd) scale and the schizophrenic (Sc) scale. T-scores on these scales were in the 70 to 75 range, slightly more than two standard deviations from the mean. Except for the social introversion and masculinity/femininity scales, all other scores were mildly elevated with T-scores in the 60 to 65 range. Interpretations of the MMPI as well as other clinical tests are compromised by the current life status of the youngsters who, when examined, were incarcerated and awaiting their court hearing. The mean profile, nevertheless, resembled the profiles of violent juveniles in general (Spellacy, 1977; Lothstein and Jones, 1978). The main difference between this group and a more generally violent group was that our sample scored lower on the manic (MA) scale. The Sc and Pd peaks suggest a clinical picture of paranoid orientation, idiosyncratic thinking, alienation, and general difficulty in interpersonal relationships including authority figures. Persons with these peaks often have been described as chronically angry but not necessarily overtly hostile or sadistic. Thus, our MMPI and Rorschach findings are clinically similar.

When the MMPI results were submitted for analysis, using adolescent norms (Marks et al., 1974), all elevations were minimized and it was difficult to distinguish our sample from a normal sample of adolescents. It is difficult to explain the absence of elevations on the MMPI scales, using adolescent norms. Given their circumstances during the assessment, the adolescents may have responded defensively. The second possibility is that the sample is heterogeneous and that individual profiles combined to modify any possible elevations (Megargee, 1970). The third possibility is that the subjects are normal.

EMPIRICAL INVESTIGATION OF TYPOLOGIES OF ADOLESCENT MURDERERS

One objective of our study of adolescent murderers was to determine whether the typology derived from the literature review could be empirically verified. On the basis of this presumed typology, we divided the 18 youths into two groups. The first group consisted of 12 youths whose homicidal offenses involved a victim who was either a relative or a close acquaintance. The crime had been perpetrated in a highly emotional interpersonal situation that may have included the perception of imminent physical danger by the offender and provocation by the victim. For these reasons, these youths were likely to represent the emotionally disturbed group in the typology. In the second group were 6 youths whose homicidal offense involved a victim who was either a stranger or a distant acquaintance. The offenses in these cases occurred in the context or service of some other deviant or criminal behavior. These youths were believed, therefore, to represent the second group of murderers referred to in the typology as the criminal or psychopathic-like group. None in our sample were believed to represent the young murderers referred to in the literature as accidental killers.

We expected the two groups to differ from each other in that the designated emotionally disturbed group would display more evidence of anxiety and depression, show greater degree of acceptance of social mores and conventions, function better intellectually and educationally, and have fewer negative contacts with legal authorities than the "criminal" group.

The typology suggested by the literature did not fare well in statistical analysis of our group. Although a few variables did show statistical significance, our analyses did not confirm the typology. From a clinical point of view, however, the variables on which the groups differed were interesting. The emotionally disturbed group had higher schizophrenia scores on the MMPI and a greater number of popular responses and total human content on the Rorschach. The disturbed group had a higher verbal-scale IQ score on the WISC-R, while the criminal group achieved a higher performance-scale IQ. Although these differences and other trends in the data might be viewed as clinically supportive of the implicit typology, this conclusion should be regarded with considerable caution.

In addition to data analyses based on the presumed typology, we analyzed the data using a somewhat different grouping of the adolescents. The circumstances of the homicides committed by this group seemed to fall into three categories. Eight homicides were perpetrated in an impulsive, highly emotional context, without apparent forethought. For example, if homicide was the end result of a fight among intimates, in which either the adolescent or a relative was threatened by imminent assault, the subject was assigned to one group. Four of the homicides in our sample occurred in what may be defined loosely as a planned act. In these cases, the adolescent may have been involved in some type of interaction or altercation with someone, left the scene, and after a period of time pursued the victim and killed him. Youths who committed homicide in this manner were assigned to a second group. Six of the youths, as already indicated, committed the crime in the context of another crime, and the homicide seemed incidental to the total situation. These youths formed the third group.

Underlying the decision to group subjects in this manner was our assumption that the nature and severity of individual psychopathology would vary in some direct way with the amount of time each subject had to consider the implications of his or her actions. More specifically, we expected examinations of psychological characteristics of the first group to disclose evidence that the homicide was the culmination of the subject's attempts to cope with an emotionally tense situation of long duration, whereas the data for subjects in the second group would reflect a more deviant adjustment in other areas of functioning, such as more previous arrests and educational achievement problems. The third group was expected to have a similar but more intense pattern of deviant adjustment than the second group, perhaps to display characteristics of classic psychopathy (that is, an inability to empathize, high psychopathic deviance scores on the MMPI, etc.).

Using the groupings of the impulsive or spontaneous murder, the planned murder, and the psychopathic-like murder (grouping that conform somewhat to those employed in criminal law), the data did not reveal any significant group differences on any of the psychological test variables.

Examination of background and behavioral factors associated with the offense, however, revealed several patterns that suggest that further work on a grouping scheme might provide useful information.

For example, the victims of the impulsive group of offenders were not only close relatives or friends of the young murderer, but they were also persons who had been a major source of tension in the offender's life for a long time. All the victims had exhibited hostility toward the offender or the offender's parents before the homicide. The homicide always occurred in the home of the offender, usually in the presence of other family members. In no case did the offender attempt to avoid arrest. In all of the cases of the first group, the homicide occurred spontaneously and, with one exception, the weapon used was a knife. The knives were household types and were, therefore, immediately available, as was the handgun used by one subject.

In the absence of firm psychological data, we can only speculate about the extent to which the elevated emotional impact of the victim's status in the family situation might have affected the adolescents in the impulsive group. The fact that all victims represented some intrusive authority figure in the offender's life suggests the possibility that the homicidal act may have involved much more than a situation-specific reaction to a threat of physical harm. If this is true, one might not expect to find evidence of severe psychopathology on psychological tests. The homicides would have provided a resolution to a realistic conflict.

A decidedly different picture emerged from examinations of the circumstances of the planned murders. All homicides by adolescents in this group occurred in public settings. The relationship between the offender and the victim was more distant, and the homicides occurred as an extension of an argument or fight in which the offender had been matched or overpowered by the victim. A handgun was used in all of these cases. The offenders left the scene and attempted to avoid detection and arrest. Thus, one could argue that, in contrast to the resolution of tension experienced by the first group, in the second group the homicide may have induced tension. If these distinctions could be shown as reliable and valid, they would identify possible areas of intervention in a substantial portion of adolescent murderers.

The third, the so-called psychopathic-like group of offenders had no common patterns of background and behavior. The victims were strangers to the offenders in this group. For the most part, the victims seemed to have appeared at the wrong place at the wrong time. Each of these homicides seemed to be particularly gruesome in comparison to the murders committed by the adolescents in the other two groups. Weapons included knives, handguns, and other instruments not usually chosen to kill someone. There was no evidence that the primary motivation of the subjects in this group was homicide. The homicide appeared incidental to the commission of another crime or deviant act. Unfortunately, the circumstances surrounding this third group of homicides leads us to believe that this kind of homicide is totally unpredictable and thus not amenable to prevention except in a general sense.

We chose to do the second within-group analysis according to the tone and direction of recent literature on the prediction of violence, particularly reviews by Monahan (1975) and Megargee (1976) that have emphasized the need to assess the context of a violent crime in combination with psychological factors. Although neither of our within-group analyses produced statistically significant findings, it would not be reasonable at this point to discard either the typology implicit in the literature or the grouping based on situational factors. Our data are preliminary to more extensive research, and our sample size is small. Larger sample sizes will allow the use of more rigorous statistical procedures, such as discriminant function analysis. In subsequent analyses, we will use more systematic criteria for dividing subjects into groups. For example, our initial division of subjects into emotionally disturbed and criminal-like groups might have been supported had we used psychological test scores (e.g., the Pd scale of the MMPI or the F+ percent of the Rorschach) or combinations of test scores and/or sociodemographic variables to establish the groups.

CONCLUSIONS

Now that we have reported our early findings, we must ask, so what? We are systematically collecting comprehensive data on psychological tests, sociodemographic variables and court histories for a larger group of adolescent murderers. We are, in addition, considering expanding the scope of our research to study violent juveniles in a broader sense. The need to develop a taxonomy of violence-prone situations and to develop measures of contextual variables cannot be overstated because, to our knowledge, neither exists. We are also cognizant of the need to develop standardized rating scales to measure such important constructs as the amount of criminal deviance, home-background instability, socialization problems, and family variables, and of the need to include biological measures that might relate to violent behavior.

It was apparent clinically that most of the adolescents in our sample were psychologically disturbed and were not hard-core criminal types. It was also apparent that, at least in our sample, adolescent murder was not a gang activity as it has been reported to be in other large cities (Wolfgang and Ferracuti, 1967). These findings seem to have some clear and hopeful implications. We have had considerably more success treating emotionally disturbed rather than criminally oriented or psychopathic individuals.

Since most of these juveniles return to society within a year or two, even if incarcerated, we must assist them in the reentry process by providing them and their families with whatever type of therapy, vocational training or rehabilitation, and support they need. The data also provide another rationale for the movement toward programs to prevent mental illness, more specifically, prevention of violence programs as has been suggested by the President's Commission on Mental Health (1978). While we may be a decade or more away from reasonably accurate prediction of juvenile homicide (if indeed this is a possibility), the identification and classification of violence-prone individuals, families, and situations is within reach. Some of the individuals involved may be amenable to clinical treatment. For the others we must be willing to examine and change the impact of such institutions as schools on their lives. Restrictions on the availability of guns seem imperative if we are serious about reducing homicide. After reviewing the circumstances involved in the murders committed by the group we studied, a conservative estimate would be that if weapons were more difficult to obtain, 25 percent of the murders would probably not have occurred.

Cognizance of the lack of generalizability of our data to other areas of the country, even as more sophisticated research strategies are developed, must be acknowledged. We need to encourage a wider sampling of violent subjects. Violence in youth has different causes, depending on the country, state, city, or rural area in which it is taking place; we could learn a great deal about violence by examining these differences as well as the similarities between violent individuals and violence-prone situations in different parts of the country. Expanding subject pools to include noncriminal violent individuals as well as the unreported criminally violent offender must be considered if an understanding of violence is desired.

We have a final consideration for future research. Is there a difference between adolescent and adult murderers? Certainly the law recognizes this distinction in the differential manner in which juveniles and adults are handled. Our findings, which revealed many similarities in the characteristics of adolescent and adult murderers and their victims, suggest that legal distinctions between adolescents and adults may not be consistent with psychological and sociological findings, at least in the instance of murder. Research on this question may have implications for both the legal disposition and psychological treatment of adolescent murderers.

REFERENCES

ADAMS, K. A. The child who murders. *Criminal Justice and Behavior* 1:51-61, 1974.

BENDER, L. Children and adolescents who have killed. *J. Psychiat.* 116:510-513, 1959.

BIALER, I. Conceptualization of success and failure in mentally retarded and normal children. *J. Pers.* 29:303-320, 1961.

BOLMAN, W. M. Aggression and violence in children. *Curr. Probl. Pediatr.* 4:3-32, 1974.

BROMBERG, N. Psychological study of murder. San Francisco and Los Angeles Psychoanalytical Societies, Santa Barbara, California, October, 1949.

CORDER, B. F., BALL, B. C., HAIZLIP, T. M., ROLLINS, R., and BEAUMONT, R. Adolescent parricide: A comparison with other adolescent murder. *Am. J. Psychiatry* 133:957-961. 1976.

EASSON, W. M., and STEINHILBER, R. M. Murderous aggression by children and adolescents. *Arch. Gen. Psychiatry* 4:27-35, 1961.

EVSEEFF, G. S. The potential young murderer. *J. Forensic Sci.* 21:441-450, 1976.

EXNER, J. E., WEINER, J. B., and SCHUYER, W. *A Rorschach Workshop for the Comprehensive System.* Rorschach Workshop, New York, 1976.

FERRACUTI, F., and NEWMAN, G. Assaultive offenses, in *Handbook of Criminology.* D. Glaser, ed. Rand McNally, Chicago, Ill., 1974.

FOODMAN, R., and ESTRADA, C. Adolescents who commit accidental homicide. *J. Child Psychol.* 16:314-326, 1977.

HAIZLIP, T. M., CORDER, B. F., and BALL, B. C. Personality and environment patterns in adolescent murders. *American Academy of Child Psychiatry,* Toronto, Ontario, October, 1976.

HELLSTEN, P., and KATILA, A. Murder and other homicides by children under 15 in Finland. *Psychiatric Quarterly Suppl.* 39:54-57, 1965.

KING, C. H. The ego and the integration of violence. *Am. J. Orthopsychiatry* 45: 695-709, 1975.

KOPPITZ, E. *Psychological Evaluation of Children's Human Figure Drawings.* Grune & Stratton, New York, 1967.

LEARY, T. *The Interpersonal Diagnosis of Personality.* A functional theory and methodology for personality evaluation. Ronald Press, New York, 1957.

LOTHSTEIN, L. M., and JONES, P. Discriminating violent individuals by means of various psychological tests. *J. Pers. Assess.* 42:237-243, 1978.

MALMQUIST, C. P. Premonitory signs of homicidal aggression in juveniles. *Am. J. Psychiatry* 128:93-97, 1971.

MANN, F., FRIEDMAN, C. J., and FRIEDMAN, A. S. Characteristics of self-reported violent offenders vs. court identified violent offenders. *Internat. J. Penol.* 4:69-87, 1976.

MARKS, P. A., SEEMAN, W., and HALLER, D. L. *The Actuarial Use of the MMPI with Adolescents and Adults.* Williams & Wilkins, Baltimore, 1974.

MCCARTHY, P. Youths who murder, in *Determinants and Origins of Aggressive Behavior.* J. DeWit and W. W. Hartup, eds. Mouton, The Netherlands, 589-594, 1974.

MCCLEARY, R. D. Violent youth. *International Journal of Offender Therapy and Comparative Criminology* 19:81-86, 1975.

MEGARGEE, E. I. The prediction of violence with psychological tests, in *Current Topics in Clinical and Community Psychology.* C. P. Spielberger, ed. Academic Press, New York, 1970.

MEGARGEE, E. I. The prediction of dangerous behavior. *Criminal Just. and Behav.* 3: 3-22, 1976.

MILLER, D., and LOONEY. The prediction of adolescent homicide. *Am. J. Psychoanal.* 34:187-198, 1974.

MONAHAN, J. The prediction of violence, in *Violence and Criminal Justice*. D. Chappell and J. Monahan, eds. D. C. Heath, Lexington, Ky., 1975, p. 15-32.

OFFER, D., MONAHAN, R. C., and OSTROV, E. Violence among hospitalized delinquents. *Arch. Gen. Psychiatry* 32:1180-1186, 1975.

PETTI, T. A., and DAVIDMAN, L. Homicidal school-age children: Cognitive style and demographic features. American Academy of Child Psychiatry, Houston, Texas, 1977.

Report to the President from the President's Commission on Mental Health. U. S. Government Printing Office, Washington, D. C., 1978.

RUSSELL, D. H. A study of juvenile murderers. *Internat. J. Offender Ther.* 9:55-86, 1965.

RUSSELL, D. H. Juvenile murderers. *Internat. J. Offender Ther. and Comparative Criminol.* 18:235-239, 1973.

SADOFF, R. L. Clinical observations on parricide. *Psychiatric Quarterly* 45:65-69, 1971.

SARGENT, D. Children who kill—a family conspiracy? *Social Work* 7:35-42, 1962.

SCHERL, D. J., and MACK, J. E. A study of adolescent matricide. *J. Am. Acad. Child Psychiatry* 5:569-593, 1966.

SENDI, I. B., and BLOMGREN, R. G. A comparison study of predictive criteria in the predisposition of homicidal adolescents. *Am. J. Psychiatry* 132:423-427, 1975.

SILVER, L. B., DUBLIN, C. C., and LOURIE, R. S. Does violence breed violence? Contribution from a study of the child abuse syndrome. *Am. J. Psychiatry* 126: 152-155, 1969.

SMITH, A. L., HAYS, J. R., and SOLWAY, K. S. WISC-R vs. culture-fair in a juvenile delinquent population. Rocky Mountain Psychological Association, 1977a.

SMITH, A. L., HAYS, J. R., and SOLWAY, K. S. Comparison of the WISC-R and culture-fair intelligenc test in a juvenile delinquent population. *J. Psychol.* 97: 179-182, 1977b.

SMITH, S. The adolescent murder. *Arch. Gen. Psychiatry* 13:310-319, 1965.

SPELLACY, F. Neuropsychological differences between violent and non-violent individuals. *J. Clin. Psychol.* 33:966-969, 1977.

STRASBURG, P. A. *Violent Delinquents*. Monarch Press, New York, 1978.

TANAY, E. Psychiatric study of homicide. *Am. J. Psychiatry* 125:146-152, 1969.

TANAY, E. Children who kill parents—reactive parricide. *Aust. N. Z. J. Psychiatry* 7:263-277, 1973.

THORNTON, W. E., and PRAY, B. J. The portrait of a murderer. *Dis. Nerv. Syst.* 36: 176-178, 1975.

TOOLEY, D .The small assassins: Clinical notes on a subgroup of murderous children. *J. Am. Acad. Child Psychiatry* 14:306-318, 1975.

WALSH-BRENNAN, K. S. Psychopathology of homicidal children. *Royal Society of Health* 94:274-277, 1974.

WALSH-BRENNAN, K. S. Children who have murdered. *Medico-Legal Journal* 43:20-24, 1975.

WATKINS, E. O. *The Watkins Bender Gestalt Scoring System*. Academic Therapy Publications, San Rafael, Cal., 1976.

WOLFGANG, M. E., and FERRACUTI, F. *The Subculture of Violence*. Metheun, New York, 1967.

ZIENTS, A. B., and ZENOFF, E. H. The juvenile murderer. American Academy of Child Psychiatry, Houston, Texas, 1977.

CHAPTER 13

The Behavioral Assessment of Rapists

GENE G. ABEL
JUDITH V. BECKER
EDWARD BLANCHARD
BARRY FLANAGAN

Assessing the treatment needs of rapists is a relatively new concept. At least two factors have limited the need for such assessment: In the past, rapists were treated primarily by incarceration, and since specific programs were not generally available for rapists in the prison system, detailed assessment simply was not needed; when treatment was provided, its orientation was dynamic. Assessment using the dynamic model was a rather global procedure, essentially similar to the assessment of other sexual deviates or, in most cases, any type of offender.

In the last ten years, behavioral approaches have been used with increasing success in assessing and treating various types of sexual deviates (Barlow, 1974; Abel, 1976; Abel and Blanchard, 1976; Barlow and Abel, 1976). Recent behavioral assessment-treatment has focused specifically on the treatment needs of rapists and other sexually aggressive persons (Abel et al., 1976, 1977b).

Psychological treatments usually include such nonspecific elements as an empathetic relationship with the patient and the acceptance by the patient that he has a problem he wishes to correct. Beyond these nonspecifics, however, each type of deviation potentially involves specific treatment needs that must be assessed. Table 1 outlines what we consider the specific treatment needs of rapists.

All rapists have excessive urges to rape. Others may or may not also have deficits in heterosexual arousal and/or various deficits in social skills. Since excessive urges to rape and deficits in arousal to nonrape stimuli are discussed in most of this chapter, the social-skills deficits will be briefly

Table 1

The Behavioral Assessment and Treatment of Sexually Aggressive Patients

Assessed Behavioral Excess or Deficits	Treatment Methods
Excessive arousal to rape stimuli	Aversion-suppression methods 1. covert sensitization 2. masturbatory extinction 3. electrical aversion 4. chemical aversion 5. biofeedback-assisted suppression 6. odor aversion
Deficit arousal to nonrape sexual stimuli	Generation of arousal to nonrape cues 1. masturbatory conditioning 2. exposure 3. fading 4. systematic desensitization
	Social Skills Deficits
Heterosocial skills	Heterosocial skills training
Assertive skills	Assertive training
Empathetic skills	Empathy training
Sexual performance	Sexual dysfunction treatment and/or sex education
Gender role behavior	Gender role, motor behavior training

reviewed first so as to give the reader a perspective on the total assessment-treatment of rapists.

Generally, these individuals lack appropriate heterosocial behaviors or they experience incapacitating anxiety and discomfort when attempting to relate socially to women. They are unable to talk with women, flirt, or ask women out on dates. We evaluate these skills by asking the rapist to interact with a woman in a role-playing scene in which he must demonstrate appropriate heterosexual skills. These scenes are videotaped and rated, using a heterosocial skill checklist (Barlow et al., 1977). Rapists with heterosocial skill deficits are then offered specific training.

Some rapists also lack adequate assertive skills; they may be unable to express their own opinions and unable to ask others to change their behavior. In other cases, they assert themselves inappropriately by explosions of anger and hostility or by the rape of an innocent victim. Assertive skills are assessed by asking the rapist to role-play scenes in which he must carry out appropriate assertive behaviors (Eisler et al., 1973; Hersen et al., 1973; Eisler, 1976). Those lacking appropriate assertive skills undergo specific assertive skills training while those with appropriate skills bypass this treatment.

The next area to be evaluated is empathy. Some rapists can appreciate the feelings and sensitivities of others, while other rapists appear cold and indifferent to others' emotions. Empathy skills are assessed by asking the rapist to demonstrate these skills to a woman while the interaction is videotaped. We then rate the presence or absence of his ability to appropriately identify the woman's feeling state, pinpoint the cause of the woman's feelings, express feelings of hurt or enjoyment to the woman, etc. When ratings of these scenes demonstrate deficits, we teach the patient empathy much as psychotherapists are trained in this skill.

Rapists likewise need an evaluation of their sexual skills. Deficits in this area may include any number of problems along a continuum, from inadequate sexual knowledge to specific sexual dysfunction, such as premature or retarded ejaculation, or impotence. Specific behavioral assessment techniques have not been developed for this aspect, and assessment is done in a psychological interview or by paper-and-pencil testing, using such tests as the Sexual Knowledge Inventory or the Male Sexological Test.

Gender-role behavior is another potential social-skills deficit. Although an uncommon problem compared to those described above, a few rapists have excessive masculine-gender behavior or inappropriate gender-motor behavior, that is, inappropriate ways of sitting, standing, or walking. We have developed rating scales to identify specific deficits in this area (Abel,

1976), and our treatment is directed at developing appropriate gender-role motor behavior through role-playing, modeling, social reinforcement, and video feedback.

THE USES OF PHYSIOLOGICAL ASSESSMENT WITH RAPISTS

After a patient's social skills are evaluated, the rapist's arousability to rape stimuli and possible deficits in his arousal to nonrape sexual stimuli are determined. To evaluate these, one needs a valid, reliable measure of sexual arousal.

Zuckerman (1971) and Abel and Blanchard (1976) reviewed the literature on methods of measuring the sexual arousal of males, and they concluded that the most objective assessment procedure is direct calibration of penile tumescence. To determine this, a penile transducer is placed around the penis and, as an erection occurs, an electrical output displays the increased penile size on recording paper. The transducer has made it possible to examine the sexual responses of rapists. Our recent findings resulting from physiologic recordings of rapists, compared to nonrapists, may be categorized into six major areas.

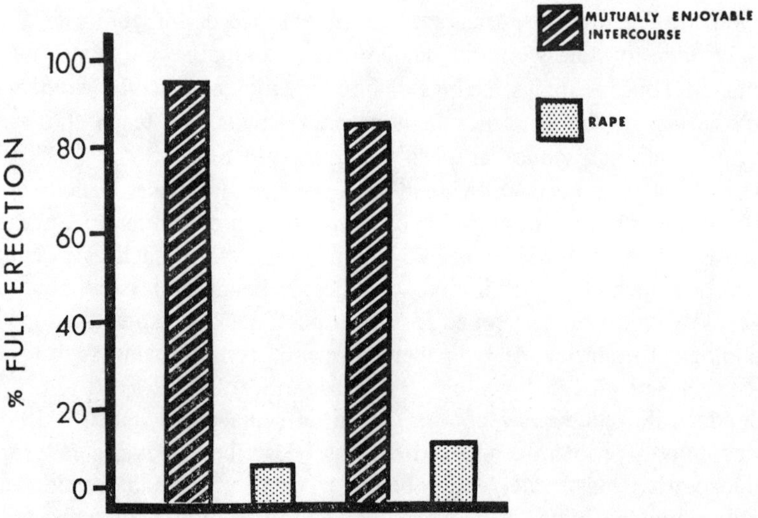

FIGURE 1. Nonrapist's erections during descriptions of intercourse and rape.

COMPARISON OF ERECTION RESPONSES OF RAPISTS AND NONRAPISTS

Comparing the erection responses of rapists and nonrapists requires measuring both groups' erections while presenting them with specific stimuli that depict either rape or nonrape experiences (Abel et al., 1977a, 1978). The patient wears a penile transducer while seated in the laboratory and listening to two-minute audiotaped descriptions of scenes of specific content (Abel et al., 1975b). The patient's greatest erection during this two-minute interval is calculated and converted into percentage of full erection. In this fashion, various types of sexual descriptions may be compared objectively on the basis of their ability to elicit sexual responsiveness.

Figure 1 indicates the typical sexual responses of a nonrapist to descriptions of scenes of either mutually enjoyable intercourse or rape. The subject had never forced himself on a female, denied having urges to rape, and had warm, empathetic relationships with women. His erections to descriptions of scenes of mutually enjoyable intercourse, rape, mutually enjoyable intercourse (repeat of the previous intercourse scene) and rape (repeat of the previous rape scene) indicated that the patient had greater

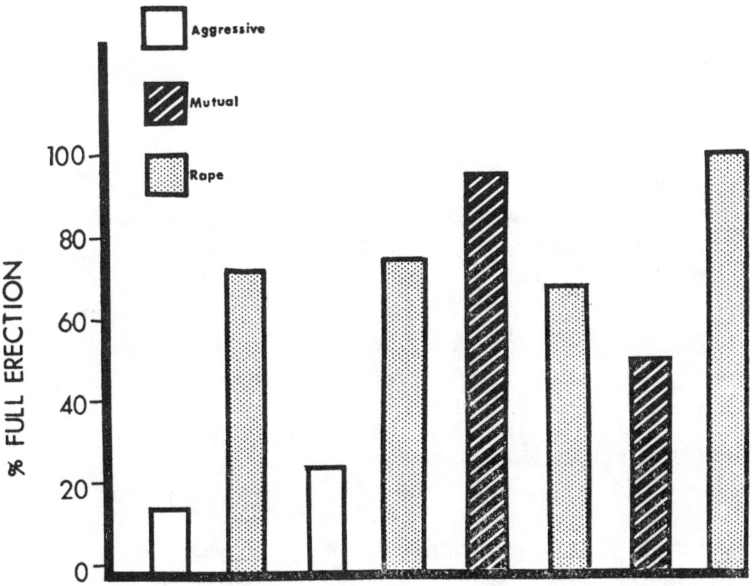

FIGURE 2. Rapist's erections to descriptions of aggression, mutually enjoyable intercourse, and rape.

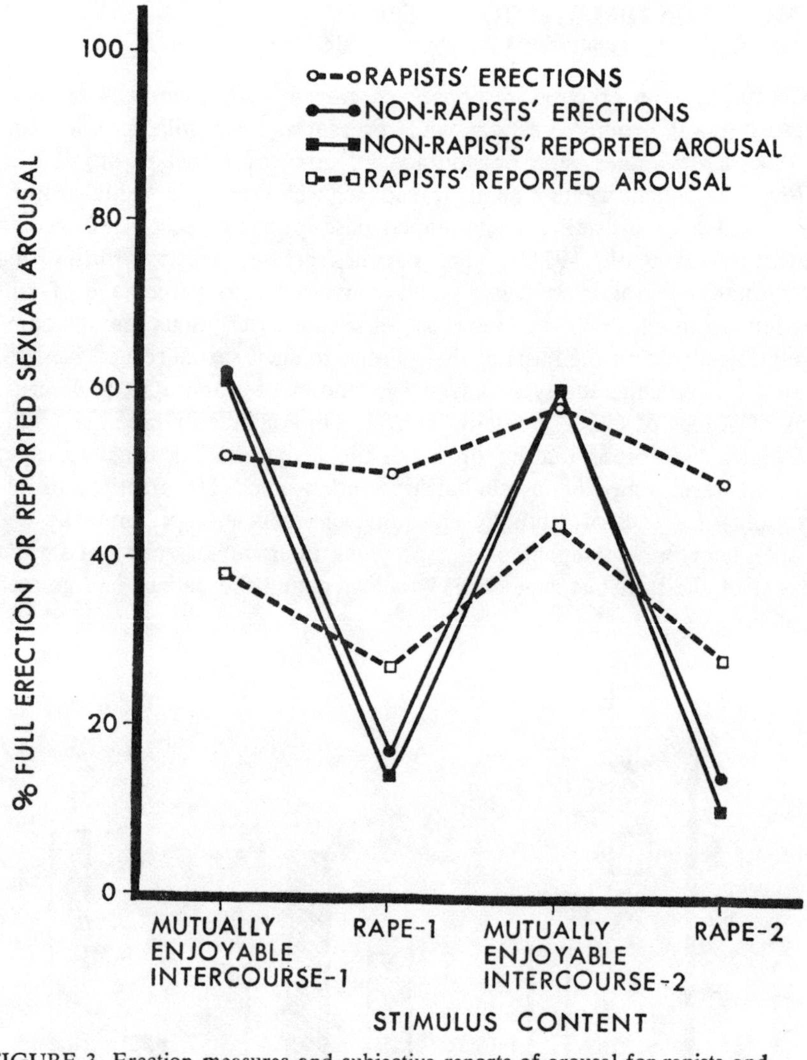

FIGURE 3. Erection measures and subjective reports of arousal for rapists and nonrapists to descriptions of mutually enjoyable intercourse, and rape. From Abel et al., *Arch. Gen. Psychiatry*, 34, 895-903 (1977a). Copyright 1977, American Medical Association.

than 80 percent of a full erection to mutually enjoyable intercourse cues, while his arousal to rape cues was less than 20 percent of a full erection. (In our laboratory, there is a 15- to 20-percent "noise" in the recording process, so values of less than 20 percent are usually ignored.)

These results are in marked contrast to those of a 19-year-old rapist (Figure 2) who had an extensive history of sexually aggressive acts since age 13. At that age he would approach women in parking lots or shopping centers, enter their car, and grab them in the vaginal area. This behavior continued intermittently until he was 19 years old. He began raping at age 17. Seeing women in a parking lot, he would follow them home, enter their home on a false pretext, and rape them. Of note in his history was his strong religious background and the patient's and his family's prominence in their church.

An examination of his erection record reveals that his arousal to intercourse descriptions is similar to that of the nonrapist, with 93 percent and 54 percent erections. Where the nonrapist failed to respond to rape stimuli, however, this rapist obtained 68 percent and 100 percent full erections to the rape descriptions.

To confirm that the responses of the two subjects reflect the responses of nonrapists and rapists in general, erections of 7 nonrapist sexual deviates were compared to the erections of 7 rapists, using descriptions of mutually enjoyable intercourse and rape. The results shown in Figure 3 confirm that both rapists and nonrapists responded equally to mutually enjoyable intercourse scenes. Obvious differences occurred, however, in their arousal to descriptions of rape scenes. Rapists' erections to rape descriptions were identical in magnitude to their erections to nonrape descriptions. By contrast, nonrapists responded to mutually enjoyable intercourse scenes, but failed to respond sexually to descriptions of rape. Thus, it appears that rapists differ from nonrapists in their physiological responses. The importance of such a finding is that it is now possible, using an objective physiological measure, to discriminate between rapists and nonrapists. If a goal of treatment is to help rapists acquire appropriate sexual behavior, then treatment should be expected to reduce the rapist's erections to rape cues. Any treatment program for rapists should employ an objective measure, such as erection responses, to assess the rapist's progress in treatment; as treatment takes effect, the rapist's erections to rape descriptions should steadily decline. If no decline occurs, one should question the effectiveness of the therapy.

COMPARISON OF ERECTION RESPONSES TO VERBAL REPORT

Rapists have traditionally been assessed by clinical interviews. After establishing a working relationship with the rapist, the therapist questions the patient about his true arousal pattern, the extent of his urges to rape, and his ability to control these urges. Since the equipment for a psychophysiologic assessment is an added expense to traditional clinical evaluation, one question arises: Is it really worthwhile to measure rapists' erection responses? If identical information were available from clinical interviews, the answer would be no.

Figure 3 provides preliminary information on this issue. The group of 7 rapists and 7 nonrapists was questioned on the extent of their sexual arousal during psychophysiologic assessment (on our scale, 0 equals no sexual arousal, 100 equals marked sexual arousal). Their verbal reports were compared to the records of erections to tapes of rape and mutually enjoyable intercourse scenes. Figure 3 shows that the nonrapist group had an extremely high correlation between reported arousal and recorded arousal, indicating that nonrapists, by and large, reported the extent of their sexual arousal accurately. Rapists, by contrast, consistently reported less sexual arousal than was recorded by the transducer. These results suggest that rapists' verbal reports fail to reflect the actual extent of their arousal.

Figure 4 depicts the erection responses of an 18-year-old single male referred for pretrial evaluation. His history revealed that, reportedly while intoxicated, he and a friend had kidnapped an 18-year-old woman, driven her to a deserted area, and raped her. The patient said repeatedly that, although he was seeking a psychiatric evaluation, he was not aroused

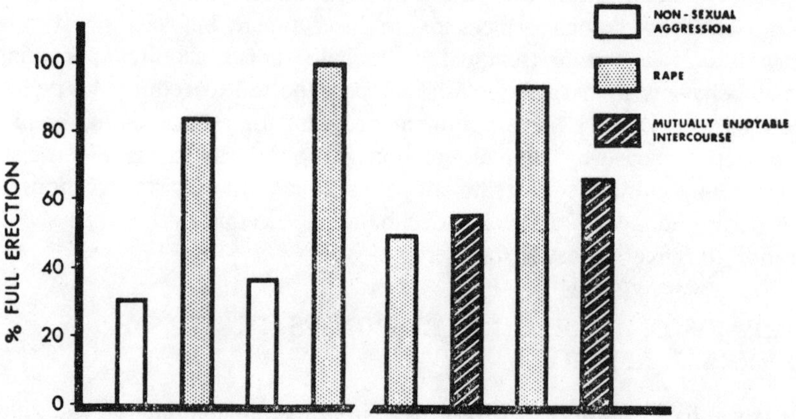

FIGURE 4. Rapist's erections to descriptions of aggression, rape, and mutually enjoyable intercourse.

by thoughts of rape and that the incident was entirely a product of his drinking. Throughout the evaluation, he consistently reported no sexual arousal to the descriptions presented to him. Erection measures, however, showed him to have greater than 30 percent of a full erection to all sexual scenes presented to him. His erections to rape scenes were 84 percent, 100 percent, 50 percent and 94 percent. The patient not only affirmed an absence of sexual arousal to all scenes, but reported sensing only minimal erections to any cues, except for a 5 percent erection to the first presentation of the rape scene and a 3 percent erection to its third presentation. During the fourth presentation, the patient volunteered that he was unable to visualize any portion of the scene described while concomitant measurement revealed that he had 94 percent of a full erection.

These results confirmed our frequent observations that rapists cannot or will not verbalize the extent of their sexual arousal to scenes depicting rape or other sexual behavior. Our laboratory results confirmed what has been suspected for some time: evaluative techniques that rely exclusively on the rapist's verbal report run a high risk of being invalid. If the intent of treatment is to conduct assessment and therapy based on valid data, erection measurement seems to be important.

CONTRIBUTION OF ERECTION MEASUREMENT TO UNDERSTANDING THE RAPIST AND HIS TREATMENT

Audio descriptions are flexible and may be altered to present a variety of unique stimuli to the patient (Abel et al., 1975b). Audio descriptions allow the examination of issues related to the rapist's arousal patterns. For example, one treatment reported to reduce deviant sexual arousal is covert sensitization (Abel et al., 1977b). This involves the pairing of aversive images, which are anxiety-provoking or distasteful to the patient, with images or thoughts of carrying out such inappropriate sexual behavior as rape. Covert sensitization usually involves gleaning information from the clinical interview and relying on the rapist's self-report as to the effectiveness of the treatment, finding out whether or not the covert cues are indeed aversive, and whether or not they reduce his arousal to rape themes. This issue may be evaluated more objectively by examining the impact of such covert scenes on the rapist's erections in the laboratory.

Figure 5 depicts the erection responses of the 19-year-old rapist discussed above. In light of his extensive religious background, we questioned whether or not religious references would elicit lower erection responses to rape compared to other references, such as the legal consequences of rape.

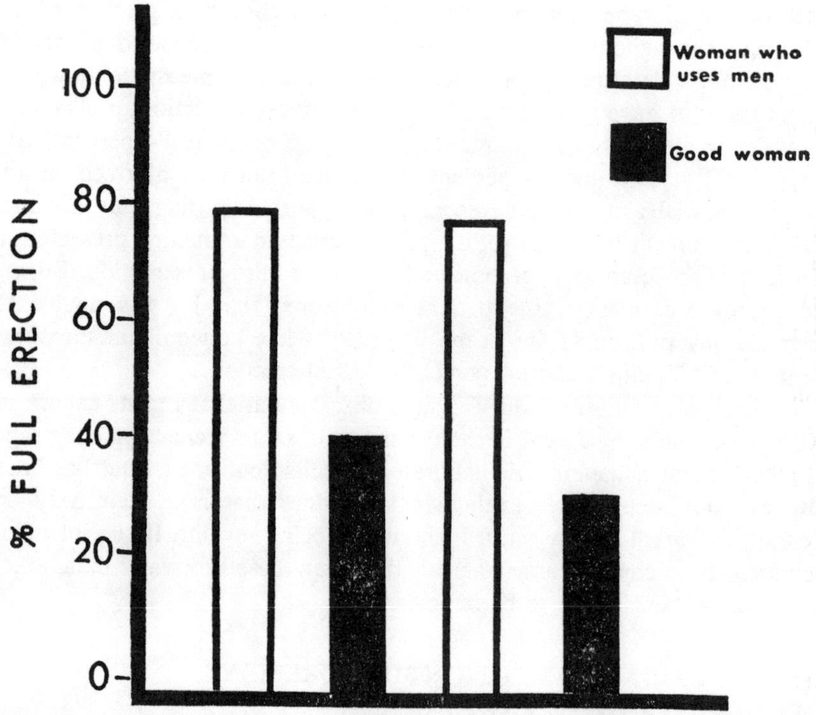

FIGURE 5. Rapist's erections as a function of the rape's consequences.

We developed two descriptions of rape. The first included references to the religious consequences of the rape—how God would feel on seeing the patient commit the rape, the church deacons' reactions to his raping, and so on. The second description concerned the legal consequences of rape—going to jail, being locked up, etc. Erection measurement during these presentations revealed that the rapist had 89 percent and 82 percent erections to types of rape scenes that included references to legal consequences. Rape scenes concomitantly depicting religious consequences produced only 24 percent and 49 percent erections. If covert scenes were to be used to reduce this patient's arousal to rape cues, references to religious themes could be expected to reduce arousal to rape cues more significantly than references to legal consequences. Using the erection measurement method, the therapist may preview the expected response to covert sensitization scenes before actually trying the treatment, so that he or she no longer has to rely exclusively on the rapist's verbal report of the effectiveness of such covert scenes.

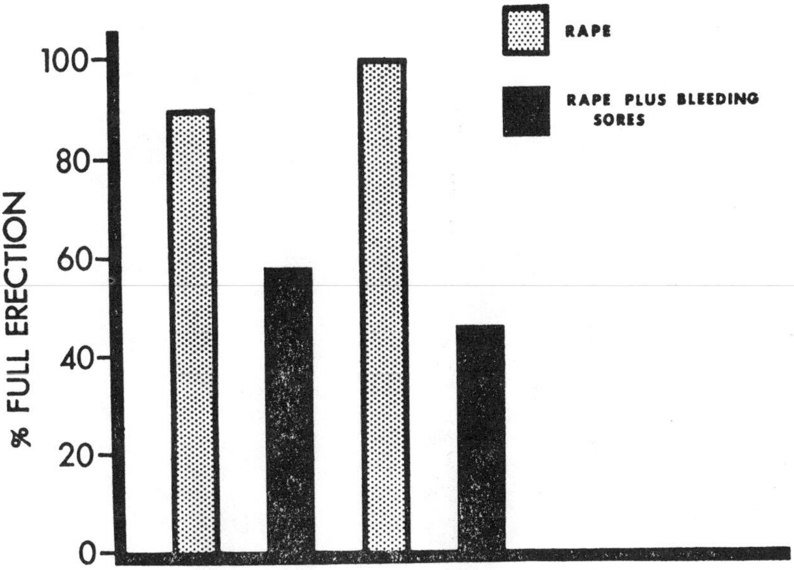

FIGURE 6. Rapist's erections as a function of aversive imagery. From Abel et al., *Arch. Gen. Psychiatry,* 34, 895-903 (1977a). Copyright 1977, American Medical Association.

Figure 6 shows the results of a similar case. After questioning the patient about potential aversive covert images, we suspected that images of the rape victim's open bleeding sores would reduce the patient's arousal to rape. Two scenes were developed, one describing rape, the other describing a rape of the same victim but including references to vulgar, bleeding sores on the victim's body. The patient's erections to the first scene were 90 percent and 100 percent, while his erections to the second rape scene were 53 percent and 46 percent.

A final example of the additional information that may be obtained by erection measurement is shown in Figure 7. In clinical interviews the same rapist revealed his tendency to categorize women into dichotomous groups; women were either good (nonmanipulative, not self-centered) or bad (using men for their own selfish purposes). He reported that he raped the "bad" women but would not assault good women. To investigate the validity of his statements, rape descriptions were developed depicting women known to the patient who, in his opinion, came from the two different groups. Care was taken that the women described were equally sexually attractive to the patient and varied only as to the "goodness" or "badness" of their

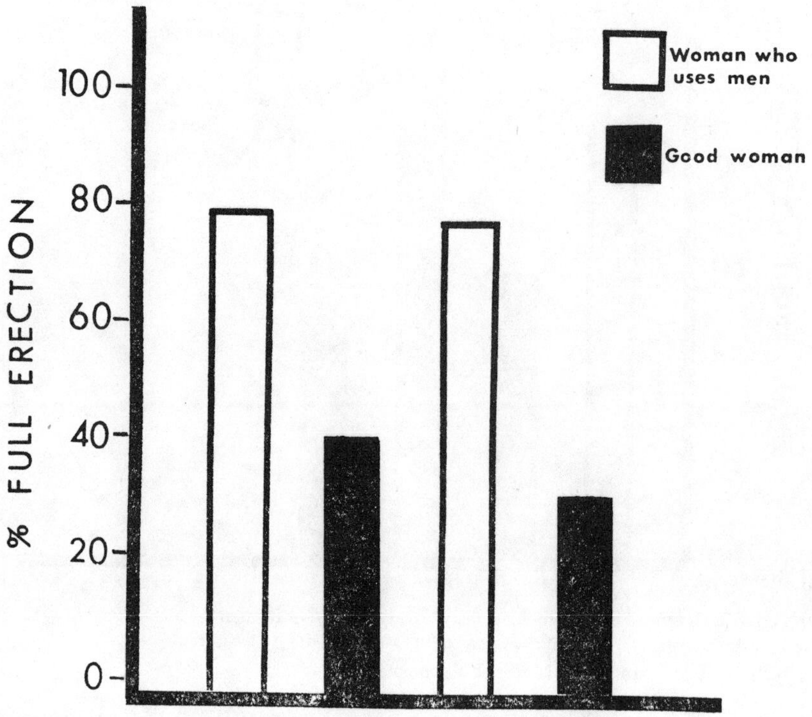

FIGURE 7. Rapist's erections as a function of victim's character.

character. The rapist's erections to these descriptions were influenced markedly by the victim's character. When the scene described the rape of a woman who uses men, he obtained 79 percent and 77 percent erections. To the scene describing the rape of a good woman, his erections were 40 percent and 30 percent. These laboratory results confirmed a clinical impression described in the literature (and by the patient) that rapists frequently divide the world into good women (not potential victims) and bad women (potential victims).

By altering the specific content of audiotaped descriptions, the therapist may evaluate the parameters that contribute to or reduce the rapist's sexual arousal. Using such physiological measurement allows an exploration of possible motives for rape and an examination of the potential effectiveness of treatment for a rapist.

PREDICTION OF DANGEROUSNESS ON THE BASIS OF ERECTION MEASURES

Evaluating the treatment needs of rapists and making decisions regarding the release of incarcerated rapists into the community raises the issue of predicting dangerousness. To examine this issue by using erection measures, 13 rapists were rank-ordered (from R1 to R13) on the basis of the number of women they had raped. R1 had committed one rape; R7, two rapes or more; R8, 10 or more; R10, 20; R11, 30; R12 about 100; and R13 clearly more than 100. The rapists' percentages of erection to rape stimuli were plotted against their rank-order number and the number of rapes committed, but no significant trend could be identified. Examination of these data revealed considerable variability regarding each rapist's responsiveness to the sexual cues, irrespective of their content. To allow comparisons despite the variability of the data, the rapists' mean percentage of erection to rape stimuli was divided by their mean percentage of erection to mutually enjoyable, nonaggressive scenes of sexual intercourse. The resultant value was termed the rape index.

Figure 8 shows this rape index for the 13 rapists (R1 to R13) as well as seven nonrapist sexual deviates (NR1 to NR7). These data indicate that a rape index of 0.5 or greater suggests that the patient is a rapist. Especially conspicuous are the rape indices of patients R10, R12, and

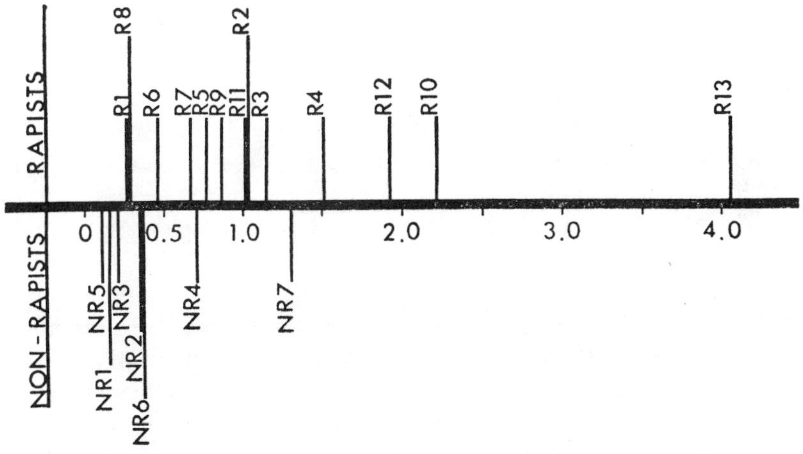

FIGURE 8. Rape indices as a function of the number of rapes committed. R, rapists.

R13. These three men had committed rape frequently and they also had the highest rape indices. If one defines a rapist as dangerous if he has raped often in the past, then the rape index seems to be able to identify dangerous rapists. It should also be pointed out that nonrapist NR4 who had a high rape index (higher than 0.5) was a sadomasochist; his rape index may be high because he was aroused by sadomasochistic activity similar to that described in the rape scenes. Nonrapist NR7 was a voyeur whose high rape index cannot be accounted for on the basis of his reported past behavior.

A second definition of dangerousness might be that the individual has severely injured his victims in the past, that is, by sadistic rape. The two most dangerous rapists in the group of 13, as defined by injury or harm to their victims, R12 and R13, also had two of the three highest rape indices. If dangerousness is defined by a higher likelihood of having injured one's victim in the process of rape, a high rape index, especially one greater than 1.5, suggests such individuals.

Another means of identifying rapists likely to harm their victims is to identify sadists, persons who respond to physical violence with sexual arousal. We developed a third type of audio description, one depicting aggression, devoid of sex. These scenes describe the same victim as do the rape or mutually enjoyable intercourse scenes, but instead of a sexual experience, the scene is of the rapist beating up the woman, injuring her, slapping her about the face, beating her with his fists, etc.

Calculating the 13 rapists' responses to these aggression cues versus their responses to rape cues, we obtained a correlation of +.98. The men's arousal to assault scenes was almost exactly 40 percent of their arousal to rape cues, which suggests that arousal to aggression and arousal to rape are directly related.

The responses of nonsadistic rapists to purely aggressive descriptions, shown in Figures 2 and 4, contrast with the responses of patient R13. This 33-year-old man, one of the sadists in our sample, had an extensive history of brutal assault of his three wives. He had stuck needles into his wife's breasts and vagina, poured alcohol over her pubic area while scrubbing her with a brush, and had recently put live electric wires into her vagina.

His erection responses to three types of descriptions are presented in Figure 9. His greatest erection responses were to descriptions of aggression. Other sadistic subjects demonstrated a similar pattern of high arousal to aggression scenes and low arousal to scenes of mutually enjoyable intercourse. Thus, it seems that erection responses to aggression cues may be used to identify sadists who are likely to injure their victims during the course of rape.

Finally, if a rapist is defined as dangerous because he selects an extremely young or old victim who is unable to defend herself against the attack, erection responses will help to identify such individuals. This is done by a generalization gradient. Rape scenes are described in which the rape behavior is held constant, but the scenes are varied by altering the

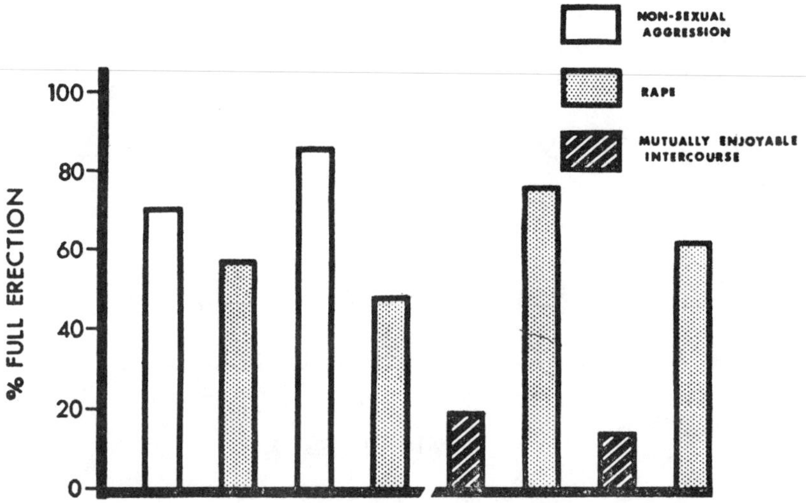

FIGURE 9. Sadist's erections to descriptions of agression, rape, and mutually enjoyable intercourse. From Abel et al., *Arch. Gen. Psychiatry,* 34, 895-903 (1977a). Copyright 1977, American Medical Association.

age of the victim. Figure 10 shows the responses of the 19-year-old rapist described earlier, as a generalization gradient. The data show that the rapist's peak arousal varied with the victims' age, from 20 to 50 years. Similar measures from patients R7, R9, and R12, the only pedophiles in our group, showed a clear skewing to the left, the patients' erections steadily increasing with descriptions of rape of progressively younger victims. It thus seems possible, using erection criteria, to identify rapists whose victims are likely to be very young or very old on the basis of generalization gradients.

It is possible to identify the more dangerous rapist, depending on one's definition of dangerous. Erection measures will assist in identifying three types of rapists: those who have raped most frequently, those who were likely to have injured their victim in the process of rape, and those whose victim was likely to be very young or very old.

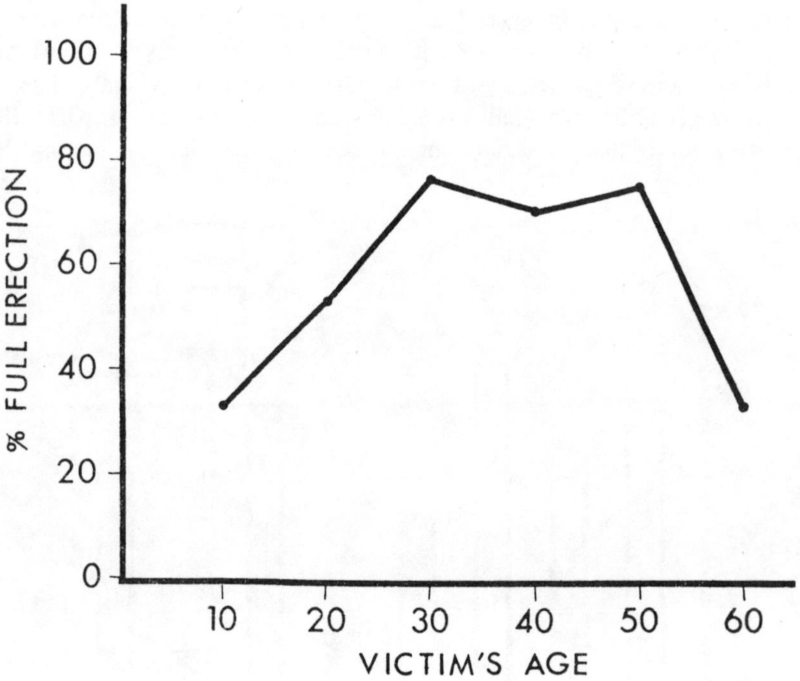

FIGURE 10. Rapist's erections as a function of victim's age.

ERECTION MEASURES AS A MEANS OF EVALUATING RAPISTS' RESPONSES TO TREATMENT

Although various treatment programs are available for rapists, evaluating their effectiveness has been difficult. One problem has been the lack of specification as to exactly what changes are to occur in the rapist if treatment is effective. In this regard, identification of specific behaviors to be altered, listed in Table 1, provides objectivity to the evaluation of the rapist's progress in treatment.

A second difficulty is that evaluation has relied almost exclusively on the rapist's report of improvement. The data reported in Figures 3 and 4 illustrate the dangers in relying on only such self-reported information. Therefore, assessment of rapists' responses to treatment should include not only the standard clinical interview, attitudinal measures, and report of the frequency of rape and nonrape sexual thoughts and behaviors, but it also requires repeated measurement of the rapists' arousal to rape and nonrape sexual stimuli.

Previous studies (Abel and Blanchard, 1976; Abel et al., 1977b) have examined modes of stimulus presentation that are most effective in generating deviant and nondeviant arousal in rapists. Our results (Figure 11) confirmed in a rapist population that videotapes or movies are far more

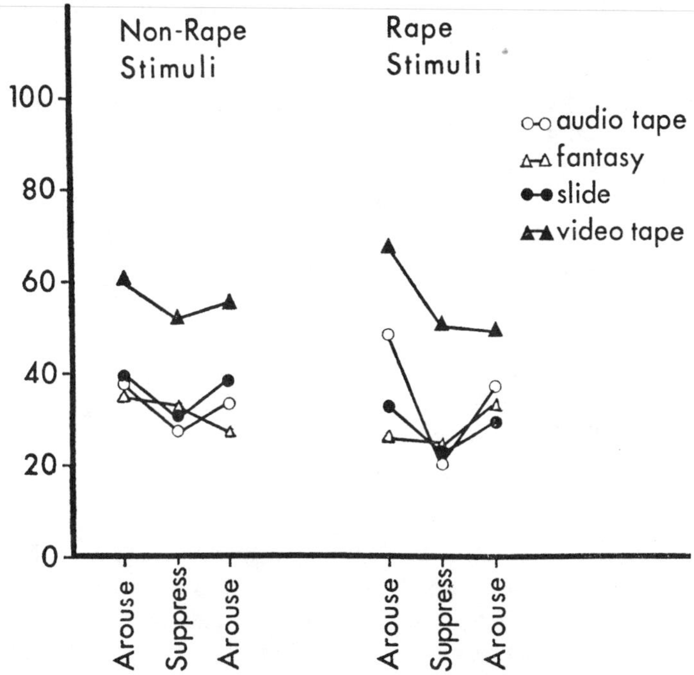

FIGURE 11. Rapists' erections to rape and intercourse stimuli as a function of stimulus modality and instructional set. From Abel et al., in *Clinical Aspects of the Rapist*. Grune & Stratton, New York (1977b), p. 174.

erotic than audiotaped descriptions, the rapist's free fantasy, or slides. These results are similar to those obtained with a homosexual population (Abel et al., 1975a).

In addition to the mode of stimulus presentation, the patient's instructional set is critical in recording erection responses. Sexual arousal as measured by the penile transducer is not simply an automatic response, completely outside the control of the rapist; rapists can suppress portions of their erections. If erection measures are to accurately reflect the patient's progress in treatment, his ability to partially inhibit his erection response must be controlled for. One method is to measure the rapist's erections under instructions to become aroused to the cues, and also under instructions to suppress that arousal (Figure 11). These comparisons provide the therapist with information regarding the rapist's ability to control his erection before treatment begins. Any reductions in arousal to rape cues may thus be evaluated in light of the known degree to which the patient can voluntarily control his erections.

Plotting or graphing the rapist's arousal to rape or nonrape sexual cues is important as treatment progresses. Recording such values assures the therapist that appropriate measures are being obtained, and it provides the therapist with a constant check on incidents that occur during treatment that may influence the rapist's responses. Ideally, as treatment progresses, one looks for a gradual but progressive reduction of deviant arousal, parallel maintenance or increase in the patient's arousal to nonrape, mutually enjoyable sexual cues, and improvement in the social skills mentioned earlier.

POTENTIAL FOR UNETHICAL ABUSE OF ERECTION MEASUREMENT

Assessment of rapists using the penile transducer has the potential for unethical abuse. Since patients' arousal to various rape themes sometimes is measured outside of their awareness, the therapist has data that are incriminating to the patient and often in conflict with what the patient reports as erotic. This is doubly dangerous when one realizes that the validity of the measures is greatest when positive responses to rape themes are recorded; we know less about the meaning of a patient's failure to respond to these themes. One solution to this dilemma is not to rely exclusively on the erection data but to incorporate them with other information (clinical interviews and paper-and-pencil tests) in arriving at a clinical judgment regarding a patient.

Another safeguard against unethical use of the erection measures is to obtain written, informed consent from the patient, explaining to him that some of the data may be obtained outside his awareness and that the information may conflict with his reports of sexual arousal. If the patient is incarcerated, we should expect the authorities to attempt to obtain the assessment results with any available means of coercion. This being the case, it is probably necessary to reach an argeement with the prison administration that no attempts to procure the test results will be made. In a research project, the data may be coded so that they cannot be decoded by anyone, including the investigators, as is done in some drug research.

A final safeguard is to organize an advisory body, separate from the assessment group, whose members will ensure the patient's understanding of the treatment, the potential for unethical abuse of the data, and who will take appropriate steps to prevent abuse.

CONCLUSIONS

Therapy for the rapist has improved tremendously in the last few years. Factors that have contributed to this advance include the following: rapists have been more accessible to psychological treatment, so that it has been possible to develop new assessment-treatment techniques; behavioral approaches to the treatment of sexual deviates seem, in general, to have applicability to many rapists, which has greatly accelerated the development of treatment programs for rapists; and recent advances in the methods of assessing rapists' sexual arousal have provided us with means of exploring etiological factors that contribute to arousal as well as means to assess the patients' response to treatment. The remaining major hurdle is to explain these advances so that society might be more willing to encourage treatment of rapists. The developments described in this paper make the treatment of rapists (as opposed to their incarceration) much more tenable.

ACKNOWLEDGMENTS

Preparation of this chapter was supported in part by the National Institute of Mental Health, Grant No. MH-27724, and the National Center for the Prevention and Control of Rape, Grant No. MH-32841.

REFERENCES

ABEL, G. G. Assessment of sexual deviation in the male, in *Behavioral Assessment: A Practical Handbook.* M. Hersen and A. S. Bellack, eds. Pergamon Press, New York, 1976, pp. 437-458.

ABEL, G. G., BARLOW, D. H., BLANCHARD, E. B., and GUILD, D. The components of rapists' sexual arousal. *Arch. Gen. Psychiatry* 34:895-903, 1977a.

ABEL, G. G., BARLOW, D. H., BLANCHARD, E. B., and MAVISSAKALIAN, M. Measurement of sexual arousal in male homosexuals: The effects of instructions and stimulus modality. *Arch. Sex. Beh.* 4:623-629, 1975a.

ABEL, G. G., and BLANCHARD, E. B. The measurement and generation of sexual arousal, in *Progress in Behavior Modification,* vol. 2. M. Hersen, R. Eisler, and P. M. Miller, eds. Academic Press, New York, 1976, pp. 99-136.

ABEL, G. G., BLANCHARD, E. B., BARLOW, D. H., and MAVISSAKALIAN, M. Identifying specific erotic cues in sexual deviation by audio-taped descriptions. *J. Appl. Behav. Anal.* 8:247-260, 1975b.

ABEL, G. G., BLANCHARD, E. B., and BECKER, J. V. Psychological treatment for rapists, in *Sexual Assault,* S. Brodsky and M. Walker, eds. Lexington Books, Lexington, Mass., 1976, pp. 99-115.

ABEL, G. G., BLANCHARD, E. B., and BECKER, J. V. An integrated treatment program for rapists, in *Clinical Aspects of the Rapist.* R. Rada, ed. Grune & Stratton, New York, 1977b, pp. 161-214.

ABEL, G. G., BLANCHARD, E. B., BECKER, J. V., and DJENDEREDJIAN, A. Differentiating sexual aggressives with penile measures. *Criminal Justice and Behavior,* 5: 315-332, 1978.

BARLOW, D. H. The treatment of sexual deviation: Toward a comprehensive behavioral approach, in *Innovative Treatment Methods in Psychopathology.* K. S. Calhoun, H. E. Adams, and K. M. Mitchell, eds. Wiley & Sons, New York, 1974, pp. 121-147.

BARLOW, D. H., and ABEL, G. G. Recent developments in assessment and treatment of sexual deviation, in *Behavior Modification: Principles, Issues and Applications.* A. Kazdin, M. Mahoney, and E. Craighead, eds. Houghton-Mifflin, Boston, 1976, pp. 341-360.

BARLOW, D. H., ABEL, G. G., BLANCHARD, E. B., BRISTOW, A., and YOUNG, L. A. Heterosocial skills checklist for males. *Behav. Ther.* 8:229-239, 1977.

EISLER, R. M. The behavioral assessment of social skills, in *Behavioral Assessment: A Practical Handbook.* M. Hersen and A. S. Bellack, eds. Pergamon Press, New York, 1976, pp. 369-395.

EISLER, R. M., MILLER, P. M., and HERSEN, M. Components of assertive behavior. *J. Clin. Psychol.* 29:295-299, 1973.

HERSEN, M., EISLER, R. M., and MILLER, P. M. Development of assertive responses: Clinical, measurement, and research consideration. *Behav. Res. Ther.* 11:505-521, 1973.

ZUCKERMAN, M. Physiological measures of sexual arousal in the human. *Psychol. Bull.* 75:297-329, 1971.

CHAPTER 14

Conjugal Violence: A Comparative Study in a Psychiatric Setting

KAREN H. COLEMAN
MAXINE WEINMAN

In the early 1970s when Steinmetz and Straus (1974) searched the literature for data on family violence, they noted a lack of material on husband-wife violence. The only empirical data on the incidence of marital violence included in their book, *Violence in the Family,* are two studies of applicants for divorce of whom a significant portion mentioned physical abuse as a factor in the dissolution of the marriages (Levinger, 1974; O'Brien, 1974).

Since that time, evidence has accumulated to document the prevalence of marital violence. In Scotland, an examination of 3020 police cases involving violence revealed that violence between unrelated males constituted the largest category (38.7 percent), the second most frequent offense (26 percent) being violence by husbands directed against their wives (Dobash and Dobash, 1977-78). A recent nationwide survey in the United States of more than 2000 couples conducted by Straus, Gelles, and Steinmetz (Straus, 1977-78) showed that during the 12-month period preceding the interviews, 28 percent of the couples had experienced at least one violent incident and 5.3 percent had experienced violence that could be considered a beating. Straus cautioned that these figures might be misleading because of underreporting of domestic violence or, at the opposite end of the pole, because violence is a normal part of life for some families. His figures included only couples living together. He suggested that the true incidence rate is probably closer to 50 or 60 percent of all couples than to the 28 percent who were willing to describe violent acts in an interview survey.

Along with current research efforts, the media have drawn attention to the problem through television shows, books, newspaper and magazine articles. How do these efforts of investigating and publicizing marital violence affect the mental health professional? More couples are talking about the problem and seeking assistance from therapists. In one clinic of the Texas Research Institute of Mental Sciences (TRIMS), between January and May, 1978, therapists reported that 340 couples and individuals presented marital violence as a major problem. This accounts for 24 percent of the patients seen in the clinic during that period. Obviously, therapists need more information regarding treatment of persons involved in conjugal violence.

One of our goals was to gather information on intact couples who were involved in conjugal violence and sought psychiatric help for the problem. A second goal was to discuss these findings in relation to treatment. Our study compared socioeconomic characteristics, backgrounds of family violence, sex-role orientations, alcohol and drug use, frequency of marital arguments, and physical punishment of children of a group of couples involved in conjugal violence (CV group) to a group of couples who have not been involved in conjugal violence (NV group), drawing some implications for treatment.

While the study was in progress, all individuals who came to the marriage and family clinic seeking assistance for interpersonal problems were invited to participate in the study on marital violence. Two couples refused to participate, and therapists reported that about 10 individuals were too disorganized to complete the questionnaires at the time of the intake interview. Since the focus of the study was on both spouses, responses from individuals coming to the clinic alone were not included. Thus the sample for this study consisted of 60 couples: the first 30 couples reporting conjugal violence within the past 18 months and the first 30 couples reporting no history of conjugal violence. All were seeking psychiatric assistance for marital problems. Although two couples were not legally married, they had lived together for more than one year and for the purposes of this study were considered a marital pair.

Although the sample size was small, our study involved a cross section of socioeconomic groups. Gross annual incomes ranged from $1000 to more than $30,000; education ranged from 8 years beyond kindergarten to college graduation. We took precautions to insure that the nonviolent group was free of conjugal violence. These included obtaining responses from the patients about the presence or absence of marital violence on a questionnaire and review by a research assistant of the marital history as recorded in the patients' charts.

At the intake appointment, each person completed a questionnaire regarding physical punishment received as a child, observation of conjugal violence as a child, alcohol and drug use, marital arguments, physical fights between spouses, and the use of physical punishment with his or her own children. For such questions as, Do you and your spouse have physical fights?, response categories of none, infrequent, occasional, frequent, and often were used and scored 0 to 4, respectively. Sociodemographic data were collected, and each individual completed the Bem Sex-Role Inventory (Bem, 1974), a psychological self-rating measure of 60 personality traits which classifies individuals according to sex-role orientation. Couples who reported violent episodes were interviewed in semistructured interviews to determine the severity and frequency of violence. Conjugal violence was defined as occurring whenever a man or woman involved in an intimate relationship suffers serious or repeated injury at the hands of the partner. Violence was classified as severe when either partner required medical attention for injuries received during the violent episode, as moderate when the physical fights occurred more often than six times a year with no injuries requiring medical attention, and as mild when there were fewer than six fights annually with no serious injuries.

RESULTS AND DISCUSSION

Sociodemographic Characteristics

Researchers of conjugal violence have suggested that the greatest amount of family violence is found in the lower class (Steinmetz and Straus, 1974; Gelles, 1974; Wolfgang and Ferracuti, 1967). The assumption that conjugal violence is associated with a family's position in the social structure was tested by analyzing the demographic data from the sample (Table 1).

Significant differences between groups were found on educational level and combined gross annual income. The CV males and females had significantly lower educational levels and reported less annual income than did their nonviolent counterparts. No differences between groups were found on age, race, and number of children. Overall, although these data support the notion that marital violence is related to social class, it is note-

Table 1

Education, Income, and Early-Violence Experience of Violent and Nonviolent Couples

	Conjugal Violence M	Conjugal Violence SD	No Violence M	No Violence SD	*t*	*p*
Husbands' education (yrs.)	12.3	2.1	13.8	2.4	2.65	<.01
Wives' education (yrs.)	12.0	2.0	13.0	1.8	2.12	<.04
Gross Family Income	11,653	62.53	15,223	67.00	2.03	<.05
Backgrounds of being hit or witnessing conjugal violence as a child						
Wives	2.8	1.9	1.8	1.5	3.55	<.001
Husbands	3.2	2.0	1.7	1.6	3.07	<.01
Couples	5.9	2.9	3.6	2.3	2.13	<.05

worthy that 40 percent of the violent men had some college education, and one man in this group had attended graduate school and was earning $30,000 annually.

Our data on the mean educational levels of the CV husbands and wives do not support O'Brien's (1974) research, which suggests that violence is frequently precipitated because husbands have less education and/or fewer job skills than their wives and are thus unable to maintain a superior position in the family.

Considering that the mean gross annual income for the CV group was $11,653 (compared to $15,223 for the NV group) and that, in many cases, both spouses' incomes were needed for the families' survival, it is possible that marital violence occurred partially as a result of the couples' response to stress and economic frustrations. Other research support this idea (Steinmetz and Straus, 1974).

Learning, Maintenance, and Transmission of Family Violence

The literature on child abuse presents strong evidence that abusive parents were frequently abused as children (Silver et al., 1969; Gelles, 1973). Owens and Straus (1975) found that an adult's approval of interpersonal violence correlated highly with his or her experience of violence as a child. Other studies indicate that individuals who were exposed to a high degree of parental punishment are more sensitive to the effectiveness of power and more likely to use physical punishment in their own families (Hoffman, 1960; Carroll, 1977).

According to Gelles (1974), violent parents provide the child with role models for the use of violence. Among the 80 families he studied, respondents who had observed their parents engaging in physical violence were in fact more likely to fight physically with their own spouses than did respondents who had never seen their parents fight. We hypothesized, therefore, that couples in our sample who were experiencing conjugal violence had experienced and/or observed significantly more parental violence than had the nonviolent couples. We also expected the CV couples to hit their own children more than did the nonviolent couples. The findings of differences in backgrounds and transmission of family violence between groups are presented in Table 1.

T-tests revealed significant differences in background of violence, both husbands and wives in the CV sample reporting that they had observed and/or experienced parental violence more often than had those in the NV group. A trend for the CV couples to hit their own children more than did the NV couples was noted. Overall, our data support the hypothesis that childhood backgrounds of family violence are related to conjugal violence.

When the husbands' and wives' scores on history of family violence were combined, the difference between the CV and NV groups became even more significant. Perhaps the experience and effect of a violent background are best described by a paragraph from an autobiography written by a man in the CV group:

> I managed to finish high school with the help of my friend's parents. They taught me that everyone that lives in a family had some kind of family trouble at one time or another but I have never seen another man beat his kids with his fists or a mother turn into a wino while the husband beat her. I've never seen one of my friends get knocked dizzy because his father shoved his head into a wall. I firmly concluded that my family was not normal. In fact, I still fear my father mentally, and now, years later, I still prefer to stay away from him. I guess the saddest part is that I have become almost as big a bully as he was.

Further analysis of the data using chi-square tests shows that the frequency of having been hit as a child is significantly related to later conjugal violence ($X^2 = 17.53$, $df = 3$, $P < .001$). There were no significant differences between groups on having witnessed conjugal violence as children.

In an earlier study (Coleman and Howard, 1978) in which we investigated the backgrounds of violence of 33 CV women and 30 NV women, we had noted no significant differences. In that study, however, 13 of the women were divorced or separated from their spouses, while in the current study all women were living with their spouses. This serendipitous information about the difference in marital status of the two groups of CV women and their backgrounds of family violence supports Gelles's (1976) finding that one of three major factors that influence a wife to stay in a violent marriage is having been struck frequently as a child.

Marital Arguments and Conjugal Violence

The notion that verbal arguments between intimates are productive and desirable has been proposed by Bach and Whyden (1974). Couples being trained to "fight fair" are told, "A fight a day keeps the doctor away." Other current therapies also advise the release of aggression by verbal and sometimes physical expression in a treatment setting (Lowen, 1966; Perls, 1969; Janov, 1970). This view is based on Freud's theory of catharsis, the "liberation of affect" through the re-experiencing of blocked or inhibited emotions (Freud 1924, [1914]). Contemporary advocates of this theory have been called ventilationists (Berkowitz, 1973: p. 24).

This view, despite its popularity, is supported by scant empirical evidence. Some social scientists, in fact, warn therapists that encouraging the expression and acting out of anger in the therapeutic situation may produce long-term effects and inappropriate behavior in other settings. Aggressive outbursts have tension-reducing effects that may reinforce future aggressive behavior. Berkowitz (1973), who for more than a decade investigated stimuli associated with impulsive violence, suggested that talking about angry feelings is preferable to directly attacking others verbally or physically, either actually or in fantasy. A review of research on the effectiveness of catharsis by Bandura and Walters (1974) suggested that participation in physically aggressive activities may actually increase violent behavior.

To test the hypothesis that verbal aggression may be a substitute for physical aggression in our sample, we included an item concerning the frequency of marital arguments in our questionnaire, finding a significant difference between the CV and NV groups, the CV group reporting significantly more verbal arguments than the NV group ($X^2 = 11.74$, $df = 1$, $p < .001$). No support for the ventilation theory was found.

Alcohol and Violence

The abuse of alcohol by husbands involved in conjugal violence is a consistent finding (Gelles, 1974; Gayford, 1975; Coleman and Howard, 1978). In our study, both husbands and wives in the CV sample reported significantly more alcohol use than did the NV husbands and wives ($X^2 = 26.28$, $df = 12$, $p < .01$) (Table 2). More than one-half of the CV men used alcohol frequently, compared with 20 percent of the NV men. There were no significant differences between groups on drug usage.

Table 2

Alcohol Use by Husbands, Wives, and Couples

	Conjugal Violence		*No Violence*	
Alcohol Use	Wives % (n = 30)	Husbands % (n = 30)	Wives % (n = 30)	Husbands % (n = 30)
None	10.0	3.4	30.0	13.3
Infrequent	20.0	10.0	16.7	16.7
Occasional	50.0	33.3	46.7	50.0
Frequent	13.3	33.3	6.6	16.7
Often	6.7	20.0	0	3.3

Sex-Role Stereotypes and Conjugal Violence

Martin (1976) asserted that the socialization of both males and females in our culture leads to unrealistic role expectations based on gender. She contended that adherence to these sex-role stereotypes determines the presence or absence of physical violence in a conjugal relationship. Straus (1977), in a study of the contribution of sexism to the frequency of wife-beating, concluded that both men and women need to be "liberated" to reduce the incidence of wife-battering. He attacked the presumption of superior authority for husbands in a family and views this attitude as contributing to physical attacks on wives. He believes that the preeminence of the wife role for women makes it difficult for wives to leave their abusive partners.

Clinical impressions of therapists who worked with the CV couples supported the idea that rigid adherence to sex roles contributes to violent episodes. One prominent characteristic of the men was their belief that to be a man, one must be strong, dominant, superior, and successful. Most of the male patients saw their major role in the family as that of breadwinner and ultimate decision-maker with little responsibility for the emotional climate of the family. "Helpfulness" to the wife frequently took the form of demanding behavior, the husband insisting that his views of financial planning, household management, and discipline of the children be accepted by her. If she refused to carry out his ideas, he felt thwarted in his managerial role and perceived her as wrong and provoking. The wives, in turn, felt totally responsible for the family's emotional climate and frequently took responsibility for their husbands' behavior. The women's tendency to define themselves first within the framework of their husbands' expectations and then within that of their families left them vulnerable to unreasonable demands from both husbands and children. Some of the wives viewed themselves as strong because they could tolerate violence, stay with their husbands, and keep the family together.

To provide some empirical evidence on adherence to traditional sex-roles by couples involved in conjugal violence, we included the Bem Sex-Role Inventory (BSRI, 1974) in this study. Specifically, we hypothesized that CV husbands and wives would be significantly more sex-typed than NV husbands and wives. The BSRI contains masculinity and femininity subscales, and the respondents received both a feminine and a masculine score. The scoring procedure uses median cutoffs to place persons into one of four sex-role categories: androgynous, masculine, feminine, or undifferentiated.

We found no significant differences between the two groups. In both groups, males were classified as masculine significantly more than females, while females were classified as feminine significantly more than males ($X^2 = 37.71$, $df = 9$, $p < .001$). Researchers using the BSRI have reported that high masculinity scores for males are associated with high self-esteem, good adjustment, a conservative attitude toward women, and low empathy. High feminity scores for women are associated with low self-esteem, excessive dependency, and poor adjustment (Deutsch and Gilbert, 1976; Bem, 1977; Orlofsky, 1977). In our study, 35 percent of all males and 22 percent of all females were classified as androgynous, a category that represents a high endorsement of both masculine and feminine items and is considered to be the most psychologically healthy category. Thirty-two percent of all women and 15 percent of men fell into the undifferentiated category. This classification represents a low endorsement of both masculine and feminine items and is related to low self-esteem (Spence et al., 1975; Bem, 1977). Overall, 77 percent of the husbands fell into the categories of androgynous or masculine, while 74 percent of the wives fell into the categories of feminine or undifferentiated.

Considering previous research that relates better adjustment to the masculine and androgynous categories, it seems that husbands in our sample were adjusted better than their wives in terms of socialization to cultural norms that value instrumental behavior. Recent evidence suggests that masculinity indeed is the norm for cultural socialization and that masculine characteristics are the clinical standards for adult mental health (Block,

1973; Broverman et al., 1970). These findings suggested that more sources of conflict exist in our society for women than for men. In attempting to conform to the traditional female role, a woman denies or represses her striving for independence and the development of instrumental skills. In a validity study of the BSRI, Bem (1975) noted that although all non-androgynous subjects have some behavioral deficiencies, females with high feminity scores have the greatest deficiencies of all. Since all of the couples in our sample complained of marital conflict, one might hypothesize that the combination of wives who have few instrumental skills and husbands who value effective behavior but have little empathy and a conservative attitude toward women leads to marital discord.

Following Bem's (1977) suggestion that investigators further analyze their data without categorizing subjects, we compared the masculinity and femininity scores of the CV and NV groups, using *t*-tests. Only one significant difference was apparent: the CV wives had a higher mean on feminity items than did the NV wives ($t = 2.10$, $df = 58$, $p = < .04$). This finding supports the impressions of volunteers and mental health professionals who work with battered women and report that low self-esteem and conformity to traditional female roles are characteristic of these women. In our study, the hypothesis that sex-typing and conjugal violence are related was partially supported for the wives but not for the husbands. The need for future research to determine which psychological factors, if any, separte abusing and nonabusing husbands is apparent.

Implications for Treatment

The high frequency of verbal arguments among CV couples indicates that encouraging overexpressive patients to engage in verbal aggression against their spouses may lead to subsequent aggressive behavior. Teaching the couples control over impulsive verbal behavior and new modes of dealing with stress that arises from everyday living is an important task in treatment.

The relationship of conjugal violence and alcohol abuse has been documented by previous research and data from our study. Interventions through existing programs for treating alcoholism might be one way of reducing marital violence.

As our study supports the hypothesis that violence breeds violence, the importance of therapeutic intervention with the whole family is highlighted. Teaching effective parenting skills and giving the children an opportunity to talk about their feelings may prevent the emergence of violent families in the future. If family violence is severe, the wife's responsibility in maintaining a chaotic relationship that endangers herself and her children must be confronted.

The high femininity scores of wives in the CV group on the BSRI reflect the women's need to develop instrumental skills so that they may function effectively in a complex society. A therapy group for women involved in violent relationship has been meeting at our institute for two years. The group provides a supportive environment in which the women may explore life options, develop adult coping skills, receive realistic feedback, and assess their strengths and weaknesses. Several graduates of the group have moved on to new jobs and relationships that enhance their sense of self-esteem.

Summary and Conclusions

This study examined characteristics of couples involved in conjugal violence who sought psychiatric assistance for their problems. Low socioeconomic level, frequent verbal arguments, backgrounds of family violence, alcohol abuse, and the women's tendency to adhere to rigid sex-role stereotypes were found to be related to conjugal violence. These form a complex picture of the eruption of violence. On one hand, the frequency of verbal arguments supports an interactional view of marital violence. On the other, the women's conformity to sex-roles and the couples' experiences of violence as children support the notion that some individuals are disposed by their backgrounds either to tolerate or instigate violent behavior. Family stress caused by low income and low educational levels contributes to the occurrence of violence; families who may never achieve some of the valued goals of society may become frustrated and react aggressively both in and outside the family boundaries. It seems that any model for the eruption of conjugal violence must integrate societal, familial, and psychological factors (Rounsaville, 1977). Straus (1973) proposes a general-systems theoretical approach to family violence. His multivariate emphasis includes psychological and societal factors which he categorizes as antecedent, precipitative, and consequent. He describes a feedback process that has the potential either to decrease or increase the incidence of family violence. The model is a comprehensible and cogent analysis of violent between family members.

Despite the growing attention being given to the problem of conjugal violence, mental health professionals still seem reluctant to ask direct questions when they suspect its occurrence. A therapist's investigation of severity of violence—use of lethal weapons such as guns and knives and possible child abuse—is essential and potentially life-saving. The attitude of many mental health professionals seems to reflect the battered wife's tendency to discount the violence so that she may keep her family together.

It is time for mental health professions to examine their views regarding family violence. However distasteful, marital violence is a problem in our society and deserves to be recognized, researched, and treated.

REFERENCES

BACH, G. R., and WYDEN, P. Why intimates must fight, in *Violence in the Family*. S. Steinmetz and M. Straus, eds. Harper & Row, New York, 1974.

BANDURA, A. and WALTERS, R. H. Catharsis—a questionable mode of coping with violence, in *Violence in the Family*. S. Steinmetz and M. Straus, eds. Harper & Row, New York, 1974.

BEM, S. L. The measurement of psychological androgyny. *J. Consult. Clin. Psychol.* 42:155-162, 1974.

BEM, S. Sex role adaptability: One consequence of psychological androgyny. *J. Pers. Soc. Psychol.* 4:634-643, 1975.

BEM, S. On the utility of alternative procedures for assessing psychological androgyny. *J. Consult. Clin. Psychol.* 45:196-205, 1977.

BERKOWITZ, L. The case for bottling up rage. *Psychology Today* 7:24-81, 1973.

BLOCK, J. H. Conceptions of sex role: Some cross-cultural and longitudinal perspectives. *Am. Psychol.* 28:512-527, 1973.

BROVERMAN, I., BROVERMAN, D., CLARKSON, F., ROSENCRANTZ, P., and VOGEL, S. Sex-role stereotypes and clinical judgments of mental health. *J. Consult. Clin. Psychol.* 1:1-7, 1970.

CARROLL, J. C. The intergenerational transmission of family violence: the long-term effects of aggressive behavior. *Aggressive Behavior*, 3:289-299, 1977.

COLEMAN, K. H., and HOWARD, P. M. Conjugal violence: What women report. Paper presented to American Psychological Association, Toronto, August, 1978.

DEUTSCH, C., and GILBERT, L. Sex role stereotypes: Effect on perceptions of self and others and on personal adjustment. *J. Counseling Psychology* 23:373-379, 1976.

DOBASH, R. E., and DOBASH, R. P. Wives: The "appropriate" victims of marital violence. *Victimology* 2:426-441, 1977-78.

FREUD, S. On the history of the psychoanalytic movement (1914), in *Collected Papers*, vol. 1. E. Jones, ed. Hogarth, London, 1924.

GAYFORD, J. J. Wife battering: a preliminary survey of one hundred cases. *Br. Med. J.* 1:194-197, 1975.

GELLES, R. Child abuse as psychopathology: a sociological critique and reformulation. *Am. J. Orthopsychiatry* 43:621-661, 1973.

GELLES, R. J. *The Violent Home: A Study of Physical Aggression Between Husbands and Wives*. Sage Publications, Beverly Hills, California, 1974.

GELLES, R. J. Abused wives: why do they stay? *J. Marriage and the Family* 38: 659-668, 1976.

HOFFMAN, M. L. Power assertion by the parent and its effect on the child. *Child Dev.* 31:129-143, 1960.

JANOV, A. *The Primal Scream*. Dell, New York, 1970.

KAUNITZ, P. E. Sado-masochistic marriages. *Medical Aspects of Human Sexuality* 11: 66-80, 1977.

LEVINGER, G. Physical abuse among applications for divorce, in *Violence in the Family*. S. Steinmetz and M. Straus, eds. Harper & Row, New York, 1974.

LOWEN, A. *The Betrayal of the Body*. Macmillan, New York, 1966.

MARTIN, D. *Battered Wives*. Glide Publications, San Francisco, 1976.

ORLOFSKY, J. Sex-role orientation, identify formation, and self-esteem in college men and women. *Sex Roles* 3:561-575, 1977.

O'BRIEN, J. R. Violence in divorce-prone families, in *Violence in the Family*. S. Steinmetz and M. Straus, eds. Harper & Row, New York, 1974.

OWENS, K., and STRAUS, H. The social structure of violence in childhood and approval of violence as an adult. *Aggressive Behavior,* 1:193-211, 1975.

PERLS, F. D. *Gestalt Therapy Verbatim.* Real People Press, Lafayette, California, 1969.

ROUNSAVILLE, B. J. Perspectives on marital violence: Evidence from a study of battered women. Paper presented to American Psychiatric Association, Toronto, Canada, 1977.

SILVER, L., DUBLIN, D., and LOURIE, R. Does violence breed violence? Contributions from a study of the child abuse syndrome. *Am. J. Psychiatry* 126:152-155, 1969.

SPENCE, J., HELMREICH, R., and STAPP, J. Ratings of self and peers on sex role attributes and their relation to self-esteem and conceptions of masculinity and feminity. *J. Pers. Soc. Psychol.* 32:29-39, 1975.

STEINMETZ, S. K., and STRAUS, M., eds. *Violence in the Family*. Harper & Row, New York, 1974.

STRAUS, M. A general systems theory approach to a theory of violence between spouses. *Social Science Information* 12:105-125, 1973.

STRAUS, M. A. Leveling, civility, and violence in the family. *J. Marriage and the Family,* 36:13-29, 1974.

STRAUS, M. A sociological perspective on the prevention and treatment of wifebeating, in *Battered Women: A Psychosociological Study of Domestic Violence.* M. Roy, ed. Van Nostrand Reinhold, New York, 1977.

STRAUS, M. Wife beating: How common and why? *Victimology* 2, 443-457, 1977-78.

WOLFGANG, M. E., and FERRACUTTI, F. *The Subculture of Violence.* Tavistock Publications, London, 1967.

CHAPTER 15

Special Problems in the Prediction of Violence Among the Mentally Ill

HENRY J. STEADMAN

The mentally ill are a group for whom predictions of violence take on special significance as well as special problems. They have special significance because the mentally ill are the only group in the United States who can be preventively detained for violence they might perpetrate rather than for violence they have performed. Such predictions are the only basis for emergency commitment in 38 of the 45 jurisdictions that have such statutes (Fagin, 1976). Rather than review the conceptual and social policy issues, which has already been done by Shah elsewhere in this volume, this paper examines some recent research that points to both empirical and conceptual problems that make the prediction of violence among the mentally ill especially thorny.

A recent comment on the special empirical and policy problems of predicting violence among the mentally ill was a brief but important article by Monahan (1978a). Monahan argues that the question about the level of accuracy obtainable in making predictions of future violence (that is, estimating dangerousness) among the mentally ill is a more open question than many contemporary analysts suggest. Specifically, Monahan asks "why one could expect that one set of circumstances—those which typically apply in the *short-term emergency commitment* of mentally ill persons predicted to be imminently violent—may be exempt from the systematic inaccuracy [of psychiatric predictions] found in the current research" (p. 198). Monahan argues that gaps in existing research make it impossible to contradict theoretical arguments that the settings in which predictive accuracy has been empirically disproved are different in critical and obvious ways from community settings that are the "truest test of predictive validity" (p. 199). While Monahan raises these concerns only for the emergency-commitment circumstance, the issues really highlight a number of general problems for making predictions of future violence for the mentally ill in most situations in which such predictions are routinely required.

To sort out the many issues embedded in Monahan's question, this paper will focus on six major problems of particular importance for understanding the special difficulties in predicting violence among the mentally ill. These issues are: factors associated with assaultive behavior in the community and in mental hospitals may be quite different; there is no evidence of any direct relationship between assaultive behavior in mental hospitals and assaultive behavior in the community; the role of medication in making accurate predictions; situational variables may be prime determinants of violent behavior despite their minimal consideration in most mental health evaluations; the almost exclusive statutory reliance on psychiatrists for predictions of violence in the mental health system; and the limited, atypical groups of mental patients for whom empirical data exist and from which policy is developed.

These issues are not intended to be a comprehensive survey of special problems, but rather highlights not brought out by the other chapters in this book.

Each of these six issues has direct and important implications for both clinical decision-making and directions for future research. It is clear that certain types of research have run their course and demand new initiatives. My intent here is to set out what these initiatives might be so that information might be developed to enable the clinician to make more accurate predictions with the limited tools currently available. Improvement is needed because of the continual expansion of statutes that require estimates of the probabilities of future violence by the mentally ill. This latter point is crucial, though a neater solution to many of the prediction problems would be the abolition of the dangerousness standard. This would avoid all over-prediction and misidentification dilemmas, but will not happen unless public attitudes change radically and social changes completely outside the sweep of the history of the United States occur. It is much more realistic to move toward social-policy revisions with more limited expectations and with a clearer picture as to what gaps exist in current research, what findings are persuasive, and what additional data are needed to diminish current mistaken notions about the prediction of violence among the mentally ill and the associated misuses of such predictions.

FACTORS RELATED TO HOSPITAL AND COMMUNITY VIOLENCE ARE DIFFERENT

When predictions of violence are made to decide on the appropriate level of security for a prison inmate, the locus of the prediction is the prison to which he or she will be committed. When the family court inquires about the probability of a father's or mother's physical abuse of a child, the setting is clearly the home or similar community setting. When a judge must decide about the possibility of a husband's assaulting his spouse, the setting of the behavior is the home or some other community setting. When a parole board assesses the probability of an inmate's repeating violence, the estimation clearly relates to behavior on the street. When questions of potential violence among the mentally ill are raised, they may relate to either behavior in the community or behavior in a hospital. Therefore the locale of past and future behaviors are often mixed and take on special significance.

Mental health professionals are asked by the court whether or not persons have demonstrated behaviors that make them a danger to self or others, that is, are they apt to be violent in the future based on their past behaviors. These past behaviors may have occurred in the community before the instigation of involuntary commitment hearings or in mental hospitals before *habeas corpus* hearings for release. Although the recent federal circuit court decision in Illinois (*Matthew* v. *Nelson*) requires no demonstration of overt acts, the courts usually depend on recent violent or threatening behavior to indicate the probability of its repetition. In the empirical research on predicting violent behavior in mental patients, the infrequent discrimination between past and future behavior either in the community or in mental hospital environments fosters many inaccurate predictions as to who will be violent. There are at least two reasons for the inaccuracies: the factors related to violence in the community usually are different from those related to in-hospital violence, and there is no demonstrated relationship between in-hospital assaultiveness and community assaultiveness. Both findings are evident in some data we have compiled recently.

Factors Related to Assaultiveness

From a long-term project assessing the accuracy of psychiatric predictions of dangerousness and the accuracy of statistical predictions as compared to clinical predictions (Cocozza and Steadman, 1978; Steadman and Cocozza, 1978), it became evident that different factors were related to assaultiveness in the hospital than in the community.

The study group, described in detail elsewhere (Cocozza and Steadman, 1978), consisted of 257 male defendants found incompetent to stand trial. Psychiatric estimations of dangerousness were made for all 257. Longitudinal data were then gathered for three years from both mental hospital and arrest records to assess the accuracy of the psychiatric predictions. From this information 53 sociodemographic and criminal-history variables were entered into a discriminant-function analysis. As seen in Table 1, seven factors were identified and weighted as most accurately discriminating between the assaultive and nonassaultive patients in the maximum-security hospitals. The seven factors correctly identified 43 of the 58 persons who were assaultive while hospitalized in maximum-security mental hospitals immediately after the finding of incompetency. The overall accuracy rate was 63 percent and the false-positive rate was 0.86 to 1. This compared

Table 1

Discriminant-Function Analysis Factors and Weighting for Predicting Hospital and Community Assaultiveness—Incompetent Defendants

Location of Assaultiveness			
Hospital		*Community*	
Factor	Weight*	Factor	Weight*
Race	–.5232	Previous convictions for property crimes	–1.2081
Previous convictions for property crimes	–.4893	Total previous incarcerations	.9218
Previous adjudication as juvenile delinquent	.3356	Previous arrests for minor crimes	–.6084
Previous arrests for fraud crimes	–.3321	Previous arrests for violent crimes	.6045
Diagnosis	–.3202	Previous convictions for sex crimes	.5332
History of family problems	.3140	Previous arrests for property crimes	.5130
Marital status	.2557	History of family problems	.3591
		Age on admission	–.2137

* Standardized discriminant-function coefficients

with the psychiatric evaluation accuracy rate of 46 percent and its false-positive rate of 0.95 to 1.

More relevant to the issues discussed in this paper was the contrast between the discriminant-function analysis and the subsequent analysis which tested the same 53 variables' predictive utility for assaultiveness in the community, as indicated by arrest for murder, manslaughter or assault, or rehospitalization precipitated by an assaultive incident. Here the 8 variables reported in Table 1 were used in the statistical prediction equation to produce an overall accuracy rate of 70 percent and a false-positive rate of 2.4 to 1. These results compared with the clinical accuracy rate of 59 percent and false-positive rate of 3.8 to 1. However, the set of 8 variables associated with community-assaultiveness predictions included only 2 of the 7 variables used for hospital assaultiveness, and their weightings were entirely different.

These analyses seemed to yield little useful information for identifying mental patients who were assaultive while hospitalized that would also be useful in identifying mental patients who were assaultive in the community. This finding is particularly problematic for clinical decision-making which relies heavily on recent behavior in assessing potential violent behavior when the nonassociation between in-hospital and community behaviors discussed in the next section is considered.

Nonassociation of Hospital and Community Assaultiveness

Data from the same study group, presented in Table 2, show no relationship between assaultiveness in the maximum-security mental hospitals and assaultiveness in the community after release. Of those patients who

Table 2

Relationship between Assaults in Maximum-Security Mental Hospital and Community Assaults after Release—Incompetent Defendants

Number of Community Assaults after Release	Number of Hospital Assaults: 0		1		2 or More	
	N	%	N	%	N	%
0	78	83.9	28	80.0	21	87.5
1 or more	15	16.1	7	20.0	3	12.5
TOTAL	93	100.0	35	100.0	24	100.0

had no record of assaultiveness while hospitalized, 16 percent were assaultive in the community. Similarly, 20 percent of those with one reported assault while hospitalized were assaultive in the community, as were 12 percent of those with two or more reported hospital assaults.

This finding did not surprise us since a very similar finding had occurred in our previous research on the "Baxstrom" patients (Steadman and Cocozza, 1974). Among those long-term patients who were transferred from maximum-security correctional hospitals to regular-security civil hospitals as a result of a U.S. Supreme Court decision in 1966, there was no relationship between number of assaults while hospitalized and assaultiveness in the community. Likewise Thornberry and Jacoby (1979), in their study of Pennsylvania's "Dixon" patients, also transferred from maximum- to regular-security hospitals as the result of a court decision, found no relationship between hospital and community assaultiveness. These research findings are especially relevant to predictions of future violence by mental patients being considered for release. The studies may also relate directly to commitment proceedings in which a demonstration of danger to others is documented by assaultive behavior during a 24- to 72-hour emergency commitment. Whether the data presented here relate as clearly to emergency commitment situations is uncertain. To our knowledge, however, there has yet to be an empirical demonstration of statistically significant relationships between assaultive behavior by mental patients in hospitals and in the community.

Thus, we are left with a situation that suggests strongly that quite different factors are related to hospital and community assaultiveness and that no relationship is demonstrable between assaultiveness in these two locations. If this factor is used for making predictions, substantial error rates will occur in identifying persons as dangerous who will not be, and identifying persons as not dangerous who will be. Yet courts demand and mental health professionals regularly supply assessments that rely heavily on situationally unspecified sets of criteria and on most recent behavior, whether or not the settings for the past and future behavior are the same. The old saw that "the best predictor of future behavior is past behavior" must be qualified for the mentally ill, or anyone really, that a prime predictor of future behavior in the community is past behavior in the community and of future behavior in hospitals is past behavior in similar institutions.

The findings reported here point to two other related issues, the effects of psychotropic medications on the behaviors in question and the role of situational factors in predicting violent behavior.

ROLE OF PSYCHOTROPIC MEDICATION

Another problem in predicting future assaultiveness among the mentally ill is the confounding effects of psychotropic medications. First, the person being evaluated for dangerousness may be on some type of emergency commitment and receiving some type of medication during this observation period. Second, if committed, the person while hospitalized is likely to be taking some type of medication that will influence his or her behavior and the accuracy of any predictions that are made. Thus the disjuncture between the setting(s) of evaluation and the setting(s) of predicted behavior is exacerbated. Not only is the person removed from the stresses and the inflammations of community situations, but, often, a mental health evaluation is performed while medication is being administered that potentially alters the behaviors and emotions of interest.

To what extent and in what types of cases particular medications affect violent behavior is a topic beyond the scope of this paper. Suffice it to note that for most other groups for whom predictions of violence are made, medication is not an issue nearly as often nor as directly. Individuals may have some domestic problems for which treatment and medication are advised, and surely offenders come into the criminal justice system with drug abuse of various sorts. For the most part, however, the types of circumstances for which predictions are made for normals or even for prison inmates will not have psychotropic medications as so clearly a confounding factor. Such a phenomenon requires a different understanding of the person and situations for which predictions are made, and it is definitely a special problem both in making accurate clinical predictions and in assessing the validity of such predictions.

THE ROLE OF SITUATIONAL FACTORS

This issue in its broadest sense is not at all particular to the mentally ill. Knowing how situational and contextual factors interact with individual characteristics is crucial for an adequate understanding of any human violence. The role of these factors does have some special significance for the mentally ill, because of the disjunctures discussed above between hospital and community behaviors and because of the infrequent use of such variables in clinical and research endeavors.

Levinson and Ramsey (1979) demonstrated the potential importance of situational factors. In a small-scale study they used mental health associates (MHA) rather than the usual psychiatrists as evaluators. The MHAs were paraprofessionals whose socioeconomic status was more like that of the clients than the psychiatrists. This was believed to be of some benefit in accurately predicting violence among the subjects being considered for civil hospital admission. Levinson and Ramsey concluded that "The data indicate that non-psychiatric health professionals with assumed advantages for predicting behavior are unable to predict dangerousness significantly better than chance" (p. 14). The researchers also found, however, that the accuracy of the predictions depended on environmental stresses. The MHA predictions were significantly better in the low-stress situations. In these, predictions of dangerousness were wrong in seven of 26 cases (26 percent) compared to being wrong in 15 of 23 cases (65 percent) in the high-stress situations. The preliminary study supports several others (Bem and Allen, 1974; Megargee, 1976; Monahan, 1977) who have suggested that individual and situational variables interact in producing violence and must be considered in the analysis and prediction of violence.

In the clinical and statistical prediction literature the conclusions are the same. The variables that have been employed and the frameworks that have produced them have been found inadequate. As a result Shah (1978), Monahan (1978b), and others have suggested that the situations and environments of violence must be examined for more productive explanations. Megargee (1976) recommended including personality factors, internal inhibitions, and situational factors. Geis and Monahan (1976) spoke of the "social ecology of violence" which would take into account not only the person but also the environment and situation with which he or she interacts.

To date, research on situational variables in violence is limited (Wolfgang, 1958; Mulvihill et al., 1969; Toch, 1969; Gelles, 1972; Curtis, 1974; Steinmetz, 1977). These studies usually report univariate descriptive statistics on homicides, assaults, and other violent offenses and do not include mental patients in the study groups. The types of variables that have been examined include: method (i.e., weapon) used; the location of the crime; when the act was committed (time, day, month); age, sex, race, and relationship of offender and victim, ostensible motive as labeled by police; and the presence or absence of alcohol. These studies are useful but limited; they only examine violence that results in arrest and conviction; they do not examine how situational variables affect variations in the outcome of aggressive encounters (for example, while many violent offenses follow an altercation of some kind, not all altercations result in violence; what situational variables affect the probability that an altercation will end in violence?); only a limited number of situational variables are examined (for example, there is not much analysis of the sequence of events in aggressive encounters); and past research has, for the most part, been descriptive. No attempt is made to predict or interpret patterns for a theoretical perspective.

All of this is to suggest that both clinical evaluation and evaluative research can profitably shift their focuses to such variables. Moreover, accurate prediction of violence cannot be expected until such a shift occurs.

OVERRELIANCE ON PSYCHIATRIC PREDICTIONS

A particular problem with making accurate predictions of violence among the mentally ill is the overrestriction by statutes and practice of professionals that may be involved in judicially mandated evaluations. In civil and criminal statutes dealing with prediction of assaultiveness among the mentally ill, there is an almost total reliance on psychiatrists for prediction. The sole profession that is judicially acceptable in most jurisdictions to provide expert opinions for assaultive potential among the mentally ill is psychiatry.

This becomes a problem because research has demonstrated clearly that psychiatrists have no special expertise as accurate predictors of dangerousness (Cocozza and Steadman, 1976). This is not to say that it has been empirically shown that anyone can do it better. Rather, there is no evidence for the belief that any professional group, by itself, is significantly more accurate than chance. Some suggestions have been made that a team approach might be most productive (Kozol et al., 1972). This suggestion seems to be on firm theoretical ground, given the increasing evidence for the need to consider situational factors in making predictions of violence among the mentally ill or any other group. The range of such factors is so great that a wide variety of skills is required and no one specialty, especially one whose paradigm focuses on the individual psyche, may be expected to have the necessary evaluative techniques. The overreliance on psychiatric opinion by courts, however, severely restricts the introduction of the range of evidence that seems to be essential for accurate predictions of violence among the mentally ill.[1]

LIMITED STUDY GROUPS

Finally, a special problem in making predictions of violence for the mentally ill based on existing empirical findings is the atypicality of the group with whom most of the predictive research has been done. Our studies (Steadman and Cocozza, 1974; Steadman and Cocozza, 1978)

[1] Part of the problem is, of course, the fact that dangerousness, the concept in which predictions of violence among the mentally ill are operationalized, is a legal concept, not a psychiatric/medical one.

were of long-term patients in maximum-security hospitals for the criminally insane and of incompetent felony defendants. Kozol's (1972) work focused on sex offenders. Thornberry and Jacoby (1979) examined long-term patients in hospitals for the criminally insane. All of these groups are rather special ones whose similarity to most civil mental patients, voluntary or involuntary, is uncertain. Yet these are the only groups for whom intensive hospital-community followups of clinical and statistical assessments of violence have been completed.

Hedlund (1973) and Depp (1976) looked at civil hospital patients and factors associated with hospital assaultiveness, but they did not study subsequent community behavior patterns nor did they assess the validity of any psychiatric predictions. In work in which we are currently involved, however, there is some suggestion that the data from research with incompetent felony defendants discussed earlier may be applicable to certain civil patients. We gathered data on a sample of 145 involuntary male patients who were committed to six New York City hospitals in 1968. As for the 25 incompetent felons reported above in Table 2, Table 3 shows that the frequency of assaults among these civil hospital patients in the community was unrelated to their assaultiveness while hospitalized. Of patients who were not assaultive in hospitals, 16 percent were subsequently assaultive in the community, while 12 percent of those with one hospital assault and 20 percent of those with multiple hospital assaults were. Not only are there no significant differences between the groups, as with the incompetent defendants, but the proportions of persons assaultive in each category, in hospital and in the community, were quite similar.

Further work remains to be done to assess the factors associated with hospital and community assaultiveness to determine whether, for this involuntary civil group, different factors are associated with assaults in hospital

Table 3

Relationship between Assaults in Civil Mental Hospitals and Community Assaults after Release—Involuntary Civil Patients

	Number of Hospital Assaults					
	0		1		2 or More	
Number of Community Assaults after Release	N	%	N	%	N	%
0	96	83.5	7	87.5	4	80.0
1 or more	19	16.5	1	12.5	1	20.0
TOTAL*	115	100.0	8	100.0	5	100.0

* 17 patients were not released during followup period.

and in community, and how accurate statistical prediction could have been in this study group. Nevertheless, the restricted and atypical study groups remain a special problem in making predictions about violence in the mentally ill.

NEEDED DEVELOPMENTS

The primary need in research relates to expanding the range of groups for whom empirical information is available. There is no shortage of popular clinical wisdom about high-risk groups or the most important factors in predicting violence. A few years ago I heard a respected psychiatrist assert that paranoid schizophrenics were a particularly dangerous group. Three weeks later I heard an equally respected psychiatrist state that paranoid schizophrenics were among the least violent groups because their personality disruptions made it difficult for them to organize their egos into any action, including violence. Both psychiatrists were equally convinced of the validity of their statements from their clinical experience. In our research and that of others, however, there is no indication that this diagnostic group is in fact particularly violent in the community.

On the other side are many clinically based notions about the frequent association of drug or alcohol abuse with assaultive behavior. Although our research has not uncovered such a direct relationship, our recent study of arrest rates of patients recently released from New York State psychiatric centers (Steadman et al., 1978) did find patients so diagnosed as more apt to be arrested after release. This was consistent with a number of other arrest-rate studies (Rappeport and Lassen, 1965; Zitrin et al., 1976) In this instance, then, there is some statistical support for clinical judgment. In terms of the prediction of violence among the mentally ill, clinical judgment alone is entirely unsatisfactory. A more satisfactory approach to improve the knowledge base is the development of longitudinal studies of a much wider variety of civil mental patients.

A second productive direction is the use of group assessments that include statistical inputs along with more traditional clinical factors. The psychological literature is most persuasive of the superior accuracy of statistical over clinical predictions for almost any type of behavior (Sawyer, 1966; Sines, 1970). More specifically, our research and others' has consistently shown that the application of statistical techniques to predict future assaultiveness would have been more accurate than the clinical predictions (Steadman and Cocozza, 1974; Steadman and Cocozza, 1978; Jacoby, 1975). This would seem to suggest a model that might incorporate statistical assessments, and their known limitations, with clinical workups to attempt some determinations of the most beneficial ways in which they might be combined to make more accurate assessments. An approach that combines clinical and statistical assessments may offer greater potential for isolating both the range of relevant individual, situational, and contextual factors in various types of groups and the dynamics that produce violence.

The third recommendation relates directly to the day-to-day practices of estimating future assaultiveness, regardless of the procedure. Little improvement in accuracy may be expected until more thorough examinations of the environments of violence of the mentally ill are introduced, since so often either the site of the evaluation of violence potential is different from the sites of prediction (Monahan, 1978a), or the locations for which the predictions are made are unspecified. This is not as often true of other groups for whom predictions are made.

This latter recommendation is closely allied with the previous point of interdisciplinary group evaluations. Analyzing the environment from which and to which the mentally ill go requires much investigative work outside any clinical evaluation center. Kozol et al. (1972) and Levinson and Ramsey (1979) described approaches to gathering and processing such information. A more theoretical discussion of the situational dynamics and potentially relevant factors is that offered by Felson (1978) from an interpersonal-interaction framework. As yet there are no adequate data to suggest the most productive approach to clinically and statistically isolating relevant situational factors for various groups. It is clear, however, that the alternatives of clinical judgments or statistical assessments based on sociodemographic, criminal-history variables hold little hope. Given the growing, albeit primarily theoretical, literature on situational factors, such a focus seems to be more promising for addressing the special problems of predicting violence among the mentally ill than most others that have been suggested and/or attempted.

ACKNOWLEDGMENTS

This paper reflects the thoughtful comments of Joseph Morrissey and Joseph Cocozza on earlier versions. The research was partially supported by the National Institute of Mental Health Center for Studies of Crime and Delinquency (PHS Grant MH-28850).

REFERENCES

BEM, D., and ALLEN, A. On predicting some of the people some of the time: the search for cross-situational consistencies in behavior. *Psychol. Rev.* 81:506-520, 1974.

COCOZZA, J. J., and STEADMAN, H. J. The failure of psychiatric predictions of dangerousness: clear and convincing evidence. *Rutgers Law Review* 29:1084-1101, 1976.

COCOZZA, J. J., and STEADMAN, H. J. Prediction in psychiatry: an example of misplaced confidence in experts. *Social Problems* 25:265-276, 1978.

CURTIS, L. A. *Criminal Violence: National Patterns and Behavior*. Lexington Books, Lexington, Massachusetts, 1974.

DEPP, F. C. Violent behavior patterns on psychiatric wards. *Aggressive Behavior* 2: 295-306, 1976.

FAGIN, A. The policy implications of predictive decision-making: likelihood and dangerousness in civil commitment proceedings. *Public Policy* 24(4):491-528, 1976.

FELSON, R. B. Aggression as impression management. *Soc. Psychol.* 41:205-213, 1978.

GEIS, G., and MONAHAN, J. The social ecology of violence, in *Morality: Theory, Research and Social Issues*. T. Lickona, ed. Holt, Rinehart and Winston, New York, 1976.

GELLES, R. J. *The Violent Home*. Sage Publications, Beverly Hills, California, 1972.

HEDLUND, J. L., SLETTEN, I. W., ALTMAN, H., and EVENSON, R. C. Prediction of patients who are dangerous to others. *J. Clin. Psychol.* 29:443-447, 1973.

JACOBY, J. Prediction of dangerousness among mentally ill offenders. Paper presented to American Society of Criminology, October, 1975.

KOZOL, H., BOUCHER, R., and GAROFALO, R. The diagnosis and treatment of dangerousness. *Crime and Delinquency* 18:371-392, 1972.

LEVINSON, R., and RAMSEY, G. Dangerousness, stress and mental health evaluations. *J. Health Soc. Behav.* 20;178-187, 1979.

MEGARGEE, E. I. The prediction of dangerous behavior. *Criminal Justice and Behavior* 3:3-22, 1976.

MONAHAN, J., and MONAHAN, L. C. Prediction research and the role of psychologists in correctional institutions. *San Diego Law Review* 14:1028-1038, 1977.

MONAHAN, J. Prediction research and the emergency commitment of dangerous mentally ill persons: a reconsideration. *Am. J. Psychiatry* 135:198-201, 1978a.

MONAHAN, J. The prediction of violent criminal behavior: a methodological critique and prospectus. National Academy of Sciences, Washington, D. C., 1978b.

MULVIHILL, D., TUMIN, M., and CURTIS, L. *Crimes of Violence (a Staff Report to the National Commission on the Causes and Prevention of Violence*, vol. 2. U. S. Government Printing Office, Washington, D.C., 1969.

RAPPFPORT, J. R., and LASSEN, G. Dangerousness-arrest rate comparisons of discharged mental patients and the general population. *Am. J. Psychiatry* 121:776-783, 1965.

SAWYER, J. Measurement and prediction, clinical and statistical. *Psychol. Bull.* 66: 178-200, 1966.

SHAH, S. Dangerousness: a paradigm for exploring some issues in law and psychology. *Am. Psychol.* 33:222-238, 1978.

SINES, J. Actuarial versus clinical prediction in psychopathology. *Br. J. Psychiatry* 116:129-144, 1970.

STEADMAN, H. J., and COCOZZA, J. J. *Careers of the Criminally Insane*. Lexington Books, Lexington, Massachusetts, 1974.

STEADMAN, H. J., and COCOZZA, J. J. The dangerousness standard and psychiatry: a cross national issue in the social control of the mentally ill. *Sociology and Social Research* 63:649-670, 1978.

STEADMAN, H. J. *Beating a Rap?: Defendants Found Incompetent to Stand Trial*. University of Chicago Press, Chicago, 1979.

STEADMAN, H. J., COCOZZA, J. J., and MELICK, M. E. Explaining the increased arrest rate among mental patients: the changing clientele of state hospitals. *Am. J. Psychiatry* 135:816-820, 1978.

STEINMETZ, S. K. *The Cycle of Violence: Assertive, Aggressive, and Abusive Family Interaction*. Praeger, New York, 1977.

THORNBERRY, T. P., and JACOBY, J. E. *The Criminally Insane*. University of Chicago Press, Chicago, 1979.

TOCH, H. *Violent Man*. Aldine, Chicago, 1969.

WOLFGANG, M. E. *Patterns in Criminal Homicide*. Wiley, New York, 1958.

ZITRIN, A., HARDESTY, A. S., and BURDOCK, E. T. Crime and violence among mental patients. *Am. J. Psychiatry*, 133:142-149, 1976.

CHAPTER 16

Development of An Actuarial Model for Predicting Dangerousness of Patients in Maximum-Security Mental Hospitals

JAMES M. MULLEN
HAROLD K. DUDLEY, JR.

With a grant from the Hogg Foundation for Mental Health at the University of Texas, the Texas Department of Mental Health and Mental Retardation is conducting a research project on the so-called dangerousness of mental patients. The goal of the project is to develop criteria for estimating the probability of a patient's committing a violent act against another person in the future.

Under Texas statutes (Articles 46.02 and 46.03, Texas Code of Criminal Procedure) a person charged with a criminal offense and found to be insane or incompetent to stand trial for that offense with no probability of gaining competency, is civilly committed to the maximum-security unit of Rusk State Hospital. Each case must be reviewed within 60 days by a Review Board for Manifest Dangerousness composed of three psychiatrists. If the board determines that the patient is *manifestly dangerous,* the patient remains on the maximum-security unit. Upon a finding of *not manifestly dangerous,* the patient must be transferred to any nonsecurity mental health facility for treatment. Given the ambiguity of the statute and the significance of the review board's decisions, it is necessary to develop criteria for making such determinations.

The development of the present exploratory study was influenced by the results of previous research in several important ways: by studies that demonstrated the utility of the multivariate approach to the understanding of violent behavior; by studies that identified variables associated with violent behavior, particularly violent behavior in mental patients and prison inmates; by studies that addressed the methodological issues of predicting violent behavior; and by studies that recommended an actuarial approach to the prediction of dangerousness.

Researchers have determined that violent behavior is not attributable to a single variable but to multiple biological, psychological, and sociological variables. Many of these variables, identified from a review of the literature (Mullen and Rollins, 1977), were incorporated into the present research protocol. Since the study was limited, however, to the information acquired by hospital clinicians (psychiatrists, psychologists, social workers) at the time of the patient's hospital admission, the study does not include biological variables that may have influenced a patient's violent behavior.

The principal question of predicting behavior, particularly violent or dangerous behavior, is how to resolve a twofold methodological problem: What is a definition of dangerousness and how is dangerous behavior to be measured? Megargee (1976) addressed both questions. Dangerousness is not a trait inherent in an individual; it is a concept that refers to a specific kind of behavior, namely, behavior that is potentially harmful to another person. The implication of Megargee's observation is that no matter how dangerousness may be defined, focus on a specific kind of behavior is essential. Behavior is usually defined as the response of an individual to the environment. Dangerous behavior may be viewed as an individual's violent response to situational cues. One aspect of behavior is internal, such as the individual's personality characteristics, while another aspect of behavior is external. Megargee (1976) identified several traits indicative of individuals who engage in dangerous behavior. An American Psychiatric Association Task Force (1974) identified situational variables commonly associated with dangerous behavior, for example, availability of a gun and the influence of drugs or alcohol. The fact is, however, that researchers and clinicians have enormous difficulties accounting for the situational cues that contribute to dangerous behavior. Reported studies on dangerousness are examples of retrospective rather than prospective research. The studies are done with prison inmates and hospital patients on whom data may be conveniently collected while a designated violent offender is incarcerated. These studies give the impression, unsupported by research, that violent individuals may be easily typed as potentially violent. Completely ignored are the situational variables that may have triggered the violent behavior for which an individual is now institutionalized.

In view of the problems of predicting dangerousness that are discussed elsewhere in this volume, many researchers currently recommended an actuarial approach as a way of improving the quality of such predictions. By considering clinical and demographic variables together statistically, along with systematic followup of decisional outcomes, methods of determining dangerousness may be improved. The purpose of the present projcet is to develop criteria, based on an actuarial method as suggested by Shah (1978), to aid decision-making. Shah's observations on the matter are important for guiding clinicians who may be appointed to review boards for determining dangerousness:

> . . . there is no reason why information provided by actuarial tables and similar devices could not be combined with specifically identified and empirically tested clinical information and also with explicit considerations of particular setting and situational factors. Systematic followup and feedback regarding the decisional outcomes would allow periodic revisions designed to improve overall predictive accuracy. . . . The fundamental value of the actuarial approach is not in the insistence on quantification. Rather, it is in an insistence that decision rules can be made explicit and that it is most desirable to make them so. Not only would this approach facilitate the teaching of novice clinicians and evaluators, but it would greatly improve th ereliability of such judgments (p. 230).

METHODS

Design of Inquiry

Our study presented a comprehensive description of characteristics of a sample of mentally ill offenders admitted to a maximum security facility of Rusk State Hospital. As part of a pilot survey of 101 mentally ill offenders, the dependent variable of dangerousness was first assessed in several ways. Dangerousness was defined by arrests for violent or assaultive crimes of murder, manslaughter, rape, robbery, and aggravated assault. Nonassaultive arrests included all other offenses cited by the Uniform Crime Code Report. Differences were then determined between patients charged with assaultive crimes and patients charged with nonassaultive crimes. Multiple discriminate analyses of psychological tests and chi-square analyses of demographic and social variables could not identify significant differences between dangerous and nondangerous patient groups as defined by violent arrests. The use of data on patient arrests for violent and nonviolent crimes as a measure of dangerousness proved to be fruitless.

A second way of defining the dependent variable of dangerousness in the pilot survey was by the Texas Department of Mental Health and Mental Retardation review board's decisions of manifest dangerousness of mentally ill offenders. By vote of the board these patients were determined to be manifestly dangerous or not, according to the criteria of Texas statutes. Again, results of multiple discriminate analyses of psychological tests and chi-square analyses of demographic and social variables could not identify significant differences between patients determined to be manifestly dangerous or not manifestly dangerous by the review board.

A third way of defining the dependent variable of dangerousness was to rate dangerousness linearly on a three-point scale: potentially most dangerous, indeterminately dangerous, and potentially least dangerous. Criteria for identifying the most potentially dangerous group included the patient's present hospital admission for murder, manslaughter, rape, robbery, or aggravated assault; an arrest record including murder, manslaughter, rape, robbery, or aggravated assault; or a history of fighting behavior, including arrests for simple assaults. The potentially least dangerous group was identified as having no records of arrests for these violent crimes. The indeterminate group included borderline patients who could not be clearly classified in the two extreme groups. An 85-year-old man, for example, committed to the maximum-security hospital for murder, had no other record of violent behavior during his lifetime. Two clinicians classified the patients into the three groups. Once again, results of multiple discriminate analyses of psychological tests and chi-square analyses of demographic and social variables could not identify differences between the most potentially dangerous and least potentially dangerous groups of maximum-security patients.

The results of the pilot survey led us to consider another dependent measure of dangerousness, that of staff clinicians' judgments. This approach promised several advantages as, unlike the review board members, the psychologist, social caseworker, and psychiatric ward technician know each patient fairly well. They know the patients' psychological test reports, social history, criminal history from the courts, treatment plan, behavior on the ward; they observe and interact with the patients and have contacts with the patients' families. Such an approach provides review board members with relevant data on which to base legal determinations. In addition, using the clinicians' judgments as linear measures of dangerousness provided an opportunity for a thorough analysis of the data.

Definition of Dependent Variable

For the present study, therefore, the dependent variable of dangerousness was operationally defined by clinicians' judgments as follows: For each patient in the sample, a psychologist, social caseworker, and psychiatric ward technician who were on the patient's treatment team were asked independently to assess the patient's dangerousness by responding yes or no to a question about the patient's dangerousness. Identical legal criteria for determining manifest dangerousness, cited in Texas statutes as the guideline for review boards were read to them preceding the question. To exclude the possible effect of group influence, clinicians' votes were taken individually.

By this process, two groups were established according to staff judgments of dangerousness: A not-dangerous group of persons (N = 163) whom two or more of three staff members believed to be not manifestly dangerous, and a dangerous group (N = 106) whom two or more of three staff members believed to be manifestly dangerous.

Analyses of Data

Multiple discriminate analyses of the psychological tests and chi-square analyses of demographic and social variables identified differences between the dangerous and not-dangerous groups. In addition, a stepwise discriminate analysis (BMD 07M) provided the predictive model.

Data Collection

The data collected for the study came from hospital medical records that included computerized record system forms, a questionnaire concerning the patient's social history, including questions about alleged criminal offenses, and psychological tests administered to each patient during the patient's admission evaluation. The psychological tests included intelligence testing (Wechsler Adult Intelligence Scale, Beta IQ Test, Wide Range Achievement Test), and personality evaluation (Holtzman Inkblot Technique [Holtzman et al., 1961], Minnesota Multiphasic Personality Inventory, and Buss-Durkee Inventory). Individual rights to confidentiality were maintained in accordance with the ethical guidelines of The Institutional Guide to DHEW on Protection of Human Subjects (1971) and as prescribed by departmental research committee requirements.

RESULTS

Development of Criteria for Dangerousness

The not-dangerous patient group included each patient whom at least two of three clinicians judged to be nondangerous. The dangerous patient group included each patient whom at least two of three clinicians judged as dangerous. Multiple discriminate analysis determined differences between the dangerous and not-dangerous groups on the psychological tests administered. Demographic and social history differences between the dangerous and not-dangerous groups were determined by chi-square analyses. Statistically significant results are reported from the Buss-Durkee Inventory, the Holtzman Inkblot Technique, and several demographic variables.

Buss-Durkee Inventory

From the Buss-Durkee Inventory, significant differences were found ($F = 3.6$, $p = .01$) between the dangerous group (N = 106) and the not-dangerous group (N = 158) by a discriminate analysis (Table 1). Although no individual scale on the Buss-Durkee Inventory showed statistically significant differences between the dangerous and not-dangerous groups, the three scales showing the greatest differences were irritability ($F = 2.9$, $p = 0.08$), resentment ($F = 3.6$, $p = 0.05$), and guilt ($F = 3.35$, $p = 0.06$). The dangerous group had mean scores higher than the

Table 1

Discriminate-Function Analysis of Buss-Durkee Inventory (BDI) for Dangerous and Not-Dangerous Patient Groups

Variable	Mean Dangerous Group (N = 106)	Mean Not Dangerous Group (N = 158)	*F* Ratio	*p*
Verbal hostility	5.9	6.4	2.01	0.15
Indirect hostility	5.1	5.2	0.11	0.75
Irritability	5.4	4.8	2.98	0.08
Negativism	3.6	3.4	0.66	0.58
Resentment	4.2	4.8	3.63	0.05
Suspicion	3.4	3.6	0.36	0.56
Assault	4.7	4.7	0.00	0.96
Guilt	2.5	2.1	3.35	0.06
Total score	34.7	35.0		

not-dangerous group on the irritability, negativism, and guilt scales. On the five other scales the not-dangerous group had higher mean scores than the dangerous group. In fact, the total of mean scores for the not-dangerous group ($\bar{x} = 35.0$) was slightly higher than the total of mean scores for the dangerous group ($\bar{x} = 34.7$). Essentially, there were no interpretable mean differences between the two groups, although the multivariate analysis discriminated between them. This outcome is the result of the statistical combination of several variables, each of which failed to achieve the .05 level of significance in chi-square analysis.

Holtzman Inkblot Technique

The dangerous and not-dangerous groups differed significantly in mean scores on four of the 22 scales of the Holtzman Inkblot Technique: movement ($p = .03$), anxiety ($p = .01$), hostility ($p = .001$), and pathognomonic verbalization ($p = .05$). On each variable, the dangerous group achieved the higher mean score. These findings suggest that the dangerous and not-dangerous groups may be differentiated on bases other than pathology alone, although they do suggest the existence of more disturbance of affect and thought process in the dangerous group. Anxiety, hostility, and pathognomonic verbalization essentially defined Factor III in this study, as in the Holtzman group's (1961) study.

Separate factor analyses of the Holtzman Inkblot Technique were performed on the dangerous and not-dangerous groups, and they revealed a different factorial structure. In each group, seven factors were extracted. For both groups, Factor I was very similar to that reported by Holtzman et al., (1961), containing high loadings for form definiteness, movement, integration, human, barrier, and popular. The dangerous group also had a very high loading (.80) for animal on this factor.

Factor II was similar to Holtzman's, being defined primarily by color and shading. The dangerous group also showed the high negative loading (—.66) for form definiteness noted in the Holtzman samples, but the not-dangerous group showed a high positive (.52) loading for the same variable.

The most striking difference between the factorial structures of the two groups was an interchange of the variables loading on Factors III and VI. The not-dangerous group closely resembled the entire sample on these factors, Factor III being defined by pathognomonic verbalization, abstract, and to a lesser extent by anxiety and hostility. Factor VI was defined by anatomy, penetration, sex, anxiety, and hostility. In the dangerous group, on the other hand, Factor III was defined almost exclusively by anatomy

(−.82) and form appropriateness (.82). Pathognomonic verbalization and abstract appeared on Factor VI. The dangerous group differed in factorial structure primarily by the association of pathognomonic verbalization and abstract with the other usual Factor VI variables and by the existence of a factor (III) defined by anatomy and form appropriateness. The not-dangerous group more closely resembled the sample as a whole. Most of the explained variance was accounted for by four factors (I, II, III, VI). In the dangerous group, these four factors accounted for 78 percent of the explained variance, in the not-dangerous group for 74 percent. In both the dangerous and not-dangerous groups the other factors seemed to be primarily residual. Reaction time and balance each defined a factor in the dangerous group, the two variables combining to define a factor for the not dangerous. This finding is at variance with the Holtzman group's data, but should be viewed cautiously pending replication, in view of the low order of these factors.

Demographic Variables

Of the large amount of demographic information collected on each patient, only six variables showed significant differences between the dangerous and not-dangerous groups. These variables were age at admission, marital status, arrest record, fighting behavior, threat of suicide, desire to be in the institution. Sample sizes varied slightly because of varying numbers of invalid responses on each item.

Age at admission

Patients were divided into five age groups: 0 to 21, 22 to 25, 26 to 30, 31 to 40, 41, and older. In the dangerous group, 48 percent were 25 or younger at the time of admission, whereas only 31 percent of the not-dangerous group were in this age range. The highest percentage of the dangerous group were 22 to 25 years old (34 percent) and the lowest percentage of this group were over 41 (12 percent). On the other hand, the largest percentage of the not-dangerous group were 26 to 30 years old (28 percent) and the smallest percentage (13 percent) were in the 0 to 21 age group. These statistically significant results ($X_2 = 9.99$, $p < .05$) substantiate the work of other researchers (Cocozza and Steadman, 1977; Henn et al., 1977) by indicating the importance of age in commission of violent crimes. The dangerous patients were younger than the not-dangerous patients. For the mentally ill offenders in this study, the crucial age range for committing violent crimes was 20 to 24 years.

Marital status

The questions about marital status identified six different groups: those never married, married but separated, widowed, divorced, married (living together), and common-law. As there seemed to be no differences between some of these classifications, the six groups were collapsed into three: never married; married but separated, widowed, or divorced; married (living together), and common law. Of the entire sample, 57 percent had never married. This category included 53 percent of the not-dangerous group and 64 percent of the dangerous group. The remainder of the dangerous group was almost equally divided between the second and third categories, while in the not-dangerous group 31 percent were in the second category and 15 percent in the third category. These statistically significant results ($X_2 = 8.22$, $p < .05$) appear to be consistent with those of other studies (Cocozza and Steadman, 1977; Mullen and Rollins, 1977; Levinson and York, 1974; Bach-y-Rita et al., 1971), which reported the problems mentally ill offenders have in establishing and maintaining marriages.

Arrests for violent crime

This demographic variance was highly significant ($X^2 = 9.14$, $p < .001$). A majority of the not-dangerous group (63 percent) was arrested for nonviolent crimes, and a majority of the dangerous group (58 percent) was arrested for violent crimes. Another interesting finding was that, among the 130 persons committed to the maximum-security unit for nonviolent crimes, 72 percent had been correctly classified as not dangerous by staff judgment. This finding lends support to the use of staff judgment as a criterion for dangerousness: patients judged not dangerous tended to have committed nonviolent crimes, while patients judged dangerous tended to have committed violent offenses. This finding is congruent with finding of previous research (Mullen and Rollins, 1977; Bach-y-Rita, 1974; White et al., 1969). Our results point up the importance the variable of arrest for violent crime has on affecting the judgment of dangerous, and they also lend support to the dictum, "The best predictor of future behavior is past behavior."

Fighting behavior

The fourth significant demographic variable was patients' fighting behavior during the six months preceding their commitment to the maximum-security hospital. Responses were divided into three levels of fighting: never, rarely, and frequently. Frequency counts based on 240 valid responses

(147 not dangerous, 93 dangerous) were statistically significant ($X^2 = 11.57$, $p < .01$).

Sixty-one percent of the dangerous group and 74 percent of the not-dangerous group reported never fighting during the period in question. Only 7 percent of the dangerous and 12 percent of the not-dangerous patients reported frequent fighting. Twice as many of the dangerous group (32 percent) reported rare fighting encounters, compared to the not-dangerous group (14 percent). Thus 26 percent of the not-dangerous group engaged in some kind of fighting, whereas a total of 39 percent of the dangerous group fought occasionally. These findings suggest that the dangerous patient may be more volatile than the not-dangerous and subsequently more prone to overt aggression, although the differences are not dramatic. Fighting behavior also was shown to have predictive value in identifying prison parolees who would violate probation (Waller, 1974).

Suicide attempts

On the question of threatening to commit suicide during adolescence, 147 not-dangerous patients and 104 dangerous patients reported threats of suicide during their adolescence. The frequency count in a 242 contingency table reflecting a dichotomous yes/no response was statistically significant ($X^2 = 4.97$, $p < .05$). The dangerous group (12.5 percent) reported more frequent threats of suicide than the not-dangerous group (5 percent). These results seemed consistent with other research in which the relationship between violence and suicide was investigated (Bach-y-Rita et al., 1971). Thoughts of suicide by the dangerous patients may reflect their recognition of serious adjustment problems.

Patients' desire to be institutionalized

The last variable concerned the patient's desire to be in the maximum-security hospital. Responses from 151 patients, 96 from not-dangerous and 55 from dangerous persons, were dichotomized into two groups: patients stating a preference to being in an institution, either hospital or prison (29.5 percent), or at home (71.5 percent). Of the not-dangerous group 77 percent and of the dangerous group 62 percent preferred to be at home. These results were statistically significant ($X^2 = 4.00$, $p < .05$). This variable is of great interest in that the choice of institutionalization by so many patients in the dangerous group may reflect knowledge of their being dangerous enough to need the restraint of imprisonment or ill enough to need treatment. It is unfortunate that in the research protocol we did not directly ask each patient, Do you think you are dangerous?

In summary, the demographic variables reflected some significant differences between the dangerous and not-dangerous groups. The dangerous patient tends to be younger at time of admission, maintains bachelorhood more often but forms more stable unions if he does marry, commits the more violent crimes, fights rarely but more often than the not-dangerous patient, is more likely to threaten suicide during adolescence, and would more often choose institutionalization over being at home.

It is also interesting to note some social and demographic variables that did not affect staff judgments of dangerousness, as measured by chi-square analyses. There are no differences between the dangerous and not-dangerous groups as to race, psychiatric diagnosis, educational achievement, and employment. Regarding family-history characteristics, staff judgments of dangerousness were not affected by parental alcoholism, broken homes, or psychiatric illness in parents. No evidence was found that the triadic behaviors of enuresis, firesetting, and cruelty to animals differentiated dangerous from not-dangerous patients. Nor did the variables of referral for treatment of emotional disorders in childhood/adolescence or the amount of physical punishment in childhood/adolescence differentiate the dangerous from the not-dangerous patients.

Stepwise Discriminate Analysis

The multiple discriminate analyses determined significant differences between the dangerous and not-dangerous groups by the Buss-Durkee Inventory, the Holtzman Inkblot Technique, and demographic variables (age at admission, marital status, arrest for violent crime, fighting, suicidal behavior, and patient's desire to be in an institution). From these results, variables were selected for a stepwise multiple discriminate analysis. In addition to the significant variables determined by univariate F tests, other variables were included (e.g., the 22 Holtzman Inkblot Technique variables and all Buss-Durkee variables), since stepwise discriminate analysis selects its own variables in producing a regression equation.

In the stepwise discriminate analysis, nine variables provided the most efficient model for differentiating between the dangerous and not-dangerous groups. They were, in contributing order: Holtzman variables of hostility, penetration, popular; Buss-Durkee variables of verbal hostility, irritability, negativism; and the demographic variables of marital status, crime and fighting. Several variables, which did not show significant mean differences between the groups, contributed substantially to the stepwise discriminate function. Others, which did show significant mean differences between the groups, did not contribute heavily to the discriminate function because of their high intercorrelation with other variables loading on the function. For example, the Holtzman Inkblot Technique variables, anxiety and movement, correlated highly with hostility.

Demographic and social history variables that were significant in differentiating between the dangerous and not-dangerous groups by chi-square analyses included marital status, crime, and fighting. In the multiple discriminate analysis, these variables also contributed in the multiple regression equation in differentiating the dangerous and not-dangerous patients. They emerged in the following order: Marital status ($F = 11.82$, $p = .001$), crime ($F = 6.54$, $p = .01$), fighting ($F = 7.6$, $p = .01$). Differences in the means between dangerous and not-dangerous groups suggest that more dangerous patients were separated/divorced, that the dangerous group committed more violent crimes (murder, rape, robbery, aggravated assault), and that the dangerous group fought more often.

Buss-Durkee Inventory variables that emerged from the stepwise multiple discriminate analysis were verbal hostility, irritability, and negativism. The irritability scale contributed to differences between the dangerous and not-dangerous groups by a univariate F test. In the stepwise equation, then, the Buss-Durkee variables were able to discriminate the function in the following order: verbal hostility, negativism, and irritability. Although these variables distinguished between the dangerous and not-dangerous groups, there were no significant differences between the dangerous and not-dangerous group means. Slight differences found in means did not always occur in the expected direction.

Holtzman variables that emerged from the stepwise discriminate analysis differed from those in the first discriminate analysis. Factor III was less well defined here, partly because of the exclusion of variables that correlated highly with some other variable and partly because of the inclusion of some variables, notably penetration and popular, that are of some value in refining the discrimination after the initial function has been developed. Interpretation of the Holtzman Inkblot Technique variables is pending, while we await analyses of replication samples.

In applying the stepwise discriminate analysis model to patients in the sample, 21 percent of the dangerous patient group were misclassified and 23 percent of the not-dangerous patient group were misclassified. Using the cutting point of .50 probability of classifying a patient correctly as dangerous or not dangerous, 22 percent of the patients were misclassified. (Other cutting points, of course, may be chosen. The actual choice of a best cutting point should be based on pragmatic rather than statistical considerations. An unwillingness to misclassify dangerous patients, for example, might dictate the choice of a cutting point that minimizes this sort of error, even at the cost of considerable misclassification of not-dangerous patients.)

Coefficient values for the nine variables which form the stepwise discriminate function model are presented in Table 2. An application of the

Table 2

Stepwise Discriminate-Function Model

Variable	Not-Dangerous Group	Dangerous Group
HIT hostility	−0.07997	−0.09648
HIT penetration	0.39495	0.25548
HIT popular	0.69031	0.51802
BDI verbal hostility	0.99855	0.83959
BDI irritability	0.14861	−0.06912
BDI negativism	−0.42750	0.00492
Marital status	8.56304	9.50760
Crime	7.32188	6.39320
Fighting	4.04673	5.02461
	Sum = −21.85623	Sum = −22.11171

HIT, Holtzman Inkblot Technique; BDI, Buss-Durkee Inventory.

prediction model is as follows: Step 1, multiply raw score values of each of the nine variables by their coefficients, and sum together with the constant term to create two numbers. Step 2, raise the base of the natural log system for both numbers (e^x or 2.71828^x). Step 3, add these numbers and determine what percentage each of the two numbers is of their sum. The percentage states the probability of group membership as dangerous and not dangerous.

DISCUSSION

An exploratory study of this nature has importance primarily in its implications for future research. The paucity of information in the literature necessitated the inclusion of many instruments in this initial study; future research may enable us to concentrate on instruments that have proved to be most valuable in differentiating between patients judged to be dangerous and those judged to be not dangerous.

Much of the confusion on this topic is, of course, related to the lack of agreement regarding a criterion of validity for predictive instruments. Our study used an operational definition of dangerousness, the judgments of members of a treatment team. These judgments do not show much agreement with those of the legally constituted review board, which comes as no great surprise. The clinical judgments used in this study were based on many days of observation, while judgments made by the board are based on an interview lasting a few minutes. Perhaps equally important, the judges in this study ran no risk that a "wrong" decision might cause problems for them or others. The members of a review board are concerned with protecting the community from potentially dangerous individuals as well as with their own responsibility of not becoming psychiatric jailers.

Nothing is known about the validity of either set of judgments; that investigation must be undertaken before one may have any great confidence in the practical value of our findings. Our study strongly suggests, however, that it may well be possible to develop a model to predict with considerable accuracy judgments that *would* be made if an individual were observed for long periods of time by experienced treatment team members. This prospect makes investigation of the validity of judgmental criteria worthwhile. The next step is, of course, the refinement of the predictive technique by behavioral measures rather than by judgments. Our findings furnish, primarily, information concerning measures that show the most promise of contributing substantially to a model that predicts the judgments of clinicians.

Of the many psychological tests administered, several proved to be of no value in this regard. The Wechsler Adult Intelligence Scale, for example, did not differentiate between criterion groups, either in chi-square analyses or as a contribution to a discriminate function. The Beta, similarly, showed no significant differences between the two groups. It seems that judgments relating to dangerousness are not related in any significant way to intellectual factors. This finding, while negative, suggests some construct validity for the dimension of dangerousness.

The two personality inventories administered also failed to differentiate between the dangerous and nondangerous groups. The Buss-Durkee Inventory did discriminate when used in a multivariate analysis, but mean differences between the groups were small. Only one scale on the Minnesota Multiphasic Personality Inventory (MMPI) showed a significant difference between the two groups in a chi-square analysis, and even this difference was found not to contribute substantially to the discriminate function in a multivariate analysis. Again, it seems that judgments of dangerousness are being made on some basis other than expressed or latent hostility (as assessed by the Buss-Durkee Inventory) and traditional psychiatric diagnostic categories (as assessed by the MMPI).

The findings that dangerousness as defined in this study seems independent of traditional intellectual or psychiatric dimensions are borne out by investigation of demographic information. No differences between groups can be attributed to race, educational level, or psychiatric diagnosis. Because much of the literature pertains to demographic variables, a great deal of this information was collected, but only a few items showed differences between criterion groups. Of these, some surely seem suspect and must await replication before being given credence. Others seem intuitively to be correct and are likely to form part of the final prediction equation.

By far the most powerful instrument was the Holtzman Inkblot Technique. Four variables, movement, anxiety, hostility, and pathognomonic verbalization, showed significant differences in means for the two criterion groups. These variables formed the basis of the discriminate function in the initial discriminate analysis. In the stepwise analysis, there was a slight change in the variables selected because of the computational characteristics of the model, but the same constellation of variables was evident. Factor analyses revealed different factorial structures for the dangerous and not-dangerous groups. Although preliminary, these results are encouraging. Whatever the statistical technique, it seems clear that the Holtzman Inkblot Technique provides a basis for differentiating the two groups.

Many other statistical manipulations of the data are possible. Our study concentrated on relatively straightforward techniques. Any effect so slight as to require an extremely powerful statistical technique to demonstrate its existence is probably of little substantial value in a prediction equation. Use of the stepwise discriminate analysis to enhance the predictive ability of the model resulted in only modest improvement.

The implications of the present study are clear. First, there is little reason to collect extensive demographic information for purposes of clarifying a predictive model. Second, neither tests of intellectual ability nor personality inventories seem to provide enough information to justify the effort and expense involved in their collection. Third, the Holtzman Inkblot Technique is a promising instrument, and replication and standardization on other groups should occur. Fourth, the study needs criterion validation.

Reliability and validity of the prediction model are now our principal concern. Replication studies are being conducted with new samples of maximum-security patients in Texas and other states. Additional data analyses are in process, including a study comparing dangerousness of Texas maximum-security mental patients with a sample of Texas prison inmates. To test the validity of results, a study is planned to follow up discharged maximum-security patients.

Finally, future research on dangerousness should concentrate on identifying situational variables that contribute to dangerous behavior and address issues of dangerousness in various populations: prison populations, the general public, as well as mental patients.

ACKNOWLEDGMENTS

This project was sponsored by the Texas Department of Mental Health and Mental Retardation and the Hogg Foundation for Mental Health.

REFERENCES

American Psychiatric Association Task Force. *Clinical Aspects of the Violent Individual,* Report 8, July 1974.

BACH-Y-RITA, G. Habitual violence and self mutilation. *Am. J. Psychiatry* 131:1018-1021, 1971.

BACH-Y-RITA, G., LION, J. R., CLIMENT, C. E., and ERWIN, F. R. Episode dyscontrol: a study of 130 violent patients. *Am. J. Psychiatry* 127:49-54, 1971.

COCOZZA, J. J., and STEADMAN, H. J. Prediction in psychiatry: an example of misplaced confidence in experts. Paper presented to American Sociological Association, Chicago, Illinois, 1977.

HENN, F. A., HERJANIC, M., and VANDERPEARL, R. H. Forensic psychiatry: anatomy of a service. *Compr. Psychiatry* 18(4):337-345, 1977.

HOLTZMAN, W., THORPE, J. SWARTZ, J., and HERRON, *E. Inkblot Perception and Personality*. University of Texas Press, Austin, 1961.

The Institutional Guide to DHEW on Protection of Human Subjects. U. S. Department of Health, Education and Welfare, National Institutes of Health, Washington, D.C. DHEW Publication No. (NIH) 72-102, 1971.

LEVINSON, R., and YORK, Z. The attribution of dangerousness in mental health evaluations. *J. Health Soc. Behav.* 15(4):328-335, 1974.

MEGARGEE, E. The prediction of dangerous behavior. *Criminal Justice and Behavior* 13:3-22, 1976.

MULLEN, J., and ROLLINS, R. Factors of deviant behavior in mental patients. *N. C. J. Mental Health* 8(6):14-21, 1977.

SHAH, S. Dangerousness: a paradigm for exploring some issues of law and psychology. *Am. Psychol.* 3:224-238, 1978.

WALLER, I. *Men Released from Prison*. University of Toronto Press, Toronto, 1974.

WHITE, L., KRUMHOLZ, W. V., and FINK, L. The adjustment of criminally insane patients to a civil mental hospital. *Mental Hygiene* 53(1):34-40, 1969.

CHAPTER 17

Violence — An Ultimate Noncoping Behavior

ROY B. MEFFERD, JR.
JOHNE M. LENNON
NANCY E. DAWSON

The word violence elicits thoughts of intense emotion, stormy infringement, forceful violation, impetuous assault, unreasoning fervor, degrading insult, brutal enforcement. We often link violence with crime-punishment, injury-vandalism, strength-weakness, poverty-wealth, psychopathy-psychoticism, drunkenness-drug addiction, fury-terror, aggression-hostility, irresponsibility-poor self-control. Our personalized constructs of violence confound the effects of the violent act; the physical, mental, and socioeconomic characteristics of both the perpetrator and victim; and finally, the value systems and personality traits of the perpetrator. We tend to reify a violent act as violence, as if the act reflects some deep underlying trait of the human condition—something inherent in human nature. Actually, we know virtually nothing about violence as a trait.

To date much of the research on violence has been directed toward the obviously undesirable criminal and psychotic violent act. Accordingly, the developing violence construct is influenced, on the one hand, by legal definitions oriented to the effects of the violent act on the victim and on the risk to society if the offender repeats such acts in the future. On the other hand, the construct is influenced by nebulous medical concepts that permit excuse from accountability because of ill-defined and indeterminate mental illness (Gardner, 1976; Guze, 1976).

The question is a matter of the definition of violence and of how to sample for its measurement. Behaviorally, the relevant issue is not the act, the situation, the legality, the victim, the society—it is solely the *person* who committed the violent act. What were his or her perceptions, feelings, expectations, intentions, justifications immediately before, during, and after committing the act of violence? Could the situation have been coped with without resorting to force? Are there habitual patterns that make him or her a high or a low risk for future violence. For example, avoiding or seeking-out situations, environments, and occupations in which the risk of violence is high? Does he or she associate with other historically violent people?

We are conditioned to accept certain escapist behaviors as expressions of noncoping behaviors—alcoholism, drug abuse, hoboism. We accept suicide as perhaps *the* ultimate active expression of a noncoping behavior. Willful destruction of property is often viewed by society as more an expression of hostility than of violence, even when the act is specifically targeted.

Perhaps because of the revulsion that violence generates, we seldom think of it as an expression of inactive, maladaptive, noncoping behavior. We fail to recognize violence as that point at which the person or group rejects all efforts to achieve his or its goals, except by force applied to others. If there is a trait of violence, the social desirability of the act is irrelevant—society may view the act in appropriate contexts as highly courageous. The *intention* of the perpetrator is the relevant issue. The question remains, was the act necessary? Was it necessary to harm another by use of force? Was there no other way to cope with the situation?

Some people obviously are violent, abusive, cruel to others including their families and animals. Wars, the use of force in exercising power, and even the frequent urging of sports fans for unnecessarily rough body contact continue to show us how little "civilized man" has accomplished in his efforts to control his urge to resort to physical force. Given the appropriate situation and opportunity, no one is immune to the development of a mental-physiological state in which he or she may become violent, at least momentarily. This is analogous to the construct of anxiety in which even the most emotionally stable people experience severe states of anxiety on occasion (Mefferd, 1980a, b).

Violence has yet to be defined in terms of a dimension of individual differences on which people who frequently commit violent acts are at one extreme and people who never entertain thoughts of a violent act are at the other. Rather, the only way we can define violence at present is in statistical after-the-fact terms of individual acts or threats. This is not a satisfactory way to describe any behavioral trait, since it is completely indeterminate. With such a definition there are only two classes of people: those who have already committed a violent act, and those who have not yet done so. Such an indeterminate classification also poses problems of validity, since a violent act may have been committed accidentally, unintentionally, and even to the extreme despair of a fundamentally nonviolent perpetrator.

It is difficult to see how we can ever expect to predict any single individual act, especially if it occurs infrequently (Megargee, 1976). An interaction between a person and a situation always accompanies an act (Petersen, 1977), and the interaction is difficult to predict. A given violent act is the result of dozens of possible starting points, for example, the decision to carry a weapon, legally or not. Once started, an almost infinite number of pathways lead to the final violent act. A tendency to associate with a group of irresponsible, hostile people may be a contributing factor, but loners also commit violent acts. No specific common antecedent of violent acts has been found.

Several factors appear generally to be related to the commission of violent acts, however. Age is the most frequently noted correlate—the older the offender, the less is the risk that he or she will commit a violent act (Rowe and Tittle, 1977; McCreary and Mensh, 1977). Different ethnic groups have different patterns of violence (McCreary and Padilla, 1977; Silberman, 1978), and violence of group against group is increasing (Silberman, 1978). Intelligence has been implicated repeatedly in criminality (Witkin et al., 1976; Kunce et al., 1976) and just as often refuted (Shawver and Jew, 1978). Psychiatric disorders are blamed for much crime, but in one particular county-jail setting fewer than 3 percent of the individuals booked were even referred for psychiatric examination (Petrick, 1976, 1978). However, other reports very widely in the incidence of psychiatric problems, which is as high as 23 percent (Swank and Winer, 1976). According to one study, no schizophrenic persons were arrested for crimes against people, while a fourth of the arrests of alcoholics were for such crimes (Durbin et al., 1977). Drug abuse and violent death are reported to be profoundly related to violence (Zahn, 1974). Several life styles seem to entail high risks for eventual violent acts, especially when other factors are involved—youth, poor emotional control, low ego-strength, hostile attitudes, need for instant gratification. Such combinations can hardly be expected to lead to anything but maladaptive behavioral patterns (Smith and Pollack, 1976).

When these behaviors are placed in the context of relative adaptability —relative ability (or willingness) to find the means to cope with life's situations and circumstances according to society's mores—it becomes feasible to identify characteristics of this hypothesized dimension of individual differences (Adams, 1977; Masuda et al., 1978). If such a dimension of coping capacity is identifiable, then it becomes feasible to predict behaviors on the basis of a person's relative position on the dimension. People who commit unnecessary but intentional violent acts upon others should be at the active noncoping extreme.

The prediction problems relative to violence hinge on the sampling procedures. Regardless of how they are defined, violent acts are rare events. What variables are used is immaterial—the most accurate prediction we can make about any particular person in a truly representative sample is *nonviolent.* This follows from the fact that in normal times most people seldom intentionally commit a violent act.

The magnitude of this sampling factor needs amplification before any of us start predicting violence. In 1978, Texas had about 12.5 million people, and about 25,000 were inmates in Texas Department of Corrections (TDC) prisons. Of these 25,000, nearly half were recidivists—35 percent from Texas and 12 percent from other state prisons (Texas Board of Pardons and Paroles, 1978). If we triple this number of career criminals in the TDC system to include people in city and county jails, then quadruple it to estimate the total number of people living in Texas who at some time were incarcerated, we have about 200,000 people. Now, if we jump this to 500,000 to include people who received probated sentences, or escaped detection (note: there are as many homicides annually in Houston alone as there are murderers in TDC), we have only about 4 percent of the total population. You may quadruple this, or halve it as you wish—the relative population of criminals is small.

When we consider how many of these offenders committed violent acts, the numbers plummet. A larger proportion of violent offenders are apprehended, convicted, and sent to prison than are offenders who commit nonviolent crimes, and the violent offenders tend to be long-term prison inmates. At any given time only 300 to 400 convicted murderers are in the TDC prisons. Even so, *all* acts of violence or threatened violence together account for no more than 10 to 15 percent of the annual prison population. When we consider a possible dimension of individual differences that relates to relative tendencies to commit violent acts as a part of the human condition, we must consider *all* violent acts, legal and criminal. However, even if we increase tenfold the number of people who commit criminally violent acts as an estimate of the total of violent acts, the numbers still remain relatively small. Now when we consider that much of the total crime is actually committed by a small percentage of all criminals, it becomes readily apparent that some people commit more than one act, and so on (Mednick and Christiansen, 1977).

A direct consequence of these statistics is that it is virtually impossible to obtain a representative sample in which degrees of violence vary. Since the only valid estimate of violence presently available is the history of actual acts, a common research practice is to build a sample by using as many violent offenders as possible, and to compare these with selected nonviolent offenders. Inevitably, this has lead to severe classification problems—to overinclusion, that is, overprediction, of nonviolent people in the violent class (Megargee, 1976; Scott, 1977).

VIOLENCE AS ONE EXTREME ON A SCALE OF COPING CAPACITY

In our early work we attempted to predict *violence* as if it were already a validated construct. Recently, we departed from this position and moved toward the concept of violence as an extreme, active form of a noncoping life style. With this viewpoint, the obvious approach became one of broadening the base of the sample to include noncriminal people who were and were not coping with some important aspect of life. We used for this purpose the job performance of industrial and business employees in the same positions that parolees and ex-offenders seek and obtain.

We reasoned that habitual "last-resort" behavior in a noncoping life would be the use of active force to achieve one's otherwise unattainable goals. When this life style is combined with hostility and/or psychopathy, extreme explosive noncoping behavior is apt to occur.

Personality traits certainly should play an important role in whether or not a crime includes violent acts. The commission of crime itself is dangerous. At all stages of crime—planning, perpetrating, escaping, hiding—a high state of excitement, anxiety, and fear may intensify the effects of personality traits that otherwise might be controlled. A highly neurotic, low ego-strength person, that is, a person with a high trait level of neuroticism or anxiety (Mefferd, 1980a), may develop such high states of anxiety that the risks of his resorting to violence increase to very high levels. A restless, easily bored, ambivalent person who is quick to anger, easy to startle, or quick to frighten can be very dangerous indeed, especially when he is armed and in a tight, potentially dangerous situation. His fists may become even more dangerous. Just as risky are people who have developed negative attitudes toward others, who have strong emotional feelings of hostility, jealousy, or hatred. Both of these cases involve measurable traits, states, and attitudes.

Personality traits other than those possibly relating directly to violence may indirectly influence the commission of violent acts. The need for excitement in restless extraverts may draw them continually into situations in which the risks for violent acts are high. On the other hand, a person may neither have the drive nor the desire to achieve, or even to cope with steady work, with steady family pressures, or with life itself. This person is passively noncoping. Some people may resort to crime in efforts to short-cut the daily requirements for stability and responsibility. The continual resort to crime undoubtedly increases the opportunity for committing a violent act. The same considerations apply to long exposure of law enforcement officers to assignments involving frequent violence.

Some people never drift into crime, even when they have difficulty in coping with life. The industrial workers who were performing inadequately are such an example. The fact that some workers do and some do not resort to crime suggests that there are patterns of personality and attitude variables that distinguish these two kinds of noncoping people. It also seems reasonable that some patterns among such behavioral variables might be correlated with tendencies for some people to resort habitually to force to meet their needs or wants.

CAN VIOLENCE BE RELATED TO COPING CAPACITY?

In view of the apparent impossibility of predicting any isolated act, and with the present limitation of defining violence in other than historical terms, we suggest an alternative strategy. Our study was heuristic: a search for some dimension on which people may be ranked so that those who have committed criminal violence are thereby identified. The hypothesized dimension is coping capacity, and the variables for determining individual probabilities were personality traits, attitudes, and social perceptions. Age, intelligence, sex, ethnic group (Oldroyd and Howell, 1977), and socioeconomic background were controlled insofar as possible, by appropriate matching of subjects.

Inmate sample. Midsentence inmate volunteers from all TDC units were paid to complete the Birkman Method (described below). About 2300 inmates responded. The procedure eliminated the illiterate, those with little English, the most obdurate, and the least motivated. Later, 1727 of these volunteers were found to have available thorough records, including arrest(s), previous juvenile and/or adult crimes in and out of Texas, education or its equivalent, and reliable results from several batteries of psychological tests. From this pool all of the following categories were retained: 92 women, 142 Hispanics, and 270 inmates who had records of having threatened (but not committed) a violent act, and 461 inmates who had been convicted of committing one or more volitionally violent acts. The 461 violent inmates were subdivided into three groups: those who had committed only one violent offense (N = 183); those who had committed an extremely brutal, heinous crime (N = 64); and those who had been convicted of more than one independent violent act (N = 214). From the remaining inmates, 270 were identified who had no record of violence except that they had threatened specific people.

The nonviolent inmate control group was developed from the remaining pool after inmates with short sentences and young offenders with no evidence of juvenile crime were removed. Since the number of violent acts depends on the relative opportunity for having committed a violent act, the violent and nonviolent inmates were matched for number of previous offenses, total time in prison, and age.

The two categories of offenders were stratified within each ethnic and gender group for number of incarcerations, age, education, and intelligence. A close match on these variables was located for all multiple violent offenders (N = 214) and for 117 of the singly violent offenders. This resulted in a nonviolent sample of 331 inmates. The proportions of gender and ethnic grouping in each of the five categories were near those of the total TDC population; women, whites, blacks, and Hispanics were around 9, 44, 40, and 16 percent, respectively.

Working people sample. A sample of working people holding jobs of the type and at the level that parolees and ex-offenders seek and obtain —unskilled and semiskilled laborers, tradespeople, drivers, salespersons, clerks, and the like—was taken from a large, privately owned data base.[1] Workers whose performance had been assessed after at least six months'

---

[1] This study was made possible by permission to use data from two sources: a private data base owned by Birkman and Associates, Inc., Houston, Texas, and from two projects of the not-for-profit Birkman-Mefferd Research Foundation, Houston, Texas: (1) UPLIFT (supported by the Texas Criminal Justice Division, LEAA grant AC-77-EO4-4207 and EA-77-EO4-4915), and (2) COPE-AIDD (Aids in Determining Disposition) (supported by the Texas Board of Pardons and Paroles, LEAA grant DS-76-EO4-0011). Grateful acknowledgment is also made to W. J. Estelle, Jr., director, Texas Department of Corrections (TDC), and to Joe E. Reed while he was the chief of research and development at TDC, and to his staff; to Nelson Fayette, director, Institutional Services Texas Board of Pardons and Paroles, to his staff, and to the board members. Although this study was not a direct part of the two projects noted, appreciation is due the staff of the Birkman-Meffered Research Foundation who were involved in conducting the projects: Joe E. Reed, program manager, and Drs. T. G. Sadler, D. E. Kirkpatrick, V. C. Eissler, and J. Bethscheider.

work for the same employer were identified. Workers from more than 50 firms were selected, and the final sample was balanced approximately across both employers and job types. An additional 90 women and minority workers were added to increase their representation in some job categories.

Inmates were matched with people from this sample of the same sex and ethic group and closely matched for age and education. This yielded 601 workers whose performance was judged to be adequate (good or average) and 550 workers judged to be inadequate (weak or poor). No information about criminal histories was available.

Behavioral measures. Prison behavior or on-the-job performance, as well as assorted aptitude and intelligence test scores were available. A nonclinical system of inventories of personality, attitudes, values, social perceptions, and interests (all making up the Birkman Method used in an earlier report on violence [Justice and Birkman, 1972]) was available for all subjects.[2] The same 125 questions are answered first for perceptions, attitudes, and belief about *most people;* then again as applied to themselves. The communication test of the Birkman Method was used, but the interest survey was not used in this study because of the homogeneity of all categories in this respect. The communication scores correlated $r = 0.92$ with the verbal IQ scores in the inmates' prison folders.

The Birkman Method develops the same ten primary constructs for both *self* and *most people* .All constructs except one, individuality, are derived from independent questions. Such higher-order constructs as neuroticism and extraversion (Eysenck and Eysenck, 1968) are also developed.[3] Four of the Birkman constructs correlate with neuroticism: self-consciousness, feelings (i.e., depression, moodiness), indecisiveness (ambivalence), and restlessness (nervousness, impatience). Three constructs correlate with extraversion: sociability, energy, and insistence (i.e., meticulous attention to details). Three constructs involve attitudes, values, and motives: materialism (grasping, greedy, or ruthless drive to get ahead), dominance (domineering, pushing, or bullying behavior), and individuality (rebelliousness, giving unpopular answers, etc.). The variables to be discussed

---

[2] The Birkman Method is a proprietary system of questionnaires and reports owned by Birkman and Associates, Inc., Houston, Texas.

[3] The Birkman secondary factors, neuroticism and extraversion, correlated $r = 0.84$ and 0.81, respectively, with the Eysenck scores (Eysenck and Eysenck, 1968) in 641 college students. Formal psychometric and validation studies of the Birkman constructs and systems have been made by the Birkman-Mefferd Research Foundation: a three-year National Science Foundation grant at Austin College, Sherman, Texas; a three-year National Institutes of Health grant at Baylor College of Medicine, Houston; a Texas Education Agency study at Sheldon Independent School District, Houston; and a series of studies (footnote 1) funded by the LEAA.

here are the ten *self* constructs and the same constructs derived indirectly from the *most people* answers. The latter are summed item-level difference scores between the *self* and *most people* answers.

RESULTS

A multiple regression predictive equation for violence developed solely from two-thirds of the inmate sample cross-validated significantly with the randomly withheld remaining third of each category. However, it grossly overpredicted violence among about 8000 semiskilled laborers of a large factory—by 78 percent. This suggested that the base of the sample should be broadened to include noncriminals so as to capitalize on both criminality and violence.

As the first step in developing such a broadened sample, the five inmate categories and the four worker performance categories were contrasted by multiple discriminant function analyses (Tatsuoka, 1970) using the 20 variables of the Birkman Method. All categories cross-discriminated from the others at $p < .01$ levels. However, the classification was weak for threatened violent × nonviolent inmates and weak × poor workers. The hits from the "dual" classification—the people in each category being contrasted who were classified correctly by both the recorded evidence and the statistical procedure—were lowest between the three violent categories, and they were highest between inmates and workers regardless of the subcategories in either group. As a result, these nine categories were reduced to four by combining the following: good and average workers—adequate; weak and poor workers—inadequate; nonviolent and threatened violent—nonviolent; and all three violent categories—violent. This reduction in categories increased the subject/variable ratio to 23/1 for the smallest group. The high ratio was desirable for the next step to be described. The final sample was developed according to the following rationale.

The criteria of different levels on the hypothesized dimension of coping capacity were job performance and criminal history. The original, *apparent* class membership was determined in one part of the sample by a court and in the other by the immediate supervisors. This apparent class membership is ambiguous in each case, as will be noted. Besides this, the assumption that membership in either of the two samples results from different levels of the same basic behavioral style—coping—seems to involve a considerable logical jump.

The apparent class membership is ambiguous in that it is strongly influenced by situational and temporal factors. Among the workers, surely some basically good workers were rated down because of a recent personality clash with the supervisor, or of temporary distracting personal problems, or of being a square peg in a round hole, misclassified and in the wrong kind of job. Surely, some basically poor workers were rated up because of their brother-in-law or because the boss liked the way they organized the Christmas party.

Within the inmate subsample surely some truly nonviolent inmates had graduated into the violent category purely by accident. Even more certainly, some of the nonviolent inmates will graduate into the violent category as they pursue their criminal careers.

Across the two subsamples, we may assume without question that some of the workers were experienced with our criminal justice system. Given different circumstances and opportunities, some of the inmates would have been in the worker sample (and will be in it in the future), and some of them almost certainly will be rated as good.

The objective of this study was to define and describe important personality and attitude characteristics of people who habitually cope with life at different levels and with different strategies. As noted above, there is a great deal of statistical "noise" involved within the samples. The procedure we used for noise reduction was conservative. We simply imposed an additional constraint for determining class membership—in addition to the *apparent* classification that resulted from fundamentally subjective judgment processes, a person must *also* be correctly classified by statistical procedures. Each person in each criterion category must be there for two reasons—judgmental and statistical. In essence, rank-order positions of these "double hits" were maintained, and some of the randomly distributed "misses" who appeared to be badly misclassified were removed. The procedure thus assured retention of the original, *apparent* classification. No subject was transferred between original categories. Statistical class membership was determined by means of stepwise multiple discriminant function analyses. When a person of one *apparent* category invaded the statistical domain of another, these statistical misses were either removed from the sample or were used to develop new intermediate categories. This procedure was expected to render the original categories more homogeneous without destroyng the hypothesized coping classification scale.

The precise "refinement" procedures for *apparent* categories 1, 3, 4, and 6 of Table 1, Part A, were as follows:

1. Any worker who entered the statistical domain of the violent category, 6, or any inmate who entered the domain of the adequate worker, 1, was removed.

Table 1

Composition and Refinement of Sample

PART A

Subjects (N = 2213)

	Workers				Inmates	
	1 good and average N = 601	2 —	3 weak and poor N = 550	4 nonviolent N = 331 threatened N = 270	5 —	6 one time N = 183 heinous N = 64 multiple N = 214
Combined Categories N = 2213						
	1 601	2 0	3 550	4 601	5 0	6 461
Contrasts	Removals and Transfers (misses)					
1 × 3,4,6[a], 6 × 3,4,6[a]	–124(out)	—	—	—	—	–178(out)
4 × 1[b], 6 × 3[b]	—	—	–49(out)	–88(out)	—	—
3 × 1[c], 4 × 6[c]	—	—	–59(out)	–106(out)	—	—
3 × 4[d]	—	—	–25(out)	–23(out)	—	—
3 × 1[e], 4 × 6[e]	—	—	214(to 2)	172(to 5)	—	—

Table 1 (continued)

PART B
Refined Sample (N = 1561)

	1	2	3	4	5	6
N	477	214	203	212	172	283
Mean Age (yrs.)	25.4	25.3	22.6	25.4	25.1	26.1
Mean IQ (verbal)	94.8	95.9	94.8	94.8	93.7	93.7

Refined Sample, Matched Ages
18-26 Yrs. (N = 797)

	1	2	3	4	5	6
N	231	105	144	105	86	126
Mean Age (yrs.)	21.5	21.8	21.2	21.9	22.0	22.5
Mean IQ (verbal)	94.1	94.1	94.1	94.1	92.6	92.6

[a] Adequate workers (1) or violent inmates (6) who were outside their respective domain when compared with any other category were removed.
[b] All inmates who entered the domain of adequate worker (1) and vice versa for workers were removed.
[c] Members of the two mid-noncoping categories (3 and 4) who entered the domain of the extreme category of their respective group by one standard deviation or more were removed.
[d] Members of the two mid-noncoping categories (3 and 4) who entered each others' domain by 0.5 s.d. or more were removed.
[e] Members of the two mid-noncoping categories (3 and 4) who "looked like" their respective extreme—adequate worker (1) or violent inmate (6)—($0.22 \leq$ s.d. ≤ 0.99) were transferred to a new statistical "potentially" adequate or violent category, 2 and 5, respectively.

2. Any violent inmate who entered the domain of any other category was removed, likewise for any such adequate worker.
3. Members of the nonviolent inmate category, 4, and inadequate worker category, 3, who entered each others' domain by half a standard deviation were removed.
4. Within each subsample, any nonviolent inmate, 4, or inadequate worker, 3, who entered either of their respective extreme categories, 6 or 1, by one or more standard deviations was removed.
5. Two new statistical categories were established from the remainder of the two nonextreme categories: nonviolent inmates and inadequate workers, who "looked" more like the extreme group, 6 or 1, than they did the nonextreme group by from 0.22 to 0.99 standard deviation. These two intermediate groups may be classified as candidates with high future potentials for either violence, 5, or adequate job performance, 2.

This procedure left people in both extreme groups who were double hits *apparent* and *statistical*. The two central noncoping categories, 3 and 4, were double hits except for some statistical overlap between themselves. The new intermediate categories were single hits apparently misclassified by the subjective criteria or because of a lack of opportunity or exposure. Finally, a special subsample was developed that included only people between 18 and 25 years of age (Table 1B). This was done to eliminate long-term prison inmates, older revolving-door multiple offenders, and older experienced workers.

The coping scale so constructed hypothesizes that coping individuals migrate to jobs they can and do perform adequately. As coping capacity —ability plus willingness and perseverance—decreases, these people will more often be in jobs for which they are not suited, and more often will lack the ability or the will to report for work on time, to perform steadily at the expected level, to stay on the same job. As this inability or unwillingness to cope becomes severe, some will resort to illegal activities to achieve their goals and desires. Extreme or persistent inability or unwillingness to cope will separate a class of people who resort frequently to force to achieve their goals. This hypothesized scale is not intended to represent a trait of personality; rather, it represents a habituational behavior pattern involved in meeting life's situations.

A significant observation was that the inmates who threatened violent acts looked no more like violent inmates than nonviolent inmates. In the combined category 4, only 42 percent of the threatened violent, as compared to 48 percent of the nonviolent, looked like the violent category. Apparently, threats of violence are as unreliable as threats of suicide.

Even so, these 42 percent could wreak considerable havoc on society if they eventually followed through on their threats.

Correlates of the coping capacity distribution. A new predictive equation was developed (stepwise multiple regression analysis) with the criterion as a six-point scale for the six categories described above. This concurrent sample was two-thirds of the total sample. The cross-validating "withheld" sample of one-third (520) of the subjects was selected at random independently from age and verbal intelligence strata within each category of the total sample. The results are shown in Table 2. The correlations between the established and predicted class memberships were $r = 0.76$ and 0.74, for the concurrent and cross-validation samples respectively. With the smaller age-matched subsample of 17 to 26-year-old subjects, the correlation was 0.69, and it was 0.55 with the original 2213 pre-refinement sample which had only categories 1, 3, 4, and 6. Thus, the refinement procedures did not destroy the rank-order positions of subjects.

The procedure by definition selected subjects from category 3 who looked more like those in category 1, and similarly for categories 4 and 6; this effect was apparent in the predicted category means of categories 2 and 5 (Table 2). These mean predicted category memberships were extremely stable in all four samples. While the means increased monotonically, the equation resulted in under prediction of the expected mean—3.5 on the criterion scale. Actually, the predicted mean was only 3.15, but by using this mean, more of the inmates in category 4 (no present evidence of violence) were classified as violent (Table 2). Manipulation of the cutting point across the entire sample will do little to clasify these people who psychologically look like those already in either extreme category. Even this procedure of using a single overall cutting point was conservative in that the category means of all three inmate categories were considerably below the expected levels. Very few people of categories 4 and below were classified as violent. At the "proven" violent end in one small validation study, the equation correctly classified 57 of 63 parole violators at readmission to TDC who had broken parole with *another* violent act.

A potentially useful development is suggested by this underprediction of violence with an equation that still predicts proven violent people. It permits adjustment of the cutting points for each category on a rational basis, for example, by adjusting individually each category mean based on its standard deviation. This procedure adjusts for differences in the true distances between scale units. For example, were the cutting point for the most violent class, 6, adjusted with its standard deviation of 1.35, 84 percent of category 6 would be correctly classified as violent on the basis of a score of 2.89 or above. Now, 57 percent of class 4 would be correctly

Table 2

Mean Regression Scores[a] of a Six-Point Scale Hypothesized to Relate to Violence

		Expected and Predicted Violence Scale[b]							
Sample	N	Workers				Inmates		Mean	Correlation[c]
Expected	—	1	2	3	4	5	6	3.50	+ 1.00
Concurrent Validation	1043	1.13 (0.85)	1.09 (0.86)	1.85 (0.97)	2.70 (1.04)	3.95 (1.09)	4.24 (1.35)[b]	2.31 (1.64)	+ 0.76
Cross-Validation	518	1.27	1.18	1.77	2.61	4.04	4.13	2.32	+ 0.74
Age-Matched	797	1.25	1.09	1.79	2.49	4.07	4.26	2.27	+ 0.69
Original[d]	2213	1.39	—	1.58	3.36	—	3.44	2.40	+ 0.55

[a] Draper and Smith, 1966.
[b] Scale based on refined sample (Table 1B: 6, violent; 5, statistically potentially violent; 4, nonviolent; 3, inadequate performance; 2, statistically potentially adequate performance; and 1, adequate performance.
[c] Correlations between the predicted scale values and the actual scale values are high in all cases. The standard deviation of the predicted scale value is included in parentheses for each category of the concurrent sample (N = 1043) and for its mean.
[d] Original sample did not contain the statistically created categories 2 and 5 (Table 1A).

classified as nonviolent, and the situation would be even better for the three worker categories.

What specific features of these paper-and-pencil self-inventories were sufficiently distinctive to distinguish these various categories? As noted in the section on behavioral measures, four of the primary Birkman constructs correlated with the higher-order construct of neuroticism. All four of these primary constructs correlated positively at significant levels with the six point criterion scale. However, the curves were not linear, with a sharp break occurring between inmates and workers. Only feelings (depression) were significantly ($p < .05$) lower in inadequately performing workers than in nonviolent inmates ($r = 0.42$ with the criterion). The decreases in scores all were significant in comparisons between violent and nonviolent inmates, and between inadequate and adequate workers. Thus, neuroticism was high in the violent category, intermediate in both the nonviolent and inadequate categories, and low in adequate workers.

The relationship of violent crimes to high self-consciousness (concern about what others think), low ego-strength, moodiness, poor emotional control, restlessness, and ambivalence supports the speculations made earlier that the nature of crime—its danger and the excitement and emotions that are elicited—could lead to a high state of anxiety during which violent acts become almost predictable. The low self-image and the behaviors and feelings that accompany high levels of these traits make it difficult for people high on these scales to cope with a mundane job, with a routine and trying family life, with the mores and rules and regulations of society (Newman, 1974).

Except for feelings (depression), both intermediate noncoping classes were similar, and both classes were approximately at the population mean level for these constructs. Thus, the nonviolent inmates were not particularly neurotic and did not suffer especially from low self-esteem, and the same was true of the noncoping workers. We suspect that in these two classes, noncoping behavior was more a matter of lack of motivation, interest, or concern for others than of *active* feelings, beliefs, attitudes, and rebellion. The difference between criminals and noncriminals does not seem to be a function of neuroticism. The major factor could be viewed as a difference in the degree of control maintained on one's basic drive or intrinsic motivation. No control plus negative self-esteem tend to lead to the use of force to achieve one's needs. High control plus positive self-esteem tend to lead to effective coping with life's situations.

With the correlates of extraversion, there was a distinction between criminals and noncriminals. The criminals were significantly more introverted—less sociable, less energetic, less careful, and less insistent on adherence to "what is right." Only the energy construct discriminated within either subsample—the adequate workers reported themselves to be significantly more energetic than all other classes. These results suggest that the inmates were more hostile, less concerned with the necessity for strict interpretation of rules and regulations, less able or willing to apply their energy to productive endeavors than were the workers.

Considering the general pattern of the two sets of results: (1) the neuroticism-related constructs (except feelings) failed to discriminate criminal and noncriminal classes, but they discriminated within each of these classes significantly, and (2) the extraversion-related constructs (except energy) discriminated the broad classes, but not the within-class categories. This suggests a possible interaction between neuroticism and extraversion on this dimension. Neurotic introverts (violent category) could have different patterns from stable extraverts (adequate workers). We have observed such interactions for several significant behaviors, for example, orienting response and habituation (Sadler and Mefferd, 1971), operant-conditioning parameters (Sadler et al., 1971), and teacher-student interpersonal relationships (unpublished manuscript).[4]

The relationship between the self-admitted or self-attributed traits of the various categories of the sample, and those that were attributed (reflected?) to *most people* reveal the beliefs, attitudes, and self-delusions of persons in these categories. All neuroticism traits may be assumed to be socially undesirable, since all classes in the sample reported that *most people* were more depressed, ambivalent, restless, and self-conscious than they were. The opposite was the case with the extraversion traits. With one significant exception noted next, all categories reported that they were more sociable, energetic, and insistent than *most people.* The exception was that the not especially sociable, violent inmates reported that *most people* were even less sociable than they were.

Interpretation of the difference scores—*self*—*most people*—requires an anchor and we used the *self* score for this. Persons in the violent category rated themselves high on the neuroticism constructs, but they rated *most people* even higher than themselves. Yet, the difference in this category was the lowest of all the categories. In part, this was mechanical because of the limited number of items in each of the constructs. Even so, people in the violent category saw themselves as more like *most people* than did those in any other category. This tendency to see others as "more neurotic than I"

---

[4] R. B. Mefferd, Jr., L. T. Dickens, and N. E. Dawson. Personality and interpersonal behavior: Effect of teacher-student personality interactions on student performance assessment.

continued with succeeding categories, but the difference became very large for the stable, high ego-strength, adequate workers. In other words, as we move from a position of low to high coping behavior, *most people* are seen increasingly as being relatively more neurotic than oneself—more depressed, moody, self-conscious, indecisive, restless.

The same considerations apply to the extraversion constructs—workers do not view other people in the same way that prison inmates do. Adequate workers report themselves as being very friendly, energetic, and careful, but see others as much less extraverted than they are in all constructs.

The results were most consistent for those constructs that reflect attitudes, values, and a tendency to answer the item differently from *most people.* The Birkman construct of dominance was designed to relate directly to willful, forceful, intimidating dominance rather than to persuasive-leadership dominance; and the construct of materialism was designed to relate directly to relative willingness to obtain the material things one desires by whatever means possible, rather than to an opposing pole of idealism, intellectualism, spiritualism, etc. Individualism is the tendency to answer questions in an unpopular way. All three scales proved to be powerful predictors of results of the coping scale.

The influence of attitudes and values on coping behavior were reflected strongly in the differences between the *self* and *most people* reports. All groups saw others as more domineering, grasping, and individualistic than themselves. In the two extreme groups, this difference was small and the real significance of the tendency to "see others as I see myself" by both the best and worst copers was apparent from the *self* scores. The violent classes had very low ego-strength; hostile, rebellious, domineering feelings and beliefs; and their attitudes *toward* others were the same. This attitude reduces to "everyone takes what he wants by whatever means are needed to get it." With this belief, one's own violent, maladaptive behaviors become fully self-justified.

The sharp contrast occurs with the adequate workers, who also see others as thinking-acting like themselves. Their high ego-strength, that is, low neuroticism, high energy level, and their very low scores on the *self* constructs related to values and attitudes indicate that these coping people have a confident, optimistic, and hopeful attitude about others. This is markedly opposed to the hostile, cynical, neurotic attitude exhibited by the answers given by the violent inmates. This same tendency was notable to a lesser extent with the nonviolent inmates. Both they and the inadequately performing workers denied resoundingly, however, that they were as domineering, materialistic, individualistic as *most people.* This possibility reflects the fact that persons in both of these intermediate noncoping categories had about the same moderate-level ego-strengths. This resulted in a combined *self* denial and *most people* attribution of traits which the noncopers realized were neither personally nor socially desirable.

The results of this analysis may be summarized as follows: violent inmates were more moody, self-conscious, ambivalent, and restless than any other category. The adequately performing workers were in marked contrast—emotionally stable with high ego-strength. Both of the intermediate noncoping categories were essentially equal in these respects, and their mean scores were at abour the levels of the population means.

Extraversion-related constructs were much less involved within either the inmate or worker categories. The principal differences in the *self* means were that they discriminated the criminal/noncriminal categories—inmates were less sociable, energetic, insistent, and concerned about following rules than were the workers of either performance category. These characteristics were reflected in the *self-most people* differences—the hostile violent class actually reported that *most people* were *more* friendly than they were themselves.

The constructs involving value systems and attitudes discriminated the categories of the "violence" scale better than the other constructs, and they reflected the most marked differences in the relative views of *self* and *most people.* The inmates seemed to justify their behavior and attitudes by believing that *most people* felt the same materialistic, dominant, individualistic way that they did, while the adequate workers saw *most people* as conforming to the predominating value systems of our society.

A factor that must be considered in searching for the cause of a propensity for committing violent acts is drive or aggression. Aggression in an intelligent, educated, ambituous person who has a socially acceptable value system is greatly admired and usually yields self-satisfying accomplishments. In a uneducated, insecure, or psychopathic person, however, aggression may emerge as overbearing, pugnacious, provocative, and socially unacceptable macho behavior. Yet violent acts may erupt from aggressive people regardless of their background—only the outward appearance of the act may be different. A predictive equation of aggressiveness that was developed by us with a different approach and criterion yielded high scores for many hard-driving executives, powerful salespersons, highly rated supervisors, outstanding productive workers, and low scores for more passive and poorer workers. Some of the inmates from each category had high scores with this equation. Since the scores of coping capacity and of this aggressionlike prediction correlated only at $r = 0.05$, a pure drive-type of aggression does not seem to be an essential element of violence.

DISCUSSION

It was possible to classify people along a dimension of individual differences that involved coping capacity. The rank order of people so classified correlated variously with violence, criminality, and job performance. The people at the extremes were either *actively* coping, that is, working in a manner judged to be adequate by the employer, or *actively* not coping, that is, resorting to force to achieve their goals, in this case, by criminally violent acts. At the center of the scale were two classes of people, those noncoping in a *passive* fashion—merely performing inadequately for any of many possible reasons, or merely not bothering with work at all and resorting to nonviolent crime for support. Two subgroups were identified as having high statistical risk for becoming active and moving toward their respective active extremes—adequate worker or violent criminal. Time will tell whether or not this prediction can be verified.

The purpose of our study was to describe pertinent classes within such a distribution. By means of an integrated personality, attitude, and social perception instrument, three major aspects of the dimension were identified. Two of these aspects involved two well-established, higher-order personality traits—neuroticism (or anxiety or ego-strength) and extraversion. With neuroticism the general trend was high scores for the violent classes, moderate scores for both of the passively noncoping classes, that is, nonviolent inmates and inadequately performing workers, and low scores for the adequately coping workers. For extraversion, the trends were opposite and qualitatively different—both classes of inmates had low scores, that is, they were introverted, while both classes of workers had high scores, they were extraverted.

Thus, neuroticism discriminated *active* versus *passive* coping capacity, while extraversion discriminated criminality versus noncriminality. Considering this result as an interaction of these traits, the criminally violent class were neurotic introverts, while the adequate workers were stable extraverts. The noncoping workers and the noncoping inmates were both intermediate relative to neuroticism, but they were different in that the workers were extraverted and the inmates introverted.

It is attractive to interpret the results of this study in terms of Maslow's (1954) philosophy. We found that the self-actualizing and time-competent individual was actually a stable extravert, while the opposite pole of Maslow's typology consisted of neurotic introverts (unpublished manuscript[5]). In our study, these categories correspond to the adequate worker and the violent inmate.

An offender who has the personality of the adequate coper—a stable extravert—has difficulty in coping with the criminal justice system for the same reasons that make for his success if he does not resort to crime. His tendencies to speak his mind, to fraternize, to be relaxed about rules and situations, and so on, do not fit well into prison and parole systems. The neurotic introvert, on the other hand, is in his element in these systems and can turn the system to his own advantage. This was shown to be the case in McWilliams' (1975) report that, upon parole (probation in England), neurotic introverted offenders were more likely to receive shorter sentences and to remain free upon probation than were stable extraverted offenders.

As to these higher-order personality traits, the perceptions of *most people* expressed by these classes were vastly different—the violent inmates saw *most people* as quite similar to themselves—neurotic introverts. On the sociability scale they believed *most people* were *more* sociable than they, even though they rated themselves relatively low. This was in stark contrast with the other classes, and it suggests a strong streak of hostility.

Adequate workers also saw *most people* as neurotic introverts, but this was very different from how they saw themselves. We might strain the interpretation of this difference and suggest that the inmates were closeted not only by prison bars, but also within themselves by their perceptual limitations. They attributed their own self-consciousness, emotional lability, restlessness, ambivalence, hostility, low drive, low insistence, to everyone else, failing to realize that this was not an accurate perception. It would be quite difficult for people wearing such blinders to understand what the stable extraverted workers are talking about when they stress the work ethic, reliability, open-handedness, reasonableness, honor, and other abstract concepts.

The third major aspect of the dimension of coping capacity involved attitudes and values. The violent inmates had almost twice the tendency of the adequate workers to answer the personality questions in contrary, unpopular directions. They also reported themselves to be willing to do almost anything to gain material things, and almost anything to gain and keep the upper hand in interpersonal relationships. They reported that they believed it was quite proper to blame others for their own mistakes,

[5] R. B. Meffered, Jr., and N. E. Dawson. Maslow's self-actualizing person and Eysenck's typology, partially funded by National Science Foundation grant listed in footnote 3.

to take the glory that was due others, to ridicule or embarrass others if it put themselves into a dominant position. All this was in marked contrast to the adequate workers.

The revealing observation was that persons in both the violent and the adequate categories saw *most people* as very nearly like themselves on these attitude and value constructs. For the violent class this means that they saw *most people* as lying, cheating, stealing, irresponsible, grasping, domineering. They had a paranoid expectancy that *most people* were out to take them by whatever means possible, and it was, therefore, only reasonable for them to respond in kind. In stark contrast was the optimistic, hopeful, confident attitude of the adequate workers. Their high ego-strength, drive, friendliness, and emotional stability, combined with attitudes of responsibility, attention to social mores, self-sufficiency, ambition, and the like, were shared somewhat by the inadequately performing workers, less so by the nonviolent inmates, and, of course, hardly at all by the violent category.

This marked tendency for the class of violent (and criminal) persons *and* the class of adequate (and probably noncriminal) workers "to see others as we see ourselves" suggests a powerful self-fulfilling prophesy. The more negative the violent class members become, the more self-justifiable become their negative attitudes, and the more cohesive becomes their society. The more positive the adequate workers become, the more self-righteous they become about the *appropriate* value systems of their society. Each class member reinforces his own value system and his own world as he grows farther and farther apart from his counterpart. Each class thus tends to move from passive to active positions as tensions mount. Alas, these basic aspects of the human condition extend to communities and to nations—one escalates, the other retaliates, or vice versa.

Both of the passively noncoping intermediate groups saw *most people* as very different from themselves, but for the nonviolent inmates (with their moderate *self* scores), this meant that they still saw *most people* somewhat like the violent class did. For the inadequate workers, their large *self-most people* difference signified a marked distrust and a very cynical viewpoint. Perhaps, such a viewpoint is justified, since these people would be expected to cope poorly with many other aspects of life, and they may well have been long-term prime targets of the more actively antisocial classes.

These differences between *self* and *most people* reporting patterns for the different classes in this study emphasize the difficulty involved in any one class's understanding what the other class feels, experiences, thinks, believes. A beginning step is to determine what these differences are. The next step involves the characteristics of human nature that are inexorably meshed with the traits we are discussing—the individual's ability and willingness to use the information in constructive ways. The final step involves a research question—will it be possible to change the negative beliefs of the violent class.

REFERENCES

ADAMS, T. C. Characteristics of state prisoners who demonstrate severe adjustment problems. *J. Clin. Psychol.* 33:1100-1103, 1977.

DRAPER, N. R., and SMITH, H. *Applied Regression Analysis.* John Wiley & Sons, New York, 1966.

DURBIN, J. R., PASEQARK, R. A., and ALBERS, D. Criminality and mental illness: A study of arrest rates in a rural state. *Am. J. Psychiatry* 134:80-83, 1977.

EYSENCK, H. J., and EYSENCK, S. B. G. *The Eysenck Personality Inventory.* Educational Testing Service, San Diego, 1968.

GARDNER, M. R. The myth of the impartial psychiatric expert: some comments concerning criminal responsibility and the declines of the age of therapy. *Law and Psychological Review* 2:99-119, 1976.

GUZE, S. B. *Criminality and Psychiatric Disorders.* Oxford University Press, New York, 1976.

JUSTICE, B., and BIRKMAN, R. An effort to distinguish the violent from the nonviolent. *South. Med. J.* 65:703-706, 1972.

KUNCE, J. T., RYAN, J. J., and ECKELMAN, C. C. Violent behavior and differential WAIS characteristics. *J. Consult. Clin. Psychol.* 44:42-45, 1976.

MASLOW, A. H. *Motivation and Personality.* Harper, New York, 1954.

MASUDA, M., CUTLER, D. L., HEIN, L., and HOLMES, T. H. Life events and prisoners. *Arch. Gen. Psychiatry* 35:197-203, 1978.

MCCREARY, C., and PADILLA, E. MMPI differences among black, Mexican-American and white male offenders. *J. Clin. Psychol.* 33:171-177, 1977.

MCCREARY, C. P., and MENSH, I. N. Personality differences associated with age in law offenders. *J. Gerontol.* 32:164-167, 1977.

MCWILLIAMS, W. Sentencing and recidivism: an analysis by personality type. *Br. J. Soc. Work* 5:311-324, 1975.

MEDNICK, S. A., and CHRISTIANSEN, K. O., eds. *Biosocial Bases of Criminal Behavior.* Gardner Press, New York, 1977.

MEFFERD, R. B., JR. How much anxiety is "normal"? In *Phenomenology and Treatment of Anxiety.* E. Fann, I. Karacan, A. Pokorny, and R. Williams, eds. Spectrum, New York, 1980a.

MEFFERD, R. B., JR. The developing biological concept of anxiety, in *Phenomenology and Treatment of Anxiety.* E. Fann, I. Karacan, A. Pokorny, and R. Williams, eds. Spectrum, New York, 1980b.

MEGARGEE, E. I. The prediction of dangerous behavior. *Criminology, Justice and Behavior* 3:3-22, 1976.

NEWMAN, D. E. The personality of violence: conversations with protagonists. *Mental Health & Society* 1:328-344, 1974.

OLDROYD, R. J., and HOWELL, R. J. Personality, intellectual, and behavioral differences between black, chicano, and white prison inmates in the Utah prison. *Psychol. Rep.* 41:187-191, 1977.

PETERSEN, E. *A Reassessment of the Concept of Criminality: An Analysis of Criminal Behavior in Terms of Individual and Current Environment Interaction. The Application of a Stochastic Model.* Halsted Press, New York, 1977.

PETRICH, J. Rate of psychiatric morbidity in a metropolitan county jail population. *Am. J. Psychiatry* 133:1439-1440, 1976.

PETRICH, J. Metropolitan jail psychiatric clinic: a year's experience. *J. Clin. Psychiatry* 1:191-195, 1978.

ROWE, A. R., and TITTLE, C. R. Life cycle changes and criminal propensity. *Sociology Quarterly* 18:223-236, 1977.

SADLER, T. G., and MEFFERD, R. B., JR. The interaction of extraversion and neuroticism in human operant behavior. *J. Exp. Res. on Pers.* 5:278-285, 1971.

SADLER, T. G., MEFFERD, R. B., JR., and HOUCK, R. L. The interaction of extraversion and neuroticism in orienting response habituation. *Psychophysiology* 8(3): 312-318, 1971.

SCOTT, P. D. Assessing dangerousness in criminals. *Br. J. Psychiatry* 131:127-142, 1977.

SHAWVER, L., and JEW, C. Predicting violent behavior from WAIS characteristics: a replication failure. *J. Consult. Clin. Psychol.* 46:206, 1978.

SILBERMAN, C. E. *Criminal Violence, Criminal Justice*. Random House, New York, 1978.

SMITH, A. B., and POLLACK, H. Deviance as a method of coping. *Crime & Delinquency* 22:3-16, 1976.

SPELLACY, F. Neuropsychological discrimination between violent and non-violent men. *J. Clin. Psychol.* 34:49-52, 1978.

SWANK, G. E., and WINER, D. Occurrence of psychiatric disorder in a county jail population. *Am. J. Psychiatry* 133:1331-1333, 1976.

TATSUOKA, M. M. *Selected Topics in Advanced Statistics: Discriminant Analysis.* Institute of Personality and Aptitude Testing, Champaign, Ill., 1970.

Texas Board of Pardons and Paroles Bulletin. Sept., 1978.

WITKIN, H. A., MEDNICK, S. A., SCHULSINGER, F., BAKKESTROM, E., CHRISTIANSEN, K. O., GOODENOUGH, D. R., HIRSCHORN, K., LUNDSTEEN, C., OWNE, D. R., PHILIP, J., RUBIN, D. B., and STOCKING, M. Criminality in XYY and XXY men. *Science* 193:547-555, 1976.

ZAHN, M. A. Violent death: a comparison between drug users and non-drug users. *Addictive Diseases: An International Journal* 1:283-296, 1974.

Part III

LEGAL IMPLICATIONS IN THE STUDY AND TREATMENT OF VIOLENCE

CHAPTER 18

The Dangerous Patient and the Duty to Warn

CHARLES J. WEIGEL, II

Duty to warn has recently been put into a new perspective although the concept of an obligation to make a person aware of danger has long been a part of tort law. A physician's duty to warn a patient of risks and dangers relative to a patient's condition or a proposed treatment, a custodian's duty to warn those in his or her charge of hazards—all this has long been accepted as an inherent part of responsibility when there is a duty-bearing relationship. More recently, however, and in a dramatic case,[1] the duty to warn has been expanded beyond those people who are in direct legal connection with each other to others who may or may not be seen as closely connected. This wide-ranging concept attracts perhaps equally unforeseeable potential consequences.

Duty to warn involves, in its new guise, at least three basic concepts: that of duty, definition of danger and its magnitude, and the rights of individuals, if they can be identified. Of these, duty is of primary importance. While it is fairly within the vocabulary of the general population, the idea of the duty-bearing relationship is one that has given lawyers unending concern for decades. A suggested definition states that when one person is placed in a position with another and realizes that that position is at-

[1] *Tarasoff* v. *Regents of the University of California. Second Pacific Reporter* vols. 529, 551. West Publishing, St. Paul, Minnesota, 1974.

tended by some danger, some risk, or some harm potential, the first person has, then, a duty to take ordinary care to avoid these possibilities. Duty, thus, is an obligation defined by the care that should be taken by one toward another under the circumstances, of both their special position toward each other and ancillary factors surrounding that position. Thus, the problem is identifying to whom duty is owed and for how long. Common law has long said that in the absence of a statute, duty of care is owed when a special relationship exists for the length of that relationship. These relationships may vary in nature, from the unilateral duty of a mother toward her infant to the reciprocal duty of motorists toward each other when using common highways. As a general rule, in the absence of any special relationship, there is no duty. If one sees a stranger who is in peril through no fault of the observer, there is no obligation in law to go to that stranger, and, indeed, if aid is proferred, the law will examine with particularity the degree of care exercised. This rather strict concept has been ameliorated to a certain extent in the United States by a variety of so-called Good Samaritan laws, which encourage aiding others by lowering the standard of care that has to be exercised. Other duties may be created by statute for particular circumstances. A classic example is the duty to stop and render aid, if involved in an automobile accident, even though fault may not be present. The legislature, for the common benefit of all, ordered this particular duty. This is consonant with the general common-law theme that when people's actions or nonactions may affect others, for good or for bad, the law will find a duty, and that duty will be to exercise reasonable ordinary care under the circumstances.

There is unquestionable duty insofar as the practitioner of the healing arts is concerned when he or she accepts a patient for treatment. That duty has been said to be a charge or obligation on practitioners to use the ordinary care of a reasonable, prudent person of their training and skill, considerating the particular facts of the case. Included in this standard of care are the responsibility of making reasonable predictions as to present and future risks and potential harms to the patient, based on his or her malady, and the modalities of therapy available for treatment. In the physical and medical models, this test works fairly well, although it is not without problems. In the realm of mental health care, applications are considerably more difficult. It is, according to those involved in the field, difficult enough to make a diagnosis of mental illness, but making a prognosis of future danger of the patient to himself or others is even more complex. Finally, there is the dilemma of how to contend with the problem of handling the prognosis if and when it is made. Courts have traditionally looked to the medical model because of the aforementioned relative facility, in working with cases that have psychiatric ramifications. It is human nature, when confronted with something novel, to refer to the closest familar thing, and go forward from there. This has not, however, worked with great advantage in making the transition from medical to psychiatric cases. The law has been able to contend with the proferred evidence of a broken leg and the predicted danger of the patient if he walks on it, or the danger to others if the patient, for example, drives an automobile without the ability to forceably apply pressure on the brake pedal at the appropriate or necessary time. The law has not had an easy time of it when the case involves a broken mind. If, indeed, the degree of mental impairment can be ascertained with some degree of certainty, the fair predictability of potential harm has proved to be far less facile. Nonetheless, the courts have persisted in looking back to the old and more comfortable orthopedic and other medical examples for guidance, even though they seem, given the state of the art and science of psychiatry, palpably inappropriate.

Prediction of danger, according to Professor George E. Dix of the University of Texas Law School, has an inherent contradiction, because it attempts to use a permanent label on a changeable condition. He points out that even persons generally accepted as dangerous have moments of nondanger, such as while they are asleep, while an otherwise benign personality might become dangerous given the circumstance of rude awakening. Thus, many factors, not all of which are readily predictable or foreseeable, go into the admixture of personality traits under a given circumstance which leaves the whole idea of forecasting hazardous behavior in a state of amorphous fluidity. It is a far different proposition when we are contending with the architectural soundness and predictability of failure of a fractured femur.

The problem was brought into sharp, if not clarifying, focus through address and resolution of the courts of California. Nine years ago, Posenjit Podar was receiving self-sought mental health therapy at the University of California Student Center Hospital. His psychologist discovered in the course of the therapy that Podar intended to kill a readily identifiable young woman in whom he had been interested. The psychologist notified the campus police, verbally and later in writing, and after consultation with two colleagues, asked that Podar be apprehended and held in detention for 72 hours, in accordance with the provisions of California law for observation and treatment. As they are discernable from the appellate opinion, the facts had some bizarre undertones. The first releasing authority of Podar seems to have been the campus police. After picking the man up, talking to him, and evaluating Podar's potential harmlessness, they received a promise from him not to carry out his threatened action, and they let him go. The psychiatry department was notified of this action. Subsequently, the head of that department ordered correspondence regarding Podar to the police department destroyed, for what purpose is uncertain, but it clouds the case and raises a question that may have had some subliminal effect on the court's final judgment. In any event, Podar, from the time of his encounter with the police, never again went back to this psychiatric service, nor did he see his therapist until he saw him from the witness stand, when Podar was being tried for the murder of the young woman, Tatiana Tarasoff. Tatiana had returned to this country about two months after Podar was picked up. He then sought her out, shot her, and stabbed her to death.

The California court, as had others before, fell into the convenient, if not particularly useful, analogy to the traditional medical case. They said, in essence, that as medical doctors may have the duty to warn and use reasonable care in the treatment of *their* patients, so also must those engaged in psychotherapy; *they* must warn to prevent overt danger. Both opinions found liability. The first opinion, the one subsequently vacated, observed that the defendants had frightened Podar off by notifying the police, thus, in effect, discouraging him from seeking help which might have prevented the homicide, and for such action were responsible. The second opinion gives us the benefit of the recital of the pleadings by caption as presented by plaintiff, Tatiana Tarasoff's parents.

As the first element of the cause of action, the parents charged the defendants with "failure to detain a patient who was dangerous to himself and others." This allegation was shown to be invalid in view of specific statutory immunity granted to the defendants concerning detention in California. In other areas of the country, failure to detain might still be a viable cause of action. The second salient point of the pleading, "abandonment of a dangerous patient," raises an old problem that may be brought forward in a new light as a result of this case. It has long been the law that once the duty is undertaken in the physician-patient context, there is a responsibility to continue until that obligation is terminated by mutual consent, the end of the need for assistance, or the procurement of other and adequate treating entities. To turn the patient out to shift for himself or herself before treatment has been accomplished or before the patient has asked to terminate the relationship has been considered in the past to be a high legal risk. In the usual situation, the patient is the potential victim of harm through abandonment, though other and earlier cases have pointed out that a doctor who prescribes a sedative may have liability to persons whom a patient/busdriver injures when under the influence of this sedative, and require a warning, not to the injured party, but to the driver. The gist of the Tarasoff case centers on the duty to warn unsuspecting third parties, and this thought was picked up by the court in accepting, for favorable consideration, the pleading of the Tarasoffs that the defendant failed "to warn of the dangerousness of this patient." The court, in dealing with pleading, said that there is a standard of care for psychiatrists, psychologists, psychotherapists, just as there is for any other health care deliverer in any other healing role and that they must observe that standard. As we have seen, the standard of care has traditionally been couched in the question of what a reasonable ordinary prudent person would do under the same or similar circumstances. The judges in both of the majority opinions found that such a standard could and did exist in this instance, and that it had not been met by the actions of the defendant. It differentiated the situation at hand from the incarceration cases in which there were less Draconian measures available, one of which was "under the right circumstances," to use the court's words, "warning those appropriate people who are (1) at risk, and (2) can take appropriate measures to alleviate risk."

Both opinions acknowledged, but did not accept, the argument of the defendants that violent expression by the patient is not necessarily equal to inevitable violent activity, and that open communication between therapist and patient is absolutely essential to successful psychiatric assistance. The rationale of the court in denying effect to these arguments was that psychiatrists and psychotherapists are better equipped than others to evaluate the potentiality of verbalized threats becoming reality, and that the benefit to the patient from assurance of confidentiality must be weighed against the danger the patient poses in light of that evaluation.

There were two dissenting opinions, the first of which observed that danger might be enhanced when a patient is frightened away from a source of available help by threats of warning to others. This same argument was advanced in the superseded majority opinion as a reason for liability. The other dissenting judge agreed with the majority that there should be a finding of liability because in his view there had been an apparent danger and the negligence of the defendants was in failure to give adequate warning rather than in assessment of potential danger of the patient. This jurist expressed a belief that there is no such thing as a standard of care in psychotherapy because of too much disagreement among practitioners and too many variables in treatment of mental patients as opposed to the treatment of medical patients. If, however, we follow his advice and stand away from the traditional standard-of-care guide, we have nothing left by which to evaluate whether or not there has been lack of acceptable care in mental health cases. The reasonable ordinary prudent person has been the hallmark and the benchmark of the negligence cause of action. If a person conducts himself or herself within the framework of that definition, when there was a duty to exercise care, then there is no liability, no matter how appalling the results. If there is no standard of care in the given frame of conduct or course of activity, how is one to gauge what may be liability-bearing conduct and what may not?

While the majority opinion leaves us with the onerous task of determining what is a standard of care and what is not in the assessment of a dangerous patient, the minority judge, in offering to do away with that standard, seems to leave us with only two alternatives. One such alternative would be couched in strict liability, and would, in effect, make the therapist responsible for all damage related to the patient's condition and the treatment or lack of it. This approach is considered, especially by those engaged in mental health care services, to be a discouraging one indeed. The other choice would be to grant immunity, excluding the therapist from liability whenever the activity results in damage. It is a treasured tenet of the law that holds that the threat of responding in damages is one of the greatest insurers of reasonable care.

The third facet of the Tarasoff trilogy of problems concerns the rights of the patient. The duty and standard of care heretofore dealt with are more concerned with those affected by the patient's activities. Nonetheless, it would be a serious omission to disregard the fact that the law has, to a greater or lesser extent, promulgated certain ideas regarding rights. If a patient-therapist relationship is created, it would seem that there is the right to expect effective treatment. Effective treatment, in the words of those who have been charged with setting a standard of care in treatment, includes, most emphatically, a need, if not a right, of confidentiality between the parties. We have been told, over and again, that trust is a *sine qua non;* without trust, the candor necessary to help would not be forthcoming. Tangential to this right is the right of the patient to know all the significant conditions of his treatment. This has been expressed in the difficult concept of informed consent. It would seem, then, that the therapist may have to explain, at the beginning of a relationship, that any latent or patent dangers to others that may be uncovered during the course of the treatment may have to be communicated to those who are perceived to be at risk. This would in some likelihood have the chilling effect that both the first majority and the second dissent in the Tarasoff case observed, that is, of deterring the patient from seeking needed help. It must further be remembered that the law has suggested that a patient does not always have to be informed fully about the nature of his proposed treatment when such information would work to the serious detriment of the patient's well-being.

Finally, there is the consideration of the patient's right to privacy, which works in somewhat the same manner as the right to confidentiality. In one instance, however, we are concerned with the effectiveness of the treatment, and in other we are confronted with the basic right of an individual to have his own private matters, including his illnesses, shielded from public scrutiny. Perhaps the situation of the mentally-at-risk patient is analogous to the medical model wherein an individual is suffering from a communicable disease. In the latter instance, the therapist would have the duty to warn the patient of the dangerousness to others, and if the patient persisted in ignoring such advice, extend the warning to those who might come in contact with the patient. This model is somewhat deficient, however, in that *anticipatory* warning without the presence or strong indication of disregard by the patient of the need for circumspect conduct is not generally found in the medical model. Professional therapists have found that translation of threat into action is rare, but that observation must be tempered by the caveat that it is not how likely this is to occur, but rather, how likely it is that this may occur in this patient's instance.

Many observers believe that the Tarasoff case has left us with a simplistic axiom of conduct for the therapist: "when in doubt, warn." It must be remembered, however, that the case had certain individualistic aspects that may not be universal to all such problems. These include the important facts that in Tarasoff we had an ascertained threat, and a definite target. The threatened harm was specific and grievous. Finally, the Tarasoff decision tells us in fairly unmistakable language that if a real threat is perceived, then not only must warning be given, but reasonable care must be taken to see that the warning is effectively communicated to the person or persons at risk.

CHAPTER 19

Sanctions on Research with Violent Individuals

S. I. SHUMAN

Although I do intend to discuss the subject suggested by the title, two clarifications should be made at the outset. First, the word sanction is misleading in this context. There surely may be sanctions imposed for engaging in improper or illegal research, be it with violent individuals or not. It is conceivable that a researcher who has engaged in such research may suffer a sanction in the conventional sense (for example, a criminal sentence). But it is more likely that, whether or not civil or criminal sanction is attached to some research activity, an investigator may suffer a sanction in the less legalistic sense, for example, loss of esteem from his peers, perhaps even loss of a position. Even more probable in this context are sanctions in the less legalistic sense in which a researcher suffers rejection by his or her peers, embarrassment in the community, loss of friends, etc. I shall not discuss these possibilities nor try to illustrate them by cases in which such consequences have attached. Over the last ten years during which the movement for the protection of human subjects burst into full bloom, there have been very few cases—or at least few that have come to public light—in which any kind of sanction, let alone an actual criminal or civil penalty, has been imposed upon a biomedical or behavioral researcher for engaging in improper, let alone illegal, experimentation. In fact, in all English-language jurisprudence, I know of only one case holding that there had been "malpractice" in a research context (*Halushka* v. *University of Saskatchewan,* 1965) and one case involving behavioral research (*Merriken* v. *Cressman,* 1973). There are other reported incidences even apart from the Nürnberg medical experiment charges, however, which have raised questions as to the propriety of biomedical or behavioral research (see the *Clonce* [1974], *Hyman* [1965], *Jobson* [1966], *Kaimowitz* [1973], *Knecht* [1973], *Price* [1976], and *Wyatt* [1974] cases, as well as the reported incident at State University of New York-Albany [1977]). But my point is the paucity of such cases and the rarity with which any kind of conventional sanction has been imposed.

The more usual consequence for a researcher who has engaged or even proposed to engage in unethical or inappropriate research is the sense of frustration the researcher is likely to suffer because he does not share the perception of those who regard the research as inappropriate. Therefore, the sanction most likely to be suffered is a sanction only in the very extended sense of the term; that is, the researcher may suffer what he or she perceives to be some intrusion into the domain of his or her personal autonomy. This is not a slight matter by any means, but it certainly does not raise questions about sanctions as that term is used conventionally. I have personally been involved in several cases in which a proposal was rejected or critically evaluated, and it was perfectly clear that the proposing researcher suffered a sense of rejection, embarrassment, and perhaps even humiliation at having someone who he believed was not qualified to make decisive judgments about the research activity, do so.

In one case this was particularly dramatic and even traumatic. The researcher was a prestigious scientist who had an international reputation and had been an officer in the leading national organization in his professional specialty. His reputation would have enabled him to abandon his academic post at any time and significantly increase his income by going into private practice. He remained an academic largely because of his commitment to medical research, and he therefore suffered all the more when his research proposal was questioned as to its humanistic significance and as to whether he had been sufficiently sensitive to the welfare of his proposed subject population. Here he was devoting his life to improving the lot of humankind but he suddenly found his motives and conduct questioned. In the extended sense of sanction previously identified, he did suffer a sanction.

It is in this sense of sanction that I wish to discuss the proposed subject, and what this means is that we will consider not the sanctions suffered by investigators, but rather the restraints upon research that make is possible for someone other than the investigator to decide whether or not certain research may be carried out by the investigator.

A second clarification as to the subject of concern is also required. While the problem of research with violent individuals is relevant, it is somewhat misleading to think of research about aggression and violence as being research with violent individuals. Much of the research aimed at discovering the mechanisms that cause violence or aggression is research with individuals who have had an episode in which they engaged in an overt act of violence but who would not be characterized as violent individuals. Furthermore, research on aggression and violence may often involve individuals who have not been convicted of a crime nor found responsible for some act of aggression which resulted in institutionalization or incarceration. Thus it may be misleading to think of research about violent individuals as the core of this subject, and it would be more helpful if, instead, we regarded the following as the area of concern: restrainsts upon research about aggression and violence.

FROM NO SANCTION TO LAISSEZ-FAIRE

One surprising aspect of the topic has been the rapidity with which the field has developed. It is almost as though the heavens over Washington opened, and regulations that had been waiting for just the right moment came tumbling forth. It is startling to realize that barely 10 years ago Michael DeBakey (1968) would still write:

> Because of their complexity, variability, and irreducibility to stereotypes, living systems, unlike inanimate nature, are not subject to formulas. Standards codified by laws are not only difficult to interpret in real life situations, but are virtually impossible to enforce. Ethical decisions in medical science must therefore depend finally on the wisdom, integrity, and self-imposed restraints of the scientist and his peers. A simple personal credo based on general ethical norms and on love and reverence for humanity has no equivalent for moral guidance (p. 134).

Dr. DeBakey, like other medical researchers at the time, was responding to the landmark article that was published just two years earlier by Henry Beecher. In *Ethics and Clinical Research* (1966) Beecher expressed concern over some questionable medical experimentation and cited 22 examples of research which raised some serious questions. His article was in part so influential because he sensed what Ingelfinger (writing more recently) has referred to as "the antitechnologic, prohumanistic temper of the sixties, and the emphasis on the individual as opposed to societal priorities" (1975: p. 264).

As an aside, we might note that Dr. Beecher, in the 1966 article, suggested how editorial discretion might effectively prevent or discourage unethical experimentation. The Committee on Editorial Policy of the Council of Biology Editors concurred in this proposal, and it is probable that there have been instances in which material was denied publication because of editorial resistance to the experimentation itself. But exercise of control by editors is obviously a source of concern to the editors. As Ingelfinger, editor of an important journal, has said, "What special insight or superior moral sensitivity gives me license not only to accuse but to judge? Occasionally the impropriety of a given protocol is flagrant, but most of the time the editor would-be-ethicist has to sort out the grays" (1975: p. 264).

Because of the difficulties he experienced as an editor, and despite what he recognized as the superfluous and perhaps absurd levels of federal regulation, Ingelfinger would have settled for institutional review boards rather than relying upon editorial discretion to deny access to the pages of a professional journal. In fact, the recommendation of the committee did not require the editor to act on his own. Rather the committee recommended that the editor should require the published report to contain a statement "that the institution's committee on ethics . . . approved the description of the proposed research." Only if, despite, such a statement, the editor believed the research "not to have been conducted in accordance with ethical principles" was he then to pursue the matter further by contacting the author and if necessary the chairman of the relevant committee at the institution where the researcs was carried out (Woodford, 1972).

Rather than pursue the issue of editorial discretion versus other mechanisms by which to prevent inappropriate research, it might be helpful if we placed this particular issue in the context of restraints generally. To do so let me suggest that the range of available mechanisms might be constructed along some linear scale in which no-sanction—laissez-faire was at one end, and explicit prohibitions upon some or all research with human subjects was at the other end. While the ordering proposed below is hardly beyond refutation, something like the following is intended to represent a hierarchy of increased prohibition:

1. No sanctions—laissez-faire.
2. Reliance upon the conscience and scruples of the investigator.
3. Peer pressure which is not institutionalized.
4. Editorial discretion in denying access to publication.
5. Institutionalized peer pressure.

6. An institutional review mechanism (which is not the same as peer review).
7. Reliance upon the conventional law of torts with liability for civil wrongdoing. This may include (if there is such liability) loss of professional status. For example, losing one's license as a physician may be a consequence of even civil wrongdoing.
8. Criminal liability for sufficiently inappropriate research which results in prosecution for a crime and which is almost certain to have, as a corollary consequence, loss of professional status.
9. Explicitly local, state, and/or federal rules regulating some or all kinds of research.
10. A flat prohibition of all or some research with human subjects.

I began by quoting Dr. DeBakey's suggestion that reliance upon conscience was sufficient, clearly a recommendation that falls near the no-sanction end of the spectrum. What is so interesting is that in the mere ten years that have elapsed since he made his public declaration in favor of conscience rather than external restraints, the movement for such restraints has exploded and moved with persistence and success toward the other end of the spectrum. We see now the possibility of a prohibition of some or perhaps even all research with human subjects or a prohibition of any research with certain types of human subjects, for example, prisoners, mentally infirm persons, children, etc. Despite the relentless march of the restraint movement toward the prohibition end of the scale, it is almost certain that biomedical and behavioral investigators continue to share Dr. DeBakey's belief that reliance upon the conscience of the investigator is sufficient. Probably between 50 and 90 percent of the investigators continue to believe that the regulations emanating from Washington are unnecessary and constitute an unjustified interference with their First-Amendment and professional rights.

The 50 percent as the floor figure is based upon a study conducter for the National Commission for the Protection of Human Subjects, the results of which are reported in its most recent set of recommendations, namely those concerned with institutional review boards (DHEW 78-0008). The report and recommendations were transmitted to the President and Senate on September 1, 1978. In connection with this study, investigators were asked about the role of their own institutional review committees. In one instance they were asked whether "the review procedure is an unwarranted intrusion on an investigator's autonomy—at least to some extent." Twenty-five percent of the biomedical researchers and 38 percent of the behavioral and social science researchers responded in the affirmative. When asked whether "the review committee gets into areas which are not appropriate to its function—at least to some extent," 50 percent of the biomedical and 40 percent of the behavioral and social science researchers answered in the affirmative. Asked whether "they felt the review committee makes judgments that it is not qualified to make—at least to some extent," 43 percent of the biomedical and 49 percent of the behavioral and social science researchers responded in the affirmative. When asked whether "the review procedure has impeded the progress of research done at [their] institution—at least to some extent," 43 percent of the biomedical and 54 percent of the behavioral and social science researchers responded in the affirmative.

On the basis of this survey we may freely conclude that while the public apparently supports or, at least, has not rejected executive and judicial action directed toward the prohibition end of the scale, the investigators who are actually conducting the research continue to perceive such external regulations as unwarranted, unnecessary, and unduly invasive of their personal autonomy.

What is intriguing about this controversy is the intensity of the commitment to the various positions that have been taken despite the absence of any hard-core data that would enable one to answer at least the following critical questions:

Is there a correlation between each or even any of the ten mechanisms for regulation and the protection of human subjects and, if so, is the correlation metricizable? In other words, are human subjects in fact better protected when something other than the conscience—no-sanction—laissez-faire attitude prevails, or do explicit rules (that do not amount to flat prohibitions) in fact produce more or better protections?

Is there a correlation between the laissez-faire—no-sanction approach to research medicine and any real advances in medicine? Or can it be demonstrated that real progress in medicine is not impeded by any form of regulation short of flat prohibition? Often mentioned in connection with this argument are the Nazi research experiments where, despite absolutely no interference of any kind, absolutely nothing worthwile emerged from the torture, torment, and abuse suffered by the subjects used in those experiments. Although the Nazi experience is suggestive, it is hardly conclusive as to the real issue which is: In the absence of something like a Nazi social system, would there be greater medical progress in the United States if investigators were unencumbered by anything other than conscience, peer pressure, and legal liability? Would editorial policy suffice to prevent experimental abuse?

A third related question would demand data as to the correlation between protection of subjects and medical progress in general. That is, even if no question were raised about protection of subjects and physicians were entirely unencumbered by any mechanism of restraint, would medicine advance? The Nazi experiments are again relevant, but again inconclusive. More relevant perhaps is the developing drug lag in the United States which nears epidemic proportions in some fields. The question is whether current Food and Drug Administration (FDA) prohibitions of new drugs (regulations that mean $50 million and five years before a drug can enter the American market) do, in fact, on balance, cause less suffering, less harm, and better health than would an absolute laissez-faire market system restrained only by civil liability or other conventional mechanisms? Even if there were a constant risk of another Thalidomide disaster, does that justify the FDA approach to new drugs? In other words, even if a Thalidomide episode is prevented, does that provide an answer to whether the risk-benefit ratio for other forms of regulation would be less favorable? The same kind of questions may soon confront us for FDA regulation of psychological devices (Schwitzgebel, 1977).

A fourth question, not answerable by data but possibly even more important than questions for which data could lead to an answer, is this: If there were in fact a demonstrable, clear, positive correlation between research that required a lower standard of protection for human subjects and medical progress, why should such research be prohibited or encumbered so long as there is no deception, there is civil liability for negligence or fraud, and compensation for those who knowingly take the risks? Little has been done on the problem of compensation for research risk-takers despite the prevailing ethic that encourages free enterprise, at least as to economic matters (Adams and Shea-Stonum, 1975). It is apparently morally acceptable to allow poor people to survive in a manner that is clearly destructive of their dignity, autonomy, and health while it is morally abhorrent to allow people, poor or not, to sell their bodily organs or knowingly to take research risks with their health. The inconsistency would not vanish, but it might be more understandable if we really believed in the old adage that "if you have your health you have everything and if you do not, you have nothing." But, in view of the fact that people are allowed knowingly to accept all kinds of industrial health risks in exchange for profit, it is difficult to understand why medical research should be flatly denied a place in the "industrial economy."Furthermore, not for a moment do I in fact support or encourage commitment to the belief that good health is always the highest value. Acceptance of even a very restricted conception of civil liberty would compel rejection of such a view in favor of what my friend, Nicholas Kittrie, has called "the right to be different" (Kittrie, 1971) and what I have elsewhere spoken about as "the right to be unhealthy" (Shuman, 1977). My point here is, however, that even if one rejects our opinions about the right, to knowingly reject good health, the argument in favor of prohibiting one from knowingly accepting health risks in research, in exchange for profit, is hardly convincing.

I have raised these four questions not because I have ready answers but rather to suggest that the regulation of biomedical and behavioral research reflects an almost paradigm example of the "pendulum phenomenon" which often occurs in a democratic society. A problem or an abuse demands correction and this requires an overreaction to correct the perceived abuse. Eventually, the matter reaches some rational resolution but, at both ends of the pendulum swing, new problems are introduced that could have been avoided if it had not been necessary to overreact in order to compensate for the original abuse. We are now living through an era in which the pendulum is swinging to the prohibition end on the scale of research regulation to compensate for the alleged and actual abuses that obtained when the pendulum was for so long at the other extreme. However, there are already signs that the pendulum is going to return to some center position despite the flurry of regulatory activity of the last four or five years. Indeed, for just this reason the last report issued by the National Commission for the Protection of Human Subjects, containing the recommendations for institutional review boards, is in my opinion likely to be the most important report issued by the commission (DHEW 78-0008). It is so important because it is the most recent and perhaps next-to-final report, and thus reflects the maturity of judgment which has come from the three years of work the commission has done. The report does lay down a general programmatic conception of research regulation which in many respects constitutes an effective compromise between the no-sanction—laissez-faire end of the spectrum and the flat prohibition tendency reflected by some of the previous commission reports.

QUESTIONS ABOUT CAUSE OF VIOLENCE AND INTERVENTION

Thus far I have been discussing the restraints and regulations upon research in general without specific attention to research concerned with the question of violence. Of course, research of the latter type is subject to all the restraints that apply to biomedical or behavioral research in general, and thus the discussion thus far is applicable to research of the special kind with which we are concerned. It is at this point, however, where we must re-examine the problem of restraints. And here the question is, Are there any restraints more likely to be applicable where the subject of the research is aggression or violence?

What is interesting here is that while there are no specific restraints directed at research about aggression and violence, a good deal of the public and civil-liberties concern for the regulation of medical experimentation has been triggered by proposals or investigations directed at the control of violence. Typical of these cases have been those in which a drug was being considered or used to control or manipulate prisoners, psychosurgery considered for the purpose of controlling an aggressive person, chemical castration used to deal with sexual offenders, token and tier economies and other forms of behavior modification designed to enable custodians to better manage their institutionalized or incarcerated clients, electronic monitoring proposals, genetic screening, electroconvulsive therapy (ECT), electrical stimulation of the brain and psychotropic drugs (Goldstein, 1974). Except for psychosurgery, there have not been thus far any specific *federal* regulations directed at the control of research projects concerned with these types of interventions. And indeed, as to psychosurgery, there are only the recommendations of the National Commission for the Protection of Human Subjects, which have not yet been subjected to rule-making by the Department of Health, Education, and Welfare (HEW) (DHEW 77-0001). The national commission forwards its recommendations to the President and the Senate, and the President then instructs HEW to proceed to exercise its rule-making powers. The Secretary of HEW rejected the recommendations of the commission. But except for psychosurgery, there have not been any specific recommendations for any of the other types of intervention at the federal level. At the state level, however, there have been a number of efforts made specifically to regulate ECT, psychosurgery, behavior modification, and the use of psychotropic substances.

One of the most difficult aspects of the problem involved in regulating these several interventions is that, with the possible exception of electronic monitoring devices (Schwitzgebel, 1967), none of these interventions is used or usable only for the control or regulation of aggression and violence. Consequently, the regulation of research involving these various types of interventions often reflects the pressure that comes from the special concern about violence and aggression, while the need for these interventions in other situations continues, but subject to the special restraints imposed because the intervention could have been used for violence control. Particularly illustrative of this phenomenon has been the regulation of ECT and the proposed regulations on the use of psychotropic substances and psychosurgery. Although it is perfectly clear that ECT has been used to control violence and even to punish for violence, and although much of the literature on the use of psychosurgery, and particularly the important book by Mark and Ervin (1970), triggered the public concern about the use of such procedures for the control of violence and aggression, and although it is perfectly true that psychotropic substances are and have been used to help "domesticate" institutionalized populations so that their custodial managers could better handle the situation, it is equally true that each of these procedures has its more frequent application, and probably its more important use, for purposes other than control of violence or aggression.

In view of this, we must now ask an important and probably crucial question, Why have these procedures been singled out for specific concern since, like so many other biomedical or behavior interventions, they can be used for a wide spectrum of medical or control purposes, and not merely for the control of aggression or violence? The answer reveals, I believe, first, a deep confusion about aggression and violence and, second, a deep-seated commitment to the protection of what I previously referred to as the right to be different, the right to be unhealthy. The confusion that almost typically characterizes discussions about the use of biomedical or behavioral interventions to control violence stems from the failure to distinguish between a violent or aggressive personality and the causes for the commission of a crime. Many violent and aggressive acts which are regularly committed are not crimes and many crimes are not the consequence of an act of violence or aggression. There is probably more overt violence and aggression between 5 and 6 p.m. on any big-city freeway than is manifested by all the criminal conduct over a year in the same city. Yet for reasons not entirely clear, freeway violence and aggression are not typically subjects of crime control. Traffic offenses are ordinarily only misdemeanors and punished by fines or the deprivation of driving privileges, but not by institutionalization or incarceration. But I use the traffic-offense situation merely to illustrate. In our daily lives there are plenty of instances in which we experience aggressive and even violent conduct which is not deemed to be criminal. There are certainly cases in which aggressive conduct is even highly rewarded. The successful entrepreneurial personality type is likely to be highly aggressive, at least in business if not elsewhere, and other occupations reward aggressiveness if not violence. On the other hand, embezzlement characteristically is a crime that does not involve violence or aggression, as does much theft, as well as statutory economic and sex crimes. Despite the obvious distinction between crime and violence once it is drawn, discussions about the regulation of the biomedical or behavioral interventions of the kinds mentioned above continue to be belabored and encumbered by the confusion between aggressive personality and the causes of crime. An overt act that later is labeled a crime (when the actor is found guilty) may have been caused by the actor's aggressiveness or disposition to violence. However, it is entirely possible and frequently in fact the case that a person disposed to the use of violence and aggression commits an act that is subsequently labeled a crime and the cause is *not* the actor's disposition to violence or aggression. In other words, people whom we might wish to label violent or aggressive personality types may commit crimes for reasons other than their disposition to violence and aggression.

There are thus several different confusions that have plagued the careful, critical understanding necessary if we are to develop rational and reasonable regulations for biomedical and behavioral research with so-called violent individuals. First, it need be recognized that, although many interventions may be used to prevent or control violence, even procedures that seem to lend themselves most specifically to such control have other biomedical and behavioral uses. Second, it need be recognized that the cause of crime is not necessarily the disposition to aggression or violence, even when the individual has been properly labeled a violent personality type. A violent or aggressive personality type with plenty of money may express aggressivity in some socially acceptable way, or at least in a way that is not criminal. The same personality, deprived of economic opportunities, may resort to violence to secure some felt need. Poverty, poor housing, bad nutrition, lack of education, inadequate parents, poor peer-group environments, bad teachers, bad schools, etc., are more appropriately recognized as the causes of crime rather than the personality types of those who commit acts labeled as criminal.

The confusion here is generated by the use of the word "cause" and, as I have tried to explain elsewhere (Shuman, 1977), there is great need to analyze how this word functions in biomedical and behavioral contexts. I tried to show the word cause is often used in scientific discussions to cover up and substitute for sociopolitical considerations. If we want to argue about what should be done with criminal offenders, then the question of responsibility for the commission of a crime may require that we recognize that whatever the cause (be it genetic, physiochemical, or sociopolitical), certain consequences are appropriately attached to the commission of an act that has been identified as the act belonging to a particular individual. In this context (of responsibility), the concept of causation is not functioning the same way as it does when we ask the following different question: Regardless of the sociopolitical consequences of having been identified as the "owner" of the act now labeled as criminal, what is it about the personality of the actor that might be changed so that, when confronted by a future felt need, a different kind of response is more likely than the one that produced the present problem? The two questions are in no sense the same, and the failure to distinguish them is responsible for much of the difficulty experienced by those concerned with the control of aggression. It is conceivable that there may be genetic or organic, physiochemical processes that are regularly found in certain types of personalities and that these personalities regularly (generally, frequently, typically, etc.) resort to a given style of problem solution (with aggressivity or violence) (Mednick and Christiansen, 1977). Upon reading this I hope you do not hear the laughing ghosts of Lambroso et al., saying I told you so. I am not suggesting a revival of phrenology. Rather, I am suggesting that for some purposes it may be appropriate to conclude that there is a statistically significant correlation between *X* personality and a certain style of behavior. From this alone, however, it does *not* follow that changing the unique organic condition typically found in X types will cause such types to behave differently. And, conversely, it is also possible that, without changing the organic condition regularly found in *X* types, they may behave differently when factors other than their organic condition are regularly changed. To put it differently, the following two sentences are not equivalent:

1. *X* types regularly are found to have *X'* organic condition and regularly manifest *X"* behavior style when confronted by a certain type of situation.
2. *X* types regularly are found to have *X'* organic condition which causes *X"* behavior style when confronted by a certain type of situation.

X' organic condition may be a sufficient condition for the regular manifestation of *X"* behavior style, but it does not therefore follow that *X'* is a necessary condition for such behavior.

It may be the case that misfiring tissue in the amygdala, if destroyed, will change one's brain function so that there is afterward less of a disposition to resort to violence in solving certain types of problems. It may be the case that electrical stimulation of the pleasure centers in the brain may effectively prevent and perhaps even stop already initiated conduct which is deemed to be aggressive or violent. The most recent work of Heath (1977) suggests this possibility. It may be the case that regular use of certain psychotropic substances makes it possible for an individual to control his or her aggressivity, etc. (Itil and Mukhopadhyay, 1978). As medical and behavioral scientists, what we want to know, obviously, is: Are these hypotheses scientifically demonstrable, and if so, can we use this knowledge to deal with the kind of personality that is regarded as so aggressive or violent as to require institutional attention, or perhaps we should say, "so aggressive and violent in the wrong way," as to require institutional attention. What the civil libertarian is asking, however, is something entirely different. He or she asks not whether the hypothesis is confirmable, or even confirmed, nor whether that now available knowledge *can* be used to change *X* types, but rather whether *X* types should be changed (at all) and if so, should they be changed by changing their organic condition, since that condition has only been shown to be a sufficient, but not a necessary, condition for *X*" behavior style.

The Mark and Ervin book (1970), the escalating concern over crime control, and the failure of the conventional mechanisms for dealing with recidivisms have all combined to encourage medical and behavioral scientists to compress into one the different *can* and *should* questions about personality modification through organic intervention.

THE ARGUMENTS FOR AND AGAINST PROHIBITION

Have there been specific sanctions or restraints upon research directed at confirming the above type of hypothesis about correlations between organic conditions and aggressive or violent personalities? In my opinion the answer is no. Rather, the restraints that have been imposed have inhibited this kind of research more than research with the same kind of intervention, when the purpose of the research is to discover something other than mechanisms that can be used to alter the personality. Here we come again to the civil-rights protest against the co-mingling of the *can* and *should* questions, and it has been this protest and the research establishment's reaction to it that has generated the cluster of emotions, feelings, and attitudes that have typically interfered with the rational development of this subject. Is there not a right to be different, a right to choose to be unhealthy, a right to be aggressive, and perhaps even a right to have a propensity for violence? Are not these rights part of the central core of rights that constitutes the kind of civil right that distinguishes an open, democratic society from a closed, totalitarian one? If so, is not the need to protect these rights at least as great as the need for security?

What I find distressing is that, even granting the comparability of the need to protect autonomy and the need for security, why should research directed at the confirmation of a hypothesis about organicity and behavior be suppressed? The overreaction to the possibility that new knowledge may be abused seems sterile, especially in light of the enormously easier, cheaper, and more readily available mechanisms for the manipulation of masses, let alone individuals. The history of man's ability and willingness to use and abuse his fellow men makes it necessary that we accord proper respect to the feelings of those who fear abuse of possible new knowledge that might facilitate deliberate personality alterations. Yet, is it necessary to encumber research about violence and aggression with all of the current regulatory machinery to protect against fears that are legitimate? Feelings are as important as facts and perhaps more reliable than factual evidence in making some important decisions, but what is regrettable is that feelings, because they are so important, often are deemed an adequate substitute for facts and evidence. It seems to me that much of the overreaction by extremists to research on aggression and violence has been the result of such a substitution of feelings for facts. Furthermore, biomedical and behavioral research cannot be locked into a Pandora's box. Medical and behavioral research is an international enterprise. Regulations that prevent or diminish the vigor of certain types of research will only effectively prevent such research within the territory where the regulation is applicable. In the absence of universal regulation, the work will be done, and it would be regrettable if the search for scientific knowledge about brain function and its relation to aggression and violence became parochialized.

The argument of the extremist civil libertarian is then something like this: It is so important that we preserve our autonomy, which at the least means the right to be what we are, that we ought not even risk the possibility of acquiring knowledge that would make it possible to manipulate human beings so that they could be forced to be other than what they are. Consequently, research that might produce such knowledge ought to be prohibited. I suggest that such knowledge will be acquired anyway, if not in Houston or Detroit, then in the Houston or Detroit of some other country. Furthermore, a society that seeks to prevent the improper manipulation of people by the suppression of the search for knowledge about how we function is anyway not likely long to endure as an open, democratic society. Hence the argument for the prohibition or heavy regulation of certain kinds of research, although embedded in civil libertarian theory, is unconvincing precisely because, on balance, we risk a greater loss of our civil liberties rather than a preservation of them when the search for new knowledge is artificially suppressed. Furthermore, persons who suffer from uncontrollable aggressivity or a propensity to improper violence are deprived of their civil liberties when they might *wish* to have available the kind of knowledge that would enable someone to manipulate them. Particularly is this the case when they, themselves, would wish to be manipulated (Kelley, 1978). In which event, the question becomes: Do you have a right to own the kind of personality that you could wish to have changed and, if so, do you have a right to have people do research that may make it possible that when you wish to be changed you can be changed? The danger that you may be changed without wishing to be changed is the basis for the legitimate concern of the rational civil libertarian. I have not recommended nor do I now propose that this argument is so thin that there is no need for regulation. Rather I have argued against prohibition of certain kinds of research and against extremist kinds of regulation that would discourage research because of fears about the abuse of new knowledge. As Carl Cohen (1977) has eloquently, and I think persuasively, argued (in connection with DNA research):

> The penetration of every intellectual frontier threatens deeply held convictions. Every striking advance in human prowess frightens many, horrifies some and appears to a few as the profane invasion of the holy of holies. The difficulty lies not in discriminating between the real holy of holies and those only mistakenly supposed; it lies in the unwarranted assumption that there are any spheres of knowledge to which ingress is forbidden (p. 1205).

REFERENCES

Adams, B. R., and Shea-Stonum, M. Toward a theory of control of medical experimentation with human subjects: The role of compensation. *Case Western Reserve Law Review* 25:606-648, 1975.

Beecher, H. K. Ethics and clinical research. *N. Engl. J. Med.* 274:1354-1360, 1966.

Cohen, C. When may research be stopped? *N. Engl. J. Med.* 296:1203-1210, 1977.

DeBakey, M. E. Medical research and the Golden Rule. *J.A.M.A.* 203:132-134, 1968.

Goldstein, M. Brain research and violent behavior. *Arch. Neurol.* 30:1-35, 1974.

Heath, R. G. Modulation of emotions with a brain pacemaker. *J. Nerv. Ment. Dis.* 165:300-317, 1977.

Ingelfinger, F. J. The unethical in medical ethics. *An. Intern. Med.* 83:264-269, 1975.

Itil, T. M., and Mukhopadhyay, S. Pharmacological management of human values. *Mod Probl. Pharmacopsychiatry* 13:139-158, 1978.

Kelley, P. M. Prisoner access to psychosurgery: A constitutional perspective. *Pacific Law Journal*, 9:249-280, 1978.

Kittrie, N. *The Right to Be Different: Deviance and Enforced Therapy.* John Hopkins Press, Baltimore, 1971.

Mark, V. H., and Ervin, F. R. *Violence and The Brain.* Harper and Row, New York, 1970.

Mednick, S. A., and Christiansen, K. O. eds. *Biosocial Bases of Criminal Behavior.* Gardner Press, New York, 1977.

Schwitzgebel, R. Electronic innovation in the behavioral sciences. *Am. Psychol.* 25: 364-370, 1967.

Schwitzgebel, R. Federal regulation of psychological devices: An example of medical-political drift, in *Psychology in the Legal Process.* B. D. Sales, ed. Spectrum Publications, New York, 1977.

SHUMAN, S. I. *Psychosurgery and the Medical Control of Violence: Autonomy and Deviance*. Wayne State University Press, Detroit, 1977.

U. S. Department of Health, Education, and Welfare. *Report and Recommendations: Psychosurgery. DHEW Pub.* No. (05), 77-0001.

U. S. Department of Health, Education, and Welfare. *Report and Recommendations: Institutional Review Boards*. DHEW Pub. No. (OS), 78-0008.

WOODFORD, F. P. Ethical experimentation and the editor. *N. Engl. J. Med.* 286:892, 1972.

CASES

Clonce v. *Richardson*, 379 F. Supp. 338,1974.

Halushka v. *University of Saskatchewan*, 53 DLR 2d 436, 1965.

Hyman v. *Jewish Chronic Disease Hospital*. 251 N.Y.S. 2d 818, Rev'd 258 N.Y.S. 2d 397, 1965.

Jobson v. *Henne*, 355 F. 2d 129, 1966.

Kaimowitz v. *Michigan Department of Mental Health*, Civil No. 73-15434-AW (Cir. Ct., Wayne Co. Michigan, July 10, 1973).

Knecht v. *Gillman*, 488 F. 2d 1136, 1973.

Merriken v. *Cressman*, 364 F. Supp. 913, 1973.

Price v. *Sheppard*, 239 N.W. 2d 905, 1976.

Wyatt v. *Aderholt*, 503 F. 2d 1305, 1974.

Smith, R. J. Electroshock experiment at Albany violates ethics guidelines, *Science* 198:383-386, 1977.

Part IV

TREATMENT OF THE VIOLENT INDIVIDUAL

CHAPTER 20

Psychological Treatment of Imprisoned Offenders

HANS TOCH

Given the unsavory reputation of rehabilitation, my willingness to address this topic labels me as a masochist with a blind penchant for anachronisms. Today, everyone accepts two fundamental premises. The first is that non-serious offenders can be left alone; the fashionable phrase for this is that they must be "maintained in the community." The second premise has to do with Institutions of Last Resort. If a criminal is worth worrying about, the experts tells us, he or she must be equitably warehoused. The storage interventions the experts prescribe are not necessarily sterile: No one opposes decency, and this means that we may provide even dangerous inmates with such remedial services as filling their cavities, giving them sleeping pills, supplying prevocational training, cubicles with teaching machines, sanctuaries from fellow inmates, and links to the outside.[1] There is also allowance made for hard-core psychiatric attention, provided an

[1] Among those who draw this distinction are Morris and Hawkins (1977), who write:

> The cage is not a sensible place in which to cure the criminal. . . . But this does *not* mean that such treatment programs as we now have in prisons should be abandoned; quite the contrary, they urgently need expansion. No one of any sensitivity can visit any of our mega-prisons without recognizing that they contain, as in all countries, populations that are disproportionately illiterate, unemployed, vocationally untrained, undereducated, psychologically disturbed, and socially isolated. It is both in the prisoners' and the community's best interest to help them remedy these deficiencies.

offender is psychotic, and as long as he or she is psychotic. If an inmate has the misfortune of periodically going into remission, it is customary for a shuttle to convey him from a mental health setting to the prison yard and back, as the occasion demands. The inmate may also be warehoused in an outpatient capacity, and maintained on medication.

At the outset, I must assert that though there has been considerable talk about a shift from a rehabilitative view of penology to some other view, I see this transmutation as illusory on both counts. The first myth has to do with the Age of Rehabilitation that is presumably coming to a close.

Some time ago, Sykes (1958), whose prison book is still the undisputed classic, wrote that "allegiance to the goal of rehabilitation remains at the verbal level, an expression of hope for public consumption rather than a coherent program with an integrated professional staff" (p. 34). Where clinicians have existed and operated in prisons, theirs has usually been a second-class citizenship, with ill-defined or circumscribed goals. The rehabilitative thrust we have aborted has consisted—with few exceptions—of organizational ghettos, of fragmented efforts that have not only been poorly conceived, but have been insulated from their settings and from the rest of their clients' careers through the criminal justice system. The sharp break between formal therapy, organizational climate and routine processing of offenders has foredoomed any possible impact therapeutic experiences might have had. Such experiences were also usually intrinsically impotent to begin with, because they were casually and inappropriately targeted, with therapists doing whatever they learned in graduate school to a hopelessly misdiagnosed group of clients, most of whom reacted indifferently, while some relieved their boredom by baiting, mimicking, or otherwise humoring their therapists. This fact is not surprising because, as Redl (1951) has pointed out, we have been "trying to develop ways of treatment for what we do not know how to treat" (p. 146).

Even this portrait is deceptive, however, and it can be overdrawn. Most inmates live and function in an environment that demands a pretense of cynicism from persons who are more vulnerable than they admit (Toch, 1975). Prison is a milieu of "pluralistic ignorance,"[2] and in our context this means that inmates labor under the mistaken assumption that aloof

---

Nevertheless, it should be recognized that rehabilitative programs to that end are not *the* purpose or even *one* purpose of imprisonment. . . . There is a sharp distinction between the purposes of imprisonment and the opportunities for the training and assistance of prisoners that may be properly pursued within those purposes (pp. 67-68).

posturing and antistaff facades are required by inmate norms. This is the same point we could make if we were talking about slum schools or about any setting in which everyone thinks that everyone else is tough, inviolate, and hostile to whoever is their keeper, while privately admitting that there is much to be said for the warmth, support, recognition, and assistance that institutional custodians (whoever they may be) could provide.

Goffman (1961) has described the fact that "typically, the inmate when with fellow inmates will support the counter-mores and conceal from them how tractably he acts when alone with the staff." According to Goffman, mental hospital patients who felt themselves heavily involved in therapy "tended to present their favorable view of psychotherapy only to the members of their immediate clique" (Goffman, 1961: p. 65). The same point has been made for incarcerated soldiers by Cloward (1956), who found these soldiers privately thirsting for rehabilitation, while publicly contemptuous of it. Hard data that are supportive of this portrait are provided by Wheeler (1961) who found that inmates favor therapeutic encounters while laboring under the impression that their peers hold antistaff norms.

The antistaff theme and the vulnerability theme are separable, though both work in the same direction. The antistaff issue relates to assumptions that are prevalent in prison about appropriate social distance. They have to do with the fact that inmates and staff each assume that their peers demand a staff-inmate chasm, which they (at some level) personally deplore. The vulnerability issue has to do with the perceived need for a cool, inviolable facade. This stance has been diagnosed by Redl among delinquents, and he writes that "admitting value sensitivity, just like admitting hunger for love, is quite face-losing in our youngsters" (Redl, 1959: p. 45).

Vulnerability is built into prisons—as it is built into hospitals—by the fact that total institutions promote regression in their clients (Goffman, 1961). Sykes (1958) pointed out that typical prison regimes pose "a profound threat to the prisoner's self-image because they reduce the prisoner to the weak, helpless, dependent status of childhood. . . . For the adult who has escaped such helplessness with the passage of years, to be thrust back into childhood's helplessness is . . . painful, and the inmate of the prison must somehow find a means of coping with this issue" (pp. 75-76).

---

[2] "Pluralistic ignorance" was a term coined by the psychologist F. H. Allport in the 1930s. The extreme version of this phenomenon is defined by Krech and Crutchfield (1948) as a state in which "no one believes, but in which everyone believes that everyone else believes" (p. 389).

From a psychoanalytic perspective, the most plausible outcome of regression is a transference relationship with staff and/or other inmates. In a controlled therapeutic milieu this fact could be welcome, but in prison it can be dangerous on two counts: prison norms create conflict for the transference-seeking inmate, and a transference in the wrong hands is a sick relationship, or at least one that must be watched. I suppose that is what some people mean when they complain that inmates are "manipulative."

Before returning to this point I should like to deal with the second misapprehension, which is the contention that prisons can be sterile warehouses in which no treatment occurs. The issue is in part a problem of semantics, and it relates to the connotations that are assigned to treatment. If treatment connotations are nineteenth-century analogs drawn from physical medicine (the much-maligned "medical model") most prisons are by definition devoid of treatment, but so is most of psychotherapy, as well as 99 percent of the familiar human services spectrum. A less restrictive definition, which may include medically based psychotherapy but provides room for other approaches, makes it less possible to run treatment-free prisons, though it allows us to run treatment-impoverished ones. It is this definition that guides me in this chapter.

WHAT IS "TREATMENT"?

The essence of treatment is its *goal,* which is the achievement of personal growth or of constructive change in people. This goal may be stated negatively, by stressing the past personal experiences whose impact we try to neutralize; it may also be stated positively, by highlighting various regenerative or growth-producing experiences we furnish through our sophisticated treatment ministrations. Realistically, psychotherapy must achieve both positive and negative ends; it must disconfirm residues of a destructive past, and it must buttress, rebuild, and provide its clients with new attitudes, values, and skills.

The goal of treatment is always change. Since procedures must be designed and targeted to achieve change, we may define treatment as *planned individual change.* In this sense, our closest ally is probably not medicine but the field of education. To be more accurate, our ally (particularly with adult offenders) is the field of re-education which, as noted by Freud, "is something quite different from education of the immature" (Freud, 1925).

The psychological perspective that is by far most germane to re-education is the social learning perspective, whose best-known exponent is Albert Bandura. Bandura has listed the practical implication of his views for therapy:

> Change programs based upon social learning principles differ from those relying heavily on conversational methods in the *content,* the *locus,* and the *agents* of treatment. With regard to content, treatment procedures are mainly applied to the actual problem behaviors requiring modification, instead of to verbal reports of troubles. .Change agents, therefore, devote the major portion of their time to altering the social conditions governing behavior rather than conversing about them.
>
> To enhance successful results, treatment is typically carried out in the natural settings in which the problems arise. It may be conducted in the home, in schools, in work situations, or in the larger community, depending on the source of the critical determinants. . . .
>
> The third factor which partly determines the success of a change program is concerned with who implements the corrective practices. Social learning approaches do not regard professionals as the exclusive dispensers of treatments. Professionals have expertise to identify the determinants of behavior and to specify the optimal conditions for producing desired changes. But the most beneficial treatments are generally carried out under professional guidance by persons who have intensive contact with the clients and can therefore serve as powerful mediators of change. They are the ones who exercise substantial influence over the very conditions that govern the behavior to be modified. Unless they too alter their practices, any changes, whether produced by professionals or otherwise, may not endure for long. (Bandura, personal communication).

It is difficult to argue that change efforts of the kind Bandura refers to are not occurring in prison. Even if we expect no behavior modification impact from prison reward structures, and we ignore experiments such as the quasitherapeutic communities prevalent in the federal system, we are left with numerous daily staff-inmate contacts in scores of prisons that in theory may have constructive influence.

Once we accept the principle that unlicensed, nonprofessional staff can be (and probably should be) the firing line of social-learning efforts, we welcome any data that show us that nontherapeutic staff can make an impact on inmates. In this connection, we owe a debt to Glaser, who demonstrated (1964) that prison workshop supervisors, correctional officers, and chaplains were viewed by reformed inmates as critical influences. We are simultaneously heartened by Glaser's finding that counselors and other formal treatment personnel were never mentioned by the inmates as having made a difference in their lives.[3]

---

[3] The feeling, apparently, is mutual. Wheeler (1961) reports that "a larger proportion of custody than of treatment staff members felt that treatment programs could be successful for 'the great majority of inmates,' and that most inmates 'desire to improve themselves' while in the institution" (p. 243, footnote 11).

Fritz Redl, who is a member in good standing of the healing profession, speaks with more authority than I do when he writes, "We are . . . deeply impressed with the great opportunities that the closeness to daily life, daily conflicts and mistakes offers the clinician, in contrast to the traditional seclusion of the action-remote interview techniques" (Redl, 1951: p. 144). "Some things can be talked down," Redl notes, "others can be listened down. There are a few that have to be lived down, or they will not budge" (p. 137). Redl recalls the lessons we can learn from play therapy, in which "it is . . . a person who is perceived by the child as part of his 'natural habitat or life space' with some pretty clear role and power in his daily living, as contrasted to the therapist, to whom he is sent for 'long range treatment' " (Redl, 1959: p. 41).

The context of treatment must be "respectable" in the client's everyday world if this is at all possible. Beside the bureaucratization and rigidity of helping professions, their artificiality is one reason that being classified as a counselor or some such becomes a serious liability to the exercise of a therapeutic role. In fact, the formal role becomes the kiss of death if the role encumbent keeps public records and makes decisions or recommendations about his or her clients, since gatekeeping hopelessly contaminates therapy, no matter where it occurs.

Glaser's examples suggest that significant impact or change may occur in custodial settings, *provided* that:

1. The place where change occurs has dominant or salient work to be done (such as plumbing, carpentry, running Sunday school, or clerking for a guard) which frames a relationship that is a vehicle for change.
2. If possible, a legitimizing peer ingroup develops which approves of staff/inmate links and/or
3. The staff and inmate(s) are ecologically insulated from pressures that emanate from the prison-at-large.
4. Staff-inmate links shift from instrumental task orientation to links featuring supportiveness, warmth and loyalty, permitting modeling, emulation, and spontaneous influence.

Three quick comments are in order by way of exegesis. First, task-oriented enclaves are not exceptional in large institutions. Tables of organization may look impressive to outsiders, but the experienced reality of institutional life consists of the immediate environment of inmates, which (with the exception of crowd assignments such as kitchen work) is apt to feature miniworlds and intimate face-to-face groups. Second, the change process described is not at variance with "depth" views of treatment. Psychoanalysis has taught us that personal relationships are change vehicles; Maxwell Jones has noted (in his version of social learning) that work is a laboratory for exploring relationships. I may downgrade the content of social learning by implying that any task that is conjointly engaged in will do to get the ball rolling. I also may be leaving the impression that the real reason for working together is to hide evolving staff/inmate intimacy from the prying eyes of inmate subcultures. There is much more involved, obviously.

THE SOCIAL LEARNING PROCESS

In his view of social learning, Bandura (1977) highlights the importance of modeling. The perspective also assumes that there must be incentives and rewards for learning, and a substantive cognitive component, which means (in part) that what is learned must be perceived as useful by the person who is learning it. The three conditions implicit here are a credible change agent, a satisfying learning experience, and useful or meaningful learning content. To put the matter even more simplistically, the person to be changed must learn through tangible success in a supportive climate that fosters internalization of change content. Maxwell Jones (1962, 1979) uses the social learning concept somewhat differently. The process involves modeling, but the change agent is also a catalyst of group process. Change requires feedback, with the accent on revealed feelings and latent agendas in behavior. The juiciest experiences are interpersonal difficulties or (even better) crises. Social learning occurs in failure experiences, provided these are analyzed and their lessons internalized in a supportive context.

I do not mean to undersell the common elements in these two views. Jones and Bandura both prize real-life learning experiences, and prefer "natural" change agents to artificial influences. Both value the "here and now" experiences of persons-to-be-changed, as learning (hence, as "treatment") laboratories. Both Jones and Bandura would see learner activity as requisite to change. Jones refers to "living-learning" in describing this link, and Bandura talks of the person exploring new opportunities that his natural environment affords. In referring to the therapeutic community inmate, Jones writes:

> If his interest can be obtained in some simple and familiar work, and particularly if the occupational therapist can enter into a supportive relationship with him, even the most elementary occupation may be therapeutic; it may bring out and direct constructively a variety of emotions which have been denied outlet, and it may do something to offset the restrictions of the mental-hospital regime. . . (an effectively utilized

constructive work group) is capable of leading to better contact with reality, to behavior more in accordance with social standards, and to the foundations of self-esteem (Jones et al., 1956, p. 343).

Not surprisingly, I am now back to my starting point, extolling supervised activities as desirable requisites of rehabilitation. But, if I take what I said seriously, I have some problems:

One problem is that my plumbing foremen may not see themselves as rehabilitation agents, and this suggests that their influence (as differentiated from their plumbing) may be unsystematic, unplanned, and haphazard. This spontaneity is a feature that any respectable social learning theorist would have to deplore. On close inspection, in fact, the average influential staff member is mainly an unself-conscious source of genuineness, benevolence, and personal interest. He claims no change technology or skill as group catalyst. He is described as a "good Joe," a "decent guy" who inspires respect, shows integrity and cares. At best, he sounds like a part-time Rogerian, but violates this description by giving homespun advice, drawing on his experiences as husband and grandfather.

Worse, everyone sees the treatment influence as extracurricular, with the foreground occupied by shared activities or work problems. Issues of group dynamics tend to be clumsily mediated, and any transparent "father-offspring" transference is matter-of-factly accepted as a corollary of age differences.

I am left, at first glance, with two choices: I can scrap Albert Bandura and Maxwell Jones to save my prison foreman, or I can process my foreman through an in-service training program, and convert him into a behavior technologist or therapeutic community catalyst. I shall do neither, and Bandura and Jones (as it happens) would not want me to. Why are the three of us so indulgent of the free-wheeling foreman? Why are we willing to live with the drawbacks of spontaneous, unsophisticated, extracurricular treatment influences, unless they become grotesque?

The foreman's influence strikes us as potent because it is transactionally framed, in the sense that the inmate determines the extent and quality of the influence. The sticky issue of "consent" does not arise for treatment, though it does with respect to job assignment and group membership. The genuineness of the changer-as-model is also enhanced by the foreman's unselfconsciousness, which reduces social distance and deletes a potential credibility gap.

The manifest content of desirable change for offenders has to do with their law-abiding citizenship, constructive interpersonal dealings and acquired work habits. Such content is communicable through a wide range of experiences, provided these include partnership in work, benevolent conflict resolutions, demonstrations of personal and work-related competence, and a model who is visibly content with a noncriminal life style.

More dynamic aspects of desirable change have to do with dependency problems that show up in expectations of, and relationships to, authority; childhood traumas that enhance the attractiveness of peer groups who value preadolescent goals (or worse) highlighting physical combativeness and short-term hedonism or displays of impulsivity; a consistently alienated perspective, which views the world as a dog-eat-dog place in which violence and expropriation are plausible means to desired ends; developmental deficits, such as complete insensitivity to the perspectives of other people. Such dispositions and frames of reference are developed through cumulative long-term experience, much of which is redundant and self-engineered. For treatment to be successful, it must disconfirm such experiences. This, to say the least, is no mean task, but our foreman, because of his lack of sophistication, is apt to be oblivious to the odds. He consistently and disarmingly becomes the dependable, nurturing, and empathetic parental figure that was absent in the lives of his charges. He disconfirms authority-related expectations by disregarding (and hence, extinguishing) behavior that is based on subcultural norms; he counters inmate cynicism with naive optimism and disarming faith. He connects and welds pipes, blissfully ignorant of the syllogism that only shortcuts produce success. What is worse, he indiscriminately praises his charges (a prized reinforcement) for modest advances to long-term goals.

The Meek-but-Sturdy Proletarian Healer of the Disaffected is an ideal portrait, and one may exaggerate its import. My point is not that prison foremen shall inherit the therapeutic spectrum, but that they can form part of it. Glaser told us that *some* inmates ascribed critical influences to *some* supervisors. Such transactions make psychological sense, and the paradigm is worth emulating.

SUPPORT SYSTEMS

We now turn to prison chaplains, whose influence, says Glaser, transcends their numbers.[4] As a treatment agent, the chaplain enjoys diplomatic immunity. For one, he offers confidentiality, and his primary loyalties are disaffiliated from the source of his paycheck. Though a chaplain can overidentify with secular authorities (one is reputed to have led a charge

---

[4] Like other prison staff, the chaplain can ensure his lack of impact by defining himself as a specialist. The chaplain whose role definition is formally religious or ministerial is equivalent to the "purely custodial" guard.

in a riot), such instances are mercifully rare. Chaplains are potential links to the community, and offenders are permitted vulnerability-lacunae in relation to significant others in the free world. The ambiguity of the chaplain's role is a clear asset. No matter how many diplomas or certificates in pastoral counseling a chaplain may display, his contacts with parishioners occur under higher auspices than Carl Rogers'. Moreover, religious participation (like welding) is activity that has nontherapeutic content, accommodating different dosages of intimacy and relatedness. And though the normative system of the Real Man in prison proscribes trust in others, it is not clear that this proscription includes chaplains. A final point relates to change content: the chaplain's sphere includes concerns with morality and ethics, which (in translation) permits frontal attacks on impulsivity; it allows the skilled chaplain to aid the inmate in shoring up control functions of his ego and superego. Along the same psychoanalytic lines, one recalls that the chaplain's role is quasiparental by definition; it permits transference but has some built-in protection against countertransference.

Despite the chaplain's assets, some chaplains are more likely to be therapeutic than others, while inmates differ in their susceptibility to religiously tinged interventions. As a modality, chaplains have special attributes, which probably lie in the assistance they may offer to conflicted inmates, and in the support they mobilize for those who feel lonely and abandoned.

The chaplain is primarily a psychological support system, and his rehabilitative impact is a testimonial to the now-unfashionable link between neurosis, vulnerability, and criminal activity. This is an issue that increasingly arises with the diversion of nonserious offenders from prison, because of the widespread tendency to equate seriousness and chronicity of offenses with portraits of professional, subcultural, and psychopathic offenders. The corollaries of the assumption that penny-ante offenders are confused and weak, while hardened criminals are sturdy and self-sufficient, are an obstacle to the appropriate targeting of prison therapy. It is a premise that must be faced and understood because it is prevalent among practitioners and criminologists, among the public at large, and among inmates themselves.

The prevalent practitioner view highlights offense history as a measure of the offender's intentional dangerousness, which is dispassionately reacted to through the length of his prison sentence. This view is understandably buttressed by the public's classification of offenders in terms of the danger they pose. Less understandably, respected criminologists concur, because (as sociologists) they view "criminal norms" as motives, and see offender lives as subculturally sanctioned "careers." Lastly, for serious offenders the perspective is face-saving, because anyone would prefer to be seen as professional, vicious, or loyal than as conflicted or vulnerable.

STRESS AND COPING

Since everyone agrees that warehousing should be humane, we find less resistance to stress-reducing interventions than to measures addressed to the cementing of resources. The permissive stance to crisis intervention is undergirded by the prison's sensitivity to suits charging staff with negligence. It is negligent, for example, to ignore despondency that may imply suicide potential, or to set aside an inmate's claims, no matter how vague, that he is in danger. As a result, "protective" settings are populated by inmates whose problems (examined in the light of day) include demonstrably long-term inabilities to cope (Toch. 1975, 1977).

In this connection, the correctional officer's role, both as diagnostician and rehabilitation agent, becomes relevant. This is the case because officers are the frontline of prison and see the inmate more continuously and more frequently than anybody else. They also talk with inmates, although in the past, officer-inmate conversation was frowned upon. Even though residual taboos may persist among inmates and officers, the officer is at least the target of inmate requests, because he mediates services to inmates. The officer's contact with inmates also supplies him with other rich data. Guards see inmates interact, and they view them at work and at play, at rest and active, eating and fasting. The range of behavioral cues in such contacts is substantial, and the patterning is often dramatic. Unavoidably, each officer encounters mood changes, developing behavioral trends and chronicity of habit that are of clinical import. The officer sees inmates withdraw into shells, or watches them as they become irritable, obsessed, or panic-stricken.

Faced with such data, the officer may ignore what he sees. He has every right to ignore it (unless he infers violence potential) because he has not been sanctified as a "shrink." Moreover, the officer's superiors see him as a walking burglar alarm and human conveyor belt.

Ironically, officers do ignore their job-empoverished mandates and react humanely to some of their charges' plights on occasion. They may react by invoking institutional resources on behalf of inmates, relaxing and modulating rules to reduce stresses, helping define problems in quasi-counseling sessions, encouraging peers to be available to the inmate, arranging transfers to congenial settings, and pressing medical or mental health personnel to define inmates as a mental health problem (Toch, 1978).

Although the officers' concerns are ameliorative, this does not preclude an inmate's experiencing long-term impact. One way in which impact occurs is by freeing persons in crisis from impediments to self-regeneration. If this statement seems ludicrous, it is well to remember that the most salient finding in therapeutic research is that control group members tend to improve. The line between treatment and nontreatment must be drawn around interventions that work in partnership with self-restorative forces where these exist.

A second feature of what guards do is that they manipulate such environmental features as inmate work, solitude, recreation, and official information. This approach is much less drastic than its counterpart, the use of medication to rearrange *people* so they can face their *environment.* By knowing himself not to be a "shrink," the officer must treat his inmate as if he were normal but upset. Though this strategy has limits, it may work better than do interventions based on the saliency of symptomatology, with their relative lack of respect for the forces of ego which, Freud tells us, are the allies of therapy.

Exceptionally dramatic incidents involving guard impact are of a different order. They involve young inmates who are usually extreme discipline problems, and who have an "arrangement" with authorities involving recurring cycles of acting out and punishment. These cycles are redundant because they confirm interlocking expectations. The authorities know that the inmate is a troublemaker, and the inmate knows, as he has known since childhood, that adults are arbitrary, cruel, and malevolent.

But this game is not half as congenial as it looks, because it is an ineffective management strategy and leaves the inmate with thwarted dependency needs. Possibly as a result of ambivalence, there are occasional instances of drastic "conversion" and behavior change when the cycle is broken through disconfirmation. Such incidents generally involve a guard who refuses to label his inmates, overlooks insubordination, and tries to form relationships with his charges. The potency of such encounters can be documented by reviewing the subsequent career of the officer's client, which is often trouble-free.

PLAYING THE NORMS

Inmates and juvenile judges have spread tales of callow youths who acquire or cement criminal values and skills while they are incarcerated—at the knees, so to speak, of seasoned offenders. These sagas are largely misleading on at least two counts: statistically, younger inmates have much more disruptive and destructive impact on older inmates than vice versa (Toch, 1977); whatever influence older, more mature inmates have on younger inmates, and on each other, is more stabilizing than it is crime-inducing.

Traditionally, prison inmates—particularly, prison senior citizens—seek to "do (their) own time" (Sykes, 1958). Many such inmates, however, have one or two select friends with whom they engage in reciprocal crisis intervention when the occasion demands it; older inmates also do amateur counseling with younger inmates (Glaser, 1964).

Spontaneous inmate force fields of this kind can be exploited, harnessed, and upgraded, as has been demonstrated by Jones and his students as well as by innovators in residential treatment programming for youth. In guided group interaction and its variants, peer pressures have their polarities "reversed" (Vorrath and Brendthro, 1974) so that gang norms support and promote non-toughness, sensitivity, collaborative behavior, and self-knowledge.

In the hands of skillful catalysts, a group culture may be created—preferably in a small institution or a protected unit—such that inmates may explore their own (and each other's) patterns of antisocial conduct and design solutions to life problems that do not involve addictive behavior, stealing, and exploding. Through the use of ancillary techniques such as sociodrama (Jones, 1949) new solutions may be tested or rehearsed despite the artificiality of the prison environment. Other rehearsal opportunities are provided through innovative deployment of furloughs (Toch, 1967) and of contacts with significant others in the outside world.

PSYCHOLOGY AND COUNSELING IN PRISONS

So far, this chapter may look like a protracted digression. My topic is the offender, and I have discussed inmates. I have also said little about "treaters" in the usual sense of the word.

The first transgression rests on the fact that currently "live" offenders of consequence are not available to us *except* in prison. This picture could be changed through aftercare or halfway facilities, should such be created, but parole as presently constituted does not help. The parole officer's 10-minute hour is largely a surface encounter, no matter what offenders may say about the obtrusiveness of their parole experience.

The second problem rests on my desire to avoid the quagmire of therapy assessment and the complexities of the civil rights issue. I am certain (as noted before) that offender treatment is in a fetal stage, and that innovative therapeutic models for offender populations remain to be invented. Documentation is not available for some potentially innovative programs.[5] Most documented interventions appear to center on inviting but unchal-

---

[5] Innovative programs for serious offenders are often expensive and/or controversial, and therefore have an excellent chance of being prematurely terminated.

lenging populations (such as amenable delinquents) which do not help us to build a model for formal treatment of serious offenders.

The complexity of the civil rights issue has been compounded by the emphasis on "consent" questions we must pose to clients who do not know to what they are consenting (Morris, 1974), and the prevalence of gatekeeper roles that get confused with treatment roles. I have already said that as long as prison therapists feed data and recommendations to decision makers, there is little point in maintaining that they can do therapy.[6] By the same token, I see no point in setting up staff members to be insulated and isolated. The danger exists now, as has been shown by a survey of the federal system, which—as of 1976—included 103 full-time psychologists, compared to only 15 in 1966, when rehabilitation was presumably "alive." This survey (Powitzky, 1978) showed psychologists complaining "that they were not being allowed to participate enough in the correctional process," while "administrators/managers requested more involvement in the overall correctional process through consultation, staff training, and general program development" (p. 9).

The key, according to a federal task force (Powitzky, 1978), lies in the range of staff involvement. Though graduate training in psychology may be some day weakened or subverted by "professional" lobbyists, the scientist-clinician model today is still in ascendance. This means that most clinical psychologists are competent scientists, as well as being formally trained as clinicians. If we enrich the psychologist's treatment role, we may simultaneously deploy him into respected nontreatment functions (such as those listed by administrators) which link the psychologist to the organization without contaminating his relationships with clients.

The prospect strikes me as particularly bright because the most obvious functions one might add to the psychologist's roster indirectly enhance his treatment impact. The functions (some, already exercised) are those of facilitating organizational reform, participation in training and research, and "consultation" with other prison staff:

Organizational development. In prison, the enlightened top administrator faces many problems that cry out for innovative solutions. These problems include the orchestration of service delivery, staff morale and job enrichment, inmate violence and victimization, alternatives to discipline, racial tensions, community links, and the converting of new ideas into new programs. To face and solve such problems, the administrator needs help in mobilizing staff participation, creating staff-inmate groups, dealing with

[6] This statement is not an *a priori* dictum, but a corollary that neatly follows from prevalent assumptions about the requisites for a therapeutic or helping relationship (Toch, 1979).

external resistances to change, designing and documenting innovations so that they may "sell." The assistance needed to get these jobs done lies in such areas as group dynamics and the ability to exercise catalytic leadership of groups, the design of change-relevant experiences and ancillary data sources, and the conducting of research that evaluates change and buttresses successful experimentation with relevant impact data.

The psychologist who can exercise such functions may make many friends in the process and win the sort of trust that makes his or her treatment role viable. He or she may also, by virtue of being a psychologist, attend to the client impact of organizational programs and bolster their resocializing influence on inmates. This statement holds whether the actual clients of the program at issue are inmates or staff, because the two are functionally intertwined. The officer whose ideas are respected, for example, will spontaneously think in terms of resolving on-the-job problems, which invariably involve his inmates. Human service programs that are designed with staff and inmate participation are most prone to be rehabilitative, because those who are likely to subvert them after implementation are partners in their design.

Participation in training and research. As a trainer, the psychologist has the job of preparing prison staff to solve human relations and mental health problems they encounter at work.[7] This function may be exercised if the psychologist is familiar with the gamut of on-the-job problems that arise in the institution, taps the ingenuity of staff members in working out innovative solutions, and designs learning experiences that are dramatic, realistic, and compatible with relevant theory and data. This is a stiff prescription, but it does not pose impossible tasks. It requires the trainer to learn by spending time in all sorts of institutional settings as a participant-observer, an experience that may prove invaluable in therapeutic work. It entails tapping the problem-solving skills of other staff members, which engenders mutual respect and colleagueship. It finally means devising non-classroom learning experiences, including role-playing, the use of critical incidents, and the deployment of supervised inmate-staff confrontations. Good training may also involve trainees in institutional research exercises that sharpen their information-gathering skills and correct for stereotypes of other staff members and inmates. Such exercises may include some that

---

[7] In such training, I am not suggesting content involving simplified definitions from the Diagnostic and Statistical Manual (DSM), listings of symptoms and "cues to watch for." Diagnosis is *not* a science, and there is no shame in admitting the fact. Once we admit that diagnosis is an art, lay persons (unencumbered by the mystique of professionalism) may contribute their own hypotheses to the assessment process. The point obviously does not apply to medical problems.

are clinically relevant, such as interviewing inmates who are under stress or participants in violent confrontations.

In-house research is potentially variegated. Though it is somewhat limited in scope, it may address problems that are relevant to their setting, which no outsider could address without prior familiarization. Such problems could include documenting the impact of subsettings on various types of inmates (Toch, 1977), the matching of services and staff to clients, inventories of unmet needs, and client reactions to prison programs and practices. Knowledge of this kind is invaluable not only to administrators but also to therapists. It facilitates the appropriate targeting of treatment and links therapy to ongoing programs and interventions elsewhere in the institution.

Staff consultation. Where the therapist cannot treat, he or she can often help exercise the function indirectly by helping other staff (or the inmate's peers) to diagnose and address inmate problems. The psychologist may do so by working with a given staff member or peer group, by linking staff groups, and by experimenting, where possible, with "teaming" of the sort that is popular, in theory at least, in hospital settings. A team member is not a ghetto resident, nor an authority figure, nor a person who "does his thing" under different auspices in reshaped groups. A team is a functional unit designed to address the unique problems posed by a client. The membership includes whatever persons (psychiatrist, chaplain, fellow-inmates, etc.) seem to best serve the interest of the client. Ideally the team also includes the client, who must not be an object dissected in *absentia* in a democratic version of a case conference.

I have some dreams about teams, but this is not the place to unveil them. Suffice it to add that consultation permits use of a number of options, beside one-to-one encounters of consultant and consultee. The aims of consultation are also varied; there is not only the presenting problem (such as "What do I do about Jones's 'Dear John' letter, and the fact that he is talking about killing himself?") but more general and long-term concerns. This means working out solutions for analogous future problems (such as other inmates who have disloyal spouses or make suicidal threats) and the development of competence in helping, and of collaborative links that may be mobilized when needed. Consultation may also involve the use of outside resources should the primary consultant feel that these can supplement his or her skills. Such resources are always best deployed in response to demand, and never because the consultant feels they might help. The same point holds for the consultant.

APOLOGIA

The problem with trying new ideas is that they never manifest themselves in the tentative, modest guise that is commensurate with their raw, untested origin. The joy of unleashed creativity tends to be exercised at the expense of caution, and (occasionally) of quality control. I ask that the reader consider this paper as an exploratory bid, which may lead to further dialogue.

ACKNOWLEDGMENTS

If this paper has redeeming features, they derive from the constructive and thoughtful criticism of an early draft by Profs. Albert Bandura and Daniel Glaser, Dr. Maxwell Jones, Pres. Vincent O'Leary, Hon. Stephen Chinlund, and Dr. Robert Powitzky. I am grateful for this assistance.

REFERENCES

BANDURA, A. *Social Learning Theory.* Prentice-Hall, Englewood Cliffs, N. J., 1977.

CLOWARD, R. Session four, in *New Perspectives for Research in Juvenile Delinquency.* H. L. Witmer and R. Kotinsky, eds. U. S. Department of Health, Education and Welfare, Children's Bureau, Washington, D.C., 1956.

FREUD, S. Foreword, to Aichhorn, A. *Wayward Youth,* 1925. Meridian Edition, Meridian Books, New York, 1955.

GLASER, D. *The Effectiveness of a Prison and Parole System.* Bobbs-Merrill, Indianapolis, 1964.

GOFFMAN, E. *Asylums: Essays on the Social Situation of Patients and Other Inmates.* Doubleday (Anchor), Garden City, New York, 1961.

JONES, M. Acting as an aid to therapy in a neurosis centre. *Br. Med. J.* 1: 756*ff*, 1949.

JONES, M. *Social Psychiatry in the Community, in Hospitals and in Prisons.* Thomas, Springfield, Illinois, 1962.

JONES, M. Learning as therapy, in *Psychology of Crime and Criminal Justice.* H. Toch, ed. Holt, Rinehart and Winston, New York, 1979.

JONES, M., POMRYN, B. A., and SKELLERN, E. Work therapy. *Lancet,* 343-344, March 31, 1956.

KRECH, D., and CRUTCHFIELD, R. S. *Theory and Problems in Social Psychology.* McGraw-Hill, New York, 1948.

MORRIS, N. *The Future of Imprisonment.* University of Chicago Press, Chicago, 1974.

MORRIS, N., and HAWKINS, G. *Letter to the President on Crime Control.* University of Chicago Press, Chicago, 1977.

POWITZKY, R. Reflections of a federal prison psychologist. *Quarterly Journal of Corrections,* 2:7-12, 1978.

REDL, F. Ego disturbances and ego support 1951, in *When We Deal with Children: Selected Writings.* Free Press, New York, 1966.

REDL, F. The life-space interview: strategies and techniques 1959, in *When We Deal with Children: Selected Writings.* Free Press, New York, 1966.

SYKES, G. *The Society of Captives* 1958. Atheneum, New York, 1966.

TOCH, H. Prison inmates' reactions to furloughs. *Journal of Research in Crime and Delinquency,* 248-262, July 4, 1967.

TOCH, H. *Men in Crisis: Human Breakdowns in Prison.* Aldine, Chicago, 1975.
TOCH, H. *Living in Prison: The Ecology of Survival.* Free Press, New York, 1977.
TOCH, H. Perspectives on treatment, in *Psychology of Crime and Criminal Justice.* H. Toch, ed. Holt, Rinehart and Winston, New York, 1979.
TOCH, H. Is a "correctional officer," by any other name, a "screw?" *Criminal Justice Review* 3:19-36, 1978.
VORRATH, H. H., and BRENDTHRO, L. K. *Positive Peer Culture.* Aldine, Chicago, 1974.
WHEELER, S. Role conflicts in correctional communities, in *The Prison: Studies in Institutional Organization and Change.* D. R. Cressey, ed. Holt, Rinehart and Winston, New York, 1961.
WHITELY, S., BRIGGS, D., and TURNER, M. *Dealing with Delinquents: the Treatment of Antisocial Behavior.* Schocken Books, New York, 1973.

CHAPTER 21

Medical Treatment of Violent Individuals

JOHN R. LION

The medical treatment of the violent individual requires that such an individual have a specific medical illness. Few violent individuals do. The vast majority of violent people in society could conceivably carry the diagnoses of antisocial personalities, and certainly, that is the most frequent diagnosis prison systems. Most violent individuals, however, do not even come to diagnostic attention but operate within the world's behavior of warfare, insurrections, civil disputes, or riots. This point is important, because more often than not the medical treatment of the violent patient is inappropriate. It is inappropriate because such individuals do not respond to treatment, nor are they motivated for it, nor do they suffer from any definable pathology. Not only is medical treatment for such patients inappropriate, it is conceptually fallacious. The idea that violent people should be "treated" as opposed to "punished" means that the medical profession should deal with a behavior that may well be relegated, and probably should be, to the criminal justice system. This argument of course cuts through current dilemmas about retribution versus clinical salvation and is seen most poignantly in society's anguish over the disposition of juvenile offenders. We are likely to struggle with this problem for some time.

Who, then, is eligible for medical treatment? Violence, at least in a medical setting, may be a symptom of a disease process (Lion, 1972a). That process may be a psychosis. Therefore, a patient may be aggressive as part of a functional psychosis such as schizophrenia or a toxic psychosis such as amphetamine abuse. Violence may be the symptom of an affective disturbance. It is not uncommonly seen among manic-depressive patients in the manic phase or among patients with certain types of agitated depression. Violence may be the manifestation of not only a thought or affective disturbance, but of a characterologic disorder like that of the explosive personality, the passive-aggressive personality, or the paranoid personality. Current thinking about aggression and the relationship to impulsivity has lead to its incorporation, in the *Diagnostic and Statistical Manual of Mental Disorders,* third edition draft (DSM III), a group of disorders of impulse control. These are formulated as intermittent explosive disorders and isolated explosive disorders, representing aggressive disease entities that stand on their own and are not linked to thought, affective, or characterologic disturbances (American Psychiatric Association, 1980).

Violence may also be the manifestation of brain dysfunction. An old concept, this is one of the most controversial areas at the neurologic/psychiatric interface. Since the development of the electroencephalogram (EEG), epileptologists have believed violence to be the manifestation of some brain derangement. Their perceptions in this regard are not surprising, for violence, phenomenologically speaking, is an epileptoid phenomenon (Lion and Penna, 1974). That is, patients often become violent paroxysmally and suddenly without any warning. Patients do not become depressed so easily, and even in manic-depressive patients with rapid switch processes, mood changes take time to develop. Functional psychoses also occur slowly.

The notion that violence may be a manifestation of brain dysfunction is easy to understand if one looks at the syndrome of minimal brain dysfunction. One must not confuse hyperactivity with minimal brain dysfunction since most clinicians would state that the majority of hyperactive children are so on a functional basis; that is, they are hyperactive because of underlying psychological difficulties. However, a true syndrome of minimal brain dysfunction exists though its etiology remains obscure. It is treatable with specific drugs and with a less-than-specific biochemical rationale. More recently recognized are syndromes of adult minimal brain dysfunction that occur in older adolescents or in patients in their 20s or even 30s who have the hallmarks of minimal brain dysfunction but have been inadequately treated, or not treated. The patients seem to react well to central nervous system stimulants. This is a "new" entity in psychiatry, which means it has been rediscovered but not formally accepted and is the subject of much debate (Bellak, 1977), some of it emotional. Yet it is not unreasonable to view the impaired ego function in some patients labeled borderline as being caused by organic dysfunction, as Harticollis (1968) and others have shown. Realizing this, in fact, makes medical treatment different. The clinician puts less stock in formal insight-oriented psychotherapy and more in limit-setting or the teaching of alternatives to problem-solving. Drugs may be used adjunctively to reduce anxiety and thus improve cognition and perception.

While minimal brain dysfunction and violence seem to be linked, less easily linked is the notion that violence may be a manifestation of epilepsy. Brain dysfunction in violence was studied by the National Institute for Neurological Diseases and Blindness (Goldstein, 1974). The book, *Violence and the Brain* (Mark and Ervin, 1974), and the best-selling novel, *The Terminal Man* (Crichton, 1972) and its movie sequel, brought to public awareness the idea that brainstorms and violence were possible. Although this concept in itself was scientifically palatable in theory, it became highly unpalatable when considered socially. Abuse became the issue. The abuse issue manifested itself in the possible psycho-surgical intervention with violent individuals, including members of racial minorities and prisoners. Abuse was also at issue in the conceptual notion that all violent people might have brain abnormalities. This is a particularly repugnant notion to Americans whose social history contains a strong heritage of normal, healthy assertiveness and aggressiveness. The treatment of refractory epileptics patients mentioned in the literature included stereotactic amygdalectomy. Although controversial, this treatment is perhaps one of the clearest examples of a medical model in which a surgical procedure is used to treat an alleged temporal-lobe epileptoid focus. Whether the indications or outcomes are good or bad does not necessarily detract from the validity of psychosurgery as a medical paradigm of intervention.

I do not wish to reactivate the controversy, but I must point out that in every group of incarcerated violent people are known individuals who are labeled as extremely violent in contrast to their peer group. Prisoners, guards, and correctional officers are quick to point out that certain individuals "fly off the handle easily" and represent a subpopulation of persons with apparent poor impulse control and paroxysmal temper outbursts. Russell Monroe discusses these individuals elsewhere in this volume. My co-workers and I have published data from our Violence Clinic in Baltimore, demonstrating that about 5 percent of patients entering that facility with a prescreened chief complaint of paroxysmal temper outbursts have discrete EEG abnormalities (Lion et al., 1976). Many of these patients have been treated with psychoactive drugs and psychotherapy and the results are inclusive, as results always are when one uses combined modalities. Medical treatment of "epileptoid" or "ictal" or episodic individuals who demonstrate sudden onset and remission of violence is a tenable proposition. Whether or not that violence is ictal, interictal, or postictal is of little concern to me as a clinician although I respect the work of colleagues who attempt to separate true epilepsy from epilepsy-like behaviors (Benson and Blumer, 1975). There are some patients with violent temper outbursts who fall into the medical category of being epileptoid; these patients may be treatable with anticonvulsant regimes. Unfortunately, the data are insufficient to state whether or not they are or should be treatable with psychosurgical techniques, and at what point, after exhaustive trials of other intervention, should such techniques be used.

The end points in medical treatment, whether it is surgical, pharmacologic, or psychotherapeutic, are always problematic (Lion, 1975). Pacification is not the end point; indeed, this is the end point that frightens not only civil libertarians, but all clinicians who value freedom of will and choice. The goal of treatment for violence is the restoration in the patient of a sense of control over violence. Rather than have the temper control him, he is able to control his temper. This is easily said, less easily done. The titration, particularly with drugs, is delicate. Yet parallels exist in other specialties. One treats the elderly patient's Parkinson's disease with l-dopa and titrates between, say, cardiovascular toxicity and a reduction in muscle stiffness. Part of the psychosurgery controversy, at least from my experience, concerned the unacceptable chronic organic brain syndromes that accompanied the pacification resulting from amygdalectomy. I was not sure, nor is or was anyone, that the cost was acceptable. Yet I have seen patients so intractably aggressive that, without radical treatment, they are doomed to chronic incarceration. For such tragic cases the only hope was the forced induction of stupor with psychopharmacologic agents.

Patients with other disease entities, of an atypical nature, may require medical treatment when violence is the presenting problem. One example already discussed is the beligerent manic-depressive patient. Belligerence is, in fact, a common chief complaint psychiatric populations. There are reports of the use of lithium in the treatment of violent individuals, and I believe the success of lithium lies not in its antiaggressive properties but in the fact that it is effective in patients who present with manic-depressive illness manifested not by typical mood swings, but by alterations in levels of irritability and frustration (Lion et al., 1975). In other words, these are not classic manic-depressive patients who become hypomanic and depressed, but rather individuals who oscillate on a continuum of frustration, irritability, and aggressiveness.

Lithium is not an antiaggressive compound, but neither is progesterone which is used to treat hypersexually aggressive individuals. A progesteronal agent will reduce the hypersexual drive state; if that drive state includes exhibitionism, then the exhibitionism will be reduced; if it includes aggressiveness, the aggressiveness will be reduced. The target symptom of aggressiveness does not alone respond to hormone control, and the lowering of serum testosterone in individuals will lower their base rates of aggression (Blumer and Migeon, 1975).

Other drugs have been touted as useful for aggression. The benzodiazepines, which, showed potent taming effects in animals, have little antiaggressive property. In fact, a paradoxical rage response has occurred that is, according to our work, merely a disinhibitory phenomenon seen more ubiquitously in alcoholic individuals in whom small amounts of a sedative drug liberate aggression. However, some of these drugs are good for paranoid patients who need acceptable reductions in hypervigilance without the obtunding effect evoked by antipsychotic drugs (Lion, 1978).

With respect to the antipsychotic compounds, none has shown clear superiority in treating verbal or physical hostility or aggressiveness. This is not surprising, really, since antipsychotic drugs exert their effects on the psychosis. Some are better in this regard than others, but their effect on aggressiveness is largely the same, dose for dose (Itil and Wadud, 1975).

Despite great advances in psychopharmacology, no antiaggressive agent has appeared on the market. Dialogue with the pharmaceutical industry several years ago led me to understand the political ramifications of discovering such an agent. More recently, my colleagues and I tested on eight patients an alleged antiaggressive compound initially marketed as an antipsychotic drug. The absence of antipsychotic properties led to a reevaluation of preclinical work in which it was discovered that the drug had some taming effect on monkeys and mice. When administered to human beings, however, it did nothing. The manner in which we found that no effect was achieved points out some aspects of the medical treatment of violent people. Before doing this research, we had attempted to study the effects of methylphenidate on hospitalized hyperactive adult patients. In the hospital, the base rates of such violent patients rapidly dropped to unmeasurable quantities. We had a difficult time determining whether or not a drug was efficacious because the nurturant environment of the hospital made these patients manageable and tractable. In assessing a new compound, then, we needed to use outpatients. This confined our population to those willing to engage in a two-month double-blind study. We were then faced with the paradox of attempting to research volatile, explosive, temper-ridden individuals who would agree to participate in a double-blind outpatient drug study for two months and show sufficient obsessive characteristics to do so. This inherent problem was solved, and another one arose—the documentation of violence. We devised daily diaries to record the quality, quantity, duration, sequelae, and other parameters of each violent outburst and gave one diary to the patient and one to the spouse. Then we discovered that patient and spouse argued violently over diary entries, and so we sealed the diaries in envelopes which the couple brought with them each time they visited the clinic (Student, 1978). The point is that the medical treatment of violent individuals usually suffers from each of attention to the methodologies of outcome and follow-up study. Behavior disorders in general remit or are altered by a variety of environmental circumstances including nurturance, kindness, more formal things that we call psychotherapy, or the more rigorous methods of treatment that we call psychopharmacology.

I have not mentioned the formal psychotherapies in connection with medical treatment because they are not necessarily medical. They may be performed by a variety of paraprofessionals. In the criminal justice system, they are often performed by highly skilled clinicians who have no medical training, nor is such training necessarily required. The psychotherapeutic treatment of violent individuals, both as inpatients and outpatients, is an arduous and time-consuming process that involves the elaboration of fantasy, the enhancement of affect, and the inevitable development of depression which either is handled somatically, acted out the context of a transference situation, or fled from unless careful monitoring is achieved. In many impulsive, violent patients the ability to premeditate the consequences of their actions is impaired, and they act suddenly, without foresight; they must be trained to think before striking out reflexly. Likewise, many patients' ability to fantasize is impoverished as is their appreciation of their own inner affective states or rage. Instead, these patients translate rage into destructive behavior. Introspection is painful, and it involves passivity that must be endured (Lion, 1976).

Several years ago I administered reserpine to a violent patient to induce a depression artificially, so that he might become contemplative and despairing rather than hedonistic and aggressive (Lion et al., 1975). The experiment worked, but I doubt that making people depressed artificially could be considered medical therapy, even if it were accomplished with drugs; in theory, it should occur in jail. However, the milieu in jails is such that aggressiveness and protective belligerence are heightened as a matter of adaptation and survival.

Behavior modification has been used to treat aggressive patients (American Psychiatric Association, 1974). Whether or not to label this as medical is problematic; it is successful to varying degrees with different populations. One "treatment" of violence is the seclusion process, the placing of patients in seclusion rooms (Wadeson and Carpenter, 1976). The practice is controversial but so common that it occurs in almost every psychiatric hospital in the country every moment of every day; yet I also do not know whether it is medical. Such measures require physicians' orders, as if the process and the laying on of hands and the deprivation of a patient's rights were in the realm of the physician; in reality, nurses and aides do most of the restraining of patients in the world. Yet we continue to demand physicians' involvements, at least from a medicolegal standpoint. The risks of seclusion are psychological and physical; there may be a worsening of psychosis as a result of sensory deprivation, and the patient may attempt suicide or harm himself. But do these risks justify the concept of seclusion as a medical treatment, or as a treatment? It may be more accurate to perceive seclusion as a medical disposition, like nursing-home disposition. Yet that, too, requires medical involvement.

Ethical considerations of medical treatment of violent individuals should probably be briefly considered, although it infringes on the concept of treatability. Physicians are often called on to render an opinion about disposition. Although not strictly medical therapy, such a process includes maneuvers that require intervention by an expert clinician, usually a physician. At this point, we must be humble and nihilistic. Given the state of knowledge about dangerousness, medical advice becomes largely a matter of guesswork and clinical experience. It is an undefined process without clear guidelines or end points. The only thing that can be said for it is that, as for all treatment modalities in medicine, good outcome is in large measure a function of follow-up.

I believe that medical treatment of the violent patient is hampered by the profession itself, which chooses to use denial in the service of isolating itself from fear and anxiety. Thus, clinicians in emergency room settings perceive belligerent alcoholics as "harmless drunks," even though we know alcohol is frequently implicated in all types of violence, including fatal automobile accidents. Clinic physicians do not ask questions about past histories of violence, ownership of weapons, convictions for assault, driving practices, or other anamnestic data that would reveal the patient's proclivities to violence. Both therapy and disposition are thus hampered (Lion et al., 1968).

While placing blame on the profession, I must also place some burden of guilt on governmental agencies which, understandably, have chosen to place restraints on research involving the use of prisoners (Lion, and Monroe, 1974).

As the former chairman of an institutional review board, I know that some limited investigations may continue if they are in the interest of the prisoner, but that may not be enough. If we are to treat the incarcerated, or learn of their treatability, then we must be allowed to study them, but obviously not to exploit them. Society cannot have it both ways. This matter will of course not be settled for a long time.

Clinicians asked to treat violent individuals should ascertain the existence of underlying treatable psychopathology while keeping a watchful eye on treatable organicity. A dual, perhaps old-fashioned, emphasis on neuropsychiatric diagnosis is important in the medical treatment of violent patients.

More arduous to resolve, however, is the question of whether or not the medical profession should bear the brunt of handling those who have committed crimes, even if they are ill. Right how the situation is completely arbitrary, almost random. The patient with the good attorney is declared medically ill; the lower-class patient is viewed as socially maladjusted. The rich get the diagnosis, the poor get custodial care; medical treatment is a luxury. Yet even so, it is a form of intervention that will always carry with it an anguish associated with misuse, as it true of the terminally ill cancer patient who is kept alive because no one dares to let him or her die, or bear the responsibility for allowing the infection to take over; or worse, disconnect the respirator. Ultimately, the physician is the one who must pronounce the patient as hopeless and render the medical decision about medical treatment. Is it fair, or should we adapt the same decision-making to the violent patient?

REFERENCES

American Psychiatric Association Task Force. *Clinical Aspects of the Violent Individual*, Task Force Report 8, 1974.

American Psychiatric Association. *Diagnostic and Statistical Manual of Mental Disorders*, 1980.

BELLAK, L. Psychiatric states in adults with minimal brain dysfunction. *Psychiatric Annals* 7:11, 1977.

BENSON, D. F., and BLUMER, D., eds. *Psychiatric Aspects of Neurological Disease*. Grune & Stratton, New York, 1975.

BLUMER, D., and MIGEON, C. Hormone and hormonal agents in the treatment of aggression. *J. Nerv. Ment. Dis.* 160:127-137, 1975.

CRICHTON, M. *The Terminal Man*. Knopf, New York, 1972.

GOLDSTEIN, M. Brain research and violent behavior. *Arch. Neurol.* 30:1-35, 1974.

HARTICOLLIS, P. The syndrome of minimal brain dysfunction in young adult patients. *Bull. Menninger Clin.* 32:102-114, 1968.

ITIL, T. M., and WADUD, A. Treatment of human aggression with major tranquilizers, antidepressants, and new psychotropic drugs. *J. Nerv. Ment. Dis.* 160:83-99, 1975.

LION, J. R. *Evaluation and Management of the Violent Patient.* Thomas, Springfield, Illinois, 1972a.

LION, J. R. The role of depression in the treatment of aggressive personality disorders. *Am. J. Psychiatry* 129:3, 1972b.

LION, J. R. Conceptual issues in the use of drugs for the treatment of aggression in man. *J. Nerv. Ment. Dis.* 160, 76-82, 1975.

LION, J. R. *The Art of Medicating Psychiatric Patients.* Williams & Wilkins, Baltimore, 1978.

LION, J. R., BACH-Y-RITA, G., and ERVIN, F. R. The self-referred violent patient. *J.A.M.A.* 205:503-505, 1968.

LION, J. R., HILL, J., and MADDEN, D. J. Lithium carbonate and aggression: a case report. *Dis. Nerv. Syst.* 36:97-98, 1975.

LION, J. R., MADDEN, D. J., and CHRISTOPHER, R. L. A violence clinic: three years' experience. *Am. J. Psychiatry* 133:4, 1976.

LION, J. R., MILLAN, D., and TAYLOR, R. J. Reserpine and the induction of depression: a case report. *Dis. Nerv. Syst.* 36:321-322, 1975.

LION, J. R., and MONROE, R. R. Future hazards for clinical research. *J. Nerv. Ment. Dis.* 158:397-398, 1974.

LION, J. R., and PENNA, M. the study of human aggression, in *The Neuropsychology of Aggression.* R. Whalen, ed. Plenum, New York, 1974.

MARK, V. H., and ERVIN, F. R. *Violence and the Brain.* Harper and Row, New York, 1970.

STUDENT, D. Methodological issues in psychopharmacological research of violent individuals. Presented to International Society for Research on Aggression, September, 1978.

WADESON, H., and CARPENTER, W. T. Impact of the seclusion room experience. *J. Nerv. Ment. Dis.* 163;318-328, 1976.

CHAPTER 22

Medroxyprogesterone Acetate Treatment for Paraphiliac Sex Offenders

PAUL A. WALKER
WALTER J. MEYER, III

Our purpose is to present data on the use of a synthetic hormone, in combination with psychotherapy, in the treatment of a specific type of sex offender. The therapeutic protocol presented is an experimental effort to devise a treatment program for men whose illegal and harmful sexual behavior is unresponsive to conventional psychotherapy alone. The conclusions drawn are tentative but optimistic.

SEXUALLY OFFENSIVE BEHAVIOR

Almost all sexual behaviors have, at some time or place, been proscribed by criminal or canon law. Current criminal law prohibits a variety of sexual behaviors, some of which are frequently described as victimless crimes. At the Gender Clinic of the University of Texas Medical Branch at Galveston, the following are treated as sexually offensive behaviors: sexual behaviors that involve harm to the self (e.g., suicidal masochism) or to the partner (e.g., rape, child sexual abuse, homicidal sadism), or that involve the nonconsent of the partner (e.g., voyeurism, exhibitionism), or doubtful consent (e.g., child or adolescent sexual exploitation). Our criteria for sexually offensive behavior therefore are based on harm and consent, rather than on legal or medical definitions of crime or pathology.

The Offender

Various types of persons may become involved in a treatment program because of the commission of an illegal "sexual" act.

Type 1—denying

Persons who are arrested and convicted for illegal sexual behavior are often ordered by the court to avail themselves of psychotherapy. Some of these men deny the commission of an illegal act, or they may admit the act but deny the harm or nonconsensual aspects of it (for example, the rapist may claim he simply took what he was entitled to, or the adult male may swear that the 9-year-old girl with whom he had intercourse seduced him, or the man arrested 7 times for public exposure may claim that a weak bladder forces him to urinate with urgency in inappropriate places). Such persons are not readily amenable to psychotherapy directed at the sexual behavior, although psychotherapy directed at the antisocial aspects of the patient's personality may be attempted.

Caveat: Occasionally, persons presenting for psychological evaluation have been advised by their attorneys not to admit certain acts, or the patient correctly assumes that no legally sanctioned contract of confidentiality exists between him and his evaluator/therapist. Such persons may intrapsychically admit to having a sexual problem, and they may desire intervention but are caught in a situation in which this cannot be readily acknowledged. In such cases, the therapist may choose to offer absolute confidentiality, knowing that a later subpoena may force him or her into an ethical dilemma and perhaps legal jeopardy regarding the preservation or violation of that confidentiality.

Type 2—disinhibited

Some persons identified by self or others as having committed a sexually offensive act may readily admit the behavior but will maintain that the act was committed only once (the time they got caught), and that it was caused by either the disinhibiting effect of alcohol or another drug, or by temporary insanity as a result of familial stress and/or other emotional duress. Such persons, therefore, do not admit to having a *sexual* problem, although they admit the illegal sexual act. Like the Type 1 offenders, such individuals are not readily amenable to psychotherapy directed toward the sexual issues.

Type 3—violent

Some sex offenders admit to the commission of an illegal act and request help, but they define the act as nonsexual, as may the therapist. Rape and beating during a burglary or robbery, or sexual assault along with physical abuse of a child may indeed be performed without sexual gain to the perpetrator (Groth and Burgess, 1977; Groth et al., 1977). Such activities may be considered acts of violence or aggression or power, devoid of obvious sexual motives or gain. It may be more appropriate to define such acts as primarily aggressive and secondarily sexual, rather than as exclusively aggressive.

Type 4—paraphiliac

A proportion of these persons, almost exclusively male, who have histories of illegal or harmful or nonconsensual sexual activity, reveal a pattern of erotic fantasies (during masturbation and/or during consensual adult sexual activity) which includes fantasies of the deviant sexual behavior. The true paraphiliac must rely totally on these deviant fantasies to achieve erection and ejaculation. Partial paraphiliacs report occasional but nonexclusive use of such fantasies during sexual activity (i.e., erection and ejaculation do occur at times following the imaging of "appropriate" sexual activity). For such men, the deviant sexual acts are clearly sexual, primarily, and they do not usually include secondary violent or aggressive components.

Paraphiliac behavior (Money, 1977) is a relatively new concept in the behavioral sciences and is not described in the *Diagnostic and Statistical Manual of Mental Disorders,* second edition (American Psychiatric Association, 1968), although it is included in drafts of the proposed third edition. Diagnosis of a paraphilia requires detailed inquiry into the patient's erotic fantasies, especially during masturbation.

Caveat: Some patients claim to have no visual fantasies, maintaining that they masturbate while perceiving only the tactile sensations. Many men are poor reporters of their cognitive experience during masturbation. At times the patient must be told to masturbate while paying attention to his cognitive experiences, and he must then be interviewed as soon as possible after ejaculation. (When the collection of semen samples is part of the research protocol, this assignment to the patient is facilitated). Under these circumstances, patients often report that erection and ejaculation followed the imagery of the deviant activity, although such imagery may be perceived as intrusive and unwanted.

Incidence: In our clinical experience, about 80 percent of men identified as having committed illegal, harmful, or nonconsensual sex acts (especially rape, exhibitionism, and child sexual abuse or exploitation outside of the family) report that their sexual fantasies are exclusively or primarily paraphiliac in content. (Curiously, fathers involved in incest rarely report such a paraphiliac pattern of erotic fantasies.) Informal discussions with other therapists and researchers professionally concerned with sex offenders reveal that our experience is not always shared by others, who find a lower percentage of paraphiliac imagery occurring in their client populations. This difference may be explained, in part, by the fact that we inquire into paraphiliac imagery. Others may wait for such information to be volunteered. In addition, our patients are primarily outpatients who have already obtained parole or probation and are, therefore, in less legal jeopardy should they admit such imagery. In many treatment programs conducted in the prison or state hospital systems, demands are high for the patients/inmates to present a "clean" picture of themselves as cured. In our case, sampling or experimenter bias cannot, of course, be totally ruled out.

Hypersexuality: Some Type 4 paraphiliacs may be considered hypersexual in that the frequency of erotic arousal, erections, and ejaculations is high (15 to 40 orgasms per week). Not all paraphiliacs display this pattern. The hypersexual paraphiliac is not necessarily sexually aroused all the time, but environmental stimuli for sexual arousal are often present. The cue for sexual arousal in the rapist, for example, may be "a woman walking alone and not wanting sex with me," or, for the exhibitionist, "a woman not expecting to see my penis," or, for the pedophile, "a child at play." Such stimuli frequently result in triggering an erectile response.

Specificity of arousal: Our investigation of paraphiliac imagery is done in an interview as patients provide a self-report. Serial sexual fantasies reported by any one individual may be highly stereotyped in content or theme; that is, paraphiliacs often report that erection and ejaculation depend on a specific fantasy image. The specificity of a cue stimulus for sexual arousal has an animal model demonstrated by Carbaugh and Schein (1961) who found that the rooster depends on the single image of the hen's head for correct copulatory orientation. The headless body does not elicit mounting behavior but the bodiless head may. Unbeknownst to barnyard voyeurs, roosters rely on a highly specific stimulus for their copulatory behavior.

Elicited versus emitted behavior: Many, but not all, Type 4 paraphiliacs can respond with an erection to stimuli depicting consensual adult non-paraphiliac sexual activity. "Acceptable" arousal may be elicited by manipulation of stimuli but, on their own, most paraphiliacs emit erections only to self-produced paraphiliac imagery. Therefore the demonstrated capacity to respond (elicited behavior) to "acceptable" stimuli does not ensure that the emitted behavior will be "acceptable."

ETHICAL CONSIDERATIONS

Confidentiality

As mentioned, absolute doctor-patient confidentiality is not sanctioned by law in all jurisdictions. The therapist/researcher, therefore, must decide carefully how much confidentiality should be promised, and he or she must guard the privacy of records, especially those containing detailed data on the patient's erotic life. In our opinion, the clinician/researcher should advise the client/patient that certain topics (e.g., lust murder or threats of masochistic suicide or child abuse) cannot be held in confidence and must, by law, be reported to the police, child welfare unit, or local mental health deputies—or, for those working in prison settings, to the parole board.

Duress to Enter Treatment

Most people go to the doctor only when they hurt. Sex (to the perpetrator, even the masochist) usually feels good. Therefore, the majority of persons engaging in harmful or nonconsensual sexual activity do not request help until or unless they are under legal pressure, real or imagined, to do so. The current regulations regarding informed consent of some university research review boards prohibit treatment of prisoners, parolees, or probationers. Sometimes we find ourselves in the position of being able to accept for therapy only those "free agents" who do not want therapy, and having to refuse to help the man to whom a judge gave the "choice" of prison versus therapy. To protect his "free will," we force him to have prison as his only alternative.

NONHORMONAL THERAPY

Many forms of psychotherapy have been attempted in treating sex offenders (Brecher, 1978). Insight-oriented, dynamic, and/or analytic therapies may have positive results that are too often dangerously delayed, allowing the patient to continue his illegal behavior until he is arrested and therapy is terminated or interrupted. Such therapies are usually not directed specifically to the sexual behavior but toward re-growth or reformulation of the personality. Theoreticians disagree as to the appropriateness, efficiency, and necessity of these methods.

Behavior therapies directed either specifically toward the sexual behavior and/or its concurrent fantasies (Type 4 paraphiliac), or toward social-skills training for exhibitionists and rapists deficient in appropriate sex-initiating behavior, have grown in favor among therapists in recent decades. Proponents of behavior therapy (Bancroft, 1970, 1975; Barlow, 1973; Freund, 1976) have warned, however, that such therapies often increase the occurrence of harmless consensual sexual activity without decreasing the deviant behavior. Brownell et al., (1977) and Hayes et al., (1978) warn that the behavioral treatment of one pattern of deviant sexual activity, in persons displaying multiple deviations, does not lead to a decrease of other deviant activities until each of these activities is treated sequentially and directly.

Shorkey and Cangelosi (1975) reviewed 24 reports of behavior therapy for heterosexual sex offenders published between 1960 and 1975. Nineteen of the 24 reports were single case studies; 59 offenders were treated. In almost all cases, therapy was described as successful although follow-up was usually only for six months or less, insufficient time to observe the usually high rate of recidivism (Frisbie and Dondis, 1965). The verdict regarding the utility of these therapies is not yet in.

HORMONAL THERAPY

Cyproterone Acetate: Behavioral Aspects—the European Experience

In the early 1960s Laschet and others (Laschet and Laschet, 1975) began to use cyproterone acetate as an antiandrogen in the treatment of sex offenders. The researchers reported high success in lowering libido in treated men. Cyproterone acetate is not available in the United States for clinical trials.

Medroxyprogesterone Acetate (MPA): Behavioral Aspects—Previous Experience

Blumer and Migeon (1975) and Money and coworkers (Money, 1968, 1970; Money et al., 1975, 1976; Meyer et al., 1977; Walker, 1977, 1978) have published the results of their work at the Johns Hopkins University School of Medicine and Hospital where they treated *XYY* sexually aggressive and "anger-aggressive" patients and *XY* sex offenders with MPA (Depo-Provera, Upjohn). Most of the *XY* sex offenders were Type 4 paraphiliacs and most of the *XYY* aggressive patients were Type 3 violent sex offenders (a few were Type 4).

Behaviorally, the men treated weekly with MPA (in dosages ranging from 100 to 400 mg, deep intramuscular injections) demonstrated inconsistent and probably insignificant decreases in nonsexual aggressive or impulsive violent behavior. The patients' sexual activity (fantasies, erections, ejaculations, acceptable and deviant overt behavior), however, decreased dramatically while the patients were in therapy. Of the 23 men studied by Money et al. (1975), 8 completed therapy and reported that their sexual arousability returned post-therapy but was either less intense or more easily controllable than before therapy. Five of the eight had a total remission of paraphiliac imagery. Six of the 23 men (26 percent) prematurely dropped out of the program; a high drop-out rate is usually the result of the patients' pronouncing themselves "cured."

MPA: Medical Aspects

MPA, a derivative of progesterone, acts like progesterone. It has weak androgenic activity and functions as an anti-androgen in males. Although MPA has been used in human beings since the late 1950s, little information has been accumulated concerning its metabolic clearance rate or volume of distribution. In 16 adult women, Gupta et al. (1977) found the volume of distribution to be 20 ± 3 l/kg/day and the metabolic clearance rate 21 ± 2 l/kg/day. Plasma concentrations of MPA after oral administration have been reported by Hiroi et al. (1975), Cornette et al. (1971), and Martin and Adlercreutz (1977). After a 100-mg oral dose, the peak plasma level of MPA was 7.3 ng/ml (Martin and Adlercreutz, 1977). Intramuscularly administered depot dosages of MPA may yield higher and more sustained blood concentrations for several months (Jeppsson and Johansson, 1976; Saxena et al., 1977; Ortiz et al., 1977). MPA sometimes is still detectable 180 days after a 150-mg injection (Ortiz et al., 1977).

Gonadal-hypothalamic Axis

The hormone's major effect is on the gonadal-hypothalamic axis. MPA was believed to be effective in treating precocious puberty, probably by suppression of gonadotropins (Kupperman and Epstein, 1962; Collip et al., 1964; Hahn et al., 1964; Kaplan et al., 1968). The suppression of luteinizing hormone (LH) and follicle-stimulating hormone (FSH) could not be documented in all individuals despite marked lowering of sex steroids (Lemli et al., 1964; Rifkind et al., 1969; Gordon et al., 1970; Mathews et al., 1970; Meyer et al., 1977). Judge et al., (1977) reported on a treatment of a male patient with precocious puberty secondary to excessive production of luteinizing hormone-releasing hormone by a hypothalamic tumor. With MPA therapy the patient's plasma testosterone concentration was lowered markedly but his LH and FSH concentrations in urine and blood were unaffected. MPA probably has a direct effect on testosterone synthesis by the testes. The minimum concentration of MPA needed to suppress testosterone has not been determined. MPA also either directly or indirectly decreases spermatogenesis (Camancho et al., 1972; Meyer et al., 1977). The effect on sperm is greatly accentuated by the addition of testosterone enanthate to the treatment program (Frick and Bartsch, 1976; Brenner et al., 1977). In addition, MPA seems to increase testosterone clearance by inducing testosterone reductase activity in the liver (Rivarola et al., 1968; Altman et al., 1972; Albin et al., 1973) and by partially displacing testosterone from sex steroid-binding protein (Forest et al., 1968). MPA interferes with the peripheral action of testosterone by changing its metabolism by fibroblasts (Saenger et al., 1973) and by intracellular binding to receptors (Keenan et al., 1975; Mowszowicz et al., 1974). MPA may also reduce the number of sex-steroid receptors in target tissues as it does in the uterus (Tseng and Gurpide, 1975). In summary MPA affects androgen production, clearance, and action at many different levels.

Other Pituitary Influences

MPA influences other pituitary functions, particularly growth-hormone and adrenocorticotropic hormone secretion. The suppression of growth-hormone secretion by MPA was first reported by Simon et al. (1967) and then supported by Gershberg et al. (1969). However, MPA has not significantly decreased the growth rate of individuals with precocious puberty (Kaplan et al., 1968). The hormone has proved ineffective in lowering growth-hormone levels in patients suffering from acromegaly (Lawrence and Kirsteins, 1970; Rake et al., 1972). Kaplan et al., (1969) reported no suppression of the growth-hormone response to insulin-induced hypoglycemia. Noting baseline growth-hormone secretion, Meyer et al. (1977) found that MPA did not affect either total integrated concentration or diurnal rhythm of growth hormone (Figures 1 and 2). Therefore, the suppressive effect of MPA on growth hormone seen by Simon et al. (1967) is either temporary or not significant.

The effects of MPA on the adrenal-ACTH axis have been shown to be varied. Urinary excretion of 17-hydroxycorticoids (Sadeghi-Nejad et al., 1971; Schoen, 1966), cortisol production rate (Sadeghi-Nejad et al., 1971), and average plasma cortisol concentrations (Hellman et al., 1976) are decreased by MPA. Camanni et al. (1963) reported the maintenance of an adrenalectomized man with MPA. Adrenal responsiveness to metopirone (Sadeghi-Nejad et al., 1971; Mathews et al., 1970; Richman et al., 1971), to exogenous ACTH (Sadeghi-Nejad et al., 1971; Schoen, 1966; Mathews et al., 1970; Richman et al., 1971; Fekete and Szeberenyi, 1965), and to insulin-induced hypoglycemia (Sadeghi-Nejad et al., 1971) are also decreased. From experiments with isolated rat adrenals, Fekete and Szeberenyi (1965) concluded that MPA had no direct toxic effect on the adrenals and that it must act by decreasing ACTH. Hellman et al. (1976) reported a generalized lowering of the average level of cortisol with some loss of normal circadian rhythm in patients treated for cancer with 400 to

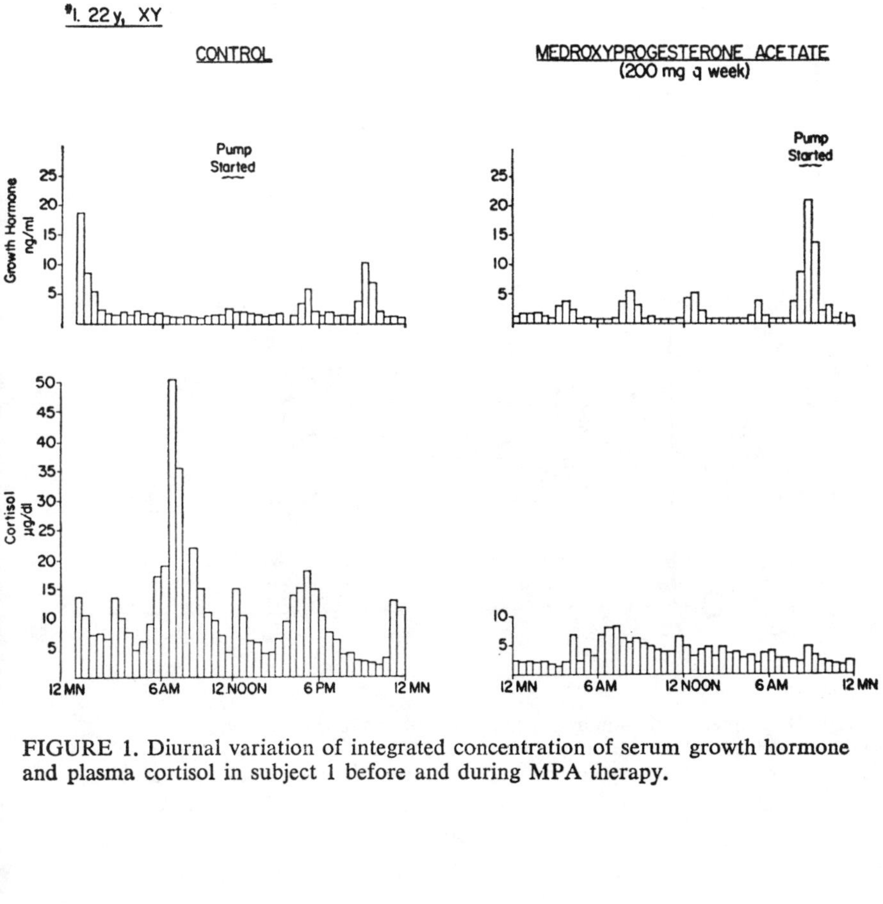

FIGURE 1. Diurnal variation of integrated concentration of serum growth hormone and plasma cortisol in subject 1 before and during MPA therapy.

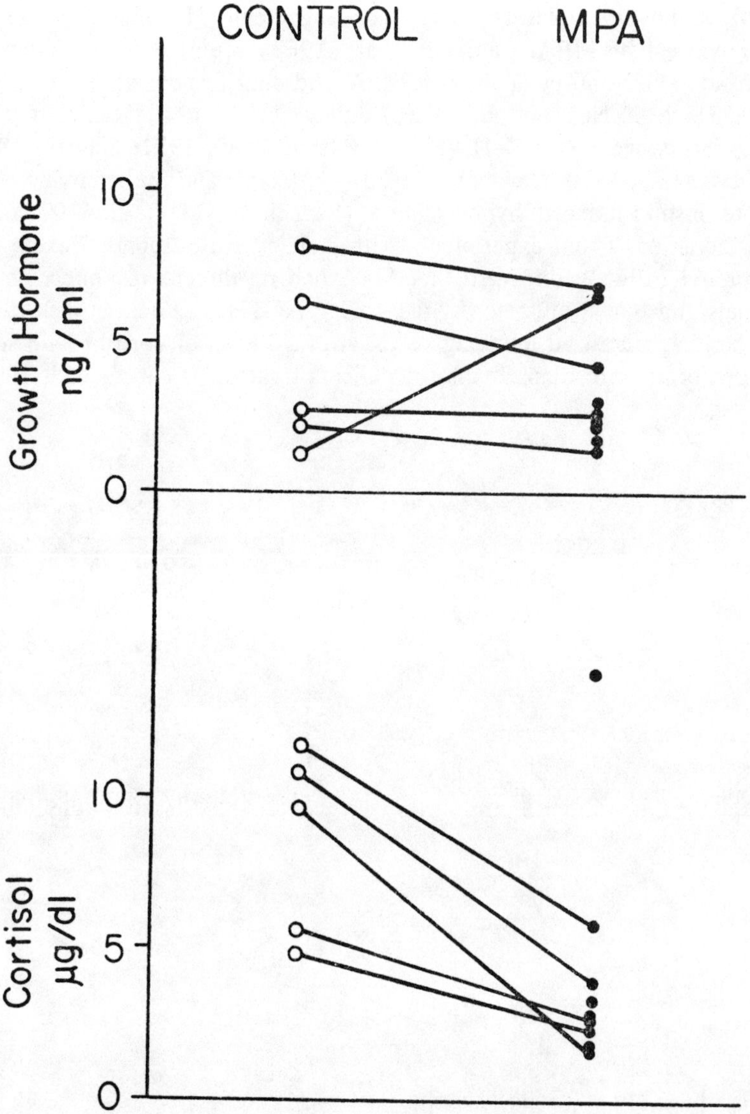

FIGURE 2. Integrated 24-hour concentration of serum growth hormone and plasma cortisol before (O) and during (●) MPA therapy. Lines connect concentrations in the five subjects studied before and during MPA therapy.

700 mg/week of MPA. In men taking 100 to 400 mg/week of MPA, there was a flattening of corticoid diurnal rhythm (Meyer et al., 1977) (Figure 1). These individuals had a marked lowering of the integrated concentration of plasma cortisol (Meyer et al., 1977) (Figure 2). The decrease in corticoid concentration does not seem to indicate a significant suppression of ACTH responsiveness to stress, since these same individuals had no significant change in cortisol response to insulin-induced hypoglycemia. Although MPA (in dosages of 100 to 400 mg/week) lowers the integrated concentration of cortisol, this should not cause concern to the treating physician; lowering of the integrated concentration of cortisol is caused by MPA's weak glucocorticoid activity. The adrenal-ACTH axis remains capable of responding adequately during stress.

Diabetogenic effects: Since MPA has some glucocorticoid action, it is not surprising that it has been implicated in producing decreased glucose tolerance. Progesterone itself is known to increase fasting insulin concentration and insulin release during a glucose tolerance test in normal individuals (Kalkhoff et al., 1970). MPA has a similar effect (Tuttle and Turkington, 1974; Vermeulen and Thiery, 1974), but this has not been demonstrable by all investigators (Beck et al., 1975; Dhall et al., 1977). Spellacy et al. (1972) reported that MPA produced an abnormal glucose tolerance in 14.7 percent of adult women receiving it for contraception. The abnormal glucose tolerance was related to their age and to weight gain while on therapy. One of the patients required insulin therapy. Gershberg et al., (1969) showed that MPA had an adverse effect on the glucose tolerance of diabetic and potentially diabetic persons. In summary, normal individuals with good insulin reserve can tolerate the mild diabetogenic effect of MPA, but those who have gained a significant amount of weight or show evidence of increased insulin resistance are at risk of developing abnormal glucose tolerance with MPA therapy. In most instances, this is reversible with cessation of therapy (Spellacy et al., 1972).

Other CNS Effects

MPA and other progesterones affect such other brain functions as degree of consciousness, seizure threshold, and ventilation control. Merryman et al. (1954) noted that women given 500 mg of progesterone intravenously were anesthetized. High doses of intravenous progesterone will also induce a sleep electroencephalographic (EEG) pattern in the rat (Komisaruk et al., 1967). MPA raises the seizure threshold in dogs (Costa and Bonnycastle, 1952), and in humans it is used to treat seizures associated with menstrual periods (Zimmerman et al., 1973). No change in EEG has been documented in adult males receiving 200 to 500 mg/week of MPA intramuscularly (Blumer and Migeon, 1975; Meyer et al., 1977). During pregnancy and the luteal phase of the menstrual cycle (periods of high progesterone levels), women have an increase in ventilation (Goodland et al., 1954); when progesterone is given to male subjects, there is also an increase in ventilation as well as a decrease in hematocrit (Goodland et al., 1953; Lyons and Antonio, 1959). Two groups have reported that MPA increases ventilation in patients with obesity-hypoventilation syndrome (Lyons and Huang, 1968; Sutton et al., 1975). Likewise, in adult men, a slight, statistically significant decrease in hematocrit ($p < 0.01$), which may indicate a small increase in ventilation, has been documented (Meyer et al., 1977).

MPA: Behavioral Aspects—the Texas Experience

In April 1977 we accepted our first MPA patient at the University of Texas Medical Branch. Our therapy program, conducted under an Investigational New Drug permit (IND #3256) issued by the Food and Drug Administration, has to date (October 1978) accepted 10 men into treatment that combines administration of MPA with rational-emotive psychotherapy. The behavioral diagnoses for the 10 patients (all karyotyped as 46,*XY*) are: rape—2, rape/murder—1, homosexual pedophilia—2, heterosexual pedophilia—2, exhibitionism—1, self-mutilation—1, frottage (touching) and exhibitionism—1.

All of the patients reveal a Type 4 complete or partial form of paraphilia; they were self-referred and began treatment as nonincarcerated outpatients. Two are currently receiving their medication while in jail for offenses committed before entering therapy.

The protocol calls for initially high dosages of 400 to 500 mg/wk i.m., for six months, followed by a gradual reduction, in 50- to 100-mg increments, every three months thereafter if the harmful or nonconsensual behavior has been suppressed. Usually therapy begins at 400 mg/wk, but for large patients the initial dosage may be 500 mg/wk. The high dosage level may be maintained indefinitely if the clinician believes that the patient's behavior is being only barely suppressed (i.e., temptations persist although, it is hoped, they are not acted out). If, after six months at maximal therapy, the patient has not acted out or imagined the unwanted behavior, an attempt may be made to wean him gradually from the medication. As the dosage is lowered, circulating levels of serum testosterone rise and libido returns. It is hoped that the patient has, in the meantime, learned in psychotherapy either to redirect his libido or to predict his sexual arousal so that unwanted sexual behavior may be aborted by the performance of an incompatible response (i.e., masturbation).

To date, one man in our sample has been in therapy at maximal dosage for 18 months. Six other patients are currently receiving MPA, four at maximal dosage and two at reduced dosages. The seven men in the program have been receiving therapy for one to 18 months.

One man, a heterosexual pedophile, ended therapy only one month before our recommended stopping time and is considered to have completed therapy. Two men, a rapist and a self-mutilator, stopped therapy after a few weeks. The two drop-outs declared themselves cured; follow-up continues. Seven new patients are currently being evaluated and are expected to begin therapy soon.

At the present time, when only one man has completed therapy, it is premature to claim beneficial long-term effects for the sample. Every patient in therapy, however, has reported a reduction (usually to zero) of masturbatory frequency and frequency of erotic fantasies. All report a total stoppage of their unwanted sexual behavior.

The patients report that their felt need or desire for sexual activity is diminished and, if sexual activity does occur, the latency to erection and to orgasm and ejaculation is greater. However, the patients are able to produce a semen sample (via masturbation) when requested. As our study continues, we plan to add new modalities of psychotherapy, especially covert sensitization.

MPA: Medical Aspects—the Texas Experience

Our patients do not report any consistent change in physical well-being. Two have reported leg pains, several reported gastrointestinal upsets and increased sleepiness. Our patients have not complained of headaches. In the World Health Organization-sponsored comparative trial of depomedroxyprogesterone, an increased incidence of spontaneously volunteered complaints of abdominal discomfort (5.2 percent), anxiety or nervousness (3.9 percent), and headaches (10.7 percent) was noted (World Health Organization, 1978).

In our sample, no significant change in physical condition has been noted. No change was observed in penis length or prostate size and consistency. Slight decreases in testicular size were noted. Half of the individuals gained weight while taking the drug (Meyer et al., 1977, and present study). Breast changes have been carefully looked for because of the carcinogenic effect of MPA on the mammary glands of the beagle bitch (Nelson et al., 1972; Berliner, 1974; Hill and Dumas, 1974; Fowler et al.,

1977; Hansel et al., 1977). To date we have not observed breast enlargement in any of our patients. Brenner et al. (1977) reported that one patient of 14 developed unilateral gynecomastia, but that patient was also receiving testosterone enanthate.

In our sample, MPA did not consistently affect electrolytes, calcium, phosphorus, uric acid, blood urea nitrogen, cholesterol, total protein, albumin, total bilirubin, alkaline phosphatase, creatinine, lactic dehydrogenase, SGOT, and SGPT (Meyer et al., 1977). One of our patients developed insulin-dependent diabetes mellitus.

Preliminary measurements show that patients in the present study typically have serum MPA concentrations of between 50 ng/ml and 173 ng/ml (measured by Davis G. Kaiser, Ph.D., Upjohn Company; Cornette et al., 1971). A fall in testosterone to near female levels occurs when the MPA plasma concentration exceeds 50 ng/ml (Figure 3). The changes in gonadotropins shown in Table 1 are similar to those observed by others (Meyer et al., 1977).

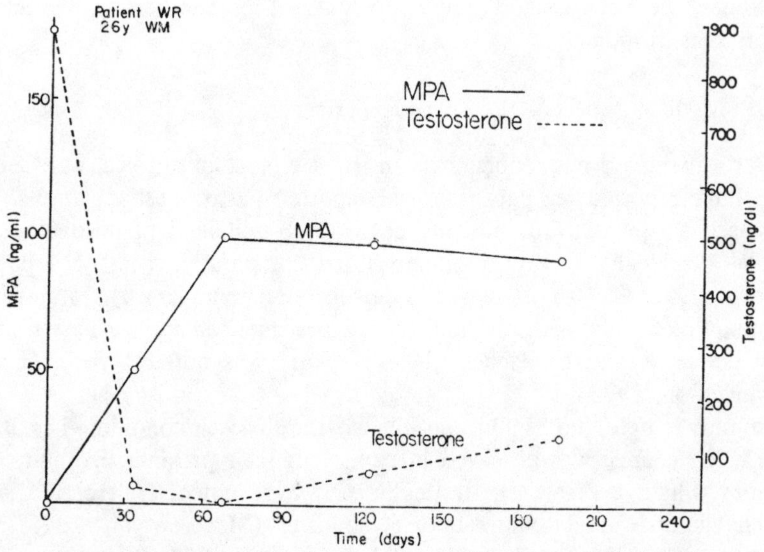

FIGURE 3. Plasma testosterone and MPA concentrations of a patient receiving 400 mg/wk of MPA.

Table 1

Dosage, Duration, MPA, Plasma Testosterone, Serum LH and FSH Concentrations Before and During Therapy

Patient	Dosage (mg/week)	Duration (months)	MPA Concentration (ng/ml)	Testosterone (ng/dl)		(mIU/ml) LH		FSH (mIU/ml)	
				Pre-Rx	Rx	Pre-Rx	Rx	Pre-Rx	Rx
1	400	15	122.1	935	126	4.7	2.25	10.0	5.3
2	300	12	105.7	889	93	2.6	1.0	8.5	1.8
3	500	3	102.7	722	13	4.0	4.0	2.7	2.7
4	400	5	97.9	875	89	12.0	4.2	14.5	4.5
5	400	10	160.4	778	187	8.0	6.5	7.8	3.0
6	500	12	149.0	766	30	6.0	2.0	8.3	4.5
7	400	6	135.3	908	42	1.9	0.95	5.2	0.4
8	300	12	173.0	383	16	5.5	1.6	7.5	4.5
Mean				782	75	5.6	3.0	8.1	3.4
Standard deviation				178	61	3.5	2.0	3.3	1.7

CONCLUSION

Medroxyprogesterone acetate has proved to be useful, in conjunction with psychotherapy, in treating Type 4 paraphiliac sex offenders. The medical risks incurred with this therapy are minimal, but they do require careful monitoring by a physician of the patient's overall physical health.

Although we have no experience with using MPA without psychotherapy, we suspect that psychotherapy is an important factor in preserving beneficial results after the patient has stopped taking the hormone. The primary advantage of MPA administration is its rapid suppression of illegal and harmful sexual activity; this occurs more quickly than may be expected from psychotherapy alone and is especially advantageous if the undesired sexual activity is highly harmful (i.e., rape murder) or is acted out frequently. Fantasies of the illegal and harmful sexual activity are also diminished. Patients report a "vacation from sex" as their fantasies no longer intrude upon their lives.

The therapist dealing with sex offenders often finds him/herself frustrated because of poor therapeutic outcome in most cases. By using MPA in addition to conventional psychotherapy, we have been able to observe quick and dramatic positive outcomes which reward our efforts, keep our patients from running the risk of another arrest, and, most importantly, protect possibly large numbers of potential victims who might have been assaulted by our patients.

ACKNOWLEDGMENTS

Supported by grants from the Hogg Foundation for Mental Health, The M.D. Anderson Foundation, and The Upjohn Company, and by funds from the departments of Psychiatry and Behavioral Sciences, and Pediatrics, The University of Texas Medical Branch. Patients were studied, in part, in the clinical research unit, The University of Texas, supported by grant RR-00073 from the Division of Research Resources, National Institutes of Health.

REFERENCES

Albin, J., Vittek, J., Gordon, G. G., Altman, K., Olivo, J., and Southern, A. L. On the mechanism of the anti-androgenic effect of medroxyprogesterone acetate. *Endocrinology* 93:417-422. 1973.

Altman, K., Gordon, G. G., Southern, A. L., Vittek, J., and Wilker, S. Induction of hepatic testosterone A-Ring reductase by medroxyprogesterone acetate. *Endocrinology* 90:1252-1260, 1972.

American Psychiatric Association. *Diagnostic and Statistical Manual of Mental Disorders,* second ed. Washington, D.C., 1968.

BANCROFT, J. A comparative study of aversion and desensitization in the treatment of homosexuality, in *Behaviour Therapy in the 1970's*. L. Burns and J. Worsley, eds. Wright, Bristol, England, 1970, pp. 12-33.

BANCROFT, J. The behavioral approach to sexual disorders, in *Psycho-Sexual Problems*. H. Melne and S. Hardy, eds. University Park Press, Baltimore, 1975.

BARLOW, D. Increasing heterosexual responsiveness in the treatment of sexual deviation: A review of the clinical and experimental evidence. *Behavior Therapy* 4: 655-671, 1973.

BECK, P., VENABLE, R. L., and HOFF, D. L. Mutual modification of glucose stimulated serum insulin responses in female Rhesus monkeys by ethinyl estradiol and nortestosterone derivatives. *J. Clin. Endocrinol. Metab.* 41:44-53, 1975.

BERLINER, V. U.S. Food and Drug Administration requirements for toxicity testing of contraceptive products, in *Pharmacological Models in Contraceptive Development—WHO Symposium Geneva 1973*. M. H. Briggs and E. Diczfalusy, eds. Bogtrykkeriet Forum, Copenhagen, 1974, 240-253.

BLUMER, D., and MIGEON, C. Hormone and hormonal agents in the treatment of aggression. *J. Nerv. Ment. Dis.* 160:127-137, 1975.

BRECHER, E. M. *Treatment Programs for Sex Offenders*. National Institute of Law Enforcement and Criminal Justice, Washington, D.C., 1978.

BRENNER, P. F., MISHELL, D. R., BERNSTEIN, G. S., and ORTIZ, A. Study of medroxyprogesterone acetate and testosterone enanthate as a male contraceptive. *Contraception* 15:679-691, 1977.

BROWNELL, K., HAYES, S., and BARLOW, D. Patterns of appropriate and deviant sexual arousal: The behavioral treatment of multiple sexual deviations. *J. Consult. Clin. Psychol.* 45:1144-1155, 1977.

CAMANCHO, A. M., WILLIAMS, D. L., and MONTALVO, J. M. Alterations of testicular histology and chromosomes in patients with constitutional sexual precocity treated with medroxyprogesterone acetate. *J. Clin. Endocrinol. Metab.* 34:279-286, 1972.

CAMANNI, F., MASSARA, F., and MOLINATTI, G. M. The cortisone-like effect of 6α-methyl-17α-acetoxyprogesterone in the adrenalectomized man. *Acta Endocrinologica* 43:477-483, 1963.

CARBAUGH, B. T., and SCHEIN, M. W. Sexual response of roosters to full and partial models. *American Zoologist* 1:62-63, 1961.

COLLIP, P. J., KAPLAN, S. A., BOYLE, D. C., PLACHTE, F., and KUGUT, M. D. Constitutional isosexual precocious puberty: effects of medroxyprogesterone acetate therapy. *Am. J. Dis. Child.* 108:399-405, 1964.

CORNETTE, J. C., KIRTON, R. T., and DUNCAN, G. W. Measurement of medroxyprogesterone acetate (Provera®) by radioimmunoassay. *J. Clin. Endocrinol. Metab.* 33:459-466, 1971.

COSTA, P. J., and BONNYCASTLE, D. D. The effect of DCA, compound E, testosterone, progesterone, and ACTH in modifying "agene-induced" convulsions in dogs. *Arch. Int. Pharmacodyn. Ther.* 91:330-338, 1952.

DHALL, K., KUMAR, M., RASTOGI, G. K., and DEVI, P. K. Short term effects of norethisterone oenanthate and medroxyprogesterone acetate on glucose, insulin, growth hormone and lipids. *Fertil. Steril.* 28:156-158, 1977.

FEKETE, G., and SZEBERENYI, S. Data on the mechanism of adrenal suppression by medroxyprogesterone. *Steroids* 69:159-166, 1965.

FOREST, M. G., RIVAROLA, M. A., and MIGEON, C. J. Percentage binding of testosterone, androstenedione and dehydroisoandrosterone in human plasma. *Steroids* 12:323-343, 1968.

FOWLER, E. H., VAUGHAN, T., GOTISIK, F., REICHHART, P., and REED, C. Pathologic changes in mammary glands and uteri from beagle bitches receiving low levels of medroxyprogesterone acetate: an overview of research in progress, in *Phar-*

macology of Steroid Contraceptive Drugs. S. Garattini and H. W. Berendes, eds. Raven Press, New York, 1977, pp. 185-210.

FREUND, K. Diagnosis and treatment of forensically significant anomalous erotic preferences. *Canadian J. Criminol.* 18:181-189, 1976.

FRICK, J., and BARTSCH, G. Reversible inhibition of spermatogenesis by various steroidal compounds, in *Human Semen and Fertility Regulation in Men.* E. S. E. Hafez, ed. Mosby, St. Louis, 1976, pp. 533-542.

FRISBIE, L., and DONDIS, E. Recidivism among treated sex offenders. *Research Monograph No. 5.* Department of Mental Hygiene, State of California, 1965.

GERSHBERG, H., ZORRILLA, E., HERNANDEZ, A., and HULSE, M. Effects of medroxyprogesterone acetate on serum insulin and growth hormone levels in diabetics and potential diabetics. *Obstet. Gynecol.* 33:383-389, 1969.

GOODLAND, R. L., REYNOLDS, J. G., MCCOORD, A. B., and POMMERENKE, W. T. Respiratory and electrolyte effects induced by estrogen and progesterone. *Fertil. Steril.* 4:300-317, 1953.

GOODLAND, R. L., REYNOLDS, J. G., and POMMERENKE, W. T. Alveolar carbon dioxide tension levels during pregnancy and early puerperium. *J. Clin. Endocrinol. Metab.* 14:522-530, 1954.

GORDON, G. G., SOUTHERN, A. L., TOCHIMOTO, S., OLIVO, J., ALTMAN, K., RAND, J., and LEMBERGER, L. Effect of medroxyprogesterone acetate (Provera®) on the metabolism and biological activity of testosterone. *J. Clin. Endocrinol Metab.* 30:449-456, 1970.

GROTH, A., and BURGESS, A. Sexual dysfunction during rape. *N. Engl. J. Med.* 297: 764-766, 1977.

GROTH, A., BURGESS, A., and HOLMSTROM, L. Rape: Power, anger, and sexuality. *Am. J. Psychiatry* 134:1239-1243, 1977.

GUPTA, C., MUSTO, N. A., BULLOCK, L. P., NAHRWOLD, D., OSTERMAN, J., and BARDIN, C. W. In vivo metabolism of progestins II. Metabolic clearance rate of medroxyprogesterone acetate in four species, in *Pharmacology of Steroid Contraceptive Drugs.* S. Garattini and H. W. Berendes, eds. Raven Press, New York, 1977, pp. 131-136.

HAHN, H. B., HAYLES, A. B., and ALBERT, A. Medroxyprogesterone and constitutional precocious puberty. *Mayo Clin. Proc.* 39:182-190, 1964.

HANSEL, W., CONCANNON, P. W., and MCENTEE, K. Plasma hormone profiles and pathological observations in medroxyprogesterone acetate treated beagle bitches, in *Pharmacology of Steroid Contraceptive Drugs.* S. Garattini and H. W. Berendes, eds. Raven Press, New York 1977, pp. 145-161.

HAYES, S., BROWNELL, K., and BARLOW, D. The use of self-administered covert sensitization in the treatment of exhibitionism and sadism. *Behavior Therapy* 9:283-289, 1978.

HELLMAN, L., YOSHIDA, K., ZUMOFF, B., LEVIN, J., KREAM, J., and FUKUSHIMA, D. K. The effect of medroxyprogesterone acetate on the pituitary-adrenal axis. *J. Clin. Endocrinol. Metab.* 42:912-917, 1976.

HILL, R., and DUMAS, K., The use of dogs for studies of toxicity of contraceptive hormones, in *Pharmacological Models in Contraceptive Development—WHO Symposium Geneva 1973.* M. H. Briggs and E. Diczfalusy, eds. Bogtrykkeriet Forum, Copenhagen 1974, pp. 74-84.

HIROI, M., STANEZYK, F. Z., GOEBELSMANN, U., BRENNER, P. F., LUMKIN, M. E., and MISHELL, D. R., JR. Radioimmunoassay of serum medroxyprogesterone acetate (Provera®) in women following oral and intravaginal administration. *Steroids* 26: 373-386, 1975.

JEPPSSON, S., and JOHANSSON, E. D. B. Medroxyprogesterone acetate, estradiol, FSH, and LH in peripheral blood after intramuscular administration of Depo-Provera® to women. *Contraception* 14:461-469, 1976.

JUDGE, D. M., KULIN, H. E., PAGE, R., SANTEN, R., and TRAPUKDI, S. Hypothalamic hamartoma—a source of luteinizing hormone factor in precocious puberty. *N. Engl. J. Med.* 296:7-10, 1977.

KALKHOFF, R. K., JACOBSON, M., and LEMPER, D. Progesterone, pregnancy and the augmented plasma insulin response. *J. Clin. Endocrinol. Metab.* 31:24-28, 1970.

KAPLAN, S. A., FRASIER, S. D., and COSTIN, G. Growth hormone secretion in idiopathic precocious puberty: effect of medroxyprogesterone. *J. Pediatr.* 75:133-138, 1969.

KAPLAN, S. A., LING, S. M., and IRANI, N. G. Idiopathic sexual precocity: therapy with medroxyprogesterone. *Am. J. Dis. Child.* 116:591-598, 1968.

KEENAN, B. S., MEYER, III, W. J., HADJEAN, A. J., and MIGEON, C. J. Androgen receptor in human skin fibroblasts characterization of a specific 17β-hydroxy-5α- androstan-3-one protein complex in cell sonicates and nuclei. *Steroids* 25: 535-552, 1975.

KOMISARUK, B. R., MCDONALD, P. G., WHITMOYER, D. I., and SAWYER, C. H. Effects of progesterone and sensory stimulation on EEG and neuronal activity in the rat. *Exp. Neurol.* 19:494-507, 1967.

KUPPERMAN, H. S., and EPSTEIN, J. A. Medroxyprogesterone acetate in the treatment of constitutional sexual precocity. *J. Clin. Endocrinol. Metab.* 22:456-458, 1962.

LASCHET, U., and LASCHET, L. Antiandrogens in the treatment of sexual deviations of men. *J. Steroid Biochem.* 6:821-826, 1975.

LAWRENCE, A. M., and KIRSTEINS, L. Progestins in the medical management of active acromegaly. *J. Clin. Endocrinol. Metab.* 30: 646-652, 1970.

LEMLI, L., ARON, M., and SMITH, D. W. The action of Depo-Provera in 3 girls with idiopathic isosexual precocity: decrease in estrogen effect without urinary gonadotropin reduction. *J. Pediatr.* 65:888-894, 1964.

LYONS, H. A., and ANTONIO, R. The sensitivity of the respiratory center in pregnancy and after the administration of progesterone. *Trans. Assoc. Am. Physicians* 72: 173-180, 1959.

LYONS, H. A., and HUANG, C. T. Therapeutic use of progesterone in alveolar hypoventilation associated with obesity. *Am. J. Med.* 44:881-888, 1968.

MARTIN, F., and ADLERCREUTZ, H. Aspects of megestrol acetate and medroxyprogesterone acetate metabolism, in *Pharmacology of Steroid Contraceptive Drugs.* S. Garattini and H. W. Berendes, eds. Raven Press, New York 1977, pp. 99-115.

MATHEWS, J. H., ABRAMS, C. A. L., and MORISHIMA, A. Pituitary adrenal function in ten patients receiving medroxyprogesterone acetate for true precocious puberty. *J. Clin. Endocrinol. Metab.* 30:653-658, 1970.

MERRYMAN, W., BOIMAN, R., BARNES, L., and ROTHCHILD, I. Progesterone "anesthesia" in human subjects. *J. Clin. Endocrinol. Metab.* 14:1567-1569, 1954.

MEYER, III, W. J., WALKER, P. A., WIEDEKING, C., MONEY, J., KOWARSKI, A. A., MIGEON, C. J., and BORGAONKAR, D. S. Pituitary function in adult males receiving medroxyprogesterone acetate. *Fertil. Steril.* 28:1072-1076, 1977.

MONEY, J. Discussion on hormonal inhibition of libido in male sex offenders in *Endocrinology and Human Behavior.* R. Michael, ed. Oxford University Press, London 1968, p. 169.

MONEY, J. Use of an androgen-depleting hormone in the treatment of male sex offenders. *J. Sex Research* 6:165-172, 1970.

MONEY, J. Paraphilias, in *Handbook of Sexology,* J. Money and H. Musaph, eds. Elsevier, Amsterdam 1977, pp. 917-928.

MONEY, J., WIEDEKING, C., WALKER, P. A., and GAIN, D. Combined antiandrogenic and counseling program for treatment of 46,XY and 47,XYY sex offenders, in *Hormones, Behavior and Psychopathology,* E. Sachar, ed. Raven Press, New York, 1976, pp. 105-120.

MONEY, J., WIEDEKING, C., WALKER, P., MIGEON, C., MEYER, W., and BORGAONKAR, D. 47, XYY and 46, XY males with antisocial and/or sex-offending behavior: antiandrogen therapy plus counseling. *Psychoneuroendocrinology* 1:165-178, 1975.

MOWSZOWICZ, I., BIEBER, D. E., CHUNG, K. W., BULLOCK, L. P., and BARDIN, C. W. Synandrogenic and antiandrogenic effect of progestins: comparison with non-progestational antiandrogens. *Endocrinology* 95:1589-1599, 1974.

NELSON, L. W., CARLTON, W. W., and WEIKEL, JR., J. H., Canine mammary neoplasms and progestogens. *J.A.M.A.* 219:1601-1606, 1972.

ORTIZ, A., HIROI, M., STANCZYK, F. Z., GOEBELSMANN, U., and MISHELL, D. R. Serum medroxyprogesterone acetate (MPA) concentrations and ovarian function following intramuscular injection of Depo—MPA. *J. Clin. Endocrinol. Metab.* 44:32-38, 1977.

RAKE, J. S., HAFIZ, S. A., LESSOF, M. H., and SNODGRASS, G. J. A. I. A trial of medroxyprogesterone acetate in acromegaly. *Clin. Endocrinol.* 1:181-187, 1972.

RICHMAN, R. A., UNDERWOOD, L. E., FRENCH, F. A., and VAN WYK, J. J. Adverse effects of large doses of medroxyprogesterone (MPA) in idiopathic isosexual precocity. *J. Pediatr.* 79:963-971, 1971.

RIFKIND, A. B., KULIN, H. E., CARGILLE, C. M., RAYFORD, P. C., and ROSS, G. T. Suppression of urinary excretion of luteinizing hormone (LH) and follicle stimulating hormone (FSH) by medroxyprogesterone acetate. *J. Clin. Endocrinol. Metab.* 29:506-513, 1969.

RIVAROLA, M. A., CAMANCHO, A. M., and MIGEON, C. J. Effect of treatment with medroxyprogesterone acetate (Provera®) on testicular function. *J. Clin. Endocrinol. Metab.* 26:263-370, 1966.

SADEGHI-NEJAD, A., KAPLAN, S. L., and GRUMBACH, M. M. The effect of medroxyprogesterone acetate on andrenocortical function in children with precocious puberty. *J. Pediatr.* 78:616-624, 1971.

SAENGER, P., SHANIES, D. D., and NEW, M. I. Influence of medroxyprogesterone acetate on testosterone metabolism by cultured human fibroblasts: a model for drug-steroid interaction. *J. Clin. Endocrinol. Metab.* 37:760-764, 1973.

SAXENA, B. W., SHRIMANKER, K., and GRUDZINSKAS, J. G. Levels of contraceptive steroids in breast milk and plasma of lactating women. *Contraception* 16:605-624, 1977.

SCHOEN, E. J. Treatment of idiopathic precocious puberty in boys. *J. Clin. Endocrinol. Metab.* 26:363-370, 1966.

SHORKEY, C., and CANGELOSI, S. *Modification of Sexual Behavior: Summary and Annotated Bibliography*. American Psychological Association, Washington, D.C., 1975.

SIMON, S., SCHIFFER, M., GLICK, S. M., and SCHWARTZ, E. Effect of medroxyprogesterone acetate upon stimulated release of growth hormone in men. *J. Clin. Endocrinol. Metab.* 27:1633-1636, 1967.

SPELLACY, W. N., MCLEOD, A. G. W., BUHI, W. C., and BIRK, S. A. The effects of medroxyprogesterone acetate on carbohydrate metabolism: measurements of glucose, insulin, and growth hormone after twelve months' use. *Fertil. Steril.* 23: 239-244, 1972.

SUTTON, E. D., ZWILLICH, C. W., CREAGH, C. E., PIERSON, D. J., and WEIL, J. V. Progesterone for outpatient treatment of Pickwickian syndrome. *Ann. Intern. Med.* 83:476-479, 1975.

TSENG, L., and GURPIDE, E. Effect of progestins on estradiol receptor levels in human endometrium. *J. Clin. Endocrinol. Metab.* 41:402-404, 1975.

TUTTLE, S., and TURKINGTON, V. E. Effects of medroxyprogesterone acetate on carbohydrate metabolism. *Obstet. Gynecol.* 43:685-692, 1974.

VERMEULEN, A., and THIERY, M. Hormonal contraceptives and carbohydrate tolerance II. Influence of medroxyprogesterone acetate and chronic oral contraceptives. *Diabetologia* 10:253-259, 1974.

WALKER, P. A. Medroxyprogesterone acetate as an antiandrogen for the rehabilitation of sex offenders, in *Progress in Sexology*. R. Gemme and T. Wheeler, eds. Plenum Press, New York 1977, pp. 205-207.

WALKER, P. A. The role of antiandrogens in the treatment of sex offenders, in *The Prevention of Sexual Disorders: Issues and Approaches*. C. Qualls, J. Wincze, and D. Barlow, eds. Plenum Press, New York 1978, pp. 117-136.

WORLD HEALTH ORGANIZATION Special Programme of Research, Development, and Research Training in Human Reproduction Task Force on Long Acting Systemic Agents for the Regulation of Fertility. Multinational comparative clinical evaluation of two long acting injectable contraceptive steroids: norethisteron oenanthate and medroxyprogesterone acetate. 2. Bleeding patterns and side effect. *Contraception* 17:395-406, 1978.

ZIMMERMAN, A. W., HOLDEN, K. R., REITER, E. O. and DEKABAN, A. S. Medroxyprogesterone acetate in the treatment of seizures associated with menstruation. *J. Pediatr.* 83:959-963, 1973.

CHAPTER 23

Treatment of Child-Abusing Families

RITA JUSTICE
BLAIR JUSTICE

In addressing the problem of treating child-abusing families we focus on five questions: How serious is the problem of child abuse? What is our role in treatment? How does child abuse occur? What is our approach to treating these families, and how do we evaluate changes that parents make so as to determine when a home is safe for a child?

Child abuse is a problem that has reached epidemic proportions (Light, 1973). Kempe (1969, 1971) reports that about 25 percent of all fractures seen in children in the first two years of life and 10 to 15 percent of all physical trauma seen in the first three years are the result of abuse by parents or parent surrogates. Estimates of the total number of actual cases per year range from Zalba's (1971) estimate of 200,000 to 250,000 with 30,000 seriously hurt, to Light's (1973) of a half-million, to Gil's (1970) of an upper limit of between 2.5 and 4.1 million. The seriousness of the problem is magnified even more by the fact that more than 50 percent of the children who are abused will be abused again if there is no therapeutic intervention (Fontana, 1964).

There are a number of therapeutic strategies of intervention in child abuse. The one we use is group therapy with the abusive parent. We began our first group in 1973 and since that time have seen 32 couples. The characteristics of our clients are: 75 percent of the parents were between 20 and 40 years old at the time of the reported incident and 25 percent were under 20 (Justice and Justice, 1976). Eighty-five percent of the men in our group hold skilled or semiskilled jobs and 15 percent are in white collar or professional occupations. Forty percent of the women are members of the labor force; 88 percent of these women hold skilled or semiskilled jobs and 12 percent are in white collar or professional positions. Two of the 32 families were receiving welfare when the abuse occurred and an additional 10 percent received other public assistance. Twenty percent of the men and women in our group had college or graduate training or degrees. Seventy percent are high school graduates and 10 percent have a grade school education. The ethnic makeup of the group approximates that of our geographic area: 63 percent Caucasian, 25 percent black, and 12 percent Mexican-American.

In our sample, 30 percent of the parents had been severely beaten as children and 13 percent had been in foster care. Five percent seem to be psychopathic or borderline psychotic and the remainder fit no single classification in the *Diagnostic and Statistical Manual of Mental Disorders, II.*

Almost all parents we have seen have been referred to us by local child welfare agencies. Sevently-five percent of the parents have temporarily lost both physical and legal custody of at least one of their children at the time they come to therapy. They enter therapy under duress; they understand from the court that their chances of having their children returned —or not removed—will be greatly enhanced by their coming for therapy. Thus, they are initially quite angry and resentful about being in group. That anger dissipates after two or three weeks. There is no screening, other than our asking that both parents in the family attend if there is both a mother and father in the household. The group meets once a week, in the evening, for an hour and a half. The parents go through the admissions procedure of the Texas Research Institute of Mental Sciences and are billed on a sliding-fee basis by that agency. Couples stay in group therapy an average of six months.

Our results with the parents have been encouraging. Of the 32 couples we have seen, three dropped out and subsequently had their parental rights terminated by the court. Among the remaining 29 couples, there has been one recurrence of abuse, but the child welfare worker did not find it necessary to remove the abused child nor any of the other children in the home.

How does child abuse happen in the first place? Child abuse is the result of a system of interaction between parents, child, the environment,

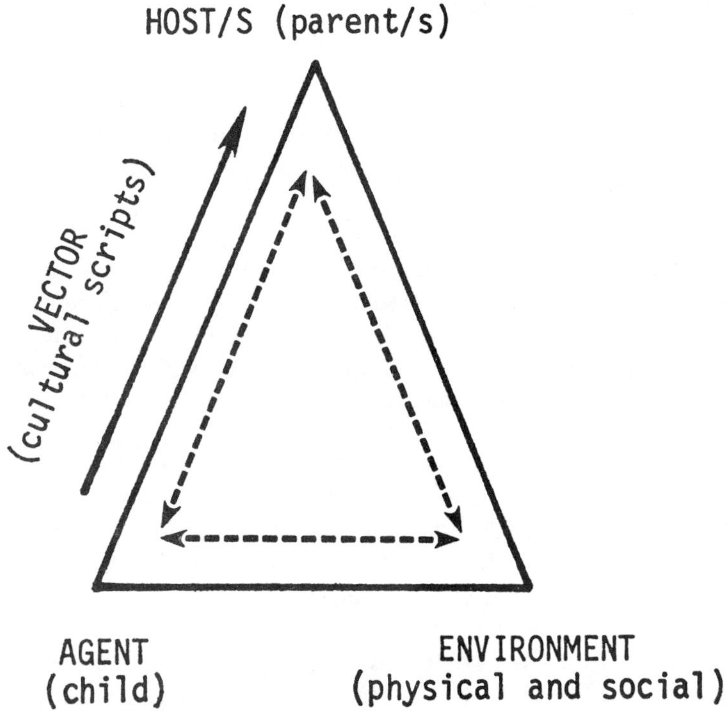

FIGURE 1. A psychosocial stress model of child abuse.

and society. This interaction is represented in a Psychosocial Stress Model of Child Abuse (Figure 1), which is our theoretical base.

We first consider the characteristics of the parents. To understand the role played by the parents, it is necessary to look in detail at the parenting they have received as children. Every abusive parent we have seen was physically and/or emotionally abused as a child. This has been true of the parent who actually inflicts the physical injury on the child and of the passive spouse.

Most abusive parents are products of what Helfer (1974) calls the "world of abnormal rearing." The cycle begins with parents' unrealistic expectations of their child. They expect to *receive* nurturing from their offspring, not give it. The child complies as well as he or she can but, in the process, the child develops a sense of distrust, becomes isolated and, consequently, the child's social skills are impaired. When grown, the child is likely to pick a mate who has similar problems. They marry with the expectations that their mate will nurture them and give them the kind of love they never received as children. Both husband and wife are disappointed, but one gives in and assumes the caretaker role most of the time. That person, the "loser" in the struggle for nurturing, decides to have a child, with the idea that a baby will give the much-needed and never-received love. When the child fails to fulfill such a heavy demand, and the parent experiences stress, abuse occurs.

Why does the parent's frustration, anger, and disappointment take the form of child abuse instead of some other expression of violence? The majority of abusing parents—and, in our sample, all of them—repeat a pattern they learned in childhood. They grew up with a model of abuse, and as adults they display such behavior toward their offspring when in crisis.

From a systems point of view, the violence is an expression of tension in the emotional and relationship system of the abusive family. To use Bowen's terms (quoted in Framo, 1972), the kind of emotional and relationship system that characterizes the abusive family is one of great intensity, force, and fusion or "stucktogetherness." Since the parents are so undifferentiated in the sense of being fused into others who make up the nuclear or extended family, they do not have a sense of separate self or autonomy. The less differentiation there is, the more likely is it that problems will occur during stress. These problems may be expressed in three ways: marital conflict, dysfunction in a spouse, and transmission of the problem to one or more children (Bowen, 1966). The marital conflict takes the form of fights between the spouses as if to see which one will obtain more of the common self. Dysfunction in one of the spouses usually means that one has given in to the other. The dysfunction may be physical, emotional, or social. Social dysfunction in a spouse spills over into violent behavior that is directed against the child. The family system must absorb so much undifferentiation that there may not only be violence by father or mother but a problem in all three areas: conflict between spouses, the dysfunction of one, and a problem with the child. The root of the problem is competition within the family system over which one will be taken care of by the other. The winner is cared for but the loser must escalate to extreme behavior—like violence—to obtain care.

At this point the child becomes a factor in the psychosocial stress model. The parent's violence is directed at a "special" child, the one the parent perceives as being most in need of attention or care and is therefore the most threatening competitor to the parent seeking the same thing. The specialness may be real or exist only in the eyes of the parent. At high risk of being abused are children who are premature, twins, retarded or handicapped, adopted, congenitally malformed, conceived during the mother's depressive illness, or children of mothers with frequent pregnancies. In short, children who are different or require more care than most children are at risk. However, the difference may be only that the child reminds the parent of someone disliked, even the parent himself or herself.

Among the children whose parents have been in our group, 67 percent were between 4 months and 3 years of age at the time of the abuse. When four-year-olds are included, the percentage rises to 79 percent. Fifty-nine percent of the abused children in our group sample are girls. Seventeen percent of the children were born to single mothers, and one-fourth of the mothers were depressed at the time the babies were born. In our sample, none of the abused children come from families with four or more children; the largest percentage (38 percent) are from families with two children. One specific child—the different one—is often the only target of abuse. Only one child was abused in 80 percent of the cases.

Some children, seemingly from birth, are more difficult to manage and apparently contribute to the likelihood of abuse. Some have a particularly grating quality in their crying; nurses and social workers have confessed understanding why a parent might batter that child (Gil, 1970). We emphasize, however, that even the most difficult-to-manage child is unlikely to be abused unless the other factors in the psychological stress model are also present.

Perhaps what most clearly distinguishes the abusive parent's environment from that of normal parents is that abusers often are in a state of life crisis at the time the abuse occurs. We compared 35 abusing parents from our groups with an equal number of nonabusers who were similar in age, education, and income (Justice and Duncan, 1976). Although the nonabusive parents also had problems with their children, none had ever abused them. We asked the parents in each group to fill out the Holmes and Rahe Social Readjustment Rating Scale (1967). The scale lists 43 events or changes that could occur in a year in the life of a person—changes that require readjustments as a means of coping. The changes range from death of a spouse as the event requiring most readjustment to minor violations of the law, judged to require the least. The abusing parents scored an average of about 234 on the scale while the nonabusers scored and average of about 124 (Table 1). A score of 200 to 299 is considered as indicating a moderate life crisis.

The changes experienced by the abusing parents constituted a series of situational and maturational crises that exceeded their ability to adapt.

Table 1

Distribution of Life-Change Scores for Abusing and Nonabusing Parents[a]

Parent group	No crisis 0-149	Mild crisis 150-199	Moderate crisis 200-299	Major crisis 300+
	Life-change scores			
Abusers (N = 35) $\bar{x} = 233.63$	4	9	14	8
Nonabusers (N = 35) $\bar{x} = 123.62$	25	5	3	2

[a] $x^2 = 25.69$, $p < .001$; $t_{ind} = 4.28$, $p < .001$.

They had no time to regroup before a new crisis occurred. In terms of Selye's (1956) three stages of response to stress (alarm, resistance, and exhaustion), no sooner had they passed through the first phase of alarm and entered the resistance stage than they were confronted with a new crisis that plunged them into exhaustion. In this third stage their defenses were lowest and their inner controls against acting out were weakest.

The final factor in the psychosocial stress model is what we call cultural scripts, the accepted and expected patterns of interaction between individuals in a society. We are concerned with the expected patterns between parent and child. One cultural script, embodied in the saying "spare the rod and spoil the child," reflects the attitude that violence toward children is not only acceptable but necessary. Other cultural myths are those of the madonna mother and the Gerber baby. Both myths are perpetrated by the advertising media that portray mothers as kind, loving, serene, and organized supermoms and all babies as cute, cuddly, clean, and easy to care for. When the facts do not match these ideal images, potentially abusive parents experience anger and guilt that further increases their tension. We have found that all factors in the psychosocial stress model—parent, child, environment, and cultural scripts—must be considered to understand child abuse and account for its occurrence.

Using the psychosocial stress model as a theoretical base in treatment of abusive parents, we concentrate on identifying and changing behaviors that contribute to the abuse. The first evening parents enter our group, we ask them to fill out a checklist of problems that are of possible concern to them (Table 2). We have found this to be a nonthreatening way for clients to identify and communicate to us the problems they are experi-

Table 2

Problems Checklist

Which of the following are areas of concern to you?
(Check here)

—— Low Self-Image—low opinion of self, think you're no good, can't do anything right.
—— Don't Have Friends—stay to self a lot, isolated from others, feel alone.
—— Temper and/or Impatience—have a "short fuse," blow up easily, or get impatient with nearly everyone.
—— Dependent—depend heavily on spouse, can't make decisions yourself, can't make it without spouse or some other relative; often irresponsible.
—— Little Support from Spouse—have to do most of decision-making yourself, can't depend on spouse to help with kids or to give "moral support," or to say nice things.
—— Stress—feel under much pressure all the time from job, kids, house, finances or other reasons.
—— Child Development and Needs—don't know much about the needs of babies and children at various ages and what to expect.
—— Sex—little or no sexual satisfaction in marriage, frustration, arguments over sex.
—— Trust—can't trust anyone, always being let down, look at people with suspicion.
—— Depression—feel down and hopeless; have trouble getting things done and making decisions; life looks bleak.
—— Child is Disappointment—child isn't loving or doesn't do what you expect or seems different from other children.
—— Child Care and Management—need to know much more about what to do for and with baby or child at various ages, and how to get child to "behave."

Make sure you have checked all the problems that are of concern to you.

Now look at the list of problems again and RANK them in terms of which are bigger problems and which are smaller problems.

For example, if Temper/Impatience is your biggest problem, put the number 1 by it in the list below. Then go down the list and see what is your second biggest problem. If Trust is the second biggest, put a 2 by it.

Put numbers by all the problems that are of concern to you so you will rank them according to importance. If two are of EQUAL weight or importance, put the same number by each of the problems.

Rank Problems by
putting number by
each concern)

—— Low Self-Image
—— Don't Have Friends
—— Temper and/or Impatience
—— Dependent
—— Little Support from Spouse
—— Stress
—— Child Development and Needs
—— Sex
—— Trust
—— Depression
—— Child Care and Management
—— Child is Disappointment

encing in their lives. Based on these problems, we set goals and make contracts using goal-attainment scaling (GAS) (Kiresuk and Sherman, 1968). GAS is an evaluation and therapeutic tool that requires identifying the main concerns of abusive couples and setting goals to be reached in therapy in each area. The typical problems we see are symbiosis, isolation, talking and sharing with mate, temper and/or impatience, child development and management, and employment.

A GAS follow-up guide is constructed for each person in the group, setting goals to be reached for each area of concern in a three-month period. The same guide is used for follow-up after the couple leaves the group.

Our therapeutic methods include transactional analysis (TA), which is both a theory of personality organization and a therapeutic tool for change; Rational Emotive Therapy (Ellis, 1973); behavior therapy, using techniques like those developed by Lazarus (1972) and Wolpe (1969); child management techniques and information on the needs of children during specific developmental stages; and group dynamics, which we use as a way to promote group support of the changes being made by individual members.

Once we have set up goals to be accomplished, what do we do therapeutically about each problem? Symbiosis is the first problem we work on because its consequences are usually the most serious. We use the term symbiosis as it is defined in transactional analysis literature, specifically in the work of Jacqui Schiff (Schiff and Schiff, 1971). When we attempt to break up the symbiotic relationships between an abusive couple, we think in terms of strengthening two separate personalities. In TA terms, we want each person to begin using Parent, Adult, and Child as his or her own ego state, and to stop trying to force the mate to be responsible for him or her. Figure 2 illustrates a symbiotic relationship of one couple in our group with the husband discounting—not showing—his feelings while the wife discounts her ability to think and be a caretaker.

A symbiotic relationship might be expressed in group, for example, when we ask the wife a question and her husband answers. We begin breaking up the symbiosis by asking that couple to agree to a contract: when we ask Jane a question, she, not John, will answer. Such a contract makes the couple aware of the extent of their stucktogetherness, and they begin seeing and changing other examples of symbiotic behavior in their lives.

Working on the problem of isolation, we ask the abusive parents to contract to do things that will break up their loneliness; to make two new friends in a specified time, to get a telephone, to go out to dinner with another couple, to meet their neighbors, and so forth. Abusive parents

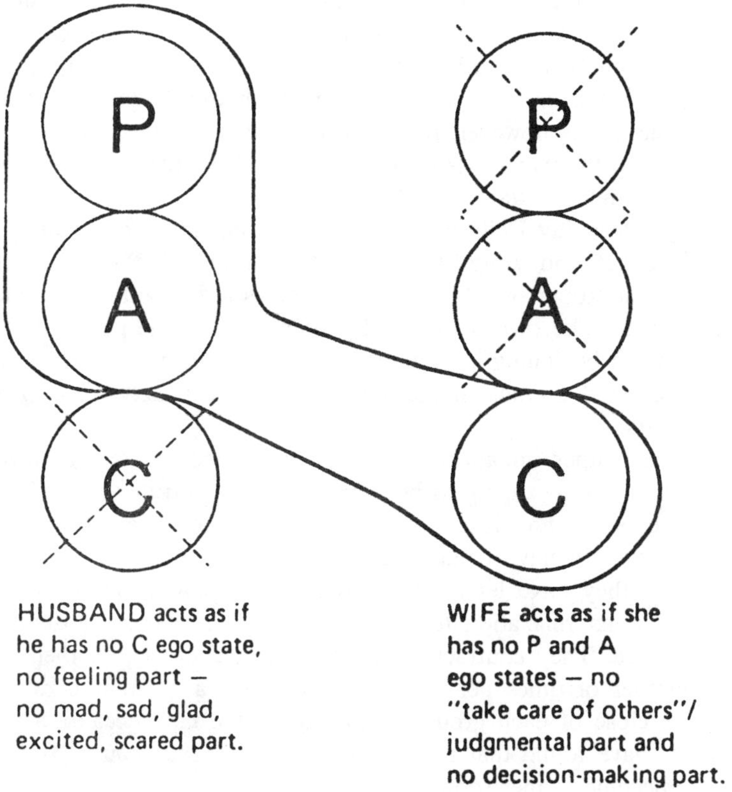
P
A
C
P
A
C
HUSBAND acts as if he has no C ego state, no feeling part – no mad, sad, glad, excited, scared part.
WIFE acts as if she has no P and A ego states – no "take care of others"/ judgmental part and no decision-making part.

FIGURE 2. A symbiotic relationship at one point in time.

are often cut off from others both in fact and in feeling. They have few contacts with people outside their immediate families. Being in group is an important first step in breaking up the isolation of abusing parents, but the group meetings are not sufficient to break up lifelong patterns. Hence, we use behavior modification contracts for changes that will increase the parents' "people contact" outside group.

In addressing the problem of talking and sharing with mate, the focus is on teaching the couples to communicate effectively. The couples entering our group invariably have marital problems. Initially they put up a united front, verbally denying they have any problem with their marriage, but the checklist filled out at the beginning of the first group session helps to bring areas of discord into the open. It is not uncommon for a couple in our group to report that they talk to each other only when necessary and that what talking they do is angry or critical. Della, for example, complained that she was lonely and ready to talk to an adult after spending the whole day trapped in the house with her two small children. When her husband Robert came home, however, he would immediately turn on the television set and pick up the paper, not even speaking to her except to say hello and to ask when dinner would be ready.

We began teaching Della and Robert the communication techniques of "active listening" and using "I messages" (Gordon, 1970). The two also contracted that Robert would spend 15 minutes a day with Della when he got home, before he turned on the TV or picked up the paper. The contract was just a beginning in getting them to start sharing with each other, but it represented a crack in the wall they had built between each other over the years.

As to the temper/impatience problem, we found the temper levels of people in our group ranging to both ends of the spectrum. The acting-out partners are often short-fused, hot-tempered people, whereas the passive partners frequently have trouble expressing anger at all, or they express it only after they have let it build up to the exploding point. In group we teach parents relaxation techniques to help them control their anger and impatience. They contract to practice the techniques on their own a certain number of times per week. We also play a 15-minute relaxation tape at the close of each group session. Since the tape became a regular feature, we have found that the parents seem to make changes faster and their lives become calmer sooner.

The point we emphasize is that people do have control over their anger, and that they get angry and impatient when their needs are not being met. We teach the parents to identify their needs and to meet them in non-exploitive ways.

Our approach to the issue of child development and management involves giving information the parents do not have. Many parents, abusive and not, are ignorant of the developmental stages of children—what children need at each stage and what a parent should and should not do. They also do not know child management techniques other than physical punishment. All parents in our group receive a chart of developmental stages and needs (Table 3) which we compiled from various sources.

Parents contract to learn the different stages, needs, and responses and to report on them in group. In doing so, they bring up questions they have about their children and they correct misinformation. The group members participate in oral multiple-choice exercises from Smith and Smith's *Child Management* (1966). Outside of group, the parents contract to read books

Table 3

Developmental Stages and Needs

Age	Stage	What the Child Needs	What Parent Needs to Do	What Parent Shouldn't Do
0-6 months (or crawling)	Early Oral (Existential)	To establish symbiosis Food and physical stroking To find that he/she has impact on the environment Talk	Feed, fondle, talk to baby When baby cries, check to see what is wrong Try out different things to soothe child	Don't withhold strokes Don't feed on schedule Don't spank Don't hover over baby when there's no discomfort
6 months-1½ or 2 years	Late Oral (Exploratory)	Move around Get into things Drop things Self-feed	Continue giving unconditional positive strokes "Baby-proof" the house Provide protection	Don't restrict mobility Don't force toilet training Don't spoon or force-feed Don't spank
1½ or 2-3 years	Anal (Separation)	To test and oppose To be negative Break symbiosis Learn to consider needs and feelings of others	Expect child to start considering others Expect child to use cause-and-effect thinking and problem-solving Institute disciplining Begin toilet-training	Don't fail to discipline (not punish) and give reason to convey expectations Don't make expectations too high or be too demanding Don't be inconsistent toward child
3-6 years (can be 2½-5)	Genital (Imaginative)	Identify differences in self and others: sex, color hair, eyes Ask questions Move away more from parents physically Invent monsters	Answer all questions with reasons Encourage problem-solving Teach how to get strokes	Don't answer questions with "because I said so" Don't get uptight over masturbation Don't tease

Table 3 (continued)

Developmental Stages and Needs

Age	Stage	What the Child Needs	What Parent Needs to Do	What Parent Shouldn't Do
6-12 years	Latency (Creative)	Argue, compete, achieve Do things, have companions Join community activity	Discuss values and state rules Listen to child's reasons Encourage task completion and setting priorities	Don't make rules and values too rigid Don't fail to discuss rules and values
13-18 years (puberty through teens)	Adolescence (Recycling)	Be contradictory Be part child, part adult Say, in effect: "Go away closer" and "Tell me what to do—I dare you." Recycle previous stages	Stick by rules and values Encourage independence but still offer "protection" and guidance	Don't give up Don't be over-protective or under-protective

on child management, ranging from simple ones like *TA for Tots* (Freed, 1974), to more sophisticated ones, like *Parent Effectiveness Training* (Gordon, 1970).

Employment may be a problem for abusive families in different ways. A job might be adding stress to already overstressed lives. Not infrequently, people in our group are experiencing some type of employment stress at the time they abuse their children. For some, the stress is from being laid off, for others it is a result of holding several jobs or working double shifts while the mate is not working at all; for still others, the stress is in working at jobs where they are unhappy. Because the types of stress from employment situations vary, the contracts among our group members also vary. In one couple's case, the husband was able to quit one of his two jobs when the wife decided, with group support, to get a job and to stop sitting at home watching soap operas while hoping child welfare authorities would return their baby.

Group dynamics come into play when one person uses the experiences of others to make a job decision. One night Al announced that he wanted to ask the men in the group what they thought about his moving from one job to another. Because Al had few friends at the time, the men in the group became a sort of peer group for him, with whom he could share feelings and ideas and make a decision with more security than he would have done without their help.

As mentioned earlier, the stress of constant environmental change is a problem reflected in all aspects of the lives of the couples we see. We address this by showing the parents how they score on the social readjustment rating scale and explaining the significance of the scores. We give them information on how to modify the effects of the stress of constant change and, most importantly, we ask them to defer changes that are not absolutely necessary. Many abusive parents do not seem to know when to say no, and they often seem not to consider factors that are likely to force them to make even more changes. For example, they may move into an apartment without a lease and then have to move again in a few months. So our work in the area of stress and change consists of teaching the parents to slow down and to plan ahead.

The final questions are those of returning the child home and follow-up evaluation. We use a quantitative method, goal attainment score, for deciding when a couple has made enough changes for the child to be returned home safely. Our follow-ups of parents since 1973 confirm that when clients obtain a GAS score of 55 or more, it is safe for the child to return home. Since we have used these criteria for the child's return and for termination of therapy (which occurs usually one to two months after the child has been returned), there has been one recurrence of physical abuse among the 29 couples who completed therapy with us. Six-month follow-ups show that expected levels of outcome and composite GAS scores of 55 are holding up.

When the couples leave the group and their child has returned home, the overall changes they made have followed this general pattern: their symbiotic relationship has changed so that they are meeting their own needs and providing mutual support for each other; their isolation has changed to mixing with people, telephoning people, and reaching out for help when needed; the talking and sharing with the mate has moved from silence or criticism to regular exchange of positive strokes and mutual support; the impatience and/or temper has changed to more relaxed behavior; child development and management have been learned so that the parents understand the needs of their children and are making appropriate parenting responses, using techniques of management other than physical discipline; employment changes center on getting a job or learning to keep from getting uptight at work or using work to avoid relationships at home; and the parents are keeping their life changes at a manageable level.

REFERENCES

BOWEN, M. The use of family therapy in clinical practice. *Compr. Psychiatry* 7: 360-361, 1966.

ELLIS, A. *Humanistic Psychology*. Julian Press, New York, 1973.

FONTANA, V. J. The neglect and abuse of children. *State J. Med.* 64:215-218, 1964.

FRAMO, J. L., ed. Toward the differentiation of a self in one's own family, in *Family Interaction*. Springer, New York 1972, p. 121.

FREED, A. *TA for Tots*. Jalmer, Sacramento, California, 1974.

GIL, D. G. *Violence Against Children*. Harvard University Press, Cambridge, Massachusetts 1970, pp. 58-60, pp. 29-30.

GORDON, T. *Parent Effectiveness Training*. Wyden, New York, 1970.

HELFER, R. E. *A Self-Instructional Program on Child Abuse and Neglet*. With Committee on Infants and Preschool Child of American Academy of Pediatrics and National Center for the Prevention and Treatment of Child Abuse and Neglect, Denver 1974, Unit 1, p. 12.

HOLMES, T. H., and RAHE, R. H. The social readjustment rating scale. *J. Psychosom. Res.* 11:213-218, 1967.

KEMPE, C. H. The battered child and the hospital. *Hospital Practice* 4:44-51, 1969.

KEMPE, C. H. Pediatric implications of the battered baby syndrome. *Arch. Dis. Child.* 46:28-37, 1971.

KIRESUK, T. J., and SHERMAN, R. E. Goal attainment scaling: A general method for evaluating comprehensive community mental health programs. *Community Ment. Health J.* 4:443-453, 1968.

JUSTICE, B., and DUNCAN, D. F. Life crisis as a precursor to child abuse. *Public Health Rep.* 91:110-115, 1976.

JUSTICE, B., and JUSTICE, R. *The Abusing Family*. Human Sciences Press, New York 1976, pp. 90-93.

LAZARUS, A. A., ed. *Clinical Behavior Therapy*. Brunner-Mazel, New York, 1972.

LIGHT, R. J. Abused and neglected children in America: A study of alternative policies. *Harvard Educational Review* 43, pp. 559-587, 1973.
SCHIFF, A. W., and SCHIFF, J. Passivity. *Transactional Analysis Journal* 1:1, 1971.
SELYE, H. *The Stress of Life*. McGraw-Hill, New York, 1956, pp. 31-33.
SMITH, J. M. and SMITH, D. E. P. *Child Management: A Program for Parents*. Ann Arbor Publishers, Ann Arbor, Michigan, 1966.
WOLPE, J. *The Practice of Behavior Therapy*. Pergamon Press, New York, 1969.
ZALBA, S. A. Battered children. *Trans-Action* 8:58-61, 1971.

CHAPTER 24

The Treatment of Psychological Emergencies

DIANA SULLIVAN EVERSTINE
LOUIS EVERSTINE
ARTHUR M. BODIN

The Emergency Treatment Center (ETC) provides a program of intensive services designed to meet the needs of family members and other persons who are experiencing psychological emergencies. The center, an independent nonprofit corporation that is affiliated with the Mental Research Institute, has been in operation since February 1975.

The seven-days-a-week, 24-hours-a-day program of the center is coordinated with the work of ten Northern California police departments to help in such emergency situations as family fights and suicide attempts as well as instances in which persons are believed to be severely emotionally disturbed; in addition, the center responds to any kind of crisis call that involves children and adolescents. The population of the area served is about 760,000, of whom about 150,000 are between 10 and 17 years of age.

The Emergency Treatment Center's basic rationale is a belief in the importance of reaching out to people when they are in crisis, as opposed to waiting passively for the properly motivated client to seek us out. Unfortunately for the person who is in a psychological emergency, the experience does not always occur between the hours of eight and five on weekdays. And if an emergency call must be made at 3:30 in the morning, it will very likely be the police who are called. Yet few police officers have either the temperament or the training to cope with these emotionally charged and highly ambiguous psychological emergencies. Moreover, many people are afraid of dealing with the police because of presumptions of racial prejudice; or, they fear that a record within the criminal justice system may be opened or an existing record expanded. Many have a not completely unfounded skepticism about the ability of police officers, considering the framework in which they operate, to be helpful or sensitive when working with *crimeless victims,* that is, with people who have not done anything culpable (Everstine et al., 1977). Those who hold that view may believe that the police approach predisposes the officer to assigning blame and to discovering a "guilty party." And the police themselves look upon their primary roles as the apprehension of criminals and the prevention of crime. For them to be present in a situation that in no way involves a crime is, in their view, taking them away from their primary function.

When people are caught up in a psychological emergency and choose to call the police, they may not have given logical thought to whether or not they were calling the right agency. They call because they want help and want it fast. They may have chosen to call the police because they did not know of any other agency or knew that only the police would respond. But their reasons for calling are irrelevant when one considers that if the emergency is truly psychological in nature, they have called the wrong agency. In the process, their expectations of help in resolving their problems are likely to be unrealized. The most a police officer can be expected to do is to take some of the electricity out of an emotionally charged situation, often more by his presence than by what he does or says. The officer may be able to defuse the crisis temporarily and, when necessary, make a referral to a more appropriate agency.

Because the ETC staff is on call every day at all hours of the day or night and is able to respond directly to the scene of the crisis, we are able to reach persons who would seldom find their way to the local mental health care delivery system. Since their first impulse was, in most cases, to call the police, they are probably reluctant to define their current problem or problems as "mental" or psychological. For that reason, even if a police officer had responded to the call and had done what he could to defuse the situation, these people would probably not have planned a visit to their neighborhood clinic on the following morning. The typical family who receives service from ETC is a working-class or lower middle-class family. In many of those families, people tend to be fearful and suspicious of "psychotherapy" because they are well aware of the stigma that is attached to being a mental patient or to showing some kind of emotional weakness or defect. The name "Emergency Treatment Center" was selected for the express purpose of avoiding that kind of labeling and allaying that fear.

The Model

The program of the Emergency Treatment Center represents a new model that is intended to take the place of earlier models of crisis intervention. The program operates as follows. Mobile teams, consisting of two persons (a man and a woman) are on call during the hours when most conventional mental health agency facilities are closed. ETC supervisory staff is always available (by telephone or radio pages) to the on-duty staff or to additional cases when the need arises.

A major source of referrals to ETC is the police officer in the field who has encountered an emergency situation. Depending upon the severity of the emergency, the officer has a choice among several options. He can: place a direct call to the ETC emergency number (292-HELP), have the police dispatcher telephone ETC, or ask the person or family to initiate the call to ETC. Other main sources of emergency calls are mental health agencies, hospital emergency rooms, crisis services such as parental-stress and suicide hotlines, the juvenile probation department, the social services (welfare) department, and family members themselves who have learned of the ETC telephone number from media public service announcements. The on-duty staff members carry radio pagers which are activated immediately by the answering service when a caller is on the line. The counselor goes to the nearest telephone, calls the answering service, and the incoming call is "patched" to the line on which the counselor is calling. Because of the efficient operation of this communications network, the team can usually reach the scene of an event within 20 to 30 minutes of the initial emergency call.

Another aspect of the ETC model is that our teams have more time flexibility than do the police. Generally, police officers can spend no more than 30 minutes off the street before their absence from regular patrol duties begins to be felt by other officers on patrol. The Center's staff members, by contrast, are not under this kind of time pressure; they can remain on the scene until the immediate emergency has been resolved. The average initial ETC visit lasts 2.3 hours, although some extremely unusual situations (such as the aftermath of a parent's suicide or the case of a person who is barricaded in an apartment) have required as many as eight hours to resolve.

When a team of ETC counselors arrives at the scene of an emergency, therapy begins at that moment, and any subsequent therapy that is necessary will be conducted by one or both members of the team. Every effort is made to ensure this continuity of service to the family. Although ETC does not provide long-term treatment, the Center staff generally sees clients for at least two, and as many as six, visits. In addition, any referral that is made for special services or long-term therapy is followed up by the Center staff until the referral connection is functioning.

The ETC model differs from that of most mobile psychiatric evaluation units, and indeed from most police family crisis intervention units such as the Bard (1960) or Schwartz and Liebman (1972) models, in this critical aspect: the people who respond to the emergency calls are trained therapists who begin and, if necessary, continue the therapy in the home, office, or elsewhere until the emergency situation is resolved and steps have been taken to prevent recurrence of the situation.

GENERAL THERAPEUTIC APPROACH

ETC staff counselors take a practical, systems-oriented approach to their work with persons and families in emergency situations. They try to avoid formal psychological or diagnostic jargon that might frighten or intimidate some clients. Our staff prefers to talk about specific problems of living and skills for managing problems. We believe strongly that it is important for our counselors to convey warmth and to be able to communicate with people of many life styles and value systems. Since the initial "cry for help" of many ETC clients is not made in the expectation that they will receive counseling or psychotherapy, we believe that our first task is to establish rapport with the clients and to gain their trust. We wish to start where they are, as as opposed to where we are, and this means that our initial expectations are essentially neutral and our preconceptions held in reserve. The client's own cognitive set is the framework for our initial dialogue. In the case of many first-time interventions, our primary goal may be simply to introduce the person or family to the concept of counseling and to gain some acceptance of its possible usefulness for them.

The basic therapeutic style of ETC counselors is, nevertheless, neither passive nor superficial. Our approach may, in fact, be described as active and intensive. Although few clients of the Center are initially motivated for change, some of them have been struggling with their problems for a long time. Once their problems have been identified and acknowledged, we point out that those problems are not likely to disappear by magical means. The converse is more likely: the problems will continue and the behavior they generate will become less and less appropriate with time. Violence might occur, or an already violent series of events might be prolonged. And even though it is essential to reach out to people when they are caught up in an emergency, it is equally important to continue reaching out to them as long as they are in need of help. This objective often requires aggressive followup activities.

FOLLOWUP PROCEDURES

Because ETC operates around the clock, and because many of our counseling sessions are conducted in the clients' homes, our program encounters the phenomenon of missed appointments less often than others do. Usually, the followup sessions are conducted by at least one of the staff members who responded to the initial call. This provision ensures continuity and takes advantage of the rapport that was developed when the team responded at the time of the emergency, when the clients' defenses were low and their need for help was most acute. The lack of such continuity accounts for the overwhelming majority of dropouts (from attempted referrals) in traditional, office-based crisis intervention programs. In a study of referrals that were made by the family crisis intervention unit of a large Northern California police department, it was found that only about 15 percent of those referrals were, in fact, followed up by the family in question. By contrast, about 90 percent of our clients who are offered followup visits actually accept the offer. Because we have reached out with help during an emergency, ETC staff members enjoy special advantages in terms of obtaining cooperation from persons who might otherwise resist help from professionals in the mental health, probation, or social service fields. That special relationship, earned by prompt responding, provides a foundation from which affirmative followup measures can be implemented, in that way capitalizing upon the momentum that has already been gained.

HOW ETC WORKS

The sequence of events in a typical ETC case will be described here in some detail. To begin with, someone calls for help; usually the call is made by a member of the family of the eventual client; often that call is made to the police. In some instances, the caller is a neighbor or passer-by, a bartender, taxi driver, motel manager, or another gatekeeper of that sort. The police officer, upon responding to the scene, evaluates the problem and decides whether or not the services of the Center will be useful. In making this decision, the officer reviews guidelines that were presented to him or her by ETC staff members at a training session. If the officer decides that intervention by ETC would be helpful, he or she gives the family some information about the Center and asks the parties involved whether or not they will consent to our being called (ETC staff will respond only when the police believe that it may be useful and when the persons involved give their consent. Only in such life-or-death situations as when a person is actively suicidal or is so psychotic as to be a danger to others, or in a hostage-taking or barricaded-person situation, will ETC take action without consent). When an initial call comes, for example, from a police department dispatcher, the staff members usually ask only for the name of the officer who called and the telephone number at which the officer may be reached. A staff member then calls the officer and asks for a description of the situation and the officer's assessment of it. The officer will also be asked whether or not he or she will remain at the scene until the team arrives or will leave as soon as the team is en route. He or she may wish to wait until a little while after the team has arrived, to see whether or not the situation can be sufficiently contained. It is often useful for one of the team members to talk, by telephone, with one or more of the persons who is involved in the emergency before starting out for the scene of the event. Sometimes, but not often, this initial conversation results in the team's deciding upon a response other than going to the scene right away. One such instance would be when one family member is reluctant to give consent for our visit to the home, while another is very much in need of help. We may arrange to meet that person on neutral ground such as a community center or a neighbor's house. Indeed, we have met our clients in the lobby of a hotel, the waiting room of a community mental health center, the lounge of an airport, and a doughnut shop; once we responded to the call of a client who waited for us in a public phone booth in the parking lot of a shopping center. When possible, however, we prefer to visit the home.

Usually, the police officer who is awaiting our arrival meets the team members outside the house or just inside the door, and gives them a few minutes' briefing. When the officer has already left, we may be sure that he or she has decided that the situation is likely to remain calm for the time being. When team members ask the police officer to stay on for a little while, the purpose is to make sure that the situation remains calm enough to conduct a useful intervention without the eruption of violence once more.

SPECIFIC THERAPY TECHNIQUES

Upon entering the home, ETC staff members talk in turn with each of the persons involved. This first session begins by our asking each person to describe what he or she sees as the main problem or problems. The response to that question may be clear or vague, and it may be interrupted by one of the other persons. When someone is interrupted, the staff members introduce firmly (if need be) the rule that only one person may speak at a time. Then we may seek clarification of initially vague problem descriptions by asking for specifics or illustrations, or for an account of what the person would like to do that he or she cannot do because of his or her difficulty. Or, we may ask what he or she would like to stop doing, were it not for the difficulty that prevents him or her from stopping.

In the context of our basic orientation to problem resolution through problem management, we believe that it is normal to have difficulties in life. Further, since the mismanagement of these difficulties converts them into problems, we inquire routinely about previous or current attempts to manage the difficulties at hand. We ask questions such as: What have you been trying to do about this so far? In the answer to that kind of question we often obtain information about the person's problem-solving skills, his or her previous efforts to solve problems, and what he or she felt was useful or not useful about these efforts. That kind of information may be helpful for contacting previous therapists (with appropriate consent), and it may save us from wasting time with interventions that have already been tried but have failed (either because they were unsuitable from the start, or because they were not offered in a manner that was acceptable to the people involved). In the first emergency session, staff members attempt to find out what the people involved might wish to achieve as a result of their talking with us. When they reply that they "simply want to feel better," or that they "want to feel less depressed," we ask them to explain what they would be able to do that they cannot do now or what they would be able to stop doing that they can't help doing now.

Another step, in the first session, is to find out what notions the persons involved may have about achieving their goals. It is useful to inquire about those ideas because it encourages the family members to think positively; the process itself stimulates rational planning; and their replies may provide us with cues about how to follow the course of least resistance to change, by encouraging change in ways that are consonant with the expectations of the persons who must do the changing.

A final but important step in the emergency visit is to summarize what has occurred and to ask the person or family members to reflect on their reactions to this initial contact. We then open a discussion about the next steps to be taken. We may suggest that the next session take place in the home or invite the family members to come to one of our offices. Or we may make an appointment for them with another agency, either at that time or by a telephone call at a later time.

Two Illustrative Cases

To illustrate how the Emergency Treatment Center works, we shall describe two cases from the first call for help through the emergency visit to the resolution of the problems involved (names have been changed).

MR. AND MRS. BURR

How and Why the Emergency Treatment Center Was Called

ETC was called, at 10:30 p.m., by an officer who had responded to a call from Mrs. Christine Burr. Mrs. Burr wanted to have her husband taken to a psychiatric hospital because she was afraid that he would become violent and harm her and her two-year-old daughter. Mrs. Burr said that her husband had previously attempted suicide.

When the officer first arrived on the scene, he realized that the Burrs had a serious problem, but he was not sure whether or not Mr. Burr should be hospitalized. When the officer asked Mr. and Mrs. Burr if they were willing to have someone from ETC visit them that evening, both consented.

How the Problem Was Presented

The Burrs were living in an expensive new apartment complex which was built around a pool and garden. When the ETC team arrived, the officer was waiting for them outside the apartment. He explained that he was puzzled by Mr. Burr and considered him to be potentially violent. For that reason, the staff asked the officer to remain for a while. He showed us into the Burrs' sparsely furnished four-room apartment, which appeared out of place in the plush surroundings of the building and its grounds.

As we were being introduced by the officer, Mr. Burr sat rigidly on the living room couch in one corner of the room while Mrs. Burr sat on a chair in the opposite corner. She was crying quietly and seemed to be frightened. Mr. Burr looked extremely agitated and hostile. He declared, to no one in particular, "I just can't stand it any more. I don't care what happens any more. She doesn't understand what's happening to me." It became clear that there was intense anger between the Burrs and that the wife's presence was agitating the husband. Because it seemed that Mr. Burr might become violent once more, we asked the wife if she would either go into another room or visit a neighbor while we talked with her husband, and she agreed to go next door.

After Mrs. Burr left, we asked the husband to tell us what the problem was. Mr. Burr said he was an ex-convict and, because of his record, had not been able to find work. He had been unemployed for more than nine months. When we asked him why he had been sent to prison, he said that he had stolen a truck from a construction site, adding that he didn't do that sort of thing any more, but even though he was earnestly trying to find work no one would hire him. He said his wife insisted that, without exception, he must tell prospective employers about his prison record. He told us that she thought everything would be all right if he was honest about his past, but each time he did so he experienced failure. Burr said being supported by his wife was driving him crazy. She had insisted that they rent the expensive apartment for the sake of appearances. She was very kind to him and seldom complained, he said, but she never stopped talking about how happy she would be when he would get a job and they could buy a house. He asked, "How do you think it makes me feel when I can't pay the rent where we are?"

We asked Mr. Burr what kind of work he would like to find, and whether or not he had some kind of special training. First he said that he would do anything, but, on second thought, he said that there were some jobs that he had done in the past that he would not do again. He had once worked for his father in the construction business, but he gave the impression that his father had set him up to fail. He had moved to this city to get away from his father. When he had been in a hospital once, he had thought about becoming a nurse because he would enjoy helping people. We said that this sounded like a good idea and asked him if he had looked into nursing training programs. He said that the reason he had not was that he thought it would be impossible to be admitted to the training, considering his record. We asked whether or not he had been in contact with one of the groups that try to help ex-convicts. He had not, because he was ashamed to associate with ex-cons. We ventured the opinion that some of those groups were worthwhile and often did a lot to help people find job training. We asked him if he would give one of them a call if we looked up their names and telephone numbers. He replied that he would call them if we thought it was worth it.

By now, Mr. Burr had calmed down considerably and was talking about how bad he felt about blowing up and hitting his two-year-old daughter. We assured him that, although he should not have struck his little girl, it was true that he had a lot of problems. We said that everyone has the right to blow up once in a while. Burr stated that he really loved his wife and daughter and did not want to let them down. When we asked him if he would be willing to get into counseling with his wife, he reluctantly agreed to do so. We explained that sometimes family members need help to work on what is reasonable to expect from one another, and they need guidance on how to work out their problems together. He said, once again, that he would be very willing to talk with a counselor because he really wanted the marriage to work.

In a brief staff conference in the hallway of the apartment, we agreed on some first impressions. We decided that, although Mr. Burr was trying genuinely to assume responsibility for supporting his family, he was immature for his 32 years of age. He seemed to be quick to blame others for his problems and slow in trying to get help for himself. We decided he would need a lot of support, such as therapy with his wife as well as peer counseling from a group that specializes in the problems of ex-convicts. We then asked if we could talk with his wife alone for a few minutes and he agreed.

Mrs. Burr appeared still frightened and shaken, although about 45 minutes had gone by and her husband was much calmer. We asked her what she thought the problem was, and her vague reply was that she didn't know what had happened. We expressed surprise at that answer and questioned her further. She said that she knew her husband was having a hard time, but that she didn't understand why he had blown up today. When we asked her whether or not she was aware of the pressure that her husband felt to provide a home for her and their daughter, she replied that she had tried hard not to push him; instead, she had told him about how good it would be when they could buy a house. We ventured the opinion that, at this point, talking about buying a home represented tremendous pressure to a man who had been unemployed for nine months. Mrs. Burr admitted that she had not thought about it in that way, and that she had only wanted to cheer him up by talking about the nice things they would do and could buy when he got a job.

Then we asked her how she and her husband had been getting along during the past few months. At first she hesitated, and then she admitted that they had not been getting along well. He had been sleeping in the living room and drinking at night for a long time. When we asked why her husband was sleeping on the couch, she replied that she didn't like him to touch her when he was drunk. We asked Mrs. Burr if she usually enjoyed sex with her husband and if he was a good lover. She said that while she enjoyed sex very much and that her husband was a fine lover, she just didn't like him to be near her when he was drunk. When we asked for her thoughts about why her husband was drinking and whether or not she had tried to get help for him, she said that he drank because he was unhappy and that she had called a family social work agency but had not gone in for an appointment. Then we asked her whether or not she thought she could help her husband. She said "maybe," but that she didn't know how. We suggested that possibly Mr. Burr needed to feel necessary and important to his family. We went on to say that she might stop talking about buying a house until they were financially more secure. She could first try to build his self-confidence. Mrs. Burr replied positively to both of those suggestions, yet we got the impression that she did not fully grasp what we were saying. We asked her whether or not she wanted to work on saving the marriage, or if she wanted help in separating. Her reply was that she really loved her husband and wanted to try to save their marriage. When we asked her if she would get some counseling with her husband, she said that she would.

We next inquired about how she felt about her husband's continuing to live at home with her and their daughter. We explained that we could arrange for a place for him to stay temporarily if she felt frightened or thought he might become violent again. She said that she felt much better now and wasn't afraid that he would become violent. When asked about how she would feel if he wanted to sleep with her tonight, she said she felt all right about it. Finally, when we asked if there was anything that she would like to say before we called her husband back into the room, she said that there was nothing else and that we could call him.

When Mr. Burr came back into the room, he was still nervous but apologetic about his blow-up. We re-introduced the idea that he and his wife should get into therapy together, and Mr. Burr said he would very much like to do that. We discussed how Mrs. Burr's talking about buying a house had upset him, and he was able to say that he needed her emotional support during this difficult period. We gave them a referral for family counseling, and told them that we would telephone the next day with information about organizations for ex-prisoners. When we called the next day, we discovered that the couple had already made an appointment for marital counseling.

Resolution and Followup

ETC made a visit to the Burrs' home a week later to discuss employment prospects. During this session, we learned that the Burrs had not followed through with the plan for marital counseling, and as a result we offered to continue seeing them. In about two weeks, with the assistance of an ex-prisoners' group, Mr. Burr found a job as a salesman.

The ETC counselors saw the Burrs 6 times during a period of two-and-one-half months. They worked diligently on some of their principal problems, such as learning how to be more supportive of each other. This change presented difficulties for them because each was selfish and immature and was relatively blind to the other's needs. We also helped them to achieve a more realistic conception of what marriage means and requires. When the marriage seemed to reach some relative state of stability, we withdrew for the purpose of encouraging the Burrs to take responsibility for each other and themselves.

MRS. SCHMITT

How and Why the Emergency Treatment Center Was Called

ETC was called by a police officer who had been summoned to the Schmitts' home by the local fire department. Mrs. Schmitt had called the fire department earlier that evening because she thought that space ships were landing in her back yard. When the firemen arrived at the house and observed Mrs. Schmitt's agitated condition, they called the police. The officer who responded to the call felt that Mrs. Schmitt should be hospitalized, but she was aggressively opposed to it. The officer hoped to avoid having to hospitalize Mrs. Schmitt by force and against her will. He called ETC because he hoped that we could help Mrs. Schmitt to enter a hospital voluntarily. He sought advice about how to assist her two sons aged 11 and 13.

The ETC staff members were met outside the house by the officer, who said that he would like to stay for a few minutes because he feared that Mrs. Schmitt was potentially violent. He was concerned about Mrs. Schmitt's sons because she was having hallucinations that the boys were hairy monsters and covered with blood. He was afraid that she might harm them in a panic, thinking that they were monsters. The officer said Mrs. Schmitt was known to have a drinking problem, and that she had been arrested on two occasions recently for driving while drunk. (That evening, Mrs. Schmitt had insisted to the officer that she had not been drinking for more than a week.)

How the Problem Was Presented

When the ETC staff members entered Mrs. Schmitt's home, they found her rushing about frantically and looking out of windows to see if any more space ships or Martians were coming. Mrs. Schmitt, a woman of medium build, was dressed in a robe, her hair uncombed, and her legs covered with large bruises. She looked as though she had not slept for a long time. One counselor approached and asked her if she would sit down and talk to both of us. She replied, in a friendly (but manic) manner, that she would be glad to sit and talk with anyone who might be able to explain why the Martians were chasing her. A counselor asked her when those strange events had begun. When she had gotten up that morning, she replied, she had found that she could not read *TV Guide*. When she had tried to read it with her father's glasses, the glasses had not helped. In the afternoon she had looked at her eldest son and he appeared to be covered with blood. She felt as though a power had come over her, but she did not know "what to fight."

Just then, Mrs. Schmitt's father entered the room and announced that he had known all along that his "poor little girl" was "crazy." He would appreciate it if we would "just get on with it," and take her to the "funny farm." He did not seem to be particularly concerned about his daughter's condition nor to be sensitive to her feelings. He went on to say that, even though he himself was a drinker, it was all right for him to drink because he worked six days a week. He told the counselors that they should think twice if they expected him to stop drinking.

The father seemed to be primarily concerned with justifying his own drinking. He continued to talk about what a fine person he was and how crazy his daughter was, and reiterated that his drinking was not a problem. While the father talked about how crazy his daughter was, we noticed that Mrs. Schmitt obliged him by acting crazy. She grimaced, struck awkward postures, and muttered strange sounds to invisible people. The father clearly preferred to view her as a crazy person, rather than as an alcoholic, because he did not want to confront his own alcoholism. Mrs. Schmitt also preferred to view herself as crazy rather than admit her own alcoholism. Finally, after the father had been talking for a while, a counselor asked him if he would mind if we talked with his daughter alone. After Mrs. Schmitt's father left the room she began to calm down, and we asked her once more if anything like this had ever happened to her before. She said nothing like this had ever happened before. The counselor asked her if she had ever been in a mental hospital or in an alcoholism rehabilitation center. That question appeared to upset her, and she replied emphatically, "No." Her extreme reaction to that question led the counselor to suspect that she might have been hospitalized but was afraid to admit it. The counselor then went on to explain that there are times when people cannot handle their problems alone and may need help. When Mrs. Schmitt said she could not go to a hospital because she had to care for her sons, we told her about a new program of the Center that might be useful to her. We had formed a network of emergency homes (shelters) in the community where children and adolescents receive short-term foster care. These homes are provided by "emergency parents" who have been trained by our staff. The child may stay for as short a time as one night or as long as two weeks.

As she listened to our description of the emergency homes program, Mrs. Schmitt seemed to become more and more angry and she suddenly gestured toward the ceiling and said, "They will make me pay for it later." We assumed she meant that if she permitted her boys to be taken to an emergency home, she would be punished for neglecting them. We assured her that no one would have to pay in any way and that we had suggested placing the sons in an emergency home only because we wanted her to get the help she needed. Mrs. Schmitt's response was to leap to her feet and declare that she was not going to a hospital and that we could not make her go. A counselor calmly pointed out that she would not have to stay in the hospital for a long time, possible no longer than three or four days, and that one of the counselors would accompany her to the hospital.

After some reflection, Mrs. Schmitt asked, "Do I really have to go?" and we assured her that it would be a good idea. When she agreed reluctantly, an ambulance was called to take her to the hospital, and one counselor followed by car while the other arranged an emergency home placement for the two sons. Both boys seemed relieved that their mother was going to a hospital because they had become fearful of her when she started seeing and hearing strange things. They told us that she had gone after them a few times recently; once they slept in the garage because they were afraid to stay in the house.

When the ambulance arrived at the hospital, a counselor was waiting there. The ambulance driver reported that Mrs. Schmitt had seen many flying saucers along the way and had expressed the certain belief that they were chasing her. During the intake interview, she continued to deny that she had a drinking problem and insisted that her father was right when he called her "crazy."

The counselor conferred with hospital staff members who checked the records to see if Mrs. Schmitt had been a patient there. She had been hospitalized several times in the past, each time for alcoholism, most recently about six months ago. In our discussion with the hospital staff, it became clear that Mrs. Schmitt should be placed in a locked psychiatric ward instead of an alcoholism rehabilitation program elsewhere, mainly because she would have to be a voluntary patient in the alcoholism program and thus would have to acknowledge that she had a drinking problem. (We learned later that her drinking had stopped about two days before the current incident, but that she had so saturated herself with alcohol that her present condition was the result of delirium tremens.) Our decision seems, in retrospect, to have been the correct one because, within a day's time, she concluded that she did not belong in the psychiatric ward and was not at all crazy. She was released the following day.

Resolution and Followup

Before Mrs. Schmitt left the hospital, the ETC counselor who had accompanied her on the day before visited her to arrange a followup appointment. When Mrs. Schmitt came to the ETC office for her followup session, she was extremely apologetic about the space-ship incident. The counselor asked about her previous drinking behavior and she admitted that she had had a drinking problem for at least ten years. This time, she vowed, she was going to conquer her problem.

Mrs. Schmitt had a favor to ask of us. She was extremely anxious about her recent arrest for drunken driving and the fact that she would soon have to appear in court. She assured us that she had not really been drunk but that the police officer had taken a dislike to her. (We had already learned that the blood test had shown her to be only one decimal point below the level that is typical of a comatose state.) When Mrs. Schmitt asked the counselor to write a letter to the judge, telling him that she was now sober and had sworn off drinking, the counselor confronted her with the seriousness of her behavior in having driven a car when she was so drunk. The counselor said she would have to stop lying to others as well as herself. We agreed to write a letter to the judge that would state only that Mrs. Schmitt had taken a first step toward getting help for her problems.

ETC counselors continued to see Mrs. Schmitt while she waited for a new alcoholics' group to be formed at a local clinic. She appeared for two more visits but canceled the fourth meeting because of illness. When she did not appear for her next appointment, a counselor called her home and received no answer. The next day, Mrs. Schmitt's eldest son telephoned the counselor to say that his mother was drinking again and he didn't know what to do. When he was asked how long his mother had been drinking, the boy replied "about two weeks." The counselor told the boy that ETC would visit his mother immediately. When we arrived, Mrs. Schmitt was very drunk and belligerent. She was furious because her son had "informed" on her. The counselor explained to Mrs. Schmitt that she would have to go to the alcoholism rehabilitation program to sober up; because she had been drinking so much, for so long, she should have medical supervision for her own safety. The idea of going back to a hospital made her even more angry, but we were able to persuade her that it was necessary. In an hour, the counselor managed to enroll Mrs. Schmitt in the rehabilitation program. The children were once again placed in an emergency home.

Eventually, because of the two hospitalizations and the possibility of losing custody of her two sons, Mrs. Schmitt began to take a more serious view of herself. By no means did she solve her problems, but she was able to remain sober for long periods and was able to find and maintain a part-time job.

SUMMARY AND CONCLUSIONS

The two histories presented above are broadly representative of the kinds of cases with which the Center deals routinely, especially in respect to these characteristics:

1. the central problem, which is often presented as the sole possession of one of the family members, is usually shared by one or more family members, because a family is a system;
2. the "presenting problem" is often a screen for the basic problem or problems;
3. a person who is experiencing a problem may not be able to describe the problem accurately or even coherently, or may be unwilling to do so, and the result is a mutual search for the problem that requires treatment.

The treatment of psychological emergencies requires:

1. responding promptly, while the emergency is still an emergency;
2. active, as opposed to passive, forms of responding, such as going to the client instead of inviting the client to seek us out for treatment;
3. following through to prevent missed referrals and relapses and to maintain the momentum of treatment.

Treatment for psychological emergencies is enhanced by:

1. visiting the home;
2. meeting as many people as possible in the client's support network;
3. considering family members to represent the components of a system;
4. conducting active, aggressive intervention into the family system as

swiftly as possible, in order to motivate change and cause the family members to take new perspectives when their resistance to change is low and their desire for change is intense.

When these principles are applied, emergencies may be subtly and deftly turned to the advantage of the clients, because they can be congratulated for having sought and pursued change and for having the courage to face its demands. From this perspective, a psychological emergency need not become a personal or family crisis, and even if it does become a crisis, pathology on the part of the person or the family system is not an inevitable result. In the work of the Emergency Treatment Center as a full-time, mobile outreach service that specializes in early detection of difficulties and resolution of problems, the major requisites of *secondary prevention* are being met.

REFERENCES

BARD, M. Family intervention police teams as a community mental health resource. *Journal of Criminal Law, Criminology, Police Science* 60:247-250, 1960.

EVERSTINE, D. S., BODIN, A. M., and EVERSTINE, L. Emergency psychology: a mobile service for police crisis calls. *Family Process* 16, 3:281-292, 1977.

SCHWARTZ, J. A., and LIEBMAN, D. Mental health consultation in law enforcement, in *The Urban Policeman in Transition*. H. Snibbe and J. Snibbe, eds. Thomas, Springfield, Illinois, 1972.

CHAPTER 25

Prevention of Violence: The Case for a Nonspecific Social Policy

JULIAN RAPPAPORT
KAREN HOLDEN

Because this volume has contributions from many disciplines, and because we are psychologists, it might be reasonable to assume that what we present in this chapter is a psychological viewpoint on the prevention of violence. So as not to mislead readers who are not psychologists, let us say that although the position we present is not only our own it would be wrong to see it as the viewpoint of mainstream psychology. In many ways, which we hope will be obvious, our position is much more a critique of the ways in which psychological views of violence are applied to so-called preventive strategies.

In E. F. Schumacher's last book, *A Guide for the Perplexed* (1977), he used the metaphor of a map to describe his discovery that the world one encounters as an adult is not as it was portrayed by others when one was a child. Schumacher recalls traveling in Russia and looking on his tourist map for the churches. Of course, as his guide explained, churches do not appear unless they have been converted to museums. For anyone interested in finding the living churches of Moscow a tourist map is useless.

So too, suggests Schumacher, are the maps for life provided by much of our educational system. His analogy is apt. As one looks at the tourist map of psychology, although there are ample places marked "violence," or in psychologists' language, "aggression," and ample places marked "prevention," looking for the intersection between violence and prevention in order to know specifically how to prevent violence is quite useless. This is not only because there are no experimental and empirical data which evaluate, in the social world, with ecological validity and methodological sophistication, any means for true (before the fact) prevention of violence. The reason the map is useless is much more basic. It is not that we simply have to do the right research, but rather that we have not asked the right questions about the right people.

To anticipate what will be a complicated argument, we suggest that the concepts of prevention are a poorly understood conglomeration of differing social intentions and ideas. We talk about prevention but do not seem to understand it conceptually, or what it requires pragmatically. It is, in short, a social-policy disaster.

The focus of our interventions tends to be on individual powerless persons rather than on organizational or institutional systems. Given what we know about the complex determinants of social behavior (violence is simply one example) or, more to the point, given what we do *not* know about human behavior, individual-level interventions with the powerless are a serious error if the aim is true prevention. If we need individual intervention at all it is with the powerful, not the powerless. Phrased in terms of the Schumacher analogy, when we look on our psychological map to ask questions about the prevention of violence, we find, rather than an exciting new tradition, a museum of frozen traditions.

To examine why this is so we need to hold several observations in juxtaposition:

1. Those interested in preventing violence most often represent, aware or not, the social-control forces of society. Although this is not necessarily a political evil, or unjust, it must be understood to be as much a concern with social stability and the well-being of the powerful in our society as with scientific understanding or the prevention of harm.

The political motivations, the judgment policies (Hammond and Adelman, 1976; Lamiell, 1979), and the powerful themselves are a legitimate topic of study. All of which is simply to say that violence can be understood only in its political context. That observation may be obvious to some, but it makes psychologists very uncomfortable, since we know very little about such matters as political context.

2. Psychological theory, and most of social science, is a *person blame* business. This is pertinent to our understanding of violence. It has im-

plications for explanation, research, treatment, and prevention. It accounts for interventions in the lives of some people (and not others) which one would have a hard time explaining on the basis of scientific evidence.

3. Theories of violence or aggression are no exception to the rule in that they almost always focus on individual blame explanations, regardless of terminology. Even social-learning and sociological explanations which begin outside the person end up converted to intervention programs for fixing up deviant individuals. If these theories have any application to prevention, it is to powerful rather than the powerless.

4. The number and kind of etiological explanations, specific independent and dependent variables, in the literature of violence are so wide-ranging that to talk of *the* prevention of violence makes no sense.

5. Preventive interventions may be classed into two major types depending on the level of analysis and point of intervention (Rappaport, 1977). They are either *specific/person-oriented* or *general/systems-oriented.* As might be expected from the dominant theoretical bias in favor of person blame, person-oriented interventions are by far the most prevalent, despite the fact that these require specific data and technology which do not exist unless one is willing to shift one's concerns from control of the powerless to control of the powerful (e.g., law enforcement, government and corporate officials).

6. The use of specific/person-oriented preventive interventions is an idea that comes directly out of public-health thinking (à la vaccination) and requires either the identification of a *specific etiology* or identification of a population at risk. We currently have the ability to do neither with regard to violence among the powerless, unless we are willing to identify an at-risk population with a high rate of false positives. That is a permissible strategy only if we are willing to ignore the next point.

7. Application of preventive interventions must take into account the unintended social costs.

8. This analysis will lead to the conclusion that, given our current state of the art, general or nonspecific social policies, rather than specific strategies for prevention of violence among the powerless, are the only ones permissible. Such a social policy has little to do with violence or so-called violent people *per se,* and a great deal to do with general strategies for improving the social conditions of life for everyone. Such general strategies need not be vague. They can and should be quite specific and testable. What nonspecific means is that they are applicable to everyone, not a small set of isolated deviants, and that such policies have potential effects on a large number of dependent variables.

9. We suggest that the best way to pursue social policy does not involve

research and intervention based on a model of specific preventive interventions aimed at such specific problems as violence, unless one is trying to control those who hold power over others. For prevention of violence among the powerless we require a model to study and strengthen the mediating structures between powerless individuals and the larger social institutions. The model should look for outcomes on a number of dependent variables, including, but not limited to, reduction of violence. This is, of course, exactly the opposite of current methods and national research policy which tends to view the powerless as people with a set of very specific problems, requiring very specific solutions, which only await discovery by the powerful.

WHAT (WHOSE) VIOLENCE DO WE WANT TO PREVENT?

The idea of the prevention of violence evokes a number of images. It probably conjures up a portrait of a violent person, to wit, the title of this book: *Violence and the Violent Individual.* In the foreword to her most recent book, which concerns itself with "the calamitous 14th century," a violent age indeed, the historian Barbara Tuchman (1978) explains that "disaster is rarely as pervasive as it seems from recorded accounts. The fact of being on the record makes it appear continuous and ubiquitous whereas it is more likely to have been sporadic both in time and place." She goes on to observe that "after absorbing the news of the day, one expects to face a world consisting entirely of strikes, crimes, power failures, broken water mains, stalled trains, school shutdowns, muggers, drug addicts, neo-Nazis, and rapists. The fact is that one can come home in the evening—on a lucky day—without having encountered more than one or two of these phenomena." She formulates Tuchman's Law: "The fact of being reported multiplies the apparent extent of any deplorable development by . . . (any figure the reader would care to supply)" (Tuchman, 1978).

Tuchman posits a psychological principle, and a very good one. Motivated perception, perceptual readiness, and so on, have a reasonable place in our literature and are currently making a comeback as explanatory principles of behavior (Silverman, 1976). The images that are conjured up when one thinks of crime and violence include a set of people very different from you and me. Here is a person who is not only different from us, but who may also be a direct and immediate threat to our physical well-being. The fact is that for most people the subjective probability of being attacked by a violent individual is considerably higher than the objective or true probability and this overestimate may be related to how much television one watches (Gerbner and Gross, 1976), a fact which would support Tuchman's Law.

Forgetting that more individual violence is perpetuated among people known to one another than between strangers, unless of course one wants to include organized violence such as wars, or recreational violence such as football games, fear of the violent stranger abounds. One attack on a New York City subway train, traveled safely by millions of passengers, is retold in news stories to the point at which people living in Boston, or Wheeling, West Virginia, or Los Angeles are afraid to ride on the bus. A recent survey (U.S. Department of Justice, 1975) found 40 percent of a national sample of respondents indicating fear of walking alone at night. We have often wondered, when walking in downtown Manhattan, why people are so orderly. Why they seem not to bump into each other, or take each other's belongings. Instead, most people seem simply to go about their own business, despite what we have been told about New York City.

The fact is that most of us are far more likely to be victimized by white collar crime committed by employees against their employers or by large corporations against the public: How many people suffer the consequences of a choice about where to put a gas tank in an automobile that proves to be unsafe, but too expensive to change, or by the pollutants they breathe, as compared to the number beat up on subways? Yet subjectively (that is to say, psychologically) we are more threatened by the individual who commits street crime than by the silent white collar criminals who cause increases in the prices we pay for the products we buy, or who commit corporate violence in the form of pollution, defective automobiles, factory negligence and so on (Monahan et al., 1977; Monahan and Novaco, 1978).

To understand violence and its prevention in our society probably requires much less, rather than much more, attention to violent individuals; but the mythology of violence suggests otherwise. In the context of this mythology of the violent person, social scientists are viewed as diagnosticians and treaters, in the hope that we will reduce, prevent, or deter individual violence. In Thomas Szasz's (1970) language we are the witch hunters. The comparison is not far-fetched. In our modern secular theology punishment and treatment are confused and the aims of social control begin to sound like the aims of humanitarian treatment, much the way exorcism was a humane way to treat a witch. In fact, diagnosis and treatment may be nothing more than a rationalization. It sounds better to talk of rehabilitation and corrections than of punishment and control. Functionally they are often equivalent (McCloskey, 1978). We are not, by the way, opposed to punishment; what we are opposed to is calling it by some euphemism that makes us believe that we are less violent than the people we are punishing.

It is not convincing to argue that capital punishment is less violent than murder, or that prison isolation is less violent than theft. This is not to say that such punishment might not be just, deserved, useful, necessary or whatever; it is to suggest that it is not necessarily less violent. And it is a bit absurd to have it carried out by a so-called department of corrections. The fact is that when we talk of the prevention of violence what we really mean is the prevention of "them" doing violence to "us." We are quite willing to tolerate violence that is justified in the form of police or military action, or violence that is recreational even if it leads annually to one and a half million young men suffering physical injury on their high school football fields while their mothers and girl friends cheer them on to "hit him again, hit him again, harder, harder!" (Underwood, 1978).

It would be comforting to think that psychologists and other social scientists have a history of combating the view that the individual criminal is different from the rest of us and not quite human. Unfortunately, the history of social science and criminology is one in which such views have been perpetuated. As the social scientists seek to become engaged in the legal system, we are often required to justify our competence where none, in fact, exists (Rappaport et al., 1980). Psychologists tend to accept, for example, the role of predictor of future behavior by means of psychological tests. That role tends to reinforce popular myths about deviants, and to perpetuate attempts to identify the so-called criminal type. Psychologists' traditional emphasis on testing, classification, and prediction of criminal behavior as a function of individual characteristics is a major preocupation. It is a preoccupation not inconsistent with much of sociology, which also focuses on differences between groups like delinquents and nondelinquents (Glueck and Glueck, 1951, 1971). This research, while intended to allow early detection and prevention, generally assumes that something is wrong with or different about the offender in some personal way and that, if he or she can be identified early, amelioration may take place and crime be prevented.

The problems with such research are both methodological and theoretical. Any two large groups of people differing on some characteristic are likely also to differ on other characteristics, without any necessary cause-and-effect relationship. The assumption that all people who break the law are somehow more like one another than they are like anyone else, or that they constitute a special type that requires some kind of treatment, or that available treatments are effective, are all highly questionable (Bazelon, 1973; Meehl, 1970). Such work is steeped in the philosophy of victim-blaming, hypothetical social pathology of cultural subgroups, and a person-blame ideology. It ignores the strengths and competencies of subgroups (Rappaport et al., 1975) and the need for basic economic and social reforms in the rules of the game, in favor of an ideology of individual treatment, which infrequently allows for legitimate access to environmental resources.

PSYCHOLOGY, SOCIAL SCIENCE, AND THE PERSON-BLAME IDEOLOGY

In an important paper on the nature and consequences of psychological research on social problems, Caplan and Nelson (1973) presented a classic analysis of social science and psychological research. These writers are particularly concerned with the social policy implications of what they term a "person-blame" bias in psychological research on social problems or, in simple terms, the tendency always to hold individuals responsible for their own problems in living. Such an approach ignores situationally relevant factors external to the individual, and ultimately has political and practical intervention implications.

What is done about a problem depends on how it is defined. Not only does problem definition tell one where to look in order to create changes, but it also suggests where not to look, what should not be done. A focus, for example, on individual psychodynamics would lead one away from a focus on social-situational variables. As Caplan and Nelson point out, to question traditional or established problem definitions is often to vie against the common sense of culture. If a given intervention is ineffective, the problem definition is rarely held responsible.

In psychology our focus on individual-difference variables has had a profound impact on the nature of our research on social problems. As Caplan and Nelson suggest, "Train a person in psychological theory and research, and suddenly a world disastrously out of tune with human needs is explained as a state of mind" (p. 202).

Even more disturbing, and here Caplan and Nelson only refer to this problem in a long footnote, is the fact that even explanations that use situational determinants, for example, much of the behaviorist writing, have little trouble construing situational relationships in terms of person blame. This is a phenomenon which William Ryan (1971) has described quite well as victim blaming. We have referred to it as environment blaming (Rappaport et al., 1975).

Whether one uses words like situation, learning, ego, or personality, one often concludes things like, It is not their fault are violent, they learned to be asked. Why, for example, do we study the poor rather than the non-ables may not account for their violent behavior, learned aggressive responses do. This rephrasing at the point of analysis is quickly converted, when one turns to intervention, so as to justify treating individuals. Whether they learned to be that way, or were born that way, becomes irrelevant after abstract analysis. What is relevant is that persons are viewed as flawed or fatally different from you and me. In short, while situational or social forces are alluded to, interventions focus on changing powerless people, rather than changing their situations. In Ryan's words:

> The formula for action becomes extraordinarily simple: change the victim. All this happens so smoothly that it seems downright rational. First, identify a social problem. Second, study those afflicted by the problem and discover in what ways they are different from the rest of us as a consequence of deprivation and injustice. Third, define the differences as the cause of the social problem itself. Finally, of course, assign a government bureaucrat to design a human action program to correct the differences (Ryan, 1971: p. 8).

Caplan and Nelson argue that the social scientist's concern with social problems most often waits in the wings while others define the questions to be asked. Why, for example, do we study the poor rather than the non-poor in trying to understand the origins of poverty? Why do we study nonachieving children rather than the public schools? Why do we study the motivations of poor tenants, rather than the motivations of landlords, in attempting to understand urban decay? Why do we study the moral development, brain waves, television-watching or wife-beating of powerless individuals, rather than the structures of local government, military institutions, reasons for lack of access to physical resources, or the aggressiveness, competition, and anger expressed against the non-college-bound child in our suburban public schools?

Is it possible that social science and social scientists are used by society to displace the blame for prior failures of our social system, or to rationalize current practices? Monahan (1977), in a recent review of our inability to predict violent behavior among juveniles, suggests that the best predictors of violent behavior, although still inaccurate more often than not, are demographic characteristics such as commission of a previous violent act, age, sex, and race. Why, asks Monahan, are the juvenile courts willing to rely on psychological tests as a predictor of whether or not a person should be released or confined when such tests are shown to be less accurate than demographic variables? Would we like a rationale that released older and confined younger persons who committed the same act simply because age is a better predictor of recidivism than psychological tests? Monahan's analysis suggests that it would be quite difficult in terms of legal rationale and public opinion for a judge to suggest that while this person who is black and this person who is white committed an identical offense, because the rates of recidivism are higher among blacks than among whites, we will confine the black child and release the white child. Instead, psychological tests enable one to label the black child as having low ego strength or lack of impulse control and thereby launder what amounts to a demographic prediction, allowing the judge's decision to seem to be motivated by sound, logical, humane, scientific reasoning, rather than demographic characteristics. Much of the psychological and sociological literature tends to serve a similar function (Seidman, 1977).

Caplan and Nelson suggest their own explanation in what they term the *latent functions* of a person-blame ideology. Person-blame offers a convenient apology for our government and our cultural institutions, which then can not be held responsible for the problem. If help is offered, one is credited with being humane, while at the same time one is able to maintain social control without changing social institutions. The ideology serves as a publicly acceptable device for control while distracting attention from systemic change. In addition, large numbers of well-educated reformers can view themselves as socially relevant while maintaining essential custodial roles for society. And finally, person-blame notions reinforce the social mythology by rewarding the middle class with self-esteem for having made it on their own: "Person blame interpretations are in everyone's interest except those subjected to analysis" (Caplan and Nelson, 1973: p. 210).

Our view in this context is that psychological theories of violence are based on similar kinds of thinking and yield similar results. Much of our theoretical explanations of violence turn out to be person-blame views, including those which use words like environment and culture, and sound like non-person-blaming views. They serve the advertent or inadvertent maintenance of status quo social conditions.

THEORETICAL CONCEPTIONS OF VIOLENCE AND AGGRESSION

Although we have no intention of systematically reviewing the literature on violence and aggression, a monumental task if done in any detail, we do want to show the general character of psychological theory and data in broad overview.

Several general characteristics in this literature are of interest. First, although the topic is violence, in psychological research the term aggression is most often used. Limiting a literature search to violence, rather than aggression, one would miss a great deal of the literature. The term aggression, however, covers a very wide range of behavior, from war and murder through physiological arousal. The range of dependent measures is so wide it is not at all clear that the researchers are studying the same phenomenon. Second, we were surprised to find that few authors concern themselves with the prevention of violence. We would be forced, if we were to think about how this literature bears on intervention before the fact, to make, with few exceptions, rather large inferences about what the authors seemed to be saying about the problem. There are, of course, a number of intervention suggestions and authors who are quite specific about what one might do to change individuals *after* they have committed some act, although in most cases the authors make large leaps of inference. That is, the empirical data are often far removed from the world of social interventions, and suggesting social policy, or even treatment, is somewhat tenuous. The gaps between theory, application, systematic testing, and evaluation are very large.

Another characteristic of this literature is its overhelming emphasis on individuals and what is wrong with them, however they got to be that way. In our own search of the literature, we found that about 75 percent of the authors used primarily person-blame ideologies. The percentage would be much higher if we had limited ourselves to the work of psychologists, or if we had limited ourselves to the most influential and prestigious psychology journals. (If you are not persuaded, we suggest that you read the more comprehensive theoretical review by Roberts et al. [this volume] and do your own count.)

The range of etiological explanations spans instinctual, genetic, psychodynamic, physiological, personality characteristics, and social learning, the latter two being the most popular.

The most traditional manner of viewing aggression is as an instinct. This view, prevalent before the turn of the century, is represented by both William James' (1968) notion of aggression as inherent in humanness, and William McDougal's "Instinct for Pugnacity." Both saw aggressive acts as unavoidable. Although the display and intensity were modifiable, the instinct was not. Freud, of course, also postulated aggression as based instinctually in the thanatos, or death instinct. He too felt aggressive tendencies were inherent in man. Konrad Lorenz (1971), a contemporary ethnologist who sees human beings in an evolutionary context, also views aggression as biologically based and instinctive. Although few accept the instinctual theory today, the influence of this thought, particularly Freud's dynamic principles, remains strong.

The early social-learning theorists, led by Dollard and Miller (1950), postulated a theory of aggression based on a reinterpretation of psychodynamics into learning terms. Viewed in this light, aggression is determined by frustration, or the blocking of a goal response. The blocking creates a situation of increased drive, which expresses itself as an aggressive act. Like Freud, Dollard and Miller viewed the expression of this drive as a major motivator. They reformulated Freud's idea of catharsis, or equivalence of drive forms, which states that the displacement of the aggressive response to an object other than the original "frustrator" does as much to lower the drive as would aggression toward the original object. What is important then is expression, not determination.

Contemporary psychologists like Feshbach, Hokanson, and Berkowitz are still interested in pursuing the drive model. Feshbach (1971) believes that television with aggressive content, when construed as a fantasy experience, may control or *reduce* aggressive acting-out. The fantasy is a *substitute* for actual aggression, providing an opportunity for the expression of anger as well as functioning as a cognitive control, being enjoyable, and facilitating new insights and cognitive reorganization. Hokanson (1970) accepts the concept of catharsis as reducing aggressive excitation, but only when the expression is directed at the *source* of the anger. He does not view the "equivalence of drive forms" hypothesis as viable. Berkowitz (1969) reinterprets this notion to state that aggression is *initiated* by frustration, but will not become behavior unless a cue in the environment elicits the act. His argument that the finger pulls the trigger, but the trigger may also be pulling the finger, illustrates this point. Berkowitz postulates that a weapon cue, eliciting the response, also allows one to emotionally remove oneself from the target, making the act seem less real, and thus increasing the probability of an aggressive act. Wilson (1975), a sociobiologist, modifies the argument further. His position is pragmatic: even if aggressive tendencies are inborn, or instinctual, they are not inevitable, as it takes a situational determinant to elicit the aggressive act.

Another set of researchers take a more moderate position. They are interested in the physiological bases of aggression. Shachter and Singer (Singer, 1971) blend the internal/external dichotomy by describing physiological arousal as having "inherent" descriptors. They believe that, since most arousal is the same physiologically, "aggressive feelings" are only labeled as such and dependent on previous learning and experience and the immediate situation. Moyer (1971), as an example of one direction taken by physiological psychologists, believes that aggression is determined by certain lesions or physical characteristics of the brain that are stimulated by situational aspects of the environment. His position is, once again, a belief that internal variables in combination with situational stimuli determine an aggressive act.

The school of thought most widely accepted today was initiated by Bandura and Walters (1963) in their early reformulation of social-learning theory. Bandura (1973) and his colleagues view aggression as a learned response acquired through modeling and reinforcement. After extensive empirical work with children who viewed aggressive models, Bandura concluded that aggression is a response that can be initially learned and modified in intensity through modeling aggressive acts. Children who are vicariously reinforced (through a model), as well as children who are directly reinforced for aggressive acts, will show an increase in aggressive behavior. The model need not be human—cartoons or fictional characters may also act as models for aggression.

Buss (1961, 1971), whose "Aggression Machine" heralded a vast amount of empirical work on the determinants of aggression, sees aggressive acts as being of two kinds: angry aggression, in which the aggressor wishes harm on the victim, and instrumental aggression, where an aggressive act implies gaining a reinforcer. Buss believes that he more prevalent case is that of instrumental aggression. Using his aggression-machine paradigm, he finds that most people will raise a shock intensity above the necessary learning base line in a bogus learning experiment, when shock is used by the subject to indicate to another person that he has responded incorrectly. Buss hypothesizes that even under conditions of minimum reinforcement (the victim's improvement), reinforcement increases aggression.

As the study of aggression is a popular one, one finds diverging schools of thought in different areas of the discipline. In contrast to the learning theorists, there are still contemporary psychologists who see aggression as a personality characteristic. Of relevance is Megargee's work on "over- and under-controlled personality types." Megargee (1973, 1976) states that individuals with few self-controls on aggressive response will exhibit a high level of moderately aggressive acts, in contrast to those highly over-controlled types, who, when slightly provoked, will remain calm, but who, when highly provoked, will exhibit an act of intense violence. The implications for prediction in this case include *a priori* personality assessment, although, judged by his chapter in this volume, Megargee may now have serious questions about this approach.

A more social-psychological viewpoint was expressed by Zimbardo (1969), using the concept of deindividuation. Zimbardo believes that a feeling of anonymity or "deindividuation" (separation from individual awareness) may cause an increase in aggressive behavior. By loss of the threatening individual identity and acceptance of a group concept, the person feels more able to aggress anonymously with less fear of retribution, as well as with less self chastisement. Other researchers in the fields of environmental psychology have identified excessive temperature and crowded conditions as being partially responsible for the elicitation of an aggressive response.

Those who posit learning views, because they talk of external-stimulus conditions, sometimes seem to be dealing with other than a person-blame ideology. This is a rather confusing situation in that people like Bandura (1973) seem to recognize the error of conceptualization that stems from basing all of one's notions on an understanding of individual behavior when one is interested in generalizing and changing behavior which is ultimately determined by the social, political, organizational, and institutional context. He concludes his influential book this way:

> Like so many other problems confronting man, there is no single grand design for lowering the level of destructiveness within a society. It requires both individual corrective effort and group action aimed at changing the practices of social systems. Since aggression is not an inevitable or unchanging aspect of man but a product of aggression promoting conditions operating within a society, man has the power to reduce his level of aggressiveness. Whether this capability is used wisely or destructively is another matter (Bandura, 1973: p. 323).

But, while Bandura devotes 78 pages of the book to "modification and control of aggression," less than five pages discuss changes in social systems. The discussion itself is simply a descriptive relabeling, in psychologists' language, of what political activists like John Gardner on the one hand, and Saul Alinsky on the other, do. It is not a contribution to thinking about aggression beyond the individual level of analysis.

While Bandura himself makes a number of suggestions for using individual-behavior principles to control socially powerful decision-makers, rather than the powerless, the thrust of behavior-modification technology leads one to use it on the powerless rather than the powerful. We contend that principles of individual behavior control are useful as a *preventive* device only when they are used to control those in power, whose behavior affects large numbers of others.

Turning to the nonpsychological literature, while we find societal determinants to be viewed as at the base of violent acts, these are usually discussed as important only because they have been internalized. One trend of thought (Lifton, 1973; Slater, 1970) views violence as behavior stemming from feelings of powerlessness, meaninglessness, and self-alienation. As society becomes more mechanized and mobile, our lives and individual "beingness" goes through such rapid change that we begin to feel "detached": because our human contacts change so rapidly, we become alienated, not only from our own identity, but from our "targets." Parallel to the Berkowitz view, these theorists believe we have drained the emotionality out of violence, leaving it a meaningless act. Both turn to the brutal and often unnecessary violence of the Vietnam war to illustrate their point. Soldiers have become so far removed from the point of the war emotionally, and from their targets physically (through arms and airplanes), that a violent act loses its "potency," allowing the soldiers to remove themselves from individual responsibility and kill without feeling or regret.

The theory originally postulated by Wolfgang and Ferracuti (1967) and concerned with the subculture of violence is a popular one. In this theory, it is group standards, morals, and values that "legitimize" violence. Individuals developing in such a group see violence as a necessary way to "survive," gaining acceptance, status, and approval. This theory was originally postulated in reference to certain "nonlegitimate" subcultures in society (such as youth gangs), but an analogy may be drawn to governmental, corporate, and other forms of institutionalized group violence, in which violent actions are condoned and praised within the group as an inherent part of certain roles. Monahan (1976, 1978), discussing these forms of so-called corporate violence (here defined simply as unnecessary and unjustified force), believes that we should remove the concept of violence from its medical model and construe it as learned behavior—often performed by legitimate authority whose expression is defined by cultural values and social relations. Taking a somewhat different viewpoint, theorists such as Gamson (1974) view violence as a political strategy, and often as the only means to get action. It is viewed as a forced-choice option—to make political gains one must use violent behavior.

Finally, we note the views of the historian Arthur Schlesinger, Jr. who, in *Violence: America in the Sixties* (1968), traces violence as a legacy of our country's "frontier mentality": a force institutionalized historically in our governmental and cultural structure, condoned and legal on certain levels, condemned on others. In his view the only prevention possible is based on each individual's taking collective responsibility to raise the consciousness of the people and start a mass movement against violent action.

We found that beyond the individual level of analysis it is rare, regardless of discipline, for authors to do more than describe or to suggest specific social interventions to prevent violence. It is even more rare (it does not occur) for anyone actually to propose, carry out, and evaluate an intervention based on other than attempts to change individuals. The most common way in which psychologists have approached the prevention of violence has been through attempts to predict its occurrence among given individual (almost always powerless) persons. We turn now to an overview of that work.

PREDICTION OF INDIVIDUAL VIOLENCE

Many reviews have concluded that our ability to predict individual violence is poor, particularly if one takes into account the large numbers of false positives. Reviews by Livermore et al. (1968), Meehl (1970), Monahan (1976), Rappaport (1977), and Shah (1978) have all concluded on the basis of the empirical literature that, in Monahan's words:

> Violence is vastly overpredicted whether simple behavioral indicators are used or sophisticated multivariate analyses are employed, and whether psychological tests are administered or thorough psychiatric examinations are performed. . . . We are left with a central moral issue. How many false positives, how many harmless men and women are we willing to sacrifice to protect ourselves from one violent individual? (Monahan, 1976).

In any attempt to prevent violence, whether through the official criminal justice system or through the apparently more benign treatment systems of mental health and education, the problem of overidentification is serious. This problem is no less serious for those who would prevent it by treatment than for those who would prevent it by punishment. Often more a semantic than a real distinction is made between the two, at least insofar as the rights of individuals subjected to such treatment are concerned.

There is a basic philosophical inconsistency between legal and psychological/sociological rationales for social control. The legal tradition emphasizes punishment for actually committed unlawful behavior and provides for protection of rights through due process. Unfortunately, the treatment and prevention literature is based on predictions of the likelihood of hypothetical future behaviors or problems. When the mental health system and the legal system combine, due process is easily lost (Kittrie, 1971; Murphy, 1974; Platt, 1969). When decisions with regard to parole, probation, civil commitment and the like are made through the judgments of behavioral scientists, the judicial system runs the risk that injustified confinement will occur. Although officially the decisions are made by judges, functionally many follow so-called expert recommendations much of the time, despite evidence that the empirical validity of prediction is questionable.

Because we occasionally have situations in which officials are forced to release persons predicted to be dangerous, some reasonable data on actual predictive accuracy do exist. Reviewing six such empirical studies, Monahan found that the percentage of true positives (those predicted to be violent and who actually turned out to be violent), using various clinical and statistical predictive methods, ranged from as low as less than 1 percent to as high as 46 percent correct. The percentage of *false* positives then, that is, the percentage of times in which one was predicted to be violent and in which violence did not actually occur, was shown to be as high as 99 percent and as low as 54 percent. What that means, of course, is that error rates are horrendous. Shah (1978), in a more recent review, draws essentially the same conclusions concerning our inability to predict dangerousness without a high rate of false positives. Despite these well-known facts, we continue to use prediction of dangerousness as a regular aspect of the criminal justice system.

There are a number of possible explanations (which combine the earlier portions of this paper) to account for our continued willingness to over-predict violence. Many of them are offered by both Shah and Monahan and include explanations such as:

1. Lack of corrective feedback: If the predictor commits a false-negative error, he is likely to find himself in great difficulty as the headline reads "Released Mental Patient Kills Wife"; false positives have no such consequences. They exist in quiet confinement and one seldom learns about them.
2. The problem of illusory correlations or systematic error which, for example, would lead one to predict that a person diagnosed as mentally ill is more dangerous or likely to commit a violent crime than others, despite the fact that that is not the case empirically.
3. Unreliability of the criterion. There is widespread disagreement as to what is violent, and even more as to what is aggressive.
4. Because the actual occurrence of "dangerous to others or self" violent acts is so low, there is a tendency toward overprediction simply on the basis of statistical error.
5. The people for whom violence is predicted tend to be the most powerless members of our society.

While each of these factors probably contributes to the phenomenon, the general problem may be summarized as a function of the person-blame ideology discussed earlier. It is clear that willingness to predict violence is not a function of scientific success.

But our focus here is on the implications of our inability to predict with regard to programs of prevention, rather than on why we continue to do it. If we are unable to predict who is violent, who will commit a violent act, and if we are unclear as to the etiology of what we are trying to prevent, specific programs of preventive intervention are neither possible nor justifiable. More general strategies of social policy are required.

PREVENTION AND ITS VICISSITUDES: A QUESTION OF SOCIAL POLICY

What has been said thus far is that our person-blame ideology in general, and theories of violence in particular, combine with our inability to predict individual violence among the powerless in a way that makes the ideal of focused and specific prevention strategies a weak social policy. To understand why, we need to consider in detail what true prevention requires.

We start here with the premise that prevention implies *before the fact,* and from a public-health stance prevention is always the method of choice. Unfortunately the situation is more complicated. If one's sole aim, independent of any other concern, were to prevent the repetition of criminal violence in the larger society by the same individual, once identified, adjudicated, and so on, all that would be necessary would be some form of punishment such as life imprisonment or execution. Obviously this is usually not our only consideration in discussions of violence prevention, treatment or punishment. We are rarely concerned with the prevention of violence at all costs, but rather with the prevention of violence within some *acceptable level of cost.* Furthermore, preventing the violence of an individual is not the same as preventing violence in a community. By waiting until an act of violence occurs, even if prevention of individual recidivism were 100 percent effective, one does not change the incidence (appearance of new cases) in a community. The only exception to this is changing the behavior of an individual who is so socially influential as to have a widespread impact on large numbers of people, such as an important government official.

The concept of true prevention is well illustrated by the metaphor of going upstream to find out who is throwing victims into the water to drown, rather than continually trying to fish them out. Gerald Caplan's writing (1964) is the best known in the field, and he is to be credited with bringing the serious application of public health principles to the mental health field. Borrowing from public health, Caplan conceptualized three kinds of prevention: primary, secondary, and tertiary.

Tertiary prevention, in this context, refers to such programs of rehabilitation as work release or therapeutic intervention. Calling these programs prevention may simply be a way to rename the existing world. In the analogy to drowning victims, it would be like arguing that prevention means artificial respiration, rather than preventing people from being thrown into the water. For this reason some authors have suggested that we ought perhaps return to the simpler designations of prevention versus treatment (Waggenfeld, 1972; Kessler and Albee, 1975).

Secondary prevention is of two sorts, both of which use, albeit in rather different ways, the notion of early detection. Early detection is a medical concept, and it implies an ongoing, if sub rosa, "disease process." The trick is to identify, early in the developmental stages of the disease, on the basis of symptoms or signs, those people who should receive immediate treatment so as to halt the disease process. The potential drowning victims would be fished out as soon as they show signs of struggle to stay afloat, after they are in the water but before they swallow too much, and then taught how to swim. An early-detection and secondary-prevention program of this sort might refer so-called aggressive, acting-out boys to a psychologist or social worker. It might involve diversion from legal processing following some minor aggressive act, coupled with a referral for counseling.

An alternate view of secondary prevention is based on the study of human development, rather than the study of a disease process. Here the theory is that if a person can get the right kind of nutrients (in social science, read experiences), he or she will develop normally. Early detection means finding those people, often children, who are "at risk" or have a high likelihood of not obtaining the "correct" experiences, or of having the wrong experiences (poor child-rearing, bad models, and so on). We would look for children who are not learning how to swim, or not learning how to swim properly before they are forced into the water. While an example of the first approach might be giving all the children in a school a psychological test such as the Minnesota Multiphasic Personality Inventory (MMPI) and sending those whose profile is aggressive to an appointment with the counselor, or to a program of some sort, this approach would involve things like finding parents who use the wrong child-rearing methods and teaching them new ones, or parents who model violence and teaching them verbal rather than physical expression of their emotions. The first case requires identification of those at risk by examining them for signs or symptoms; the second case also requires knowing something about the specific etiology of the problem.

Notice the similarity in both forms of secondary prevention. It requires individuals to be identified as at risk, either because of a relatively mild problem or because of a presumed lack in their experience, so that they have some defect to be fixed up. For those with a legal bent, the rule of law may seem stretched by such intervention; but it is much easier to justify coerced treatment or education than it is to justify punishment—even if the client views the treatment or education as punishment.

If one puts legal and ethical questions aside, there are only two valid public-health criteria for evaluating a preventive outcome. Does the incidence (the number of new cases) decline, or does the prevalence, the total number of cases, new and ongoing, decline? To evaluate these sorts of outcomes it is necesary to do epidemiological research. Such research requires careful identification of cases so that incidence and prevalence can be evaluated before, during, and after intervention. Time-series designs are a good device for such work. To do it, however, the criterion for violence needs to be quite precise, or one gets into very difficult research problems. We note that the criteria for violence are hardly precise, and words like aggression have little social agreement (Wiggins et al., 1975).

The effects of a true prevention program cannot be evaluated by demonstrating that a given treatment works for a given sample of patients. Prevention is a public-health measure, and its evaluation requires epidemiological statistics. A given treatment may be quite effective at preventing violence in a given individual or group but be useless vis-à-vis an impact on incidence and prevalence. Using the earlier metaphor for prevention, the phenomenon we wish to prevent is people being thrown into the river. We may be able to fish out certain of such people, give them artificial respiration, and if necessary teach them how to swim better, but presuming limited resources, less than 100 percent effective life-saving techniques (treatments), and a large-scale epidemic of being pushed into the water, our ability to deal with the problem in this way will not affect the total number of people in the water. If there is an epidemic, many will drown.

If the problem were one of low incidence (few people being pushed in), and if we have high treatment success rates, and if we have unlimited resources, we may not need to worry about preventing the initial push into the water. In the case of violence and aggression among the powerless in our society, none of these conditions hold, unless one is willing to use only a limited definition of violence, such as repeated commission of a legally dangerous act, in which case we have given up prevention as our aim. By any other definition, the rates are high, the treatments considerably less than 100 percent effective, and the resources hardly infinite.

This brings us to primary prevention. If secondary prevention seeks to reduce prevalence by reducing duration, primary prevention seeks to reduce it by reducing incidence, or reducing the number of people pushed into the water in the first place. True primary prevention is what we have called here a nonspecific social policy. According to Caplan's definition:

> Primary prevention is a community concept. It involves lowering the rate of new cases . . . in a population over a certain period by counteracting harmful circumstances before they have had a chance to [operate]. It does not seek to prevent a specific person from becoming [violent]. Instead it seeks to reduce risk for a whole population so that, although some become [violent], this number will be reduced. It thus contrasts with individual patient-oriented psychiatry (and social science) which focuses on a single person and deals with general influences only insofar as they are combined in his unique experiences (Caplan, 1964: p. 26).

For reasons discussed below, although primary prevention is more difficult to get a comfortable handle on, and at first blush would seem to require more rather than less knowledge, historically this seems not to be the case. When our state of knowledge has been similar to our understanding of violence, primary prevention, a *general or nonspecific social policy* rather than a specific one, has proved to be the most effective strategy.

THE CASE FOR A NONSPECIFIC SOCIAL POLICY

For the prevention of violence, as for most social problems, our level of understanding, the focus of our theory, our technological capacities, and the ethical responsibility to engage in prevention only within acceptable social costs, severely limit the usefulness of specific/person-oriented treatments as a social policy. Prevention would require *nonspecific* or general forms of social-change intervention, rather than those specifically aimed at violence or any other single dependent variable. Although reduction of violence may be a by-product of nonspecific social changes, it would be only one of many intended as well as unintended effects.

In arguments for a social policy of prevention, this distinction must be clear: Person-oriented treatment and system-oriented prevention programs cannot be lumped together. The two intervention strategies are not interchangeable; they require both differing information and intentions. By nonspecific social policy we mean two things: The interventions proposed are not so specific as to be aimed at a single person-type predicted to be at risk, and the interventions are not aimed at some specific presumed disease process or a narrowly conceived change in one suspected etiological mechanism.

Nonspecific does not mean vague, fuzzy, or poorly thought out. Nor does it mean vaguely suggesting to "improve the quality of life." A nonspecific prevention strategy may be very specific about what to do. What is nonspecific about it is its expected multiple effects on a range of people, rather than its expected specific effect on a single target population. The suggestion that IQ tests be dropped from use in public schools is, for example, a specific suggestion about social policy, but one which may have multiple effects. Reduction of labeling and expectation effects in public schools might well be *one* such outcome, although surely not the only one, and it, in turn, would have other effects, some predictable and others not. The target population for the intervention would be *all* school children, not simply those identified as at risk.

As another example, the suggestion that nonprofessionally staffed and controlled crisis intervention centers (McGee, 1974), or advocacy centers (Edelman, 1973), or self-help groups (Mowrer & Vettano, 1975) be made available on a widespread voluntary basis is a general/system-oriented preventive strategy. It is nonspecific in that such centers are proposed as places where people with a variety of problems in living might find access to a support system (Rappaport, 1977). This does not require identification of a specific at-risk population; but it does attempt to provide a support system, with easier access than the usual mental health system, available to more people. One possible outcome is reduction in the violence of suicide, but such centers need not be targeted for such specific outcomes to have that result. They might have a number of other effects, both good and bad, and would require continuous evaluation.

While specific person-oriented treatment strategies require knowing the specific etiology and the specific population at risk, or exactly what to deliver to exactly whom, general/system-oriented preventive strategies need not require identification of those at risk since everyone in the population will be affected by the change. Putting fluoride in the water system, for example, does not require identification of those prone to tooth decay, since everyone will drink the water. Even where etiology is reasonably clear but has a multiple environmental causality and a number of possible interactive determinants, as in the case of heart disease, system-oriented strategies like public education may be necessary for a significant and general impact on a society (Maccoby et al., 1977; Maccoby, 1979). It is widely acknowledged that public health measures, rather than clinical medicine, account for the health status of a population.

When the etiology is unknown or multiple and where there are a variety of suspected predisposing, precipitating, and perpetuating factors, and where individuals at risk are difficult to identify, history suggests general rather than specific strategies (Bloom, 1975; Kessler and Albee, 1975). The medical analogy would be something like this: When Edwin Chadwick advocated the independent circulation of water and sewage on the basis of a mistaken theory of disease (Susser, 1968), he may have prevented more disease than any other single public-health measure had done, even though he did not understand the etiology and could not propose a specific vaccine for people at risk. The change did not come about by isolating a specific cause-and-effect relationship between a germ and a disease; Chadwick did not even believe in the germ theory. Instead, he took a logical step toward improving the quality of life based on observation of a relationship between a problem and an environmental condition.

Like Chadwick, we need not isolate a specific cause-effect relationship, or a population "at risk." The possible causes of violence, as well as the large numbers of ways in which it may be expressed, make up a matrix of so many possibilities that to view it as reducible to a simple linear cause-effect relationship is highly suspect. Consider the possibilities. How many different ways can violence be expressed? How many different human situations might instigate violence, in how many different settings? The permutations and combinations grow very quickly. Unless one is willing to suppose that a single mechanism causes a single response, it makes no sense to look for specific techniques aimed at individuals.

Similarly, even if we are willing to ignore the problem of specific etiology and instead apply a broad-band treatment, but only to a high-risk population, we would still have difficulties. To do so would require identifying a population, before the fact, which is more likely than others to show the disorder. The only case in which this will make sense is when the population at risk can be shown to affect large numbers of others because of their own powerful linking roles in society—for example, law enforcement officers and administrators. Likewise, those government officials or corporate executives who may control decisions at the level of organizational violence could be identified as at risk and their behavior modified by changing reinforcement contingencies, teaching them self-control, modeling, treating, and so on (Bandura, 1973; Monahan and Novaco, 1978). We suggest that the individual, or specific/person-level strategy, may best be applied to the powerful, rather than the powerless, and this of course requires a reversal of our usual images of prevention of violence and of who is the violent individual. We cannot accurately identify a comparable high risk for dangerousness group among the powerless. To talk of individual change as a preventive measure for any but the most powerful members of our society is to ask the wrong intervention question.

If one is concerned with prevention in the general population, nonspecific social policies are required. A view similar to ours was well presented by Nevitt Sanford (1972) in the context of mental health, and again most recently by Goodstein and Sandler (1978). These writers suggested that the prevention of emotional disturbance is less desirable and ultimately different from interventions designed to foster development of effective human functioning. Intervention aimed at prevention of a specific problem is different from that aimed at a furtherance of health, or general well-being. Fostering competent communities as a goal is different from preventing illness or disruption as a goal (Iscoe, 1974). The shaping of a general public policy and of our social institutions, rather than the people in them (other than the most powerful), may be a more sensible target of intervention than direct attempts to prevent violence *per se*.

SOME SPECIFIC SUGGESTIONS FOR A NONSPECIFIC SOCIAL POLICY

In his recent book, *Medical Nemesis* (1976), Ivan Illich discusses ways in which the professional treatment establishment may create more harm than good. To clinical iatrogenesis (the commonly acknowledged direct negative side effects of a treatment), which may account for as much as 20 percent of medically related health problems, he added social and cultural iatrogenesis. These terms encapsulate the suggestion that we have become consumers rather than producers of our own well-being. The same may be said about the nonmedical pursuits of happiness. If iatrogenesis is a problem for medicine, it is exponentially greater in mental health, education, and welfare programs, in which unintended consequences are often more powerful than those intended.

One such culturally iatrogenic effect is the widespread reliance on professional expertise to solve our social and interpersonal problems in living. As national health insurance catches on and psychiatry and psychology become included, we are likely to see an even wider spread of the cultural expectation that all problems in living are best handled by quasi-medical diagnosis and treatment by a "licensed professional." It will be perfectly reasonable for the public to demand, given this cultural expectation, that the social science-medical-psychiatric, now government-approved, establishment "cure" the problem of violence and the violent individual. Were we to be straightforward in our response, we would be honest about our inability to predict and prevent violence among the poor and powerless, and likewise candid about how much could be prevented by control of the powerful.

Unfortunately, we also need to acknowledge Edward Banfield's (1968) distinction between what is feasible and what is acceptable. We probably have feasible means to control the problem of corporate violence (that is, strategies that are physically possible and, if implemented, would work); what we lack is acceptability. Control over who-and-how decisions regarding so-called acceptable levels of risk are reached by government agencies and corporations is one example. To lower the risk level in the production of a variety of products (including energy) is a feasible but politically tenuous strategy for preventing violence. To gain acceptability once a feasible strategy is established with data and analysis, a political, rather than a scientific, campaign is required. Ralph Nader's auto safety campaign has prevented directly and indirectly more violence than any contributor to this volume, or anyone else who is likely to read its papers. The social scientist may have a place in such campaigns by advocating implementation and by supplying empirical information, analysis, and outcome evaluation of strategies for change (Fairweather, 1972).

There is validity in the suggestions of Monahan (1976), that

> A "system-centered" rather than a "person-centered" (approach) . . . is less likely to result in "blaming the victim" . . . . It shifts the emphasis from early case identification to the modification of those factors which give rise to violence . . . . (p. 29).

Monahan's emphasis on modifying environmental characteristics like lighting in urban areas or increasing public transportation and public education to advise women about the dangers of hitchhiking situations, and about self-defense, may do more to decrease rape than treatment programs for sex offenders. Similarly, his suggestions concerning better gun-control laws, and limiting the availability of weapons as well as increased penalties for drunk driving (which accounts for more deaths each year than the entire Vietnam war did in ten years) are all sensible. In our view, however, such suggestions are still too focused and somewhat superficial. We do not see these suggestions as incorrect; they clearly are an advance over current approaches that emphasize prediction of who is violence-prone. Yet, they are both too limited and too focused on reliance at the level of centralized authority.

We do agree, as Monahan also suggests, that, if we must change individuals to reduce violence, we should be working on how to change violent individuals who control corporate decision-making policies that affect hundreds of thousands of people each year (Monahan and Novaco, 1978). We would want to go a step farther than situational control of powerful individuals, however, and move in the direction of social policies that favor local community control and genuine involvement of people in the decisions that affect one's life.

Our earlier suggestion for the use of crisis intervention or advocacy centers would include the notion that these not be under the aegis of either the formal mental health system or the criminal justice system, but under the control of local citizen's groups, neighborhood-based and voluntary. Similarly, many city police departments are centrally administered, and selection, training, policy, and the like are largely out of the hands of the people who live in the patrolled neighborhoods. Often this creates mutual confusion and disrespect between citizens and police. Instead, suppose each neighborhood were to have its police officers and policies selected and determined by a neighborhood group. At present the police frequently represent a lifestyle and set of values that differ from the style and values of many neighborhoods. They often function in an adversary relationship, not only with criminals but with law-abiding citizens as well. What would happen if the policies of law enforcement were set at the local neighborhood level? Local groups could select the kind of police officers best equipped to understand and respect local residents and vice versa. Often people indigenous to the neighborhood might be selected. Such a plan could change the relationship between police and citizens in such a way as to have multiple impacts on the community. The reduction of violence is only one possible outcome.

The kind of nonspecific social policies we have in mind go still a step farther. One such is to encourage the creation and development of autonomous alternative settings where people are in direct control of the policies and decisions that affect their lives (Rappaport, 1977). Several such successful settings have been developed and evaluated in both the mental health (Fairweather et al., 1969) and the criminal justice systems (Goldenberg, 1971). The small-group literature in social psychology, studies of cohesiveness, the history of ethnic organizations (Guttentag, 1970), and of communes (Kanter, 1972) suggests the desirability of such efforts.

Perhaps one of the most consistent findings of social science, in work ranging from rats in mazes to people in prisons, from problems of depression through the ability to learn, from laboratory, field, and historical analysis, and from what is variously called locus-of-control or alienation studies, is the finding that people benefit from a sense of control over their day-to-day lives (Seligman and Maier, 1967; Gurin and Gurin, 1970; Guttentag, 1970; Lefcourt, 1972; Seeman, 1972; Phares, 1973; Rotter, 1975; Seligman, 1975; Phares and Lamiell, 1977). General social policies that enhance people's control over their lives, however that may be done, may do more to prevent violence in a community than do direct attempts to control so-called violent people. Required are social policies that change the real-world contingencies in people's lives by making resources available, rather than by so-called training programs that simply provide false expectations or "self-control" and acceptance of things as they are.

The kind of nonspecific social policy we are suggesting is quite compatible with what Berger and Neuhaus (1977) call *empowering people through mediating structures*: "Those institutions standing between the individual in his private life and the large institutions of public life." Sarason (1972) has called them "settings." Between the private search for meaning and identity and the modern megastructures with which we must interact lie settings that mediate the demands of our society directly; these are the places where most of us are touched in our own lives—neighborhoods, families, churches, voluntary associations, as well as ethnic and racial subcultures. When such settings are outside the mainstream, yet serve the same function for people, we have elsewhere referred to them as "autonomous alternative settings" (Rappaport, 1977).

We require a conscious public policy that recognizes the validity of, and imaginatively supports, such settings. In these places one finds the psychological sense of community. The argument is for more than decentralization of government; it is one in favor of finding ways in which government may actively support such settings by conscious recognition that most people know what they need better than anyone else, and that in these settings they can express those needs constructively.

The key kinds of research questions raised and social policies required include learning how to strengthen rather than weaken the local neighborhoods.

> Decentralization can give the people in the neighborhoods the feeling that they are being listened to, and even participating, but it has little to do with development and governance unless it means the reality as well as the sensations of power. Neighborhood governance exists when—in areas such as education, health services, law enforcement, and housing regulation—the people democratically determine what is in the interest of their own chosen life styles and values (Berger and Neuhaus, 1977: p. 15).

Berger and Neuhaus are particularly concerned with a social policy that will support rather than destroy families (both traditional and nontraditional) as an institution. Their bias is explicit in favoring parents over experts and it is quite consistent with what we have suggested elsewhere (Rappaport, 1977, see chapters 6 and 7) vis-à-vis the black family. They also point out how current educational policies of the public schools are representative of the white middle-class family and teach contempt for one's own family, should it be the "wrong kind" (see also Rist, 1970). One suggestion is for public policy that breaks the monopoly of public education, for example, a voucher system that could be used to support families, churches, and voluntary organizations, including ethnic groups, to develop their own educational settings.

A public policy that support families and neighborhoods is not a direct attempt to prevent violence, but it is an example of the nonspecific kind of social policy we have in mind. That it may indeed have an effect on the prevalence of violence is suggested by epidemiological statistics. The Dohrenwends (1974, 1978) present a compelling case for the application of a psychosocial stress model to understand the problems of psychopathology, of which violence and aggression may be seen as one component. Bloom (1975) suggested that marital disruption is one such stressor which in 1975 alone involved more than three million people (U.S. Department of Health, Education and Welfare, 1976), and several studies (Schneidman and Farberow, 1961; National Center for Health Statistics, 1970) linked suicides to divorce and separation. In addition, homicide and motor vehicle accidents are higher among the divorced; the accident rate during the six months before and after divorce is doubled (McMurray, 1970); and loss of a spouse through death, divorce, or separation are the three most stressful life events measured in terms of who is likely to become ill.

CONCLUSION

In addition to a concerted effort to control the individual violence of the most powerful members of our society, we have asserted that for prevention of violence among the powerless, a nonspecific or general/systems-level social policy is required. One aspect of such a social policy might include increasing the availability of crisis or advocacy centers. We have advocated elsewhere the desirability of community development, community control of schools, elimination of intelligence testing, and an ecological view of society that looks for ways to mobilize the strengths and resources in a community, rather than continuously looking for deficits to repair (Rappaport et al., 1975; Rappaport, 1977). Such policies are to a large extent under the control of the education, mental health, and social science professions. We could implement them if we wanted to, but the cost would be a number of changes in the role relationships between professionals and communities, and the problems encountered are more political than scientific.

A second aspect of a general/systems-oriented social policy will require the study of naturally occurring helping systems that evolve in families, neighborhoods, and social networks where people find meaning in life and a psychological sense of community. By understanding these systems, when they work well, we may be better able to provide alternatives for those who do not fit in than by trying to force such people into existing limited options as defined by professionals who are government-approved.

A third aspect of such social policies might involve support for community organization and social advocacy as a specific strategy with nonspecific goals (Weber and McCall, 1978). The goals of such strategies can be various, depending on the group's values. Specific is the assumption that power resides in social organization as an unrealized potential, and its stimulation among the powerless will create positive effects. For some it will enhance self-esteem (Zurcher, 1970) if the expectations are met; for others it will reduce alienation; and for still others it will simply mean increased material resources. It is a strategy in the best traditions of American politics—particularly of political organizations and labor unions (Cooke, 1973).

Our guess is that by social-policy steps like the serious mobilization of community development corporations (Hampden-Turner, 1975; Katsaros, 1978), as well as neighborhood organizations and churches that are truly under the control of the people involved, we may do more to prevent the violence of street crime in poor neighborhoods than by designing programs aimed at prediction and control of violence among the powerless.

REFERENCES

BANDURA, A. *Aggression: A Social Learning Analysis.* Prentice-Hall, Englewood Cliffs, N. J., 1973.

BANDURA, A., and WALTERS, R. H. *Social Learning and Personality Development.* Holt, Rinehart and Winston, New York, 1963.

BANFIELD, E. C. *The Unheavenly City: The Nature and Future of Our Urban Cities.* Little, Brown, Boston, 1968.

BAZELON, D. L. Psychologists in corrections—Are they doing good for the offenders or well for themselves?, in *Psychologists in the Criminal Justice System.* S. L. Brodsky, ed. University of Illinois Press, Urbana, Illinois, 1973.

BERGER, P. L., and NEUHAUS, R. J. *To Empower People: The Role of Mediating Structures in Public Policy,* American Enterprise Institute, Washington, D.C., 1977.

BERKOWITZ, L. *Roots of Aggression.* Atherton Press, New York, 1969.

BLOOM, B. L. *Community Mental Health: A General Introduction.* Brooks Cole, Monterrey, Calif., 1975.

BUSS, A. H. *The Psychology of Aggression.* John Wiley, New York, 1961.

BUSS, A. H. Aggression pays, in *The Control of Aggression and Violence: Cognitive and Physiological Factors.* J. L. Singer, ed. Academic Press, New York, 1971.

CAPLAN, G. *Principles of Preventive Psychiatry.* Basic Books, New York, 1964.

CAPLAN, N., and NELSON, S. D. On being useful: The nature and consequences of psychological research on social problems. *Am. Psychol.* 28:199-211, 1973.

COOKE, A. *America.* Knopf, New York, 1973.

DOHRENWEND, B. S. Social stress and community psychology. *Am. J. Community Psychol.* 6:1-14, 1978.

DOHRENWEND, B. S., and DOHRENWEND, B. P., eds. *Stressful Life Events.* John Wiley, New York, 1974.

DOLLARD, J., and MILLER, N. E. *Personality and Psychotherapy.* McGraw Hill, New York, 1950.

EDELMAN, P. B. The Massachusetts task force reports: Advocacy for children. *Harvard Educational Review* 43:639-652, 1973.

FAIRWEATHER, G. *Social Change: The Challenge to Survival.* General Learning Press, Morristown, N. J., 1972.

FAIRWEATHER, G., SANDERS, D. H., CRESSLER, D. L., and MAYNARD, H. *Community Life for the Mentally Ill: An Alternative to Institutional Care.* Aldine, Chicago, 1969.

FESHBACH, S., and SINGER, R. D. *TV and Aggression.* Jossey-Bass, San Francisco, 1971.

GAMSON, W. A. Violence and political power: The meek don't make it. *Psychology Today* 8:35-41, 1974.

GERBNER, G., and GROSS, L. The scary world of TV's heavy viewer. *Psychology Today* 9:41-45, 1976.

GLUECK, S., and GLUECK, E. *Unraveling Juvenile Delinquency.* Harvard University Press, Cambridge, Mass., 1951.

GLUECK, S., and GLUECK, E. *Toward a Typology of Juvenile Offenders.* Grune & Stratton, New York, 1971.

GOLDENBERG, I. I. *Build Me a Mountain: Youth, Poverty and the Creation of New Settings,* Massachusett Institute of Technology Press, Cambridge, Mass., 1971.

GOODSTEIN, L. D., and SANDLER, I. Using psychology to promote human welfare: A conceptual analysis of the role of community psychology. *Am. Psychol.* 33: 882-892, 1978.

GURIN, G., and GURIN, P. Expectancy theory in the study of poverty. *Journal of Social Issues* 26: 83-104, 1970.

GUTTENTAG, M. Group cohesiveness, ethnic organization and poverty. *Journal of Social Issues* 26:105-132, 1970.

HAMMOND, K. R., and ADELMAN, L. Science, values and human judgment. *Science* 194:389-396, 1976.

HAMPDEN-TURNER, C. *From Poverty to Dignity.* Doubleday, New York, 1975.

HOKANSON, J. E. Psychophysiological evaluation of the catharsis hypothesis, in *The Dynamics of Aggression.* E. I. Megargee and J. E. Hokanson, eds. Harper and Row, New York, 1970.

ILLICH, I. *Medical Nemesis: The Expropriation of Health.* Pantheon Books, New York, 1976.

ISCOE, I. Community psychology and the competent community. *Am. Psychol.* 29: 607-613, 1974.

JAMES, W. Moral equivalents of war, in *War.* L. Bramson and G. W. Goethals, eds. Basic Books, New York, 1968.

KANTER, R. M. *Commitment and Community: Communes and Utopias in Sociological Perspective*. Harvard University Press, Cambridge, Mass., 1972.

KATSAROS, B. *Towards a New Partnership in Community Development: Community Organization and the Housing and Community-Development Acts of 1974 and 1977*. Master's Thesis, Department of Urban Planning, University of Illinois, Urbana, 1978.

KESSLER, M., and ALBEE, G. W. Primary prevention. *Annu. Rev. Psychol.* 26:557-591, 1975.

KITTRIE, N. *The Right to Be Different: Deviance and Enforced Therapy*. The Johns Hopkins Press, Baltimore, 1971.

LAMIELL, J. T. Discretion in juvenile justice: A framework for systematic study. *Criminal Justice and Behavior* 6:76-101, 1979.

LEFCOURT, H. M. Internal vs. external control of reinforcement revisited: Recent developments, in *Progress in Experimental Research in Personality*. B. A. Maher, ed. Academic Press, New York, 1972.

LIFTON, R. *Home from the War*. Simon & Schuster, New York, 1973.

LIVERMORE, J. M., MALMQUIST, C. P., and MEEHL, P. E., On the justifications for civil commitment. *University of Pennsylvania Law Review* 117:75-96, 1968.

LORENZ, K. *On Aggression*. Bantam Books, New York, 1971.

MACCOBY, N., and ALEXANDER, J. The three community study: Using mass media in the primary prevention of heart disease risk, in *Research in Social Contexts: Bringing about Change*. R. F. Munoz, L. R. Snowden, and J. G. Kelly, eds. Jossey-Bass, San Francisco, 1979.

MACCOBY, N., FARQUHAR, J. W., WOOD, P. D. and ALEXANDER, J. Reducing the risk of cardiovascular disease: Effects of community based campaign on knowledge and behavior. *J. Community Health* 3:100, 1977.

MCCLOSKEY, H. J. Crime and punishment: Deviance and corrective social therapy. *American Philosophical Quarterly* 15:91-98, 1978.

MCDOUGAL, W. The instinct of pugnacity, in *War*, L. Bramson and G. W. Goethals, eds. Basic Books, New York, 1968.

MCGEE, R. K. *Crisis Intervention in the Community*. University Park Press, Baltimore, 1974.

MCMURRAY, L. Emotional stress and driving performance: The effect of divorce. *Behavioral Research in Highway Safety* 1:100-114, 1970.

MEEHL, P. E. Psychology and the criminal law. *University of Richmond Law Review* 5:1-30, 1970.

MEGARGEE, E. I. Recent research on overcontrolled and undercontrolled personality patterns among violent offenders. *Sociological Symposium* 9:37-50, 1973.

MEGARGEE, E. I. The prediction of dangerous behavior. *Criminal Justice and Behavior* 3:3-22, 1976.

MONAHAN, J. The prevention of violence, in *Community Mental Health and the Criminal Justice System*. J. Monahan, ed. Pergamon Press, New York, 1976.

MONAHAN, J. The prediction of violent behavior in juveniles. Paper presented at a national Symposium on the Serious Juvenile Offender. Department of Corrections, State of Minnesota, Minneapolis, Minnesota, 1977.

MONAHAN, J., and NOVACO, R. W. Corporate violence: A psychological analysis, in *New Directions in Psychological Research*. P. Lipsitt and B. Sales, eds. Van Nostrand, New York, 1978.

MONAHAN, J., NOVACO, R. W., and GEIS, G. Corporate violence: Research strategies for community psychology, in *Community Psychology and Criminal Justice*. T. Sarbin, ed. Human Sciences Press, New York, 1977.

MOYER, K. E. The physiology of aggression and the implication for aggression control, in *The Control of Aggression and Violence: Cognitive and Physiological Factors*. J. Singer, ed. Academic Press, New York, 1971.

MOWRER, O. H., and VATTANO, A. J. *Integrity Groups: The Loss and Recovery of Community*. Integrity Groups, Urbana, Ill., 1975.

MURPHY, P. T. *Our Kindly Parent . . . The State*. Viking Press, New York, 1974.

National Center for Health Statistics. *Mortality from Selected Causes by Marital Status* (Series 20, Nos. 8A and 8B). Department of Health, Education and Welfare, Washington, D.C., 1970.

PHARES, E. J. *Locus of Control: A Personality Determinant of Behavior*. General Learning Press, Morristown, N. J., 1973.

PHARES, E. J., and LAMIELL, J. T. Personality. *Ann. Rev. of Psychol.* 28:113-140, 1977.

PLATT, A. M. *The Child Savers: The Invention of Delinquency*. University of Chicago Press, Chicago, 1969.

RAPPAPORT, J. *Community Psychology: Values, Research, and Action*. Holt, Rinehart and Winston, New York, 1977.

RAPPAPORT, J., DAVIDSON, W. S., MITCHELL, A., and WILSON, M. N. Alternatives to blaming the victim or the environment: Our places to stand have not moved the earth. *Am. Psychol.* 30:525-528, 1975.

RAPPAPORT, J., LAMIELL, J. T., and SEIDMAN, E. Know and tell: Conceptual constraints, ethical issues, and alternatives for psychologists in (and out of) the juvenile justice system, in *Who is the Client? The Ethies of Psychological Intervention in the Criminal Justice System*. J. Monahan, ed. American Psychological Association, 1980.

RIST, R. C. Student social class and teacher expectations: The self fulfilling prophecy in ghetto education. *Harvard Educational Review* 40:411-451, 1970.

ROTTER, J. B. Some problems and misconceptions related to the construct of internal vs. external control of reinforcement. *J. Consult. Clin. Psychol.* 43:56-57, 1975.

RYAN, W. *Blaming the Victim*. Random House, New York, 1971.

SANFORD, N. Is the concept of prevention necessary or useful?, in *Handbook of Community Mental Health*. S. E. Golann and C. Eisdorfer, eds. Appleton-Century-Crofts, New York, 1972.

SARASON, S. B. *The Creation of Settings and the Future Societies*. Jossey-Bass, San Francisco, 1972.

SCHLESINGER, A., JR. *Violence: America in the Sixties*. Signet Broadside, New York, 1968.

SCHNEIDMAN, E. S., and FABEROW, N. L. *The Cry for Help*. McGraw Hill, New York, 1961.

SCHUMACHER, E. F. *A Guide for the Perplexed*. Harper and Row, New York, 1977.

SEEMAN, J. Social learning theory and the theory of mass society, in *Applications of Social Learning Theory of Personality*. J. B. Rotter, J. Chance, and E. J. Phares, eds. Holt, Rinehart and Winston, New York, 1972.

SEIDMAN, E. Justice, values, and social science: Unexamined premises, in *Research in Law and Sociology*, vol. I. R. J. Simon, ed. JAI Press, Greenwich, Conn., 1977.

SELIGMAN, M. E. P. *Helplessness: On Depression, Development and Death*. W. H. Freeman, San Francisco, 1975.

SELIGMAN, M. E. P., and MAIER, S. F. Failure to escape traumatic shock. *J. Exp. Psychol.* 74:1-9, 1967.

SHAH, S. Dangerousness: A paradigm for exploring some issues in law and psychology. *Am. Psychol.* 33:224-238, 1978.

SILVERMAN, L. Psychoanalytic theory: The reports of my death are greatly exaggerated. *Am. Psychol.* 31:621-637, 1976.

SINGER, J. L. The influence of violence portrayed in television or motion pictures upon overt aggressive behavior, in *The Control of Aggression and Violence:*

Cognitive and Physiological Factors. J. L. Singer, ed. Academic Press, New York, 1971.

SLATER, P. *The Pursuit of Loneliness.* Beacon Press, Boston, 1970.

SUSSER, M. *Community Psychiatry: Epidemiologic and Social Themes.* Random House, New York, 1968.

SZASZ, T. S. *The Manufacture of Madness: A Comparative Study of the Inquisition and the Mental Health Movement.* Harper & Row, New York, 1970.

TUCHMAN, B. *A Distant Mirror: The Fourteenth Century.* Knopf, New York, 1978.

UNDERWOOD, J. An unfolding tragedy. *Sports Illustrated* 49:68-82 (August 14, 1978).

United States Department of Health, Education and Welfare. Births, marriages, divorces, and deaths for 1975. *Monthly Vital Statistics Report* 24, 1976.

United States Department of Justice. *Public Opinion Regarding Crime: Criminal Justice and Related Topics,* U.S. Government Printing Office, Washington, D.C., 1975.

WAGGENFELD, M. O. The primary prevention of mental illness. *J. Health Soc. Beh.* 13:195-203, 1972.

WEBER, G. H., and MCCALL, G. J. eds. *Social Scientists as Advocates: Views from Applied Disciplines.* Sage, Beverly Hills, Calif., 1978.

WIGGINS, N. S., JONES, L. E., and WASSERMAN, R. *Racial Differences in Perception of Faces.* Unpublished Study, University of Illinois, Urbana, 1975.

WILSON, E. O. *Sociobiology.* Belknap Press of Harvard University Press, Cambridge, Mass., 1975.

WOLFGANG, M., and FERRACUTI, *The Subculture of Violence.* Tavistock, London, 1967.

ZIMBARDO, P. G. The Human Choice: Individualism, reason and order vs. deindividuation, impulse and chaos, in *Nebraska Symposium on Motivation.* W. J. Arnold, and D. Levine, eds. University of Nebraska Press, Lincoln, Neb., 1969.

ZURCHER, L. A. The poverty board: Some consequences of "maximum feasible participation." *Journal of Social Issues,* 26:85-107, 1970.

Index